SWINGIN'
CHICKS
of the
'60s

a tribute to 101 of the
decade's defining women

by CHRIS STRODDER

Cedco Publishing Company
San Rafael, California

Like Michelle sang in '67, this is dedicated to the one I love...

Cover and interior design: Teena Gores
Photo Editor: Krista Osteraas

ISBN: 0-7683-2232-4

Published in 2000 by
Cedco Publishing Company
100 Pelican Way
San Rafael, California 94901
For a free catalogue of other
Cedco products please write to the address above,
or visit our website: www.cedco.com

Printed in Spain

1 3 5 7 9 10 8 6 4 2

FOREWORD

twenty questions with angie dickinson

If anyone would know about the swingin' '60s, it's Angie Dickinson. Not only is she a true movie star, but she hung out with many of the decade's most illustrious people, from political leaders to trend-setting entertainers. I interviewed this Hollywood legend to get an insider's take on the swingin' '60s.—C.S.

1 *What words summarize the 1960s?*
Horror, jubilation. Horror, because of the assassinations of John Kennedy, Robert Kennedy, and Martin Luther King, plus the Vietnam War and civil rights atrocities. Jubilation, thanks to Elvis, the new styles in fashion and behavior, the freedom of expression, and the hope that everyone felt.

2 *Who symbolizes the 1960s?*
The Beatles and the diversities of Woodstock.

3 *Who were your heroes in the 1960s?*
President Kennedy, the astronauts, and Mickey Mantle and Roger Maris of the New York Yankees.

4 *What were some of your favorite movies of the 1960s?*
Bonnie and Clyde, Butch Cassidy and the Sundance Kid, The Graduate, and *Midnight Cowboy.*

5 *What were some of your favorite songs of the 1960s?*
"You've Lost That Lovin' Feelin'" by the Righteous Brothers, and "Walk On By" and "Don't Make Me Over," both written by Bacharach and David.

6 *What was the best thing about the 1960s?*
Fashion. It was great because it came after the most horrible decade of style and forever took care of the hemline issue. I gave away nearly all of my outfits from the '60s, except for three I couldn't part with. My favorite is a pink crocheted mini dress. It doesn't fit, but I love to look at it.

7 *What was your favorite fashion of the 1960s?*
The miniskirt was my favorite fashion for women. For men, just the idea of some fashion variety was great. The Nehru jacket looks silly now, but at least it gave men an option. And colorful tuxedos enabled men to find a little individuality. The classic look was great, but not everyone could look unique in it like Sinatra did.

8 *What was the silliest thing about the 1960s?*
The portrayal of the family on '60s TV shows such as *Ozzie and Harriet, Make Room for Daddy, Father Knows Best, The Donna Reed Show,* and *The Brady Bunch.*

9 *What was the worst thing about the 1960s?*
That they ended.

10 *If the '60s were a color, what would it be?*
The '60s would be all colors, but not bright and strong. More soft and peaceful, like a Pucci dress.

11 *Is there anything you did in the '60s that you wish you wouldn't have done?*
I wouldn't have worn hot pants.

12 *Is there something you didn't do in the '60s that you wish you would have done?*
I wish I would have marched with or for Martin Luther King and his people.

13 *What was the best party you attended in the '60s?*
There were many great parties in the '60s given by Dominick Dunne and Milton Berle and the Ira Gershwins and the Lew Wassermans. But there was one party that stands out. It was in July 1960 at the home of Pat and Peter Lawford in Santa Monica. Ostensibly it was to celebrate the birthday of Eunice Kennedy, I believe; but we all knew who and what it was for. The entire contingent of Hollywood supporters of Senator Jack Kennedy was there, and the air was hot with excitement and rivalry as the election approached. This was great because we were all young and we all danced and the dark days were yet to come. Teddy Kennedy was boisterous and funny and performed for his family, and the best of the best were there. It went on very late, and during the floor show, I'll never forget the sheer joy of Senator Kennedy, laughing and finding relief from the heavy duties that were now his on this, the eve of the opening of the Democratic Convention at the Hilton in Beverly Hills. Most of those party-goers are now gone, but the memories from that night will stay with me forever. There are still great parties, but that was one to remember for all decades.

14 *Can you compare the mood of the '60s with the mood of the twenty-first century?*
Similar.

15 *How would you define the word "swingin'" as in "swingin' '60s"?*
Free and fun and harmless.

16 *Do any current actresses remind you of the great swingin' actresses of the '60s?*
Cameron Diaz.

17 *Do you have any favorite or least favorite '60s slang terms?*
My least favorite terms are any that might have led to the current use of the word "like" in ways that don't refer to liking a person or a thing, or in ways that don't mean similar to. Like, you know what I'm like talking about?

18 *What woman defines the term "swingin' '60s"?*
Jane Fonda. Jane was smart but not competitive, and she was hot but not over the top. She was sexy and confident and had classy looks and attitude. And of course, she was very beautiful and worldly, and she was the best of the role models to lead women into the bustin'-out '70s.

19 *This book is called Swingin' Chicks of the '60s—who were the swingin'est men of the '60s?*
Sinatra, Elvis, President Kennedy, the Beatles, the Rolling Stones, Dean Martin, Dustin Hoffman, Robert Redford, and of course Burt Bacharach.

20 *What lesson do you think the 1960s taught us?*
We should remember that despite the fun and frivolity and fashions, the good times of the '60s were ultimately overshadowed by the three horrendous assassinations—John Kennedy, Robert Kennedy, and Martin Luther King.

INTRODUCTION

Angela Cartwright made me write this book. Not literally, but in a way, she's the reason the Swingin' Chicks of the '60s projects were born. Before I saw Angela in 1965, the only movies or TV shows I'd ever seen were war movies. My first big-screen experience was *The Great Escape* at a California drive-in back in 1963. Two hundred and fifty minutes of cool strategy and epic chases, perfect for an awestruck young first-grader wearing pajamas and watching from the front seat of a station wagon with wood on the sides. But there wasn't one girl in the whole movie. That classic was followed a few months later by *PT-109*, which had one hundred and seventy minutes of exciting sea-going adventure—again with no girls. Meanwhile my favorite TV show was *Combat*—was this a conspiracy? Weren't there any girls in World War II?

Finally, in 1965 *Lost in Space* made its debut, and I got my first crush. The oh-so-lucky girl was Angela Cartwright, who played Penny, aluminum-foil-wearing teenage daughter in the peripatetic Space Family Robinson. I watched mesmerized for at least a couple of episodes, until I caught a glimpse of Barbara Eden's bare midriff in *I Dream of Jeannie*, and I was a goner. A few weeks later, along came Barbara Feldon's cheekbones in *Get Smart*, followed eventually by Joey Heatherton's sparkly dress on *The Dean Martin Show*, Twiggy's big eyes in a magazine, Cathy Rigby's fit form on the balance beam, then for the rest of the decade a new true love every week. The whole world, I was discovering, was filled with exciting, wonderful, beautiful, girls, most of 'em in miniskirts. Suddenly there was more to suburban life than Little League baseball and Stingray bikes cherried out with banana seats and raised handlebars. And for the first time I realized that Becky Leonard, an older woman (she was 11 years old), lived just two houses away...

Three decades later, with the twentieth century lumbering to its close, I started to think back to the energetic, bright, eternally youthful girls I had admired so long ago. I wondered whatever happened to Becky, the first neighborhood girl I ever noticed.

I assumed she had been living in a convent lo these many years, disheartened because I'd never followed up on the one kiss I lightly touched to her cheek back in 1967. While Becky wasn't findable, Angela Cartwright certainly was, so I did some research (in a public library—I wasn't stalking her or anything). I put together a respectful biography about Angela, built a single simple Web page, and posted it on the Internet. I gradually added more career summaries and where-they-are-now stories about various '60s actresses to my little site, often fulfilling the requests of the few people who wrote to me, so that by the spring of 1998 I'd written some fifty biographies about the '60s women I fondly remembered. For each one I described how she looked, told what I knew about her post-'60s life, and explained why I thought she was so great, so admirable, so representative of the swingin' '60s. This was just a fun, lightweight, low-tech endeavor, not the desperate cry for help that some high-tech Web sites can be. No fiendish plan for global conquest, no scandalous photos, no harsh language, no merchandise to sell, just gentle biographies that made up in accuracy what they lacked in malice. (Federal regulatory agencies have confirmed that no swingin' chicks were harmed in the making of any of my '60s projects.) Buoyed by rare photos and little-known anecdotes sent to me by some '60s survivors, and my sails filled with a friend's encouragement, I rechristened my growing site with a new,

affectionate title: Swingin' Chicks of the '60s. I added some spinny psychedelic graphics, and in July of '98 I launched this new enterprise into the vast Internet sea to see what messages might eventually wash up on my shore.

I didn't have to wait long. To my utter astonishment, within two weeks the biggest directory in Webdom, Yahoo, named my swinginchicks.com a Cool Link and a Pick of the Week. Not only had my ship suddenly come in, that ship was the *Queen Mary*. The result was like having your phone number printed next to the words "dial this" on the front cover of the phone book. Tens of thousands of men and women a day, some merely curious, most of them fans of the '60s, surfed on over, as did the national and international media. I've been updating and supplementing the site ever since, so that as of this writing swinginchicks.com bulges with around 150 long biographies of famous starlets, singers, athletes, and writers of the '60s. I humbly confess that it isn't so much my writing and graphics that are popular as it is the subject itself. People seem to love those fun, attractive, talented,

colorful women of the '60s—my Swingin' Chicks—and they're hungry for information about them. I've discovered that there is something about the '60s that appeals not just to baby boomers like me, but yea, to all mankind. Grandparents, busy executives, hip TV producers in Hollywood, young radio DJ's in Australia, journalists in lands as far away as Russia, the Middle East, and Finland, and Generation X. Why, Zee kids who weren't even born then have all swung by for a look. That's what's so great about the '60s: They exploded with so much life, so much energy, so much diverse style that you can't NOT find something interesting to look at, listen to, or read, no matter what your twenty-first-century life is like. Just think for a sec how dense that decade was: packed into it were the continuing exploits of '50s queens like Ava Gardner and Jayne Mansfield, the ring-a-ding years of Frank's Rat Pack, the Beatles' juggernaut, revolutions on our campuses and in our streets, day-glo flower power, and luminaries as disparate as Brigitte Bardot, the Kennedys, Diana Rigg, Martin Luther King, Mary Quant, Stanley Kubrick, Peggy Fleming, Andy Warhol, Goldie Hawn, the Maharishi, the Singing Nun, Sandy Koufax, Julie Christie, Muhammad Ali, Tina Turner, Joe Namath, Raquel Welch, Ed "Big Daddy" Roth, Jane Fonda, Craig Breedlove, Hayley Mills, the amazin' astronauts, the amazin' Mets, Mia Farrow, Dustin Hoffman, Wilma Rudolph, and Batman. There were stars we still know by a single name (Jimi, Janis, Elvis, Cher, Twiggy, Mick, Veruschka, Dick and Liz, Lulu, John/Paul/George/Ringo, Marilyn) and heroes whose mere initials are enough to elevate the stature of airports (JFK) and stadiums (RFK). In the '60s, giants were still walking the earth.

Think too of the decade's wide-ranging styles. The '60s cinema encompassed everything from the fun 'n' frisky beach flix in the first half of the decade to the solemn and artful *Midnight Cowboy, 2001,*

and *Easy Rider* in the second half. The best of TV began with the traditional, if inspired, wit of *The Dick Van Dyke Show* and ended with the free-spirited psychedelic lunacy of *Laugh-In*. Bob Dylan and the earnest folkies, Dean Martin and the cool loungies, Motown's soulful singers, the lively British Invasion, and the dark experiments of acid rock served up a still-relevant, still-remarkable sonic banquet where, like four wise men once said, a splendid time was guaranteed for all. Toss in the summer of love, the winter of Altamont, the civil rights and anti-war protests, the feminist movement, ecological awareness, colorful miniskirts, vinyl go-go boots, Nehru jackets, love beads, pop and op art, then sprinkle in a little granola and a couple of sugar cubes, spice it all up with a dash of Woodstock and a pinch of sages like Truman Capote, Joseph Heller, Tom Wolfe, Helen Gurley Brown, Hugh Hefner, Kurt Vonnegut, Arthur C. Clarke, and Jacqueline Susann, garnish with a Twist, label it with a peace sign, and you emerge with an unforgettable feast of fads and fashions, movements and moments. Does anybody recall the '80s or '90s with such a colorful rainbow of strong images? Or with such affection? Such reverence?

There was something for everybody in the '60s, just as I hope there's something for everybody in this book. I wrote it to celebrate those glorious, sometimes goofy, sometimes profound times, and to help preserve the memory of the decade's wonderful women. Marilyn Monroe, Liz Taylor, and some of the other megastars profiled in these pages don't need my, or anybody's, help to be remembered, of course; their work and their lives will be venerated for generations to come. But some other people whom you might not be as familiar with—Chris Noel, for instance—are equally as inspiring. All of them we should honor, with affection; thank, with admiration; and remember, with respect, for the women of the

'60s paved the way for all the Farrah Fawcetts, Christie Brinkleys, Diane Keatons, Mary Lou Rettons, Debbie Harrys, Danielle Steeles, Pamela Andersons, Drew Barrymores, Gwyneth Paltrows, Courtney Loves, Sharon Stones, and Madonnas who followed.

Chris Strodder
Mill Valley, California

CONTENTS

THE BEACH GIRLS

While the terrible tragedies, protest marches, and angry revolutions of the '60s made it one of the noisiest decades of the century, there was also a sweet side to the era. It was a decade of assassinations and war, but also flower stickers and VW Beetles; of protest marches and inner-city riots, but also love-ins and Woodstock; of acid rock and the first X-rated movies, but also the Beach Boys and Elvis flix. The fun, lighthearted side of the '60s was best expressed in the gentle, frothy wave of "beach movies" that rolled into drive-in theatres across the country throughout the decade. The formula was simple: Let wholesome kids frolic on sunny sands, throw in a few splashy musical numbers, and *voila*, the audience is on Spring Break for an hour and a half. Here are a few of the great girls on the beach who helped make drive-ins a vacation destination for millions of teens in the '60s.

ANNETTE FUNICELLO

who adored her and girls who wanted to emulate her. *The Mickey Mouse Club* led to a number of other Disney projects, including her own "Annette" show-within-a-show in '58 (in which she played a character named Annette McCloud) and a role as the starring girlfriend in *The Shaggy Dog* ('59).

The '60s brought more Disney work her way (*Babes in Toyland* in '61, *The Monkey's Uncle* in '65), but it took the series of fun-loving mid-decade beach movies to put her into a bathing suit and more mature situations. *Beach Party* ('63), *Muscle Beach Party* ('64), *Bikini Beach* ('64), *Pajama Party* ('64), *How to Stuff a Wild Bikini* ('65), *Dr. Goldfoot and the Bikini Machine* ('65), and *Beach Blanket Bingo* ('65) all had similar settings, often the same cast of actors and actresses, and lightweight plots that were merely excuses for good-looking teens to woo, sing, and dance on camera.

Annette surfed the surging swell of popularity into a decent singing career, even though she would later describe herself as being nervous as a vocalist. From the late-'50s to the mid-'60s she recorded seventeen albums and had thirty-one hit songs, starting with the zippy "Tall Paul." The songs were nice 'n' easy, and the albums were usually good-natured party collections (you could tell they were for parties because the titles told you so—*Annette's Beach Party*, *Muscle Beach Party*, etc.).

Unfortunately, by '67 the wave of '60s beach movies had crested, and Annette's movie momentum had wiped out. But the public still had (and has to this day) a nostalgic affection for her prim, sweetly romantic '50s–'60s image, so in the '70s she made lots of happy peanut butter commercials. In '87 she produced and starred in one more beach picture, the bouncy *Back to the Beach* (which playfully referenced her TV career as a peanut-butter-sandwich-makin' mom). Sadly, during the making of that movie she began to feel symptoms of what would eventually be diagnosed as multiple sclerosis.

Bravely maintaining her smile and generous spirit, she stayed cheerfully busy in the '90s by raising money for MS research and pursuing a wide range of interests. She established her collectible teddy bear company, came out with a perfume called Cello, and in '94 wrote her autobiography, *A Dream Is a Wish Your Heart Makes*, still with nary a bad word to say about anyone. "Even sitting in my wheelchair," she said in a TV bio, "life does not have to be perfect to be wonderful."

SWINGIN' '60s CREDENTIALS: The only actress with the words "fun," "nice," and "cello" in her name, this all-American Disney girl enjoyed a busy '60s career that included over a dozen films, frequent TV appearances, and successful record albums.

WORKIN' IT: One of the most popular actresses of the late '50s and early '60s, and one of the few who is still known by just her first name, Annette Funicello became an overnight sensation in '55 when, at the age of 13, she first appeared on a new afternoon TV show. Her appearances as a pretty, intelligent, talented, and dignified Mouseketeer helped make *The Mickey Mouse Club* the most popular children's show of the '50s and soon established her as America's sweetheart, recipient of over a thousand letters a week from boys

HER '60s LOOK: Pretty, well-groomed, with a ready smile and big, kind eyes—basically she was Walt's ideal Disney girl and America's ideal teenager. She had "infinite grace," according to one of her best friends, Shelley Fabares. She had a wholesome sexiness, too, especially when the beach movies revealed the curves that had developed since her Mousketeer days. But in keeping with her wholesome image, in most of those movies she wore the most conservative clothes of anyone, even though she was the star of party beach—watch how often she's wearing hostess pants and blouses, or turtlenecks and sweaters, while the girls around her are in skimpy outfits. She has said that she didn't think it would be proper for her to wear a bikini, and Walt Disney himself had asked her not to wear one when she started making the non-Disney beach movies in the early '60s.

BEHIND THE SCENES: What's nice in this era of tabloid scandals is the lack of gossip about Annette. Her peers still worship her and reveal nothing indiscreet about her, so she has kept her image as America's sweetheart. Annette's first crush was on *Spin & Marty* star Tim Considine. Her first boyfriend came in '57, when she got romantic with Paul Anka. He wrote "Puppy Love" about their relationship, and she recorded the *Annette Sings Anka* album in '59. Annette lived at home until she married her first husband, Jack Gilardi, who was also her manager, in a big wedding in '65, followed by a honeymoon in Mexico. Shelley Fabares was a bridesmaid. Exactly nine months later daughter Gina was born, followed by Jack Jr. in '70, and Jason in '74. Annette and Gilardi got divorced in '81. She married horse trainer Glen Holt in '86, and he's stayed faithfully by her side through the difficult health problems she's endured since the late '80s.

was usually billed simply as Annette ... though it's easy to make fun of Annette's beach movies, they did have remarkable casts—*Pajama Party*, as just one example, boasted Dorothy Lamour, Elsa Lanchester, Buster Keaton, Don Rickles, and future video star Toni Basil in cameo roles ... Frankie Avalon, the co-star with whom she's usually associated, summarized her appeal: "She's the perfect girl next door, she doesn't have a bad bone in her body. She's the sweetest girl I know, and nothing's ever changed."

BONUS SWINGABILITY: Her nickname—"Dolly" ... her exotic birthplace—Utica, New York ... after three thousand kids auditioned

for the first season of *The Mickey Mouse Club*, Annette was the twenty-fourth and final Mousketeer chosen, and the only one personally selected by Walt Disney ... the custom-made mouse ears cost $50 each, so when Annette lost three pairs $150 was deducted from her salary ... on her records, she

A DATE WITH ANNETTE

October 22, 1942	Annette Funicello is born
October 3, 1955	Walt Disney introduces his new *Mickey Mouse Club* show
February 2, 1959	"Tall Paul" enters the *Billboard* charts (it will reach #7)
December 14, 1959	"First Name Initial" enters the *Billboard* charts (it will reach #20)
March 7, 1960	"O Dio Mio" enters the *Billboard* charts (it will reach #10)
June 20, 1960	"Train of Love" enters the *Billboard* charts (it will reach #36)
September 5, 1960	"Pineapple Princess" enters the *Billboard* charts (it will reach #11)
December 14, 1961	*Babes in Toyland* is released
November 11, 1964	*Pajama Party* is released
January 9, 1965	Annette marries Jack Gilardi
August 18, 1965	*The Monkey's Uncle* is released

DONNA LOREN

SWINGIN' '60s CREDENTIALS: This talented, sweet-faced young teen was a multi-dimensional star who excelled at the three M's— music, movies, and modeling—during the '60s.

WORKIN' IT: You may not instantly recognize the name, but if you were anywhere in America during the '60s, you undoubtedly encountered the image or the voice of young Donna Loren. She got her start at only 5 years old when she won second prize on an amateur show, which led to appearances on *Playhouse 90* and on a live radio show called *Squeakin' Deacon*. At 8 she sang on her first commercial, at 9 she cut her first record, "I Think It's Almost Christmas Time," and at 10 she appeared on *The Mickey Mouse Club* TV show in the "Talent Round-Up" segment. Still not of driving age, Donna continued making records on various labels, so that by the end of the '60s she'd released eighteen singles, among them such easy-goin' pop songs as "Honey Buggie," "The More I See Him," "Hands Off," "I'm in Love with the Ticket Taker," "On the Good Ship Lollipop," "Muscle Bustle," "Blowing Out the Candles," and "So, Do the Zonk."

Donna was more than just a pretty voice, however; her pretty face took her to another level of popularity in '63 when she was chosen to be the first and only "Dr Pepper Girl." For the next five years she represented the soft-drink company on the radio, in a huge billboard campaign, in magazines, at personal appearances around the country, in calendars, and on Dick Clark's *American Bandstand* and *Caravan of Stars* shows.

Her wholesome image as a sweet, talented all-American girl made her a natural for the big screen, and in '64–'65 she got prominent roles in five popular teen movies—*Bikini Beach, Muscle Beach Party, Pajama Party, Sergeant Deadhead*, and the classic *Beach Blanket Bingo*, in which she sang a solo number, "It Only Hurts When I Cry." During these years she was also a frequent presence on TV, especially as a featured vocalist every week on *Shindig* and as a guest star on *Batman, The Monkees, The Red Skelton Show*, and even the *Hollywood Squares*. As one of the most ubiquitous teens of the decade, she was selected to write two monthly columns for *Movie Life* magazine in '66 and '67: One column, "Let's Talk It Over," gave personal advice, while the other, "Donna Loren's Young Hollywood," described what other young stars were doing. Just when she was about to get her own TV series, *Two for Penny*, in '68, Donna decided to retire from show biz to get married and raise a family.

In the '80s she tried a comeback as a singer, recording the country-flavored "Wishin' and Hopin'," her debut song on *Shindig*; the late-'90s saw a new limited-edition CD called *The Best of Donna Loren* and a new CD soundtrack of *Beach Blanket Bingo*.

By this time, though, Donna had ventured into another career: fashion. Even as a child she could sew; in fact, she designed and sewed most of the clothes she wore onstage as a young girl. She'd even done a commercial in '63 for the Simplicity Pattern Company. Thus it was only fitting that Donna would reinvent herself as a fashion designer. Now living on the big island of Hawaii, she designs clothes under the ADASA Hawaii label and has her own ADASA boutique (the name ADASA comes from her great-grandmother). In March '98 Donna was named one of Hawaii's top designers by *Honolulu* magazine, and her clothes were shown in the '98 coffee-table book called *Hawaii: Heaven on Earth*. The career may be different from what she did in the '60s, but Donna Loren is still one of the most successful girls on the beach.

HER '60s LOOK: With those big dark eyes and that big bright smile, Donna's image in the '60s was that of the wholesome all-American teen: pretty, fit, stylin' and smilin', hip enough to hang at the beach with the gang, but smart enough to get all her homework done. It's no wonder she made several covers of *Teen* magazine during the '60s; more importantly, it's no wonder Dr Pepper wanted to spotlight her for the teen audience—she looked right at home in company ads that showed her listening to records and drinking Dr Pepper, or reading a book and drinking Dr Pepper, or yakkin' on the phone while holding a Dr Pepper, or getting ready for the prom within arm's reach of a Dr Pepper. No matter what she was wearing she always looked great; what's more, she always looked *sincere*— when she was modeling an elegant white dress with long gloves, you really believed that she was the prettiest prom date you ever saw, and when she was wearing jeans and a gingham shirt she looked like she was just about the cutest dang cowgirl who ever rode the range. Recent photos of her (check her Web site) are proof of the "grace" in "aging gracefully."

'60 her name is listed as Donna Dee ... unlike Sophia Loren, who puts the emphasis on the *-en* in her last name, Donna's last name is pronounced to rhyme with "foreign" ... her exotic birthplace—Boston, Massachusetts ... other actresses who sang solos in different beach movies during the '60s included Annette Funicello, Deborah Walley, Leslie Gore, and Linda Evans ... often the other actresses in the beach movies played characters with unusual names like Sniffles, Animal, Lady Bug and Sugar Kane, but not Donna—in three of the beach movies her character was also named Donna ... refreshingly, she was a real teenager in the beach movies, unlike some of the other "teens": In '65's *Beach Blanket Bingo*, Frankie was 26, Annette and Linda Evans were 24, and Jody "Bonehead" McCrea was 31 ... also in *Beach Blanket Bingo* was Donna Michelle, *Playboy* Playmate of the Year in '64 ... when she appeared in an episode of *The Monkees* in '67, Donna played the daughter of a sheik who ordered her to choose a husband; her choice was Davy Jones ... Donna has her own fun and informative Web site—http://www.adasa.com.

BEHIND THE SCENES: Donna retired at the end of the '60s to devote herself to a marriage and a family. Happily married, she lives in Hawaii. Her son Joey Waronker plays drums for R.E.M., and her two beautiful daughters are following in Donna's footsteps in the music and fashion industries.

BONUS SWINGABILITY: Her moniker—Donna was born with the last name Zukor, but at age 14 she changed her last name to Loren ... however, on the "Honey Buggie" single in '60 her name is listed as Barbie Ames, and on the "The More I See Him" single in

 A DATE WITH DONNA

March 7, 1947	Donna Loren is born
November 11, 1964	*Pajama Party* is released
March 2, 1966	Donna's first appearance on *Batman*
September 25, 1967	Donna guest stars on *The Monkees*

girls

CHRIS NOEL

SWINGIN' '60s CREDENTIALS: Lovely Chris Noel walked away from a budding acting career to entertain the troops in Vietnam for the last half of the '60s.

WORKIN' IT: In the late '60s, every American soldier knew Chris Noel. More accurately, they knew her voice. It's still the first thing one notices about her, that marvelously husky, tomboyish voice that cracks then soothes with the warmth of a summer afternoon. To hear her is to remember a picnic on a sunny California hillside, or a swimmin' hole on a Midwest river, or white sand on a hot Florida beach.

That voice, and her remarkable looks, made her a Hollywood star before she became a G.I. legend. A Florida girl born during World War II, Chris Noel was modeling, winning beauty pageants, and cheerleading for the New York Giants while still a teen. In '63 Hollywood scooped her up and put her all-American appeal on the silver screen. *Soldier in the Rain* ('63) with Steve McQueen was her first film, quickly followed a year later by *Get Yourself a College Girl*, *Honeymoon Hotel*, and *Diary of a Bachelor*. *Beach Ball* ('65) was her breakthrough to stardom. Though it was just one of the many

lightweight beach pics of the mid-'60s, this one at least gave her star billing and featured her bikinied image in the print ads ("Nothing Bounces Like Beach Ball," read some of the ad lines). Elvis' *Girl*

Happy ('65) cast her as a pretty sidekick to Shelley Fabares, *Wild, Wild Winter* ('66) gave her another starring role in a beach-style movie (this time ski slopes replaced surf 'n' sand), and *The Glory Stompers* ('67) put her opposite Dennis Hopper in a biker epic. Throughout the '60s Chris was getting guest spots on dozens of popular TV shows, everything from *Bewitched* and *Perry Mason* to *My Three Sons* and several Bob Hope specials.

The turning point, not just in her career but in her entire life, came when she toured a veterans hospital in '65. The sight of the broken, mutilated casualties of the Vietnam War brought home the reality of what was happening ten thousand miles away. She asked to audition for the Armed Forces Network, and in '66 she began hosting her own hour-long radio show. "Hi luv," she'd say at the opening of *A Date with Chris*, and then would follow music, dedications, interviews, and Chris's own spontaneous chat. "I tried to keep it upbeat, positive, happy and full of energy," she told an interviewer, "but as the years went on it got harder." The show ran from '66 to March '71 and made her "the Voice of Vietnam," the cheery darling of war-weary G.I.'s everywhere. Thousands carried her picture with them into battle; thousands more wrote her loving, grateful, nostalgic letters. That first year she taped the show in California for broadcast in Southeast Asia, but by '67 she was actually in Vietnam for months at a time, voluntarily touring the bases and visiting the hospitals and flying into war zones too remote for Bob Hope and his big showy productions. For the next four years she sang, she autographed, she joked, she talked, she comforted, she mothered, she healed, and she brought "home" to the boys on those distant and dangerous front lines. Twice her helicopter was shot down, mortar fire sometimes exploded around her, and bullets whizzed past her more times than she could count. She was so popular and influential that the Viet Cong put a $10,000 bounty on her head.

Returning to Hollywood after the war, Chris tried to revive her screen career. She put in some minor movie and TV appearances in the '70s, but soon found that she was suffering from the same post-war syndrome that was plaguing vets all across America. Migraines, flashbacks, depression, and rage were the symptoms of the emotional storm roiling deep within. Years of therapy enabled her to cope with her pain, her nightmares, and her scars. In '85 she was in *Cease Fire*, a riveting movie that exposed the trauma faced by Vietnam vets. Her own autobiography, *A Matter of Survival*, was published in '87, another attempt to exorcise the wounds of war. To help others who also continued to suffer from memories of Vietnam, she traveled around the country to support veteran organizations and joined the boards of a dozen Vietnam-related councils and groups. In the '80s she organized the Women's Interaction Network to help women cope with the war's lingering fallout. Since '93 she's run the Vetsville Cease Fire House, a homeless shelter that she founded for disenfranchised vets in Florida. Chris does whatever it takes to keep Vetsville going—performing household chores, paying the bills, organizing fundraisers, and befriending the troubled souls who came seeking solace. Today Chris Noel still runs Vetsville, now with shelters in three cities. She's still tirelessly fighting the good fight and providing a beacon of hope for those who first heard her voice some thirty years ago.

HER '60s LOOK: Blonde, green-eyed, brightly smiling Chris projected the perfect girl-next-door image—if, that is, you happened to be lucky enough to live next to a stunning starlet with 36-23-34 measurements. She graced about a dozen magazine covers in the '60s, including *Good Housekeeping* in June of '69. On screen her wonderful 5' 6" 115-pound figure was shown off in bikinis; on tour she sported white go-go boots and tight miniskirts—in fact, she's usually credited with being the woman who introduced the mini to the Far East.

BEHIND THE SCENES: In '65 Chris was dating singer Jack Jones when she learned of the Armed Forces Network. While in Vietnam,

she married a Green Beret captain in '68, but tragedy ended their life together before it could really begin. After returning home, and suffering from delayed-stress syndrome, her husband of eleven months committed suicide at Christmas in '69. Twice remarried and divorced, she now lives in south Florida.

BONUS SWINGABILITY: Her exotic birthplace—West Palm Beach, Florida ... Chris's last name is pronounced with the accent on the second syllable, like "gazelle" ... while growing up Chris was often compared to another blonde beauty—Marilyn Monroe ... one of Chris's talents: baton twirling; in fact, she was once the national champion ... Chris's films often featured other great women of the '60s: Nancy Sinatra and Mary Ann Mobley were in *Get Yourself a College Girl*, Jill St. John and Anne Helm were in *Honeymoon Hotel*, all of the Supremes were in *Beach Ball*, Shelley Fabares and Mary Ann Mobley were in *Girl Happy*, Yvette Mimieux was in *Joy in the Morning*, and Mary Ann Mobley and Lana Wood were in *For Singles Only* ... Chris recorded an album called *Forgotten Man*, dedicating it to vets everywhere and donating the profits to a vet group; another collection of songs, *Nashville Impact*, came out in late '99 ... as you might guess, Chris has been honored with tons of humanitarian awards, among them the Distinguished Vietnam Veteran award from the National Vietnam Veterans Network in '84 ... contact Chris via her own Web site—http://www.chrisnoel.com.

 A DATE WITH CHRIS

July 2, 1941	Chris Noel is born
April 11, 1963	Chris makes her TV debut on *The Eleventh Hour*
April 14, 1965	*Girl Happy* is released
May 5, 1965	*Joy in the Morning* is released
January 5, 1966	*Wild, Wild Winter* is released

DEBORAH WALLEY

SWINGIN' '60s CREDENTIALS: This fun-loving bikini babe-ette romped through a dozen '60s movies, including Elvis' *Spinout*, *Gidget Goes Hawaiian*, and three movies with the word "bikini" in the title.

WORKIN' IT: If Annette was the queen of the drive-in, Deborah Walley might've been the princess. Born in '43 to parents who were professional ice skaters with the Ice Capades, Deborah started skating with them at age 3. She continued skating until she was bitten by the acting bug and headed for brighter lights as a teen actress. When a Hollywood producer spotted her in a Broadway production of Chekov's *The Three Sisters*, he whisked her westward and her screen career was off and running.

With lots of theatre work and a couple of TV appearances on her résumé (*Naked City* and *Route 66*, both in '60), at 17 Deborah landed the plum role of the title character in *Gidget Goes Hawaiian* ('61), the sequel to the popular *Gidget* movie of '59 (the first one cast Sandra Dee as Gidg, while another sequel in '63, *Gidget Goes to Rome*, starred Cindy Carol).

Dual Disney flix (*Bon Voyage* in '62, *Summer Magic* in '63) and a role alongside Peter Fonda in *The Young Lovers* in '64 led to the beachy-keen drive-in movies that dominated Deborah's next few years. The titles told the tale: *Dr. Goldfoot and the Bikini Machine* ('65), *Beach Blanket Bingo* ('65), *Ski Party* ('65), *The Ghost in the Invisible Bikini* ('66), *It's a Bikini World* ('67), and more, often with perky, enthusiastic Deborah filling the lead bikini. Other mid-decade faves included the comical *Sergeant Deadhead*, which put her in an Air Force officer's uniform, while *The Bubble* had her encountering an alien invasion—in 3-D no less. In the King's *Spinout* ('66), Deborah played the tomboyish "Les," the drummer in Elvis' band and one of three characters contending for his affections.

She finished the decade as the cute newlywed Suzie on the Desilu sitcom *The Mothers-in-Law* ('67–'69). Though it was a critical fave, *The Mothers-in-Law* never caught on with audiences and disappeared after two seasons. So did Deborah, leaving the biz and living the Malibu life for awhile.

She came back to make two movies—*The Severed Arm* and *Benji*—in the mid-'70s. More recently, she's done an episode of *Baywatch*, three different voices on *Chip 'n' Dale Rescue Rangers*, and she's turned her talents to writing books and screenplays. *Grandfather's Good Medicine*, her book based on her childhood experiences, was published in '92.

Actually, her career has come full circle, because Deborah has returned to the stage in the last decade, this time running the show instead of starring in it. In the '90s she founded several children's theatre companies (including a touring company called Pied Piper Productions and the Sedona Children's Theatre Company), she worked with the Educational Theatre Company in Arizona and California, and she became the Artistic Director at the Charles W. Raison Theatre in Sedona, Arizona. A partner in an Arizona film/theater production company called Swiftwind, Deborah now divides her time between L.A. and Arizona.

HER '60s LOOK: The quintessential Southern California girlfriend, she was a dynamite redhead, all smiles and energy in a petite package. Not only did she appear to be more athletic than

your average teen queen, she *was*: In her *Gidget* movie, Deborah actually did her own surfing, the only actor or actress in the cast to do so. When you see Gidget climbing up on the shoulders of a surfin' beach boy, it's really Deborah. Later, in *Beach Blanket Bingo* her character Bonnie is supposedly a skydiver, and we see her jumping through a hula hoop while freefalling; OK, so it probably *wasn't* Deborah doing the aerials, but she *was* fit and fun enough to make the stuntwork seem believable.

BEHIND THE SCENES: In '62 Deborah married teen idol John Ashley, who co-starred with her in *Beach Blanket Bingo* and *Sergeant Deadhead*, both made in '65. He was also in such '50s drive-in fare as *Motorcycle Gang*, *Hot Rod Gang*, *T-Bird Gang*, and *Dragstrip Girl*. They met on a prearranged "date" set up as a photo op by a movie magazine. She gave birth to their son, Anthony, in '63, but she and John divorced in '66. Deborah then got involved with the King during the *Spinout* filming. However, the side she saw of Elvis was a side few people ever did: She respectfully maintains that he was an influential spiritual instructor who bought her many philosophical books and opened her up to mystical Eastern teachings. Deborah has also told us that she had a platonic love affair with actor Basil Rathbone, who was fifty-two years her senior when they met on the set of *The Ghost in the Invisible Bikini* in '66. They were preparing to team as father and daughter Capulets in a Broadway production of *Romeo and Juliet* when he died in '67. Late in the decade she was married briefly to rock drummer Chet McCracken. She met her third husband, a crewmember named John Reynolds, on the set of *Benji*, and they have a son, Justin. Together she and Reynolds wrote and produced *The Vision of Seeks-to-Hunt-Great*, which won numerous film-festival prizes.

BONUS SWINGABILITY: Her exotic birthplace—Bridgeport, Connecticut ... her next film after *Gidget Goes Hawaiian* was Disney's *Bon Voyage* in '62, which was filmed in Europe. Her chaperone on the Atlantic crossing via the liner *United States* was Walt Disney himself ... many of Deborah's '60s films paired her with other top teen stars: *Summer Magic* in '63 was with Hayley Mills, *Ski Party* was with Yvonne Craig, *Beach Blanket Bingo* was with Donna Loren, *Dr. Goldfoot and the Bikini Machine* was with Annette, and *Spinout* was with Shelley Fabares ...

Deborah has named Susan Hayward as one of her major screen idols. "The heartbreak of my career," as Deborah tells it, came when she was set to costar with Hayward in the '64 flick *Where Love Has Gone*; unfortunately, the part Deborah was hired for was taken away at the last sec and given to Joey Heatherton ... still a respectful admirer of "the inner Elvis," Deborah often celebrates his legacy by attending the Elvis Week festivities held every August in Memphis.

A DATE WITH DEBORAH

August 12	Deborah Walley is born
November 9, 1960	Deborah appears on *Naked City*
November 11, 1960	Deborah appears on *Route 66*
May 25, 1961	*Gidget Goes Hawaiian* premieres in Hawaii
June 21, 1961	*Gidget Goes Hawaiian* is released
March 4, 1962	Deborah appears on *The Ed Sullivan Show*
April 24, 1962	Deborah marries John Ashley
May 4, 1963	Deborah gives birth to her son Tony
June 30, 1965	*Ski Party* is released
April 1, 1966	Deborah and John divorce
November 23, 1966	*Spinout* is released
September 10, 1967	*The Mothers-in-Law* debuts

girls

THE BOND BEAUTIES

In the '60s there were certain requirements for actresses who wanted to be Bond Bombshells. First, they had to be born outside of the U.S. (the first American actresses didn't appear in major roles until '71, when California-born Jill St. John and Lana Wood learned that *Diamonds Are Forever*). Second, it helped to have won a beauty pageant (Daniela Bianchi was Miss Italy in '60, Claudine Auger was Miss France in '58). Third, the '60s Bonds valued experience (Honor Blackman was 38 in *Goldfinger*, Luciana Paluzzi was 34 in *Thunderball*, and Diana Rigg was 31 in *On Her Majesty's Secret Service*). Finally, Bond women had to be prepared to die, since grisly deaths often awaited them (Diana Rigg's character, Tracy, was killed on the very day she wed George Lazenby's Bond. Double-oh-seven, call nine-double-one).

URSULA ANDRESS

SWINGIN' '60s CREDENTIALS: This statuesque Swiss goddess decorated several key '60s movies, including Bond's *Dr. No* and Elvis' *Fun in Acapulco*.

WORKIN' IT: Having made movies in Europe in the '50s, Ursula cleavaged her way through a dozen major English-language films in the '60s. Her impact was immediate and international—the moment her wet bikini-clad Honey Ryder character emerged from the sea halfway into *Dr. No* ('62), 26-year-old Ursula instantly became one of the most desirable actresses in Hollywood. In fact, she won the Golden Globe Award in '64 as Most Promising Newcomer.

Bond is so impressed when he first sees Honey on that beach in *Dr. No*, he forgets his perilous mission and starts crooning to her from the bushes (this wasn't Connery's first musical foray—he sang "Pretty Irish Girl" in '59's *Darby O'Gill and the Little People*). Not until the last scene of *Dr. No* is Bond able to make the big play for Ursula's character. While the pair is drifting in a small boat, he keeps his rescuers waiting so he can get a taste of Honey.

Other decade highlights for Ursula included a starring role alongside the King in *Fun in Acapulco* ('63), Frank and Dino's *4 for Texas* ('63), the Woody Allen-scripted *What's New, Pussycat?* ('65), the adventure classic *She* ('65), and the Bond spoof *Casino Royale* ('67).

She continued to make movies throughout the '70s and into the '90s, notably *The Fifth Musketeer* in '79, *Clash of the Titans* in '81, and *Falcon Crest* in '81. She also made many cheap foreign films with titles like *Slave of the Cannibal God* and *The Secrets of a Sensual Nurse*. Though her career spans decades, she's probably never been hired for her skills as a thespian—"statuesque" describes her acting as well as her looks. Her voice, certainly her singing, appears dubbed in *Dr. No*.

HER '60s LOOK: A remarkable beauty, Ursula had the icy sex-goddess look down to perfection, and the curvature under her *She* toga would make any man walk into fire (as her young lover did in the movie). In '63 her stats were listed by *Movie Life Yearbook*: 5' 6", 121 pounds, 36-21-35. Interestingly, in Ian Fleming's novel *Doctor No*, when her character first walked out of the sea, she was nude (except for a belt). He described his "elegant Venus": "It was a naked girl, her back to him. She was not quite naked. She wore a broad leather belt around her waist with a hunting knife in a leather sheath at her right hip. The belt made her nakedness extraordinarily erotic....It was a beautiful back. The skin was a very light uniform *cafe au lait* with the sheen of dull satin. The gentle curve of the backbone was deeply indented, suggesting more powerful muscles than is usual in a woman, and the behind was almost as firm and rounded as a boy's. The legs were straight and beautiful....Her hair was ash blonde....She was Botticelli's Venus, seen from behind." When Ursula later made *Fun in Acapulco*, supposedly Elvis was so intimidated by her figure that he told his pallies, "I was embarrassed to take off my damn shirt next to her!" Audiences got an eyeful of Ursula in that movie as she again made her entrance by climbing out of the water in a wet bikini. Later in the picture, she flaunted another skimpy two-piece suit and a pair of white pants painted on so tightly you could almost see her veins. Although she wasn't allowed to, Ursula might've liked to have done a few nude scenes in her movies—after all, she bared almost everything in *Playboy* in '65 and '66. The dozen pages that *Playboy* devoted to her in '65 were at the time the most the magazine had ever given to one woman in one pictorial (husband John Derek snapped the sexy photos). In '69 she explained why she liked to pose nude: "Why do I do it? Because I'm beautiful." Little wonder, then, that in January '99 *Playboy* ranked her as one of the "100 Sexiest Stars of the Century," with two other vivacious vixens, Kim Novak at #18 and Gina Lollobrigida at #20, forming a delectable Ursula sandwich.

BEHIND THE SCENES: In *Fun in Acapulco*, Ursula played a vamp who didn't take coffee breaks, but rather "man breaks." Played it quite believably, too. She was married from '57 to '66 to John Derek, the actor (*Exodus*, '60) who later married Linda Evans and Bo Derek; however, there are rumors that during the marriage she had an affair with Sean Connery on the *Dr. No* set. Later, after Connery became an international star, she would say about him, "What I like about Sean is that he's still the same down-to-earth person he was when he was unknown." Other famous names with whom she's been linked include James Dean, Marlon Brando, John DeLorean, Dennis Hopper, Ryan O'Neal, and Peter O'Toole. From '78 to '82 she lived with one of her co-stars in *Clash of the Titans*, actor Harry Hamlin, who is fifteen years her junior; in '80, at 44 years old, she had his love child, Dimitri. She now lives in Italy.

BONUS SWINGABILITY: She's used a fake moniker— on some films she was credited as Ursula Parker ... Elvis' nickname for her was "Ooshie" ... the most common joke about her name was to mispronounce it as Ursula

Undress ... in the *Mad* magazine spoof, they call her Bond movie *Dr. No-No* and her character Miss Yes-Yes ... her exotic birthplace— Berne, Switzerland ... her father was a Swiss diplomat ... she and husband Derek were both in *Once Before I Die* and *Nightmare in the Sun* (both in '65); later she and boyfriend Hamlin were both in *Clash of the Titans* ('81) ... she almost didn't get the role in *Dr. No*—supposedly Julie Christie was the favorite, but ultimately the producers decided she wasn't voluptuous enough ... not impressed by *Dr. No* (or was it her rumored 600-skins-a-week salary?), she called the movie "ghastly" ... though she was the first major Bond Beauty in a Connery Bond film, she wasn't the first Bond conquest—that honor went to actress Eunice Gayson, whose Sylvia character slept with Bond in *Dr. No* before Ursula's character appeared.

A DATE WITH URSULA

March 19, 1936	Ursula Andress is born in Berne, Switzerland
January 16, 1962	Shooting begins on *Dr. No*
October 5, 1962	*Dr. No* is released in the U.K.
May 8, 1963	*Dr. No* is released in the U.S.
November 27, 1963	*Fun in Acapulco* is released
December 25, 1963	*4 for Texas* is released
April 18, 1965	*She* is released

CLAUDINE AUGER

SWINGIN' '60s CREDENTIALS: This lithe French beauty played Domino, the Bond Beauty who swam her way into 007's heart in *Thunderball*.

WORKIN' IT: "Who? She was a Bond girl?" you might ask. Well, yes, she was—a pretty good one, too. Whereas most of the other actresses in this book bring several formidable films to the discussion, Claudine's here because of just one movie, the hugely popular

Thunderball ('65), which she made when she was only 23. Though she did get to kill the movie's crime crumb, Largo, with a spear gun, her impact on audiences was probably diminished by Bond's own infidelity— she was only one of three love interests in *Thunderball*. The movie poster touted *Thunderball* as "the biggest Bond of all," when in reality, he should have been the sleepiest Bond of all by the time he Bonded with Patricia Fearing (played by Molly Peters) in a shower, Fiona Volpe (Luciana Paluzzi) in a hotel room, and then Domino in the ocean.

Claudine's stature as a Bond Beauty might also be diminished by observers who claim that her voice was dubbed in the movie. Nothing, however, could diminish the film's thunder at the box office, which at the time was tremendous. The follow-up to the mega-hit *Goldfinger*, *Thunderball* finished first at the box office in '66, helped along by the Tom Jones theme song and the Oscar-winning special

effects. The movie also revealed Bond to be a cannibal: After he bites a poison spine out of Domino's foot, he declares, "The first time I've tasted women; they're rather good." Is that what critics mean when they talk about actors chewing the scenery?

As for Claudine's later career, she appeared in fifteen other '60s movies (nearly all of them French), she made thirty more foreign flix in the '70s, '80s, and '90s (often with titles that translated into English as things like *The Black Belly of the Tarantula* and *Cauldron of Death*), and she did some elegant ads for the French *Concorde*.

HER '60s LOOK: Eminently photogenic, she always looked like the sleek, sexy 5' 8" beauty contest winner she was (she was voted Miss France in '58 at only 15 years old). In *Thunderball* Bond first sees her character Domino under water in a slinky one-piece swimsuit. He then meets her again in a swank casino, her long hair upswept elegantly, her tan contrasted by a white gown and glittering diamonds. Claudine's magnificent measurements, given in '66 as 36-23-37, were best displayed in the stunning black-and-white bikini she wore in the last half of the film.

BEHIND THE SCENES: She married a businessman. Without any additional information available about her personal life, let's focus instead on Ian Fleming's description of Miss Dominetta Vitali in the novel: "She had a gay, to-hell-with-you face that, Bond thought, would become animal in passion. In profile the eyes were soft charcoal slits…fierce and direct with a golden flicker in the dark brown that held much the same message as the mouth. The general impression, Bond decided, was of a willful, high-tempered, sensual girl—a beautiful Arab mare who would only allow herself to be ridden by a horseman with steel thighs and velvet hands." Bond unsuccessfully tried to saddle up one page later.

BONUS SWINGABILITY: She uses a fake moniker—her real name is Claudine Oger ... her exotic birthplace—Paris, France ... others considered for the role of Domino in *Thunderball* include three official Swingin' Chicks of the '60s: Julie Christie, Faye Dunaway, and Raquel Welch ... Raquel was supposedly slated for the role, but she was released from her contract so she could star in *Fantastic Voyage* ... *Thunderball* was remade in '83, this time retitled *Never Say Never Again*, again with Connery but with Kim Basinger as Domino.

 A DATE WITH CLAUDINE

April 26, 1942	Claudine Auger is born
December 29, 1965	*Thunderball* is released in the U.S.

DANIELA BIANCHI

SWINGIN' '60s CREDENTIALS: This sexy young actress was the choker-wearin', Bond-wooin', train-ridin' SPECTRE-bait in *From Russia with Love*, one of the best Bond movies and a box-office smash.

WORKIN' IT: Unless you're talking with true Bond fans, few people would know the name Daniela Bianchi: "Bianchi? That's a red wine, right? Sweet, full-bodied, good legs, fine nose. Yeah, a '62 Bianchi, that was some year." Only the red wine part would be wrong. The Bond movie she starred in, '62's *From Russia with Love*, was a brilliant Bond film, one of the half-dozen best of the long series and the one that most closely paralleled the book on which it was based. As Tatiana "Tanya" Romana, she was the stereotypical Bond girl—easy on the eyes but not expected to do much besides look scared or laugh at Bond's quips (a stereotype that didn't get seriously challenged until the majestic Diana Rigg showed up in *On Her Majesty's Secret Service* in '69). Like Mie Hama in *You Only Live Twice*, Daniela got to pose as 007's wife (her *nom de mariage* was Caroline Somerset, his was David). But Daniela went Mie one better: traveling with him for half the movie, her character logged plenty of sacktime with 007 (Mie only got a final make-out scene with Bond). It was also the only film in English Daniela Bianchi made during the decade (watch closely—some say her voice was dubbed throughout the entire film because she barely spoke English).

Outside of her Bond-age, she put in some TV appearances (*Dr. Kildare* in '61), and she made a dozen foreign flix. Of these the most notable was the Italian *Operation Kid Brother* in '67, a lame-brained Bond rip-off that starred Sean's younger brother Neil Connery, plus Bond regulars Bernard Lee, who usually played M, and Lois Maxwell, who usually played Miss Moneypenny. In that movie Daniela was shown in bed with Neil and given the line, "Your brother was never like this." A year later she made her last movie.

HER '60s LOOK: In the novel author Ian Fleming described her character as a "young Greta Garbo" with "fine dark brown silken hair brushed straight back from a tall brow and falling heavily down almost to the shoulders, there to curl slightly up at the ends…a good, soft pale skin with an ivory sheen at the cheekbones; wide apart, level eyes of the deepest blue under straight natural brows…the lips were full and finely etched." Indeed. Luv the black choker she wears with 007, and the tantalizing train trousseau she models in the last half of the movie. Actually, the choker *is* her trousseau—as she's undressing on the train, he hands the choker to her as the only thing she needs to wear. Oh, James.…

BEHIND THE SCENES: A youngster born in 1942, she was an Italian model who had just busted the deuce when she made her Bond movie. After leaving the screen at decade's end, she began the '70s married to an Italian millionaire.

BONUS SWINGABILITY: Her exotic birthplace—Rome … she was Miss Italy of 1960, which made her a competitor in the Miss Universe pageant, where she was first runner-up … when she first met 007, Daniela's character was waiting for him in his bed, wearing only the choker … her love scenes with Bond were pretty risqué for the times, because two enemy agents were watching and filming as she and Bond hit the rack … a telling line in *From Russia With Love*: Tatiana tells Bond she has a small mouth, but he says, "It's the right size—for me, that is."

 A DATE WITH DANIELA

January 31, 1942	Daniela Bianchi is born
May 27, 1964	*From Russia with Love* is released

JACQUELINE BISSET

SWINGIN' '60s CREDENTIALS: After working as a London model, this stylish British beauty played "Miss Goodthighs" in the Bond spoof *Casino Royale* and then memorable movie love interests for Frank in *The Detective* and for Steve McQueen in *Bullitt*.

WORKIN' IT: With those looks, Jacqueline Bisset didn't need much talent. Yet she's probably a better actress than most people realize, as verified by the numerous acting awards she's been nominated for: Golden Globes in '69, '79, and '85, and an Emmy for Outstanding Supporting Actress in '99 for *Joan of Arc*. Steve McQueen said of his young *paramour* in *Bullitt*: "She catches good; she can throw it back to you with a great depth for a girl of that age."

Jacqueline's star rose rapidly in the '60s, but her greatest fame came in the '70s. She started as a 20-year-old model in '64, then she worked as an extra in *The Knack...and How to Get It* in '65, which led to a burst of two films a year for the rest of the '60s. Her character in the boister-ous *Casino Royale* ('67), Miss Goodthighs, had a three-minute scene with Peter

Sellers in a hotel room, where she simultaneously seduced and drugged him; she was later killed off by Ursula Andress's character, Vesper Lynd. Among Jacqueline's other '60s roles was a small but memorable part as a sexy but sick traveler in *Two for the Road*, a starring vehicle for Audrey Hepburn. Jacqueline's role in *The Detective* ('68) was supposedly intended for Mia Farrow until Frank Sinatra, playing the shamus, told his young wife to am-scray. *The Sweet Ride* ('68) brought Jacqueline a Golden Globe nomination as the Most Promising Newcomer, while the powerful *Bullitt* ('68) pro-pelled her to further stardom and set her up for the great decade to come. The '70s got off to a high-flyin' start for Jacqueline with the role as Gwen, the sexy stew who had Dean Martin's love child in *Airport* ('70). That same year she received critical acclaim for her dramatic performance as a young Canadian country girl who plummets to the depths of Vegas prostitution in *The Grasshopper*. Later roles included *The Life and Times of Judge Roy Bean* ('72), *Day for Night* ('73), *The Thief Who Came to Dinner* ('73), *Murder on the Orient Express* ('74), *The Deep* ('77) with its legendary wet T-shirt action, *Who Is Killing the Great Chefs of Europe?* ('78), *The Greek Tycoon* ('78), *Class* ('83), *Under the Volcano* ('84), *Wild Orchid* ('90), and *Dangerous Beauty* ('98). She's now got about sixty films on her résumé. Not just a gor-geous star, Jacqueline's also listed as Producer of *Rich and Famous* ('81).

HER '60s LOOK: Jacqueline has one of the most perfect faces in movies—a timeless look that transcends fashion, considered by no less than Steve McQueen to be the most beautiful of any actress he worked with. *Newsweek* agreed, naming her in '77 as the most beautiful actress, not just of the year, but *ever*. Standing over 5' 6", she was also curvy, leggy, and athletic (the rare triple), a great look only hinted at in most of her '60s movies. In *Casino Royale* she was dressed only in a short nightshirt for her one scene, revealing her long legs to good advantage. All her formidable assets were revealed to more stunning effect in 1977's *The Deep*, by itself justification enough when *Playboy* ranked her #86 on its list of the "100 Sexiest Stars of the Century" in January '99.

BEHIND THE SCENES: Young and stunning, she was romantically linked to several '60s superstars, including Frank, Dean, Steve McQueen, Terence Stamp, and Marcello Mastroianni. In '68 she moved in with actor Michael Sarrazin, the guy in *They Shoot Horses, Don't They?* For much of the '80s Jacqueline took up with Alexander Godunov (real name: Boris), a Soviet dancer who defected to the U.S. in '79. He died at the age of 46 in '95.

BONUS SWINGABILITY: Her full moniker is Winnifred Jacqueline Fraser-Bisset, though she's sometimes credited as Jackie in her films (in *Casino Royale* she's billed as Jacky) ... her last

televised interview that she didn't like the name Goodthighs because she didn't think she had particularly good thighs, and the name just brought attention to what she felt were two of her weakest attributes ... what's more, though her *Casino Royale* scenes only took two days to film, the producers kept her on the set for ten weeks, working her into the backgrounds of other scenes as one of Orson Welles' gang members ... in '69 when Jacqueline was nominated for the Golden Globe as the Most Promising Newcomer, the award was won by another Swingin' Chick of the '60s, Olivia Hussey, who was in *Romeo and Juliet* ... how's this for prestige: at Thanksgiving in '99, Jacqueline reportedly had an audience with the Pope, who had enjoyed an advance screening of the Biblical movie *Jesus*, in which she played Mary.

name, by the way, is pronounced "BISS-et" ... her exotic birthplace—Weybridge, England ... Miss Goodthighs was one of three Bond characters with a "good" name: Dr. Holly Goodhead, played by Lois Chiles in *Moonraker*, and Mary Goodnight, played by Britt Ekland in *The Man with the Golden Gun* ... Jacqueline claimed in a

A DATE WITH JACQUELINE

September 13, 1944	Jacqueline Bisset is born
April 28, 1967	*Casino Royale* is released
May 28, 1968	*The Detective* is released
October 17, 1968	*Bullitt* is released
March 5, 1970	*Airport* is released

HONOR BLACKMAN

SWINGIN' '60s CREDENTIALS: In *Goldfinger* this formidable film femme played Pussy Galore and flung Bond to the ground before succumbing to his charms. But Honor had established her rep in the '60s even before *Goldfinger*, especially with her popular role on *The Avengers*.

WORKIN' IT: Long before *Goldfinger* was even a gleam in producer Cubby Broccoli's eye, Honor was appearing in dozens of movies in the '40s and '50s, among them *A Night to Remember* in '58. British audiences also knew her as Mrs. Catherine Gale, karate-chopping, leather-wearing partner to John Steed, on *The Avengers* TV series from '62 to '64 (pre-Diana Rigg). *The Avengers* was so

popular in England that Honor and Patrick Macnee, who played Steed, were deemed worthy to cut a single for Decca Records. "Kinky Boots"/"Let's Keep It Friendly" floundered when it was released in February of '64, but astonishingly it resurfaced to became a top-ten hit in the U.K. in '90! Later in '64 Honor recorded an album, *Everything I've Got*, but it barely caused a ripple on the music seismograph. It didn't matter, though—she'd already decided to let her *Avengers* contract run out and go for the gold. *Goldfinger*, that is.

Easily one of the top-three Bond movies ever, *Goldfinger* presented Honor at her peak as a sexy, assured aviatrix in command of five female pilots. Interestingly, she was 38 in that '64 movie, four years older than Connery, which was quite a departure from the usual pairings that matched Bond with someone younger (sometimes *much* younger).

She made another film with Connery in the '60s, *Shalako* ('68), which also starred another Swingin' Chick of the '60s, Brigitte Bardot. Among the dozen other movie and TV roles she played during the decade was Hera, Queen of the Gods, in Ray Harryhausen's *Jason and the Argonauts* ('63). After the '60s and into the '90s, Honor had roles in various screen projects, most notably an uncredited appearance in *The Three Musketeers* ('74), the female lead in *The Age of Innocence* ('74), a regular role in the British TV series *The Upper Hand* ('90–'93), and the part of Joy Adamson in *To Walk with Lions* ('93). She also performed a one-woman show called *Dishonorable Ladies*. Versatile and durable, Honor Blackman is today something of an English national treasure.

HER '60s LOOK: Athletic, glamorous, beautiful, and smart, as Pussy Galore she was able to roughhouse successfully and believably with Bond, tossing him, and then falling for him, in the hay in Goldfinger's barn. She looked and acted like an athlete or a judo champion, though she dressed a little more provocatively in the film. Ya gotta love Honor's great riding outfit and jump suits, all of which managed to expose her ample chestal assets (her measurements in the early '60s were listed as 36-24-37). But her real fashion influence was felt when she played Cathy Gale on *The Avengers*. Honor was probably the first TV star to wear black leather clothes (usually tight suits, but also a long leather dress), often accessorizing the look with long leather boots (hence the record she made with Macnee). Said Patrick of his sexy co-star: "We had Honor Blackman in black leather, partly because it was better than wearing skirts when she was doing lots of violent action. It was an idea before its time to show women in the positive sense and not in the repressive, submissive sense, and I found that exciting and interesting. We used a lot of sexual fetishes—leather, bondage, whatever—in a very, very light way. In other words, we titillated." Indeed.

BEHIND THE SCENES: Honor was married to actor Maurice Kauffman from '61 to '75. She's got a daughter named Lottie and a son named Barnaby. And entering the new millennium, she was still single. Now let's go behind the scenes of her *Goldfinger* character.

In Ian Fleming's original novel, Pussy Galore is more clearly a lesbian who gets "cured" by Bond. The character's name is one of the most famous from all the Bond films, but the producers were nervous about using it; had the press reacted negatively to the moniker, the studio was ready to change it to Kitty Galore. Fortunately, after the London premiere of the film, a congratulatory photo of Honor being presented to Prince Philip ran in all the English papers. The name became a non-issue—the British Empire, and the producers, were saved. When Bond hears her name for the first time, he smiles and says, "I must be dreaming," but this was not what was originally written for the film. The first version was, "I know you are, but what's your name?" Unlike most Bond Beauties, Honor's character beds 007 twice in one movie, and she lives to tell about it; many do him once, and then die (see Shirley Eaton, following).

BONUS SWINGABILITY: Her exotic birthplace—the swingin'est, London, England ... as a teen Honor worked during the war as a messenger for the Home Office ... *Avengers* alums Honor, Diana Rigg, and Patrick Macnee all starred in Bond films—Rigg in *On Her Majesty's Secret Service* in '69 and Macnee in *A View to a Kill* in '85 ... when Honor left *The Avengers* in '64 to star in *Goldfinger*, a new character played by Elizabeth Shepherd was going to be introduced on *The Avengers* as the next partner for John Steed; however, after one Shepherd episode was filmed, the producers decided to replace her, Diana Rigg was quickly brought in, and the show zoomed to whole new levels of popularity ... the vehicles driven by the different actresses on *The Avengers*: Honor rode a motorcycle (in keeping with the leathers she wore), Diana Rigg drove a blue Lotus Elan sports car, and Diana's successor, Tara King, drove a deep-red AC Cobra.

A DATE WITH HONOR

February 6, 1922	Patrick Macnee is born
August 22, 1926	Honor Blackman is born
August 25, 1930	Sean Connery is born
January 7, 1961	*The Avengers* debuts in the U.K.
September 29, 1962	"Mr. Teddy Bear," Honor's first episode on *The Avengers*, airs in the U.K.
June 19, 1963	*Jason and the Argonauts* is released
March 21, 1964	"Lobster Quadrille," Honor's last episode on *The Avengers*, airs in the U.K.
December 25, 1964	*Goldfinger* is released

SHIRLEY EATON

good girls, bad girls, military girls, and science girls. When you look that good, directors will find a place for you, no matter what kind of movie they're making.

A child actress in the late '40s, she graduated to lots of movie activity as an English ingenue in the '50s, especially in the popular *Carry On...* comedies (*Carry On Sergeant* and *Carry On Nurse*, both in '58, *Carry On Constable*, '60). She appeared in films through most of the '60s, though none were nearly as big as *Goldfinger*—which for awhile was in the *Guinness Book of World Records* as the fastest-grossing movie ever. On the Bond Market it is still perhaps the most highly regarded of all time ("drenched in cliff-hanging suspense," heralded the *N.Y. Times*). And after three decades of Bond movies, hers are still among the best, sexiest Bond scenes ever filmed, though there are only seven minutes of them. It is while her character Jill Masterson is nuzzling his neck that Connery's Bond talks to Felix Leiter on the phone and delivers one of the best Bond quips ever: "Something big's come up." Bond is so overwhelmed after having sex with her that when he goes to retrieve champagne from the 'fridge, he is oblivious to the hulking Oddjob, who stomps up from behind to knock him out. Oddjob then kills Jill with skin-suffocating paint. Thus, like so many other Bond Beauties, she pays for her dalliance with 007 with her life.

Later Shirley starred in the classy *Ten Little Indians* ('66), but most of her other '60s roles came in routine adventure flix à la *Rhino* in '64, *Around the World Under the Sea* in '66, the cult-fave *The Million Eyes of Sumuru* in '67, *Eight on the Lam* with Bob Hope in '67, and *The Blood of Fu Manchu* in '68 (in which she wore a long black wig and co-starred with Frankie Avalon). Regrettably for movie audiences, she has only one movie credit after '69—the obscure *Future Woman* in '75—as she left the biz to spend more time with her family and went on to live in France for a while. An accomplished painter, sculptor, and singer, she found time to write her autobiography, *Golden Girl* ('99), and she's working on a book of poetry. She also performs a lot of charity work in England and makes frequent appearances on British television, sometimes as a participant in live debates. For Bond fans worldwide, she will always be a golden memory from the '60s.

SWINGIN' '60s CREDENTIALS: The beautiful Shirley Eaton became an international sex symbol (and a *Life* magazine cover girl) thanks to her brief but memorable role as the playful, enthusiastic gold-painted girl in *Goldfinger*.

WORKIN' IT: Shirley's versatility enabled her to appear in adventure films, comedies, serious mysteries, even sci-fi, playing

HER '60s LOOK: A 27-year-old playmate in *Goldfinger*, Shirley was a healthy, active blonde who still ranks as one of the prettiest of all the Bond Beauties. When Bond first sees Jill Masterson in *Goldfinger*, she is in a Miami hotel room, lying on her stomach in only a black bikini, spying through a telescope to help Auric Goldfinger cheat at cards. Shirley's character surrenders to Bond's charms in about ten seconds (but she has the decency to wait until that night to bed down with him and then start wearing his shirt).

Here's Ian Fleming's description of the Jill Masterson character in his novel *Goldfinger*: "It was at the top of the afternoon heat and she was naked except for a black brassiere and black silk briefs. She was swinging her legs in a bored fashion.... She was very beautiful. She had the palest blonde hair. It fell heavily to her shoulders, unfashionably long. Her eyes were deep blue against a lightly sunburned skin and her mouth was bold and generous and would have a lovely smile.... She was tall, perhaps five feet ten, and her arms and legs looked firm as if she might be a swimmer. Her breasts thrust against the black silk of the brassiere." Five minutes later, of course, she wore the best costume ever worn by any actress in any Bond movie. The image of her all painted up in gold is one of the classic icons of '60s cinema. Shirley generated awesome bikini heat, too, with a modern silhouette that signalled the transition from the full-figured, big-hipped sexpots of the late '50s (Marilyn Monroe, Jayne Mansfield, Sophia Loren) to the more slender, more youthfully active vixens of the late '60s (Jacqueline Bisset, Jane Fonda, Sharon Tate).

BEHIND THE SCENES:

Shirley was married to building contractor Colin Lenton-Rowe from '57 into the mid-'90s, when he died from cancer. She's now got two grown kids and currently lives about twenty miles north of London. She still receives daily fan mail, most of it from the U.S. and most of it about *Goldfinger*.

BONUS SWINGABILITY:

Her exotic birthplace—the swingin'est, London, England ... 17-year-old Shirley made her movie debut doing the horseback-riding scenes for Janet Leigh in '54's *Prince Valiant* ...

the introduction to Shirley's book was written by Mickey Spillane, with whom she starred in the '63 movie *The Girl Hunters* ... Shirley was actually wearing a G-string for her big paint scene in *Goldfinger*, and a patch of skin on her stomach was left exposed so she wouldn't die during filming ... Shirley's "gold paint" was actually thick skin lotion loaded with millions of real gold particles; actual paint would've dried and cracked under the hot lights ... by the way, another actress in film history was once "killed" by being smothered in paint—see *Bedlam*, a 1946 Boris Karloff movie ... when she attended the London premiere of Goldfinger, Shirley was shocked to see that most of her lines in the movie had been dubbed. (Every line except "Not too early," which she speaks as she's tempting Bond back to bed, and not to build a cool little fort out of the pillows if you know what we mean and we think you do.) She also saw that her name hadn't been credited with the prominence that was spelled out in her contract, so she challenged the studio and won a hefty settlement ... it was in Jill's presence that Bond mentioned the proper serving temperature for Dom Perignon '53 ("passion juice" as he called it): 38 degrees Fahrenheit.

A DATE WITH SHIRLEY

January 12, 1937	Shirley Eaton is born
August 5, 1957	Shirley gets married
November 6, 1964	Shirley makes the cover of *Life* magazine
December 25, 1964	*Goldfinger* is released
April 26, 1967	*Eight on the Lam* is released

DIANA RIGG

SWINGIN' '60s CREDENTIALS: A slinky sophisticate as good with a gun as she is with a Shakespeare soliloquy, regal Diana had two memorable '60s roles: She was judo-choppin', sports-car-drivin', smooth-talkin' Emma Peel on *The Avengers*, then she was Tracy, Bond's wife in *On Her Majesty's Secret Service*.

WORKIN' IT: This graceful, beautiful, intelligent actress is one of the most respected of all the stars from the '60s. Born in England in '38, Diana lived in India from age 2 to 8, then returned to England to finish her schooling. From '59 to '62 she was a rising star with the Royal Shakespeare Company. Then came the role of Emma in *The Avengers*.

The great English spy series starring Patrick Macnee as elegant John Steed had been on the air in the U.K with Honor Blackman in the role of Steed's partner, Cathy Gale. When Honor left in '64 to go make *Goldfinger*, Diana entered as Mrs. Emma Peel, Steed's new platonic partner (the "Mrs." referred to her husband, Peter Peel, a fly-boy who had mysteriously disappeared in South America). Diana played the role from '65 to '67 (though her shows were still broadcast into '68). She brought to the show a saucy charm and liberated spirit that perfectly balanced Steed's conservative old-school mannerisms (she wore leather, he wore a bowler). Emma was a rich, fascinating character, able to pick a lock, karate chop a villain, and read both *Basic Nuclear Physics* (a book actually shown in Emma's home) and *Advanced Ventriloquism* (a book we actually see her reading). Diana gave her opinions about Emma in *The Avengers Companion*: "Emma Peel was definitely a different type of character for television. For the first time a woman in a TV series was intelligent, independent and capable of looking after herself. That is why the show became such a success—it reflected what was happening to women throughout the world in the '60s." Validating her impact on popular culture, *TV Guide*'s October '99 list of "TV's 50 Greatest Characters Ever" placed Emma Peel at #8 (only one other woman was in the top ten—Lucy Ricardo at #3).

After a brief return to the Royal Shakespeare Company for the role of Viola in *Twelfth Night*, Diana Bonded in '69. *On Her Majesty's Secret Service* introduced Australian model George Lazenby for his one shot at 007, and it also married Bond off after a decade of his philandering (though the bride got killed on her wedding day). Although Connery was sorely missed, it was still a cracking-good story, and Diana is still hailed as perhaps the strongest, and the best, of the Bond women.

Diana's career continued, blending lightweight projects (*The Hospital* in '72, a quickly canceled TV series in '73, *The Great Muppet Caper* in '75, and hostess of the *Mystery* TV series in the '90s) with prestigious classics (the films *Julius Caesar* in '70 and *King Lear* in '84) and a long stage career (highlighted by star turns in '94's *Medea* and '97's *Who's Afraid of Virginia Woolf?*). She's also compiled the text for the book *No Turn Unstoned: The Worst-Ever Theatrical Reviews* (including some written about her).

Major awards punctuate her long career: She received two Emmy nominations for *The Avengers*, a '72 Golden Globe nomination as Best Supporting Actress for *The Hospital*, a '94 Tony Award for *Medea*, a '97 Emmy as Outstanding Supporting Actress for *Rebecca*, and, most impressive of all, knighthood, bringing with it the exalted titles Dame Diana Rigg and Dame Commander of the British Empire.

HER '60s LOOK: Hers was an iconic beauty, representing the very best that TV had to offer in the '60s. Her big smile, big cheekbones, and big Breck flip gave her a wholesome, yet playful appeal. Her long lean 5' 8+" figure was perfectly adaptable to the athletic stunts and varied costumes she displayed on *The Avengers*. It's a toss-up what looked better—Emma in a swingin' mod outfit, or Emma in her fightin' jumpsuit— but either way it's easy to see why in July '99 *TV Guide* voted her the sexiest woman *ever* on TV. Interestingly, a costumer for *The Avengers* once said that the tight leather suit Emma was so identified with was rarely worn on the show because it had the tendency to tear during action sequences. However it was such a great outfit that the few times Diana did wear the suit, it made a lasting impression on the audience. Ironically, Diana didn't seem at all to be the actress author Ian Fleming would've wanted for the role of Tracy in *On Her Majesty's Secret Service*. Here's his description of her in the novel: She had "golden arms, a beautiful golden face, with brilliant blue eyes and shocking pink lips ... a bell of golden hair down to her shoulders."

No matter. *Playboy* anointed her #75, ahead of supermodel Kathy Ireland, on its January '99 list of the "100 Sexiest Stars of the Century."

BEHIND THE SCENES: Far too classy for scandals, she's generated no simmering '60s stories, which is just about right for our smart Emma. Later on, Diana divorced two husbands, one in '76 after three years of marriage and the other in '90 after eight years and one daughter.

BONUS SWINGABILITY: Her exotic birthplace—Doncaster, England ... like Honor Blackman, who was 38 in Goldfinger, Diana was also in her thirties—31—when she starred in her Bond movie ... Brigitte Bardot and Catherine Deneuve were serious contenders for the role of Tracy ... at one point in pre-production for her Bond flick, producers considered an opening sequence that showed Connery going in for plastic surgery and coming out as George Lazenby, thus accounting for the difference between the old Bond and the new ... not sure how the differences in their accents—Connery's Scottish, Lazenby's Australian—would've been explained ... in Diana's last episode of *The Avengers*, "The Forget-Me-Knot," we got a glimpse of her long-lost husband, Peter Peel—his clothes were identical to Steed's and in fact Patrick Macnee played the role, though he was only visible in a long-distance shot ... in that episode, Steed called Emma by her first name for the first and only time ... Emma's replacement, who passed the departing Emma on the stairs up to Steed's flat, was Agent 69, Tara King, played by Linda Thorson ... Tara's relationship with Steed was quite different from Emma's: The most physical affection we ever saw between Steed and the married Emma was a peck on the cheek in their last episode together, but when Steed was paired with the single Tara, there was the clear implication that they had a physical relationship ... the show was canceled a year later.

A DATE WITH DIANA

July 20, 1938	Diana Rigg is born (the same day as Natalie Wood)
March 28, 1966	*The Avengers* debuts in the U.S.
September 1, 1966	"The Town of No Return," Emma Peel's first episode on *The Avengers*, airs in the U.S.
March 20, 1968	"The Forget-Me-Knot," Emma's last episode of *The Avengers*, airs in the U.S.
December 18, 1969	*On Her Majesty's Secret Service* is released
September 14, 1997	Diana wins an Emmy for *Rebecca*

beauties

MIE HAMA

SWINGIN' '60s CREDENTIALS: This perky, subservient Japanese doll had key roles in two swingin' '60s movies—the Woody Allen spoof *What's Up, Tiger Lily?* and the Bond bonzai bonanza *You Only Live Twice.*

WORKIN' IT: A huge dramatic talent, one of the greatest actresses of her generation, a major player on the global stage—Mie Hama was none of these. She was, however, a cheerful, athletic, attractive presence in all of her movies.

Born in '43, Mie hit the '60s at only 17 and quickly found a place in the Japanese cinema. By the time she was 24 and appearing with Connery in *You Only Live Twice* ('67), she'd been in over fifty Japanese films. To English-speaking audiences she didn't have much resonance back then: her only other main role was in Woody Allen's Japanese-movie-turned-American-spoof *What's Up, Tiger Lily?* ('66). She wasn't even the top-billed Bond Beauty in her one Bond movie (though she was the cutest). Half of *You Only Live Twice* goes by before she enters, but as soon as she does, she marries 007. Although it was only another pretend marriage (similar to the one Daniela Bianchi briefly enjoyed with Bond in *From Russia with Love*), at least Mie got an actual ceremony out of it (Diana Rigg's character married Bond for real two years later in *On Her Majesty's Secret Service*). Mie's character is no pushover and quickly puts the kibosh on Bond's amorous plans: "No honeymoon," she confidently announces to a surprised Bondo-san (as he's called in the book), "this is business." An hour later, Mie's character surrenders in a life raft, where we learn Bond's position on off-shore drilling. After Bonding, she didn't appear in any other major English-language films and today remains anonymous to American audiences. In Japan, however, she'd still be instantly recognized, for she was a huge Japanese movie star during the '60s. Graham Rye's book *The James Bond Girls* said that back then she was "the most photographed girl in Japan," the equivalent of "the Japanese Brigitte Bardot." In the '70s she became a popular TV hostess, giving her career a chance to live twice.

HER '60s LOOK: A sweet face framed by stylin' bangs—so '60s! As a 5' 4" Bond bikini babe, she was athletic and pert and healthy-looking, all of which fit in with Ian Fleming's original depiction of Kissy in the novel. On his pages she had "almond eyes," a "snub nose," and a "petalled mouth. She wore no make-up and did not need to, for she had that rosy-tinted skin on a golden background—the colors of a golden peach...Her arms and legs were longer and less masculine than is usual with Japanese girls, and...her breasts and buttocks were firm and proud...her skin...glowed with a golden sheen of health and vitality." "Firm and proud," that's our Ian.

BEHIND THE SCENES: The closest thing we have to juicy gossip about her is a rumor that she married a Japanese businessman.

BONUS SWINGABILITY: Her exotic birthplace—Tokyo, Japan ... in Cantonese, her first name means "beautiful" and is pronounced as two syllables, MEE-yay ... we hear she was a tough negotiator: In the mid-'60s she supposedly spoke almost no English, and the producers of *You Only Live Twice* allegedly told her she would be fired from the film because she couldn't learn her English dialogue quickly enough. The story goes that she very calmly told them that if she were fired, she would commit suicide because of the dishonor. They decided to keep her on ... she also had a talent for finding roles in which her characters had great names—in *Tiger Lily* she was Teri Yaki, with Bond she was Kissy Suzuki, and in *Kingukongu no gyakushu* ('67) she was Madame Piranha.

A DATE WITH MIE

November 20, 1943	Mie Hama is born
June 13, 1967	*You Only Live Twice* is released

THE ELVIS GIRLS! GIRLS! GIRLS!

Elvis Presley starred in twenty-seven movies during the '60s (*four in 1966 alone!*). This prodigious output—coupled with the kind of sexy roles he played, usually along the lines of a singin' race car driver, a singin' boat skipper, or a singin' whirlybird pilot—demanded an enormous bevy of beautiful actresses for Elvis to chase, dance with, sing to, or rescue. Occasionally legendary stars like Barbara Stanwyck and Angela Lansbury would grace the King's movies, but typically his supporting cast was well-rounded out by young, pretty actresses better suited for the raucous clambakes, lu-wows, and pool parties called for by the movies' slim plots. The focus is on a divine nine here, but a complete list of Elvis' co-stars would add other famous names like Ursula Andress, Donna Douglas, Barbara Eden, young Anissa Jones, Hope Lange, Barbara McNair, Mary Tyler Moore, Sheree North, Pat Priest, Nancy Sinatra, Stella Stevens, Deborah Walley, and Raquel Welch. With these wonderful women as allies, the King was takin' care of big-screen business, indeed. Welcome to paradise, Elvis style. Viva las '60s!

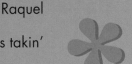

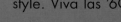

ANN-MARGRET

especially her performance of the song "Bachelor in Paradise" for the '62 Academy Awards, brought her national attention. *Bye Bye Birdie* ('63), in which she was a 22-year-old playing a ninth grader, made her a household name. The movie broke the box-office record at Radio City and put her on the cover of *Life* magazine.

JFK certainly appreciated her exciting talent—for his birthday in '62, Marilyn Monroe cooed a sultry "Happy Birthday" to him in Madison Square Garden, but in '63 it was Ann-Margret who sang "Baby, Won't You Please Come Home" to him at his private party.

A year later *Kitten with a Whip* turned up the heat, but her high-powered pairing with the King was even more electric. In *Viva Las Vegas* ('64), she was as confident and sexy as Elvis, and it was the first time he shared the big screen with an actress of equal wattage. Hers were the best duets any actress ever did with Elvis, especially the spunky "The Lady Loves Me," which ended with her pushing him into a pool. Off the screen, she headlined Vegas in '67 in a big, splashy, five-week engagement at the Riviera Hotel. She also made two tours of Vietnam with Bob Hope, and her '60s recordings covered jazz, country, and Broadway tunes.

After a brief slump due to a bout with alcohol, her career revived in '71 with *Carnal Knowledge* and an Oscar nomination for Best Supporting Actress. She had little time to enjoy her success, however, before misfortune struck. The following year she fell twenty-two feet while performing on the stage at the Sahara Hotel in Lake Tahoe. It was a terrible accident—she was in a coma for two days and suffered a broken jaw and broken facial bones. Amazingly, within three months she reopened in Vegas to standing ovations.

Throughout the '70s and '80s she continued to headline Vegas, looking more beautiful and drawing bigger crowds than ever. Her film career showed similar resilience, and she made dozens of movies from the '70s through the '90s, including *Tommy* in '75 (bringing her a second Oscar nomination) and *Grumpy Old Men* in '93. In '99 she got her fifth Emmy nomination for the TV movie in which she played Pamela Harriman. Her autobiography, *My Story*, was published in '94 and became a *New York Times* bestseller. Unlike other '60s sex kittens whose work never matured to a higher artistic level, today Ann-Margret is an acclaimed actress, widely respected and much loved.

SWINGIN' '60s CREDENTIALS: The decade's most versatile performer, this voluptuous rock-em', sock-em' fireball, "the female Elvis" as she was called, starred in *Bye Bye Birdie*, Elvis' *Viva Las Vegas*, and a dozen other '60s movies, with many TV specials, Vegas shows, and record albums filling out her '60s résumé.

WORKIN' IT: Ann-Margret had a meteoric rise to international stardom, and her stardom has had staying power. Even when her movie career has slowed, as it did in the late '60s, she has found some way to stay in the spotlight—often with live Vegas shows that have only enhanced her reputation as a dynamic performer.

Ann-Margret got off to a fast start, landing an agent at 16 and stints with a Midwestern vocal quartet called The Subtle Tones. When the group got gigs in Hollywood nightclubs, talent scouts spotted her and tested her, and she was quickly signed to an RCA record contract and a seven-year deal with Twentieth Century Fox. TV appearances,

HER '60s LOOK: Ann-Margret has always flashed big hair that's had a suitably reckless style. The color, though, has changed throughout her career. She was a brunette until she went fiery red for the film *State Fair* in '62, and then she went blonde for the gritty *Kitten with a Whip*.

Her kitten-with-a-sexy-pout face made every man want her and every man think she wanted him. But it's the "oooh la la" figure that's most memorable. Wearing black tights for Elvis, a clingy bathing suit poolside, and spangles for the stage, her eye-popping curves were so captivating that the director of *Viva Las Vegas* supposedly had the cameraman shoot a four-minute close up of her behind—footage that wasn't shown in public. Once when she was on *The Tonight Show*, her shawl fell off from around her shoulders, revealing a gown cut so low the audience gasped, thinking she was actually topless. Johnny did one of his classic double-takes at the sight of her awesome anatomy. So sexy was she, when *Playboy* announced its list of the "100 Sexiest Stars of the Century" in January '99, Ann-Margret was among the elite at #13, right between Kim Basinger and Anita Ekberg.

BEHIND THE SCENES:
The press has linked her romantically to Johnny Carson, Eddie Fisher, Steve McQueen, and Elvis. It was with the King, whom she met on the set of *Viva Las Vegas*, that she got the most attention. She wrote in her autobiography that when she and Elvis met in '63, they simultaneously said the same words to each other: "I've heard a lot about you." Their on-screen pairing was so hot, the chemistry so obvious, that when the studio released a publicity shot for the movie that showed them getting married, the fan magazines jumped all over the rumors that the couple really was married. Supposedly while in Vegas together they hid out in the Sahara for a weekend, only opening the door for room service. At one point Elvis' Memphis Mafia was said to have been so concerned that they slipped burning newspapers under their door, hoping the smoke would drive them out. She later wrote: "We both shared a devil within….At heart Elvis was no saint or king, but rather a kid….We were indeed soul mates, shy on the outside, but unbridled within….His wish was that we could stay together, but of course we both knew that was impossible….We talked about marriage…but we were never engaged." They broke up in '64 after a year of dating, possibly because Elvis was focusing on Priscilla, who had just graduated high school, and possibly because he and Ann-Margret each had too many career commitments that kept them separated. Singer Bobby Darin once said: "Elvis Presley confided in me soon after he did *Viva Las Vegas* with Ann-Margret that he was considering marrying her. I'm not implying that anything untoward ever occurred between them, but they had a marvelous chemistry. " After Elvis died in '77, she admitted that she would "never recover from Elvis' death. He is a part of me…and that will never go away." That isn't to say she didn't still experience true love. In '61 she'd met actor Roger "77 Sunset Strip" Smith, who was almost ten years her senior; they hooked up again in '64, and after a three-year courtship they married in Vegas in '67, moving into the Hollywood house formerly owned by Humphrey Bogart and Lauren Bacall. They've been each other's best ally ever since. He nursed her after her '72 accident, and when he later got a rare degenerative nerve disease that left him bedridden, she halted her career for two years to take care of him.

BONUS SWINGABILITY:
Her full name is Ann-Margret Olsson … her exotic birthplace—Valsjobyn, Sweden … in the mid-'50s she went to New Trier High School near Chicago, the same school that

produced Rock Hudson and Charlton Heston … she was the voice of Ann-Margrock, a character styled to look just like her, on *The Flintstones* in '63 … Tina Turner's autobiography reveals that Ann-Margret's first date with Roger Smith was to an Ike and Tina Turner concert … supposedly Ann-Margret almost got the starring role in the movie version of *Gypsy*, but the part went to Natalie Wood … she's said that she loves to ride motorcycles, especially Harleys … one of the presents she kept from Elvis was her bed: round and pink … throughout her career, whenever she opened a new live show Elvis would send a huge bouquet of flowers in the shape of a guitar … his nickname for her was "Rusty," the name of her character in *Viva Las Vegas* … she has her own official Web site— http://www.ann-margret.com.

 ## A DATE WITH ANN-MARGRET

December 18, 1932	Roger Smith is born
April 28, 1941	Ann-Margret is born
August 21, 1961	"I Just Don't Understand" enters the *Billboard* charts (it will reach #17)
January 11, 1963	She makes the cover of *Life* magazine
April 5, 1963	*Bye Bye Birdie* is released
May 20, 1964	*Viva Las Vegas* is released
May 1, 1967	Elvis marries Priscilla
May 8, 1967	Ann-Margret marries Roger
September 10, 1972	She falls from the stage in Lake Tahoe
August 16, 1977	Elvis dies

YVONNE CRAIG

SWINGIN' '60s CREDENTIALS: This personable, perky actress was virtually unavoidable during the '60s as she livened up the big and small screens with dozens of cheerful appearances. Among her most prominent roles were the bubbly bunkmates in two Elvis movies and a bubbly Batgirl on *Batman*.

WORKIN' IT: Looking over her credits one might think, "*Dang*, this girl was in everything!" That "everything" lasted over ten years. Maybe fans were confusing effulgent enthusiasm for deep acting talent, but there's no denying Yvonne Craig's wholesome, fun appeal and the exuberant energy she brought to her roles.

As a youth Yvonne had trained as a serious dancer, moving to L.A. in hopes of dancing, not necessarily acting. But at 22 she played Nan in the first, best *Gidget* movie ('59), and her Hollywood momentum built rapidly, bringing her parts in a decade's worth of prominent movies and TV shows: Bing Crosby's *High Time* ('60), two Elvis movies (*It Happened at the World's Fair* in '63 and *Kissin' Cousins* in '64), *Ski Party* ('65) with Frankie and Annette, *Mars Needs Women* ('66) with Tommy Kirk, *In Like Flint* ('67), *Voyage to the Bottom of the Sea*, *The Man from U.N.C.L.E.*, *The Big Valley*, *Wild Wild West*, *Star Trek* (as a sultry green alien), *The Mod Squad*, *The Many Loves of Dobie Gillis*, *77 Sunset Strip*, *My Three Sons*, *Dr. Kildare*, *McHale's Navy*, *My Favorite Martian*, *It Takes a Thief*, *Love American Style*, *Mannix*, and more.

In the second season ('67-'68) of the campy *Batman*, Yvonne's Batgirl character was a librarian named Barbara Gordon, daughter of the Gotham City Police Commissioner and a crime-fightin', motorbike-ridin', cape-flarin', high-heel-boots-wearin' ally to the Dynamic Duo. Though her only appearances were in the show's last season, it's still her most popular role.

More hit TV shows, like *The Six Million Dollar Man*, *Kojak*, *Land of the Giants*, and *Fantasy Island* followed in the '70s. In the '90s Yvonne built a career in L.A. real estate—successful, no doubt,

because who wouldn't want to buy their house from Batgirl? Her humorous, candid autobiography, *From Ballet to the Batcave and Beyond*, came out in the spring of 2000.

HER '60s LOOK: With her short hair and youthful features, she was more like a cute reliable girlfriend than a steamy sex goddess. A lean, compact 5' 4" tall with great hips, she had amazing versatility—not many other '60s actresses could successfully pull off a bikini, batgirl vinyl, western duds, and hillbilly garb like she did in her roles.

BEHIND THE SCENES: Rumor has it that she had romantic relationships with David Nelson of *The Adventures of Ozzie & Harriet*, Bill Bixby of *The Courtship of Eddie's Father*, comedian Mort Sahl, and… ahem…Elvis. She's been married twice, the first time for two years in her early twenties to singer Jimmie Boyd ("I Saw Mommie Kissing Santa Claus"), and then in the late '80s to her current husband, a real estate developer.

BONUS SWINGABILITY: Her exotic birthplace—Taylorville, Illinois … in *It Happened at the World's Fair*, Elvis sings the sexiest song of his movie career, the seductive double-entendre-filled "Relax" as he's leaning over Yvonne … *Batman* was so popular in its first year, it was shown in two-part episodes that ran on consecutive nights … Yvonne has proudly said that she did her own motorcycling on *Batman* … many other Swingin' Chicks of the '60s appeared on the show, including Julie Newmar as Catwoman, Jill St. John, Linda Harrison, Carolyn Jones, and Victoria Vetri … Yvonne has her own official Web site— http://www.yvonnecraig.com.

 A DATE WITH YVONNE

May 16, 1937	Yvonne Craig is born
April 3, 1963	*It Happened at the World's Fair* is released
March 1, 1964	*Kissin' Cousins* is released
January 12, 1966	*Batman* debuts
March 14, 1968	The last original episode of *Batman* airs

SHELLEY FABARES

SWINGIN' '60s CREDENTIALS: This classy teen singer had a number-one hit, "Johnny Angel," in '62 before graduating to roles as sweet girlfriend material in three Elvis movies.

WORKIN' IT: Even before she hit the top of the music charts with the cloud-soft "Johnny Angel" in '62, Shelley Fabares was already well known to American audiences. She'd been acting since she was 3 years old and appearing on TV and in movies all through her childhood. That same year, seasoned 14-year-old Shelley landed the part of daughter Mary Stone in the classic '50s series, *The Donna Reed Show*.

She moved on to popular teen flix like *Ride the Wild Surf* ('64), three mid-decade Elvis flix (*Girl Happy* in '65, *Spinout* in '66, and *Clambake* in '67), then *Hold On!* ('66) and *A Time to Sing* ('68). Her recording career continued through much of the decade, too. In *Girl Happy* she sang "Spring Fever" with Elvis, and eventually she released five albums: *Shelley!*, *The Things We Did Last Summer* (with Shelley on the cover in pink pants holding a beach ball), *Teenage Triangle* and *More Teenage Triangle* (with James Darren and Paul Peterson), and *Bye Bye Birdie* (with James Darren, Paul Peterson, and the Marcels). From these came three modest singles—"Johnny Loves Me," "The Things We Did Last Summer," and "Ronnie, Call Me When You Get a Chance."

After the '60s came more cool TV work, especially episodes of *Love, American Style* in '71, *McCloud* in '72, two years on *The Brian Keith Show* in the early '70s, *The Rookies* in '75, *Vega$* in '78, three years on *One Day at a Time* in the early '80s, *Newhart* in '87, *Murder She Wrote* in '89, a long run on *Coach* from '89 to '97 (bringing her an Emmy nomination in '93), and over a dozen TV movies.

HER '60s LOOK: Non-threatening to parents, but attractive to other '60s teens, Shelley had styled Breck hair, a pretty face, and a sincere smile. She played it youthfully cool and conservative with her clothes, favoring Capri pants instead of minis for her lithe and limber figure. Shelley told *16* magazine in November '62 that she was 5' 4" tall and weighed 103 pounds and that she "prefers casual clothes, by this I don't mean just Capris but comfortable day dresses, they must always be neat and I always like to look feminine. I feel some of the styles nowadays are not feminine enough." Amen to that.

BEHIND THE SCENES: Shelley described her favorite date to *16* magazine in '62: "I like to go to dinner and a show sometimes. But most of the time, I love to get together with a small group of friends at someone's home and just talk, relax and have a good time." Some rumors suggest a possible romance with Elvis in her past. According to printed sources, in *Spinout* she and the King ignored the director's order to "Cut!" and instead continued their kissing scene for three minutes in front of the crew. She got married in '64 to producer Lou Adler, the mover behind the Mamas and the Papas and *The Rocky Horror Picture Show*. She married actor Mike Farrell, he of TV's *M*A*S*H*, in '84 and has worked with him to raise funds for various causes, notably Alzheimer's research.

BONUS SWINGABILITY: Her full name is Michelle Anne Marie Fabares ... her exotic birthplace—Santa Monica, California ... she had quite the impact on Elvis—he claimed she was his favorite co-star ... actress Nanette Fabray is her aunt ... according to an interview she did with *Teen* magazine in '62, when "Johnny Angel" hit #1, Shelley was home in bed with mononucleosis ... Shelley wasn't the only actor on *The Donna Reed Show* to have a hit song—her "brother" on the show, Paul Petersen, scored a hit with the novelty song "She Can't Find Her Keys" in '62 ... when Shelley left *The Donna Reed Show* in '63, Paul's real-life sister, Patty, joined the show's cast as a newly adopted daughter in the Stone family ... Shelley is a close friend of another Swingin' Chick of the '60s, Annette Funicello—in fact Shelley was a bridesmaid at Annette's first wedding in '65.

A DATE WITH SHELLEY

January 19, 1944	Shelley Fabares is born
September 24, 1958	*The Donna Reed Show* debuts
April 14, 1965	*Girl Happy* is released
November 23, 1966	*Spinout* is released
November 22, 1967	*Clambake* is released
February 28, 1989	*Coach* debuts

ANNE HELM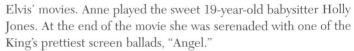

SWINGIN' '60s CREDENTIALS: A lovely guest star on many '60s TV shows, Anne made her biggest splash alongside the King in *Follow That Dream*.

WORKIN' IT: Early in her teens Anne Helm and her mother moved from Canada to New York, where Anne studied ballet and began modeling. Success came quickly: at 16 she became a showgirl at the Copa, where Sinatra was the headliner. Anne was also doing Broadway and off-Broadway theatre at this time.

She made her first TV appearance (playing Miss America on *The Phil Silvers Show*) in the late '50s. Dozens of TV roles followed, including shots on standards like *Rawhide*, *Alfred Hitchcock Presents*, and *Wagon Train*. *Desire in the Dust* ('60) put her onto the big screen, and the fantasy flick *The Magic Sword* ('62) put her in her first starring role (as Princess Helene, alongside Gary "2001: A Space Odyssey" Lockwood and Basil Rathbone).

The Princess got the King in '62. Based on Richard Powell's '57 novel *Pioneer, Go Home*, 1962's *Follow That Dream* was one of the most heart-warming and sincere of Elvis' movies. Anne played the sweet 19-year-old babysitter Holly Jones. At the end of the movie she was serenaded with one of the King's prettiest screen ballads, "Angel."

The immediate years A.E. (After Elvis) brought three more '62 movies for the busy Anne—*The Interns, The Couch*, and *The Iron Maiden*—plus lots of prominent TV appearances, including *The F.B.I.*, *The Big Valley*, *Airwolf*, *The Streets of San Francisco*, and *Hawaii Five-O*. Later in the decade she did some cornball classics of '60s cinema, such as *Honeymoon Hotel* in '64 and *Nightmare in Wax* in '69. A year on *General Hospital* and the TV movie *A Tattered Web* (both in '71), James Caan's *Hide in Plain Sight* ('80), and a role in "The Doll," one of the best episodes of Steven Spielberg's *Amazing Stories* TV series ('86), highlighted her subsequent screen work.

In the '90s she successfully pursued other careers away from the camera. A talented artist, she has had paintings exhibited in Southern California art galleries. Currently, as Annie Helm, she writes and illustrates children's books.

HER '60s LOOK: In the '60s there was something sweetly old-fashioned about her appeal, so her TV roles back then usually put her in traditional western garb. (Note that her conservative Elvis movie was the antithesis of the hip, happenin' *Viva Las Vegas*-style movies he's usually known for.) Dark-haired and pretty, she made a perfect princess in *The Magic Sword*.

BEHIND THE SCENES: Anne married novelist John Sherlock in '67 and had one son with him. After a divorce, in '72 she married actor Robert Viharo, who had played the director in *Valley of the Dolls* ('67). She and Viharo were in 1980's *Hide in Plain Sight* together, and with him she had a daughter, Serena.

BONUS SWINGABILITY: Her exotic birthplace—Toronto, Canada … her brother, Peter Helm, is also an actor with lots of TV appearances and three movies—*The Longest Day* in '62, *Inside Daisy Clover* in '65, and *The Andromeda Strain* in '72—to his credit … unlike other Elvis movies, *Follow That Dream* was top-heavy with men—the credits list fifteen actors and only three actresses … alternate titles considered *for Follow That Dream* were *It's a Beautiful Life*, *What a Wonderful Life*, and *Here Come the Kwimpers*.

 A DATE WITH ANNE

September 12	Anne Helm is born
April 11, 1962	*Follow That Dream* is released
May 14, 1969	*Nightmare in Wax* is released

SWINGIN' '60s CREDENTIALS: This adorable All-American beauty queen, one of the most famous and popular of all the Miss America winners, wooed Elvis in *Harum Scarum* and *Girl Happy*.

WORKIN' IT: Mary Ann Mobley's rep was made, of course, in '59 when she reigned as a popular 19-year-old Miss America. A year later, her eyes set on Hollywood, Mary Ann became a regular singer on the 1960 variety show *Be Our Guest*. She hit her stride in '64 with her first starring role, *Get Yourself a College Girl*. Two Elvis movies, *Harum Scarum* and *Girl Happy*, followed in '65, with Jerry Lewis's *Three on a Couch* ('66) and a Golden Globe as the Most Promising Newcomer close behind. After appearing as April Dancer on an episode of *The Man from U.N.C.L.E.*, she came close to landing the same part when it was spun into *The Girl from U.N.C.L.E.* series in '66, but Stefanie Powers got it instead. She also signed on for the role of Batgirl on *Batman* in '67, but according to

Gary Gerani's *Fantastic Television* ('77) Twentieth Century Fox Television moved her into the new *Custer* series at the last sec, and Yvonne Craig stepped into her high-heeled bat-boots.

Post-'60s work meant more TV for Mary Ann, including regular appearances on *Diff'rent Strokes* and *Falcon Crest*, *Sabrina the Teenage Witch* in '99, and mattress commercials with her husband, who seemed to do all the talking. She's also found success as a documentary filmmaker and was the only woman in the first American film crew allowed to shoot in communist Cambodia.

HER '60s LOOK: Cute, dignified, and wholesome with a fit figure, Mary Ann would've made a great Disney girl. To her credit, she has matured into a regal beauty who looks even more glamorous now than she did in her Miss America prime.

BEHIND THE SCENES: Mary Ann married actor/talk show host Gary Collins in '67 and has had one daughter with him. At the

official Miss America Web site, it's noted in her bio that she has been married to the same man, lived in the same house, and had the same phone number since the late '60s. Mary Ann has done lots of publicity work over the years for organizations such as March of Dimes, Mother's March Against Birth Defects, and the Exceptional Children's Foundation for the Mentally Retarded.

BONUS SWINGABILITY: Her exotic birthplace—Brandon, Mississippi, which is less than two hundred miles from Elvis' birthplace in Tupelo ... her husband Gary Collins was in the '70s classic *Airport*, on board the plane with sexy stew Jacqueline Bisset ... Mary Ann was a University of Mississippi student when she won the Miss America crown—ironically, another U of M student, Lynda Lee Mead, won it the next year; in fact there have been three Ole Miss winners overall, the most from any one university.

 A DATE WITH MARY ANN

April 30, 1938	Gary Collins is born
February 17, 1939	Mary Ann Mobley is born
September 6, 1958	Mary Ann wins the Miss America title
January 27, 1960	*Be Our Guest* debuts
April 14, 1965	*Girl Happy* is released
November 24, 1965	*Harum Scarum* is released

JULIE PARRISH

SWINGIN' '60s CREDENTIALS: Young and lovely, slim and graceful, Julie Parrish got her start as a model, jumped to a couple of early-'60s Jerry Lewis movies, then landed key roles in some mid-'60s teen flix, including Elvis' *Paradise, Hawaiian Style*.

WORKIN' IT: While not a major star, Julie was certainly a durable one, appearing in a wide variety of popular '60s projects. All she

'50s, she won the Miss Cinerama beauty contest, then enrolled in modeling school in Toledo, Ohio, where she won the Young Model of the Year contest at age 21. First prize was a small role in Jerry Lewis's *It's Only Money* in '62. She graduated to a classroom role in Jerry's *The Nutty Professor* ('63), and her screen career was on its way.

In addition to starring in the teeny-boppin' *Winter a Go Go* ('65), *Fireball 500* ('66), and *Paradise, Hawaiian Style* ('66), she was busy all decade with roles in dozens of TV shows, including *The Many Loves of Dobie Gillis*, *My Three Sons*, *Gunsmoke*, *Burke's Law*, *The Smothers Brothers Show*, *Ben Casey*, *Gidget*, *The F.B.I.*, *Bonanza*, *Star Trek* (the popular "Menagerie" episodes), *Death Valley Days*, and *Family Affair*. She starred in the underrated TV series *Good Morning, World*, which came and went in '67. Julie also made many appearances on TV talk shows, on game shows including *The Dating Game*, and in numerous late-'60s commercials for everything from Sterling Beer to National Airlines to Ajax detergent.

During this time she also began a career in live theatre that continued into the late '80s, and for six years she worked on and off with a comedy improv group. In the '70s, '80s, and '90s she appeared in dozens of movies, TV movies, TV shows, and commercials. Her major movies included *The Doberman Gang* in '72 and *The Devil and Max Devlin* in '80. Among her prominent TV appearances were roles as one of the major leads on the NBC series *Return to Peyton Place* in the early '70s, a stint as a principal player on the CBS series *Capitol* in the '80s, plus the Joan Diamond role on *Beverly Hills 90210* in the '90s. What's more, in the '90s she released a collection of country-flavored songs called *When We Dance*, and she flashed

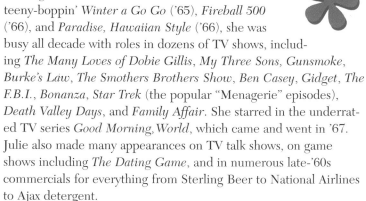

lacked was the one boffo award-winning movie on her list of credits to push her over the top to superstardom.

Modeling dominated her pre-'60s work, though Julie herself has said that she decided it was "an actor's life for me" after her first school play at age 6. As a teen living in Tecumseh, Michigan, in the her writing skills with many published essays, articles, and book reviews. Somebody please notify us if they find something Julie Parrish *can't* do well.

HER '60s LOOK: A dark-haired beauty who only seemed to get more attractive as she got older, Julie has always radiated intelligence, no matter the role. In her Elvis movie she looked positively brilliant compared to the King, who blithely sang the dimwitted "A Dog's Life" to her while she struggled gamely with recalcitrant pooches. That movie put her in several fetching ensembles, including swell bare-midriff blues and wonderful wahini reds. Unlike so many other curvy actresses of the mid-'60s who looked like they might balloon up any second, Julie always looked fit and healthy, like someone who took care of herself and laid off the Pop-Tarts.

BEHIND THE SCENES: She was scandal-free during the '60s, which is a relief because we like to think of sweet Elvis Girls as really being just that sweet. At her own Web site, Julie has written about her early days in the biz and what it was like being a young, hopeful actress: "I came to Hollywood in 1961. An almost innocent time it seems now. We girls still had to deal with white-haired old men chasing us around the audition desks, and we were taught to find a quick and safe way out of the office, without hurting the geezer's feelings. Mainly because if 'grandpa' was big enough, you might not work for him again, and that makes agents nervous. But all in all, people were kinder then." One person she thought was kinder was Elvis, with whom she got to smooch in *Paradise, Hawaiian Style* (she's on the record proclaiming him to be "a good kisser"). They didn't pursue anything more than a friendly relationship off-camera, however. Late in the decade she was involved with actor James Caan, who later

hit it big with *The Godfather*. Julie was then the steady girlfriend of comedian Albert Brooks for two years. The saddest part of her story is what happened in the '70s, when Julie became involved in a verbally-abusive relationship, but even that has something of a positive ending, because later she was elected to the Board of Directors of the L.A. Commission on Assaults Against Women, and she even worked on their hotline. Throughout the '90s she frequently worked as a counselor at Haven Hills Shelter for Battered Women, and she still speaks to audiences about domestic violence, also visiting schools to discuss dating violence.

BONUS SWINGABILITY: She uses a fake moniker—her real name is Ruby Joyce Wilbar, and she's billed as Joyce Wilbar in *It's Only Money* ... her exotic birthplace—Middlesboro, Kentucky, but she grew up in Lake City, Tennessee ... before she started modeling in the late '50s, she had a paper route, worked as a phone operator, and as a typist. As an actress she later won a typing contest for charity, competing against other actresses who played secretaries on different TV shows ... also in the cast of her series *Good Morning, World* was Goldie Hawn, a young unknown who was soon to make a splash on *Laugh-In* ... Julie's first live performance as a singer came at a packed L.A. Forum—she sang the national anthem before a Kings game in the '70s ... talented and hard-working, Julie is also a classic survivor who has battled illness through the '90s, undergoing constant treatments as she's overcome cancer ... she declares herself to be a vegan and a meditator, and she says she leans strongly toward the Buddhist philosophy and way of life ... Julie has her own official Web site—http://www.JulieParrish.com.

 A DATE WITH JULIE

October 21, 1940	Julie Parrish is born
March 16, 1961	Julie makes her TV debut on *The Untouchables*
June 4, 1963	*The Nutty Professor* is released
June 8, 1966	*Paradise, Hawaiian Style* is released
September 5, 1967	*Good Morning, World* debuts
September 17, 1968	*Good Morning, World* concludes its one-season run in primetime

PRISCILLA PRESLEY ✳

wrote at the end of *Elvis and Me*, "He was, and remains, the greatest influence in my life."

SWINGIN' '60s CREDENTIALS: Long before she became a TV and movie star, Priscilla Presley was one of the world's most-watched, most-envied women in the '60s, thanks to her one big catch: She married the King on May 1, 1967, and bore the fruit of his loins exactly nine months later.

WORKIN' IT: Molded by the King and loyal to his cause, Priscilla maintained a career in the '60s as the full-time Mrs. Elvis. She was living in Graceland in '63, married to E in '67, and by his side for most of the decade. Her own Hollywood success didn't start until Elvis' life sadly ended in '77. First came a co-hosting job on *Those Amazing Animals* in '80, followed by five years as country-girl Jenna Wade on *Dallas*. Her comedic flair was shown off, wonderfully and glamorously, in the three *Naked Gun* movies ('88, '91, '94), while more TV roles (including frequent appearances on *Melrose Place*, '96) continued to enhance her rep as a talented working actress. Meanwhile, she published an enormous bestseller, *Elvis and Me* ('85), produced several Elvis-themed films (including the TV movie of her book), and came out with her own perfume (*Moments*). A savvy businesswoman, she has steered Elvis Presley Enterprises into major profitability. Deeply loyal to the King's memory, she has continually defended him and reminded the public of his generosity, his goodness, and his triumphs. As she

HER '60s LOOK: When Elvis first saw Priscilla, supposedly one of his first comments was "She looks like an angel!" In the '60s she had the biggest, tallest hair this side of the Supremes, dyed nice and black just the way Elvis liked it (he dyed his black, too). But before anyone gets too critical of her 'do or the heavy make-up he liked her to wear, listen to this testimony about her striking beauty from one of Priscilla's contemporaries, Myra Lewis. (Myra was the 13-year-old cousin of 22-year-old Jerry Lee Lewis. She became his third wife and stayed married to him until she was 26.) In the book *Rock Wives* Myra described her meetings with Priscilla at the local Memphis beauty parlor in the '60s: "Priscilla was always so pretty, so striking, a totally different kind of pretty than she is today. She had the dyed black hair with the false eyelashes and the artificial made-up look, she was glamorous, she was photographed all the time, she looked beautiful.... If I saw Priscilla comin', I would hide. The girl followed me home one day from the beauty shop, actually got in the car and followed me all the way home. When I drove up my driveway, I rushed into my house so I wouldn't see her. It wasn't because I didn't want to know her, it was because I was too intimidated by her. If I hadn't been so insecure and afraid of being around Priscilla because she was such an attractive woman, she and I would have had more in common than any two women on the face of the Earth." In addition, Priscilla had and still has a remarkable figure, though her conservative clothes back then didn't reveal it (her sexi-

ness wouldn't become obvious until the '70s and '80s, when her TV career and the *Naked Gun* movies flaunted her curves). In the early '90s *People* magazine named her one of the fifty most beautiful people in the world, and today she's matured into a sophisticated beauty with a more appealing, healthy look than that created for the King.

BEHIND THE SCENES:

Take away her incredibly lucky break—being in Germany at exactly the right moment to meet Elvis—and she was just one of about a billion Elvis fans in the world. But there she was, 14-year-old Priscilla Beaulieu, daughter of a military man who was stationed in Germany, when who should show up in '59 but recent draftee Elvis Presley, 24 years old and the hottest talent on the planet. Their courtship lasted eight years. While they were in Germany, chaperones accompanied their dates, and Priscilla had to be home by 11 p.m. Returning stateside in the spring of '60, they stayed in contact while the King resumed his movie career in Hollywood. After a couple of years she moved into Graceland (platonically) and then graduated from a Memphis high school in '63. Bearing a three-and-a-half karat diamond engagement ring, Elvis got down on one knee and proposed to her in the winter of '66. Finally, on the first day of May in '67, 21-year-old Priscilla and 32-year-old Elvis married in Vegas. Exactly nine months later, Priscilla gave birth to Elvis' pride and joy, Lisa Marie. (In the mid-'90s Lisa Marie would be in a high-profile marriage with Michael Jackson.) Infidelities and pressures would drive them to divorce in '73, but for the '60s, Priscilla was Queen to the King, a claim nobody else could make back then. In the mid-'80s Priscilla found a new companion, Brazilian writer Marco Garibaldi, and gave birth to his son in '87.

BONUS SWINGABILITY:

Her exotic birthplace—Brooklyn, New York ... she has said that Elvis gave her her first kiss, and he wanted her to stay a virgin until they were married ... Elvis' graduation present to her in '63: a new red Corvair ... Priscilla wrote in her book that in the mid-'60s she and Elvis experimented briefly with drugs, including LSD on one night in '65 ...

after the Vegas wedding ceremony, Priscilla and Elvis flew to Palm Springs in Frank Sinatra's private Lear jet, the *Christina* ... at the May 1 wedding reception in Vegas, the 100 guests enjoyed oysters, clams, salmon, lobster, chicken, roasted pig, and a six-tiered $3,500 cake ... the newlyweds danced to the first Elvis song she'd heard in Germany: "Love Me Tender" ... at the second reception, held in Graceland on May 29th for everybody who couldn't come to Vegas, the couple danced to "Let Me Call You Sweetheart."

A DATE WITH PRISCILLA

January 8, 1935	Elvis Presley is born
May 24, 1945	Priscilla Presley is born
September 13, 1959	Elvis and Priscilla meet in Germany
March 2, 1960	His military career over, Elvis leaves Germany
May 29, 1963	Priscilla graduates from Immaculate Conception High School in Memphis
May 1, 1967	Elvis marries Priscilla in Las Vegas
February 1, 1968	Priscilla gives birth to daughter Lisa Marie Presley
October 9, 1973	Elvis and Priscilla divorce
August 16, 1977	42-year-old Elvis Presley dies of a heart ailment at Graceland

girls! girls!

JULIET PROWSE

SWINGIN' '60s CREDENTIALS: This long-limbed dancin' dazzler kicked up her heels in a half-dozen '60s flix, including Elvis' *G.I. Blues* and *Can-Can*.

WORKIN' IT: Juliet Prowse's '60s debut caused an international ruckus, appropriate for this most international of Elvis girls. Born in Bombay and raised in South Africa, she was a ballet dancer brought to Hollywood for *Can-Can* in '59. The movie had a ring-a-ding cast—including Frank Sinatra and Shirley MacLaine—and of course the leg-kicking, skirt-lifting, pulse-raising cancan dance itself. When Nikita Kruschev visited the set during rehearsals and saw the riotous dancing and revealing costumes, he was appalled. "Immoral," the Russian leader declared. Subsequent articles in the international press brought only more attention to the movie, and Juliet's career quickly picked up steam.

Soon she was starring opposite the King in *G.I. Blues*, in which her limited acting range was balanced by more of her dynamic dancing. Unfortunately, her talents barely overcame the goofy musical moments that were too common in Elvis' movies. The best (or lamest) example was the ski-lift scene that contains some of the most unbelievable lip-synching by two performers in movie history. Still, the movie was a hit, she survived to do more '60s movies (*The Second Time Around* in '61, *Who Killed Teddy Bear?* in '65), and mid-decade she even got her own series, *Mona McCluskey*. This George Burns-produced sitcom put Juliet in the role of a glamorous movie star married to a military man. When she tried to get by as an ordinary housewife living on her husband's limited salary, comedy would ensue. The show lasted one season.

For the next couple of decades she took her stunning stems to live stages. Vegas, nightclubs, and big shows like *Sweet Charity*, *Mame*, and *The Pajama Game* kept her busy and popular, with the occasional TV appearance (a pantyhose commercial, a variety special, or a TV movie) thrown in for fun. Sadly, Juliet died of pancreatic cancer in L.A. in '96 at the age of 60.

HER '60s LOOK: "A most appealing newcomer," *Playboy* declared in June of '60 when it got a first look at Juliet in *Can-Can*. You gotta love those exotic eyes and big pillowy lips (though the sexy overbite might have done some damage). At close to six feet tall, she had possibly the most famous gams in the biz (though her height probably impeded her ballet career). Strangely, the director of *G.I. Blues* didn't think much of her looks—Norman Taurog said she was "terribly tall, gawky and only nice-looking rather than sexy and hard-to-make looking," and his choice would've been another Swingin' Chick of the '60s, Elke Sommer. Elvis set him straight, though, saying, "She has a body that would make a bishop stamp his foot through a stained-glass window."

BEHIND THE SCENES: In the early '60s, you couldn't beat those royal references: Juliet was romantically linked to Elvis, then she was engaged to Frank Sinatra (the star of *Can-Can*) for five weeks in '62.

Supposedly her relationship with the former was broken up by the latter in a Vegas dressing-room confrontation. Somehow, the story goes, Frank and his two bodyguards managed to compel Elvis to stop seeing her. A philosophical Frank was quoted in *The Way You Wear Your Hat* ('98) as having said back then, "Juliet has been my one romance. I'm 46 now—it's time to settle down." However, he decided not to marry her because she wouldn't relinquish her career. According to Kitty Kelly's *My Way*, he'd been so devastated by the Ava Gardner experience that he wanted a wife who would stay home. Juliet eventually reversed her field, but when she called Frank, he said "Forget it, baby!" and hung up on her. (The official reason given in a press release was "conflict of career interests.") *The Way You Wear Your Hat* offers up a last line by Dino (who got more than his share of them): On stage one night he announced, "Frank and Julie broke up. Julie wanted Frank to give up his career, but he wouldn't." Frank, of course, was at his Rat Packin'est at the time; he was also twenty-one years her senior. In '72 she married an actor nine years her junior, John McCook, but they divorced seven years later.

BONUS SWINGABILITY:

Her exotic birthplace—Bombay, India—though some sources say she was actually born in Durban, South Africa. Certainly she spent her childhood in South Africa ... Juliet performed at the JFK inaugural gala that Frank organized in '61, and she later took the stage at Frank's Cal-Neva Lodge in Tahoe ... there's a story that in the late-'80s she was mauled by a leopard while preparing for the TV special *Circus of the Stars*, but she gamely went on with the show; later she supposedly tried to do her routine for *The Tonight Show*, but the cat mauled her a second time and she had to go to the hospital for stitches ... during her lifetime she won numerous awards from dance and theatrical organizations, and one year she was named the Las Vegas Performer of the Year ... when she died, Juliet had been hosting *Championship Ballroom Dancing* on PBS for thirteen years. Her successor, Barbara Eden, hosted a tribute show to Juliet and said "I've always admired dancers and my dear friend Juliet Prowse was truly one of the greatest and best dancers of all time."

A DATE WITH JULIET

December 12, 1915	Frank Sinatra is born
September 25, 1936	Juliet Prowse is born
March 9, 1960	*Can-Can* is released
November 23, 1960	*G.I. Blues* is released
January 19, 1961	Juliet performs at the JFK inaugural gala
September 16, 1965	*Mona McCluskey* debuts
September 18, 1966	Juliet guests on *The Andy Williams Show*
December 18, 1969	Juliet guests on *The Bing Crosby Christmas Special*
September 14, 1996	Juliet dies of cancer

THE LOOK

When people think fondly of the '60s, it's often the fun fashions they're remembering. Never before had such unconstrained, unconventional, unabashed creativity been expressed so uniquely on the world's fashion runways. While it's easy to remember the wild colors and the wacky designs, it's probably harder to recall how impractical many of those styles were. Miniskirts and hot pants froze many a London leg, paper dresses and moccasins were useless in the slightest rainstorm, and just how does one clean a metal vest or a cellophane blouse? But if the fashions were foolish, the motivation was not. Fun was in, rules were out, and suddenly a pair of striped bell bottoms, a tie-dyed chartreuse shirt, a fur vest, granny glasses, and love beads all went together, whether you were Sonny OR Cher. Fashion fear was so '50s, man. Here are some of the innovators and the instigators, the models and the mentors, who led the fashion revolution.

PATTIE BOYD

SWINGIN' '60s CREDENTIALS: An adorable buck-toothed British bird who modeled and had a cute bit-part in *A Hard Day's Night,* Pattie married one of the decade's most eligible bachelors—Beatle George Harrison—and became the muse for some of rock's most famous songs.

WORKIN' IT: Pattie Boyd was in a movie. A big movie. Beatles big. But her role was tiny: In *A Hard Day's Night,* her part was defined as "Girl on train." And her film career was limited to a single word. While dining on the train ten minutes into *A Hard Day's Night,* she was told the lads are really prisoners; she replies "Prisoners?", emotes confusion, and skedaddles off. Five minutes later she sat on a crate, all coy and flustered, as the boys serenaded her with "I Should Have Known Better." While her impact on film history was small, her impact on Beatle history was huge. When she and George Harrison first met on the set of *A Hard Day's Night,* the story goes that he was signing autographs for fans and drawing a kiss

under each signature, but for hers he drew *seven* kisses and started pestering her for a date, which she turned down because she already had a boyfriend. However, Beatles weren't to be denied in those heady days. A year later she and George were living together, and married soon after that, when she was only 21. Pattie went from model to muse: inspired by their love, George wrote some of his best songs to/about/for her, among them "I Need You," "For You Blue," and the classic "Something," which Frank Sinatra once called "the greatest love song in the last fifty years." Still inspired by her in the '70s, George wrote "So Sad" as he and Pattie were splitting up.

But their split was not the end of Pattie—she's always had more going for her than the Beatle marriage that catalyzed her international fame, even as far back as her pre-George teens. Before, during, and after *A Hard Day's Night,* Pattie was a working model. In the early and mid-'60s she did print ads in London papers and magazines, promoted English potato chips as the Smith's Crisps girl, appeared with Twiggy in Mary Quant's Paris shows, and went to the U.S. as an ambassador of "Cool Brittania." Back in London in the late '60s, Pattie and her sisters briefly ran a fashion boutique called Juniper, named after the Donovan song "Jennifer Juniper" (a song inspired by Pattie's sister Jenny, who had spent time with Donovan during the Beatles' famous trip to India in '68). Unfortunately, her modeling career never really advanced to superstardom. Published sources say that George might've even discouraged her, hoping she'd be a stay-at-home Northern wife like Maureen Cox was for Ringo. She briefly got back into modeling in '74, but she never became a major fashion force, even though she looked more and more attractive as the years went by.

HER '60s LOOK: Early in her career she looked blonde and innocent. Her beautiful blue eyes were what most people, including George Harrison, noticed first. She was so in tune with the times and the styles that in '65 she wrote a regular column for *16* magazine called "Pattie's Letter from London." In it she would give fashion advice such as how to have bangs like hers (long on the sides, short in the front, she said). As she matured she at times sported deep tans, then darkened hair, eventually evolving a more glamorous, more sophisticated look worthy of the modeling superstar she never quite became. As expected for a swingin' girl in swingin' London, her clothes were mod, gear, fab—all those Carnaby Street adjectives. The dress she wore in *A Hard Day's Night,* by the way, was a Mary Quant mini. Mary later outfitted George and Pattie with his-and-hers fur coats for their January '66 wedding.

BEHIND THE SCENES: Pattie landed a Beatle and got a couple of scenes in a Beatle movie, so she was definitely hangin' in the right

the look

circles. Once she agreed to go out with George, they supposedly fell in love instantly and were looking for houses within a month. Their romance stayed a secret until they went to Ireland later in '64, and the press invaded the castle where they were staying.

Once their relationship was public, she became more visible at Beatles' events, including recording sessions—she joined in for the choruses of "All You Need Is Love" and "Yellow Submarine." Pattie is also credited with being the person who got the Beatles interested in India and the Maharishi in early '68. However, it's not clear if that was such a good thing, given the fiasco that resulted when the group, plus friends like actress Mia Farrow and Beach Boy Mike Love, made a pilgrimage to the Maharishi's India ashram. As chronicled in John's song on *The White Album*, "Sexy Sadie," the Maharishi—"Sadie"—seemed more interested in the Beatles' women and money than in their spiritual growth (John sang, "Sexy Sadie, you made a fool of everyone"). Pattie and George made all the scenes in those days, including the infamous "Stones Party" in February '67 that ended with Marianne Faithfull and several Stones up on drug charges. But thanks to the intervention of Beatles lawyer David Jacobs and Beatles manager Brian Epstein, Pattie and George were allowed to leave without being arrested. They would be soon, though. In '69 Pattie was at home when the cops, led by notorious publicity-hound Sgt. Pilcher, busted them for possession of hash. The fine: 250 pounds.

When interests and careers put the Harrisons on divergent paths late in the decade, another rock star entered Pattie's life. Eric Clapton's feelings for Pattie were expressed to her in his most famous song, "Layla" ("I'm begging darling please," he wailed in '70). Pattie was listening, but wary of his obsession for her. Finally, in '77 she divorced George Harrison and took up with Clapton. They married in '79. Just as George had once done, Clapton wrote songs for her, including "Wonderful Tonight" and "Old Love." But in '89 this marriage would also end, for reasons Clapton explained to the *L.A. Times* in June '99. He confessed that his behavior as a

"full-blown, practicing alcoholic" had ruined their marriage during the 1980s. "Everyone used to walk around me on eggshells," he said. "They didn't know if I was going to be angry or whatever. When I'd come back from the pub I could come back happy or I could come back and smash the place up." He'd also fathered children by two other women during this time. After their split, Pattie pursued photography and charity work, and she is today what she's been for four decades—a scene-making member of rock royalty.

BONUS SWINGABILITY: For unexplained reasons her first name gets varied spellings as either Patti or Pattie ... John Lennon affectionately called her "Battie" ... her exotic birthplace—Hampstead, England. She lived in Kenya for a while before moving to London ... when she and George got married in Surrey, Paul was the only Beatle to attend. He and Beatles' manager Brian Epstein were "best men" ... Brian threw a party for the couple that night. Among the guests were Paul and Jane Asher, George Martin, and Cynthia Lennon ... George and Pattie honeymooned in Barbados ... Pattie's sister Jenny was married to Mick Fleetwood, and they lived in San Francisco's Haight Ashbury district in '67. Pattie, George, and some friends went to visit Jenny that year, making George the only Beatle to visit the Haight during the Summer of Love ... supposedly Paul McCartney decided to include "Wild Honey Pie" on *The White Album* because Pattie liked it ... "Birthday," on the same album, may also be about or for her ... at the reception after her wedding to Clapton, a good-natured George showed up and played some songs with Paul and Ringo ... reflecting on the '60s, Pattie once said, "They were good times, with so many laughs. I don't regret a thing. I still try on an old miniskirt once in a while. I just cannot believe we really wore them that short."

A DATE WITH PATTIE

February 25, 1943	George Harrison is born
March 17, 1944	Pattie Boyd is born
March 30, 1945	Eric Clapton is born
July 6, 1964	*A Hard Day's Night* is released in the U.K.
August 11, 1964	*A Hard Day's Night* is released in the U.S.
December 25, 1965	Pattie and George Harrison get engaged
January 21, 1966	Pattie and George wed
February 15, 1968	Pattie, George, John and Cynthia Lennon fly to India
March 12, 1969	George and Pattie are busted for drugs in their London home
March 27, 1979	Pattie marries Eric Clapton

SWINGIN' '60s CREDENTIALS: This lanky model/actress played small roles in several late-'60s films, but her legacy really rests on the drug-addled, sexually liberated companionship she provided to the Rolling Stones, especially Stones-founder Brian Jones and guitarist Keith Richards.

WORKIN' IT: A teen model before she became famous as anything else, Anita Pallenberg did some work for *Vogue* early in the decade. In March '67 she signed up with a London agency called English Boy Ltd., but according to Michael Gross's '95 book *Model*, the agency's founder said she "never turned up" for the shoots and "was too beautiful to get out of bed." As an actress, Anita's greatest claim to screen fame came in the role as the Black Queen in *Barbarella* ('68); that same year she had a minor role in the cult classic *Candy*. In '69 her sex scene with Mick Jagger in *Performance* seemed so real that many observers, including an outraged Keith Richards, assumed it was. Of Anita in *Performance*, Danny Peary in his book *Cult Movies* said she was "beautiful," "the film's most energetic per-former," and her scene is "one of the most erotic moments in cinema history." She sup-posedly produced an obscure Italian movie in the '60s starring Mick and Keith, though the title, and anyone who'll admit to having seen it, remain elusive.

Anita also has some claim to music fame: She sang "oo-oo" with the chorus in "Sympathy for the Devil," and she maintains that she wrote "Honky-Tonk Women" and "You Can't Always Get What You Want" with Keith (though she's not listed as one of the composers). To hear her tell it, she was a vital cog in the Stones' machinery: According to Tony Sanchez's *Up and Down with the Rolling Stones*, Anita once said, " I feel as though I'm rather like the sixth Rolling Stone. Mick and Keith and Brian need me to guide them, to criticize them and to give them ideas." Pervasive drug abuse, unfortunately, marked her life with and after the Stones. By the end of the '70s she'd lost all her beauty and sleekness, almost becoming a poster girl for the wretched results of '60s excess. However, she turned herself around in the mid-'80s, kicked drugs, lost weight, and was able to establish once and for all a life apart from any Rolling Stones.

HER '60s LOOK: In Sanchez's *Up and Down* book, he calls Anita "the foxiest blonde I had ever seen," adding, "She had only to walk along the street to cause a string of traffic accidents. She had tumbling, shining blond hair, a long lithe body and wickedly beautiful cat's eyes." Anita embodied the classic London look, à la Mick's blue-eyed girl, Marianne Faithfull. However, Anita's alluring beauty had a knowing depravity lurking below the apparent blonde innocence. She was also a fab dresser in all the kookiest mod rock gear, a worthy complement to the extravagant fashions sported by the Stones themselves. Photos of her back then show her looking groovy and relaxed in a wide range of casual but colorful clothes that were often perfectly parallel to what one of the Stones was wearing at the time.

BEHIND THE SCENES: Anita certainly had a knack for hangin' out with cool people. Based on various biographies and histories of

the look

the '60s, it would seem that she did everything and everyone for half of the decade. (Some stories even put her in beds with Marianne Faithfull and Princess Margaret.) Having met and quickly fallen for Brian Jones in '65, she left him in '67 after he continually beat her. In the book *Rock Wives* she said, "I think Brian was a terrible person really," adding that he was "a tortured personality, insecure as hell" (he drowned in '69). After Brian she turned to Stones-guitarist Keith Richards in '67 for comfort. A dozen years later they were still together, with a son, Marlon, and a daughter, Angela *nee* Dandelion. (Another son, Tara, died at ten weeks in '76.) "Loneliness and boredom," she told *Rock Wives*, drove her to drugs and affairs while she was with Keith. So reckless and incessant was her drug use, Sanchez reports in *Up and Down with the Rolling Stones*, that she was still doing heroin in the months before her daughter was born; she was also arrested for hash possession in '77. Eventually Keith left her and married American model Patti Hansen in '83. Devastated, Anita said, "I thought I could never have another love in my life—where can you go after you've been in love with Keith Richards? What else is there? But it heals, it really does, you can actually get over a person." Supposedly she'll explain how to do that in the autobiography she's writing, which must have all the Stones very, very nervous.

BONUS SWINGABILITY: Her exotic birthplace—Rome, Italy ... it was Anita's idea for Brian to wear the uniform of a Nazi SS officer and stomp on a doll in an infamous photo he did for a German magazine ... believing that she was a witch, Anita supposedly practiced black magic, one time stabbing a voodoo doll of Brian Jones and causing him to have stomach cramps ... according to *Up and Down with the Rolling Stones*, for a while she also carried garlic with her to keep vampires away, and she would cast spells in secret rituals ... in '68 she, Keith, Mick, and Marianne flew to Peru to check out the ancient culture and the modern drugs; they ended up beachin' it in Rio where the boys wrote the album *Let It Bleed* ... in '79 a 17-year-old kid was found shot to death in the bed of Keith and Anita's upstate N.Y. home, but the couple wasn't implicated. They were cited, however, for illegal gun possession... a recent Anita sighting occurred in March '99 when she attended the Paris launch party of *Numero*, a new fashion magazine ... a movie about Brian Jones is allegedly in the works, with Courtney Love the rumored choice for the Anita Pallenberg role.

A DATE WITH ANITA

February 28, 1943	Brian Jones is born
December 18, 1943	Keith Richards is born
January 25, 1944	Anita Pallenberg is born
May 27, 1965	The Rolling Stones' "(I Can't Get No) Satisfaction" hits #1 on the U.S. charts
August 10, 1968	Marlon Richards is born
October 10, 1968	*Barbarella* is released
July 3, 1969	Brian Jones drowns
July 5, 1969	In London's Hyde Park, the Stones perform a free concert in tribute to Brian

EDIE SEDGWICK

SWINGIN' '60s CREDENTIALS: The archetype of the "poor little rich girl," electric Edie blazed across Manhattan as a meteoric fashion model, a photogenic star of Andy Warhol's underground movies and parties, and a world-famous scene maker with Dylan, Jagger, and the '60s Pop Art crowd.

WORKIN' IT: An heiress who could've had the vast Sedgwick fortune, 21-year-old Edie fled from her old-money New England heritage and chose instead a rebellious life of fashion, art, and

parties. She hit New York City in '64 and was an instant sensation, quickly getting modeling jobs and recognition from *Vogue* magazine as a '65 "youthquaker." Drawn to Andy Warhol's hip art crowd, she became one of his "superstars" and a vibrant attraction at the celebrity-filled parties he threw in the Factory, his silver-painted studio. From '65-'67 he put her in a number of his bizarre underground films, including *Vinyl*, *Kitchen*, and *Chelsea Girls*, all of them pointless and amateurish but all of them showing Edie to be an eminently watchable actress. Sadly, her career ended almost as fast as it had started. Those who were there say that when Edie had an affair with Bob Dylan, Warhol lost interest in her and turned his attention to another "superstar." (Some have speculated that conflicts over money contributed to Edie and Andy's separation.) Her movie career in shambles, her modeling career wavering between inconsistent and nonexistent, Edie drifted away from the Factory family as drugs beckoned. Burned out, drugged out, and kicked out, she went to the West Coast, where her career—and her life— would soon unravel completely.

HER '60s LOOK: Hers was one of the '60s' defining looks. With eyes "as big as teacups" that were the color of "twice-frozen Hershey bars" (according to two Factory regulars), Edie had a striking, unforgettable beauty that blended optimism with tragedy, energetic youth with pained experience. One could see in her the possibilities of both the night and the morning after. In the *Vogue* "youthquakers" article, the magazine gushed that Edie had "legs to swoon over." Showing off those long legs in her black tights and Betsey Johnson fashions, and balancing her short bleached hair with long chandelier earrings, she summarized what it meant to be a hip New Yorker in the mid-'60s. Rock poet Patti Smith later described the first time she saw Edie's stick figure in *Vogue*: "She was like a thin man in black leotards and a sort of boat-necked sweater, white hair…she was such a strong image that I thought, that's it, it represented everything to me…radiating intelligence, speed, being connected with the moment."

BEHIND THE SCENES: She spent most of the decade partyin' with, hangin' with, and doin' cool rock stars such as Bob Dylan, Lou Reed, and possibly Mick Jagger, all of whom gathered around Andy and indulged in the Factory's pleasures. Edie's talents were for being noticed (by celebrities and top fashion magazines) and for handling massive amounts of drugs, a potent combination that made her the Queen of Manhattan nightlife for a few years. Andy certainly took to her, though it's thought to have been a purely platonic relationship. Truman Capote guessed that "Edie was

the look

something Andy would like to have been. He was transposing himself into her à la Pygmalion. Have you ever noticed a certain type of man who always wants to go along with his wife to pick out her clothes? I've always thought that's because he wants to wear them himself. Andy Warhol would like to have been Edie Sedgwick. He would like to have been a charming, well-

born debutante from Boston. He would like to have been anybody except Andy Warhol." Her influence helped shaped rock history, too, as it's widely inferred that Dylan wrote "Just Like a Woman," and possibly "Like a Rolling Stone" and "Leopard-Skin Pill-Box Hat," about her. At the end of her life Edie attempted a new start by moving back to Santa Barbara, her birthplace. Unfortunately, her life got even more bleak and desperate as drugs continued to take their toll. Busted for drugs in August '69, she was sentenced to five years of probation and was placed in Santa Barbara's Cottage Hospital—the same hospital where she'd been born and where her father had died in '67. While in the hospital she took lovers, and when granted leaves she continued her descent toward destruction by drinking, taking heavier doses of pills, and even doing heroin. In the summer of '69 she got silicone injections to pump up her breasts, in hopes of landing movie roles. She did manage to make one last movie, the chaotic, little-seen *Ciao! Manhattan*, which was shot partially in Santa Barbara and released after her death. For the first six of months of '71 Edie returned to Cottage Hospital, this time getting shock treatments. While there she met another patient, Michael Post, and in July of '71 they married. Sadly, four months later, her glamour long gone and her health irrevocably broken by years of heavy smoking,

drinking, and drug abuse, she died from what the coroner listed as a barbiturate overdose. A small country cemetery in the tiny town of Ballard, located in the Santa Ynez Valley just north of Santa Barbara, is her final resting place. Her grave is marked by a modest rectangular stone carved with a simple inscription that makes no reference to the glittery life she once knew: "Edith Sedgwick Post, wife of Michael Brett Post, 1943-1971."

BONUS SWINGABILITY: Her full moniker was Edith Minturn Sedgwick ... her exotic birthplace—Santa Barbara, California ... a reckless guest, she almost burned down the Chelsea Hotel single-handedly in '66 ... the classic biography about her is Jean Stein's *Edie*; in it, a friend of Edie's in the '60s, Sandy Kirkland, said "Edie was very frail and vulnerable. She was just psychologically scattered: She never finished a sentence, she never looked you in the face, she was never there. I used to hang around her apartment ... chaos! Piles of clothes on every piece of furniture" ... another '60s friend, Chuck Wein, said in the same book: "Edie could keep everybody busy getting her things ... eight guys calling her up from eight different social strata. She'd be off to a jet-set party here and an underground party there, and also rapping to the guy from the deli. And everybody on each level believed that her life on that level was her real trip. She kept everybody going!" ... according to Jean Stein's biography, at the very end of her life Edie attended a fashion show held at a Santa Barbara museum. She sat in the crowd and watched the young models with rapt attention; afterwards, she went backstage and tried on a red chiffon dress she had admired. "I haven't seen clothes like this in so many years," she told the designer. "I have been away."

 A DATE WITH EDIE

August 6, 1928	Andy Warhol is born
May 24, 1941	Bob Dylan is born
April 20, 1943	Edie Sedgwick is born
July 24, 1971	Edie marries Michael Post
November 16, 1971	Edie dies in Santa Barbara
February 22, 1987	Andy Warhol dies after a gall-bladder operation

JEAN SHRIMPTON

cover in '65, and she was the subject of a documentary called *The Face on The Cover*. By mid-decade Jean was making the then-extravagant sum of $60 an hour and writing a book, *My Own Story—The Truth About Modeling*. She reached a new peak—and established herself as perhaps the first true supermodel—when she inked a three-year deal to represent Yardley cosmetics and hair products on TV and in magazines. Like Twig and Veroosh, she graduated from still photography to film photography, but the movie she was in, *Privilege*, in '67, was a box-office bust and gave her a rep as a "wooden" actress. (Consort Terence Stamp said that "Jean trying to act is rather like me trying to perform complicated brain surgery.") Jean continued her modeling career until about '72, though at the insistence of photographer David Bailey she did some late-'80s hair-color ads. She wrote another book—*Jean Shrimpton, An Autobiography*—in '90. But most of her post-'60s years have been spent out of the spotlight. She ran an antique shop in the '70s and has owned and operated the 300-year-old Abbey Hotel in Penzance, England, since the early '80s. Intentionally staying out of the public eye and away from the camera lens, she told *People* magazine in August '99 that "it is nice to be at the end of the world."

HER '60s LOOK: A fat face, a weak left profile, small eyes, big feet, and bags under her eyes—that was once her own assessment of her looks, to which she added: "if you take off the make-up, I'm ugly." But photog David Bailey knew otherwise from the first moment he saw her in '61, a moment he described for *Vogue* in November '99: "I was up in the *Vogue* studios, which lots of photographers used, and I saw this girl being photographed for some print ad campaign. I just thought she was wonderful, absolutely compelling. It was Jean Shrimpton....I don't think there had been anything like Jean. She was a kind of beauty of the century in a democratic way. She appealed to men, women, everybody." In a '67 *Vogue* article called "The Changing Face of the Fashion Model," legendary photographer Cecil Beaton said the "most coveted" model of the

SWINGIN' '60s CREDENTIALS: All legs and arms (and hair and face and lips and eyes and...), stunning Jean was one of the most famous and influential models of the '60s, a swingin' rival to Twiggy and Veruschka for global fashion supremacy.

WORKIN' IT: One-third of the internationally famous triumvirate of Twiggy, Veruschka, and Shrimpton, Jean was the first international fashion goddess of the decade. Though her goal in the late '50s was to become a secretary, in 1960 she enrolled in modeling school, and within a year she was the star of a fourteen-page *Vogue* spread entitled "The Young Idea." The following spring she got her first British *Vogue* cover. *Glamour* dubbed her Model of the Year in '63, and from then on her face and figure graced all of the popular magazines that didn't have *Mechanix* in the title. *Elle* named her "The Most Beautiful Girl in the World," *Newsweek* put her on its

the look

mid-'60s was "Jean Shrimpton.…Miss Shrimpton's appeal is not so much in her baby-boy eyes, cleft underlip and cozy round cheeks but in the length of her extremities, and the underwater manner in which she wields them." Those long extremities were what gave her the classic stick-girl image à la Veruschka and Twiggy, but Jean's 5' 9" physique was a robust 34-23-35, and she weighed in at 120 pounds. It was a sexy figure that made fashion history in the fall of '65. That November she caused a world-wide fashion scandal when she wore a miniskirt, no stockings, no gloves and no hat to the toney opening-day ceremonies of the Melbourne Gold Cup in Australia. Mary Quant was already making minis in England, but Australian high society had never seen anything like them. As Jean wrote later, "The day of the races was a hot one, so I didn't bother to wear any stockings. My legs were still brown from the summer, and as the dress was short it was hardly formal. I had no hat or gloves with me, for the very good reason that I owned neither. I went downstairs cheerfully from my hotel room, all regardless of what was to come." When she arrived at the races, both the men and women were stunned by her amazing look and her brash fashion gaffe. Her scandalous attire landed her on front pages worldwide, and the miniskirt revolution was on its way to cultural conquest.

BEHIND THE SCENES: Because she was one of the preeminent faces of the decade, her ups and downs were followed in the press, especially her engagement to swingin' photog David Bailey and her subsequent affair with Bailey's pal, actor Terence Stamp. She later wrote that when she first met Bailey in '60, who at the time was married, they shared an instant mutual attraction. They worked together closely, Bailey got divorced in '63, and in early '64 he and Jean were engaged. That same year, however, Jean became attracted to Stamp, a handsome actor who in the '60s starred in *The Collector* and *Far From the Madding Crowd.* (Later he would appear in *Wall Street, Superman II,* and *Star Wars: The Phantom Menace.*) By the summer of '64 she and Stamp were living together in L.A.; by the summer of '67 Jean was living in New York with someone else. In her 1990 autobiography she wrote that "Terry and I were really only happy together when we were abroad and on holiday. In London, my life with him was empty. I was bored, and we must have been exceedingly boring to others. I found life trivial then, and looking back I do not understand why I stuck with it. We were so vain that we continued to dress ourselves up and go out to be looked at. Terry always looked amazing, and I had to look good to match. I was so insecure that I was always fiddling in the bathroom or running to the ladies to check my appearance. It was pathetic. Here I was, at the height of my fame, behaving like this. I was just an accessory to this beautiful star, and it was his beauty that I was in love with and that

kept me with him—not the man himself. I was under a spell, but had no energy to break it." Break it they did in '67. More than a decade later Jean married a photographer named Michael Cox, and today, still together, they have one son, Thaddeus.

BONUS SWINGABILITY:

Her exotic birthplace—High Wycombe, Buckinghamshire, England … her nickname was "the Shrimp," a name she disliked … her younger sister is Chrissie Shrimpton, herself an actress/model and a prominent girlfriend of Mick Jagger's in the early '60s before Marianne Faithfull swept him off his feet … Chrissie was supposedly the subject of the Stones' "19th Nervous Breakdown" and "Under My Thumb" … Jean was mentioned in the first line of a 1985 song by the Smithereens, "Behind the Wall of Sleep": "She had hair like Jeanie Shrimpton back in 1965" … colleagues say that Jean was the most tireless of models, always punctual and professional … Bailey pointed out her work ethic to *Vogue* in '99: "One of the things I loved about Jean was that she took modeling with a bit of dignity … With Jean you never had to reshoot anything, ever, she was always in perfect sync with the camera" … she once said that she existed throughout her whole career owning only one evening dress … she's quoted in *People* in August '99 as saying "it was great fun becoming famous, but I got tired of it."

A DATE WITH JEAN

January 2, 1938	David Bailey is born
July 22, 1939	Terence Stamp is born
November 6, 1942	Jean Shrimpton is born
May 10, 1965	Jean is on the cover of *Newsweek*
November 2, 1965	Jean wears a mini in Australia
March 8, 1966	*Privilege* begins filming
July 24, 1967	*Privilege* is released
January 12, 1979	Jean marries Michael Cox

TWIGGY

SWINGIN' '60s CREDENTIALS: Still the person most synonymous with "swingin' London" and fab Carnaby Street fashions, doe-eyed, ninety-pound Twiggy was the most famous model in the world during the '60s.

WORKIN' IT: A teenager for almost the entire decade, Twiggy had an impact that was instant and international. As *People* magazine said in August '99, she "set the fashion standard on both sides of the Atlantic." Hers is still one of the most recognized names in the world, even though her four-year modeling career ended more than thirty years ago.

In her prime, Twiggy's elfin face was on the cover of *Vogue* four times, her name and image were merchandised on dolls (the Twiggy Barbie), Mattel purses, "Trimfit" hosiery, Yardley cosmetics ("for those great big Twiggy eyes"), and lunchboxes. She made records (the single "When I Think of You"/"Over and Over" in '67), she wrote a book (*Twiggy: How I Probably Just Came Along on a White Rabbit at the Right Time and Met the Smile on the Face of the Tiger*), and she owned her own boutique and hair salon. She was deemed so newsworthy that in '67 ABC devoted three separate "Twiggy in New York" TV specials to her, just to follow her around Manhattan. And then suddenly, all of 19 years old, she retired in '69 to devote herself to her budding acting career.

Proving there was genuine talent and intelligence behind the pixie image, in the '70s she starred in *The Boy Friend* ('71), won two Golden Globes as Best Actress and Most Promising Newcomer, wrote another autobiography, and recorded two albums, *Twiggy* and

Please Get My Name Right. Continuing to distance herself from her modeling days, in the '80s she reinvented herself once again, this time as a tap-dancing, Gershwin-belting, Broadway-starring, Tony-nomination-earning, musical sensation in *My One and Only* alongside towering tapboy Tommy Tune (her co-star in *The Boy Friend*). The '90s found her starring in an off-Broadway musical called *If Love Were All,* writing another book (*Twiggy in Black and White*), and releasing more albums (notably *London Pride: Songs from the London Stage* in '96). She's achieved all this public exposure despite having stage fright: "Getting up on stage was my big hurdle," she told *People* in August '99. "I'm not an extrovert at all." She's even done a little modeling again, including an adorable, much-noticed turn in September '98 for the opening of London's Fashion Week. These days Twiggy seems to be at peace with her past: "I used to be a thing," she said in the '95 book *Model* by Michael Gross. "I'm a person now."

HER '60s LOOK: Was there any face more perfect for the '60s? The press didn't think so. She was anointed by London's *Daily Express* as "the face of 1966," and more recently by *Time* magazine as one of the twentieth century's twenty most beautiful stars in the June 14, 1999 issue. "Not for everyone, our Twiggy," gushed *Time*, "but her kindling body and ember eyes started many a fire." And the great photographer Richard Avedon declared, "Women move in certain ways that convey an air of the time they live in, and Twiggy, when she's in front of lights, is bringing her generation in front of the camera." Beaming with brightly colored eye-enlarging make-up (the secret: three pairs of false eyelashes above the eyes, penciled-in eyelashes below), crowned by a distinctively short boyish haircut (it took eight hours to perfect the first time it was cut), and with a spray of freckles across her nose, Twiggy's was a face that expressed both the boldness and

the look

the innocence of the age. Yet the remarkable kisser wasn't the novelty that made her so special and brought her the name. With 31-22-32 measurements and barely 90 pounds on her 5' 6" frame, Twiggy in a lime-green mini and green tights represented a bold departure from the softer, rounder shapes of '50s and early-'60s models dressed in sophisticated Chanel suits. "It's not what you'd call a figure, is it?" she once said of her physique. A *Newsweek* cover story called it "the frail torso of the teen-age choirboy," and "four straight limbs in search of a body." But it wasn't just what Twiggy had, it was how she had it. In a '67 *Vogue* magazine article called "The Changing Face of the Fashion Model," legendary photographer Cecil Beaton said, "It is not the baby stare that makes Twiggy a success; rather it is her concave droop, as of a punctured marionette, the almost 'triumph over the spastic' appeal that sends her to the top of the class." A glance at all the waifs in early and mid-'90s fashion magazines shows that she's still much imitated. Kate Moss is often referred to as the Twiggy of the '90s—they're virtually the same height, and Kate has a similar figure at 33-23-35. Twiggy's no longer the model, but the Twiggy look is still the style.

BEHIND THE SCENES: Twiggy was born in 1949, which meant she hit the '60s at only 11 and spent most of the decade as a minor. Growing up in a working-class suburb of London, Twiggy worked in a hair salon and struggled to keep up with the mod fashions starting to emerge. At 15 years old she met her manager/boyfriend, who was ten years her senior and married at the time. They promptly started seeing each other, and he began to steer (some would say control) her '60s career, speaking alongside her at press conferences and making business decisions for her. They got engaged in '68, but Twiggy broke free in the '70s when she quit modeling and set her sights on the movies. In '77 she married actor Michael Whitney, who was in her second movie, *W* ('74). They had a daughter, Carly. In '83

Whitney died of a heart attack. In '88 she married the respected English actor Leigh Lawson (who was formerly with Hayley Mills). Lawson directed Twiggy in *If Love Were All* in the late-'90s, the off-Broadway musical that brought them both rave reviews. They now live in England.

BONUS SWINGABILITY: She uses a fake moniker—her real name is Lesley Hornby, and sometimes spelled as Leslie ... supposedly her childhood nickname was Sticks ... her exotic birthplace—the swingin'est, a suburb of London, England ... eager for publicity

for its new car, in '65 the Ford Motor Company loaned Twiggy one of its first Mustangs to drive around ... Twiggy is partly responsible for discovering a popular singer of the late '60s; when she heard then-unknown Mary Hopkin sing on the TV show *Opportunity Knocks* one night in '68, Twiggy recommended Mary to Paul McCartney, who quickly signed her to the new Apple Records label; at the end of '68 Mary's one huge hit, "Those Were the Days," knocked the Beatles' "Hey Jude" from the top of the British charts ... to *People* in August '99 she reflected on her '60s career: "I loved it, but it was a long time ago. It was great, and it gave me my break, but it's the past."

 A DATE WITH TWIGGY

September 19, 1949.	Twiggy is born
April 27, 1967, May 25, 1967, & June 23, 1967.	The "Twiggy in New York" TV specials air
June 26, 1999	Backstage after a performance of *If Love Were All*, Twiggy meets Kate Moss

VERUSCHKA

SWINGIN' '60s CREDENTIALS: The wild, mysterious Veruschka was one of the most exotic and erotic models of the decade, appearing on many magazine covers and making an unforgettable appearance in the classic film *Blowup*.

WORKIN' IT: One of the first international supermodels, Veruschka has led a life that is as much legend as it is fact. During the '60s she intentionally let her life be clouded in mystery, so that queries into her past often raised more questions than they answered. This much is true, as disclosed by Veruschka herself in Michael Gross's *Model*: Born in '39, Veruschka grew up as Vera von Lehndorff in the eastern part of Germany during World War II. Her parents were both of royal blood—he was a count, she a countess—

and they lived in a castle on an immense estate. When the Gestapo discovered that Veruschka's father, a German officer, was part of a plot to assassinate Hitler, they executed him in '44. Veruschka, only 4 years old, was imprisoned with her mother and sisters. After the war, having lost everything, Veruschka's family moved constantly in search of friends to stay with. Young Vera attended over a dozen different schools, and ended up in Hamburg studying art in the late '50s.

By '62 she was attempting an artist's life in Italy. Her striking looks brought her an invitation to try modeling in Paris, but when that proved unsuccessful, she moved to New York, where she again received a lukewarm reception from the fashion magazines. She was, they all felt, too tall, too hard to fit, and simply too unconventional for the established magazines. So in '64 Vera returned to Italy and reinvented herself. She dressed all in black, changed her name from Vera to Veruschka (German for "little Vera," her childhood nickname), and she let her background drift from fact into myth. She began implementing her own fashion ideas into her shoots—not content to just wear the clothes, she collaborated with the stylists, photographers, and editors on how the clothes would be presented.

Her career zoomed when she appeared in *Blowup*, Michelangelo Antonioni's innovative movie about an arrogant, handsome fashion photographer (David Hemmings playing David Bailey, most viewers assumed) on the prowl in swingin' London. Four minutes into the strange world of the movie, Veruschka appears with the loaded announcement, "Here I am." Then, as Hemmings kneels over her with his camera, she undulates on the floor, tossing her hair and throbbing herself into the sexual frenzy that he is trying to capture on film. The punchline comes when he prematurely evacuates at the height of her floor-play and nonchalantly retreats to another part of the studio just as she is about to foam at the mouth with lust. The startling scene quickly made her a fashion fave. *Life* put her on front of a '67 issue, and *Vogue* ultimately gave her eleven covers.

By the early '70s she was one of the most-photographed models in history, prancing and leaping in fashion mags around the world. She was frequently sullen; never monotonous. "For me, modeling was just an extension of the theater," she said in Ian Halperin's *Shut Up and Smile* ('99). "I liked being on stage dressed up in costume. I like expressing myself. If I would have had to be a model who just got up there in pretty outfits I would gotten bored quickly." In the '70s and '80s Veruschka made the occasional movie appearance—the bizarre, experimental *Salome* in '72, the atmospheric *The Bride* in '85—but as she got older her real passion turned to body painting.

Long before a '92 cover of *Vanity Fair* showed a naked Demi Moore looking like she was wearing a man's suit, Veruschka was pioneering the art of body painting. Nude but for the paint, she would look like she was wearing a gangster's suit, or wearing a dress that parodied current fashions. Veruschka did abstract works, too, camouflaging herself into a rocky background or making it look like she had been carved from marble. Some believe she did most of the painting herself, amazing if true. *Playboy* presented features on her body painting in '71 ("Stalking the Wild Veruschka") and in '74 ("Painted Lady"). In '86 she released the book *Veruschka: Transfigurations*, which disclosed her motivations for painting her body: "I thought it would make a more interesting photograph if I changed the color of my skin, giving the image a strangeness that would distract attention from the often very boring dresses." In '92 she appeared on the cover of Suede's record "The Drowners," her body painted to look like she was wearing a man's blue suit (replete with a hat on her head). Today her continuing status as a pop-culture icon has received a unique validation: one of the most colorful Swatch watches you can buy is named "the Veruschka."

HER '60s LOOK:

As opposed to Twiggy's "innocent waif" look, Veruschka was elegant, regal, exotic, dangerous, and sexually charged. Some sources say she was 6' 4" tall, others 6' 3", still others 6' 1" (again, the Veruschka mystery). Whichever stat is true, she's the tallest Swingin' Chick of the '60s, with a look and an attitude that was all her own. "Veruschka had more of an alternative look than any model I've ever seen," said ex-model Estelle Bergeron in *Shut Up and Smile*. "Her presence was mesmerizing. She was totally into expressing herself artistically." The fashions she wore were usually otherworldly *haute couture* inventions from designers like Scaasi rather than whimsical mod looks. Veroosh was casual with the partial nudity, too. No wonder *Life* called her "The Girl Everybody Stares At." Stare they all did, because she was so eccentric, so far beyond functional fashions or traditional beauty. This was especially true when she began painting her face and body, in some cases actually attaching objects to herself for the photographs. She explained her experiments to *Playboy*: "The body does not arouse me sexually," she said. "I regard it as one element in nature. But, that doesn't mean I'm frigid. I have sexual feelings just like any woman."

BEHIND THE SCENES:

"Sexual feelings," she said. No kiddin'. When David Hemmings' character asks hers "who the hell were you with last night?" in *Blowup*, she sort of shrugs out an answer that implies she had places to go and people to do. One has the feeling that this was pretty close to Veruschka's reality. She told Michael Gross in *Model* that from '66 to the early '70s she lived with a photographer named Franco Rubartelli, who made an Italian film about her in '71. Peter Fonda wrote about his flings with Veruschka in his autobiography, *Don't Tell Dad* ('98). In '65 he saw her in Rome and was immediately overwhelmed by her astounding beauty. He

pestered her until she consented to go out with him; once she did, they spent the next several days and nights together, rolling around on tiny twin beds that were far too short and narrow for their lanky physiques. They reunited in Paris shortly thereafter and fell deeper in love, but they split up after a few days so that Fonda could return to his wife and child in L.A. He wrote that they rendezvoused only three more times in the next six years, though they exchanged many letters during that time. Their "farewell bash," as Fonda called it, came in '71 when they holed up in a luxury hotel suite in Manhattan. A tryst of fate: The exciting evening alone was interrupted by an impromptu visit from two of the '60s' most dazzling couples—Jane Fonda/Roger Vadim, and Warren Beatty/Julie Christie. According to Peter Fonda, after the party finally died down he and Veruschka finally got down to business, which they did several times, once with his sister Jane watching from the open doorway.

BONUS SWINGABILITY:

She uses a fake moniker—her real name is Countess Vera Gottlieb von Lehndorff, often billed as Veruschka, Veroushka, or Verushka; the latter is used in *Blowup*, and her own book in '86 is credited to Vera Lehndorff ... her exotic birthplace—what was then called East Prussia, now Poland ... Veroosh had one other scene in *Blowup*: Ninety minutes after the *photographus interruptus* with Hemmings, her character materializes at a London pot party in a reptilian body suit; he asks her why she isn't in Paris—"I *am* in Paris," she replies, and saunters off ... in the '70s Veruschka did print ads for Lanvin perfume, but she refused to endorse another product she was pitched—Veruschka Vodka.

 A DATE WITH VERUSCHKA

1939	Veruschka is born
December 18, 1966	*Blowup* is released
August 18, 1967	Veruschka makes the cover of *Life* magazine

VICTORIA VETRI

SWINGIN' '60s CREDENTIALS: A voluptuous dark-haired Italian beauty who appeared in seven issues of *Playboy* during the '60s, Angela Dorian was named a Playmate of the Month in '67 and Playmate of the Year in '68. Reverting to her real name, Victoria Vetri, she went blonde a year later for the starring role of the sexy half-clad Sanna in the fantasy epic *When Dinosaurs Ruled the Earth*.

WORKIN' IT: Born in '44 to a father who was a prominent L.A. restaurateur and a mother who had sung on Broadway, Victoria Vetri was first spotted by a Hollywood talent scout while attending Hollywood High in L.A. She auditioned unsuccessfully for the film

version of *West Side Story*, but she did get named Four Star Television's "Deb Star of 1962." Victoria landed some film (*Kings of the Sun* in '63) and mid-decade TV work (including *Wagon Train*, *Perry Mason*, *The Man from U.N.C.L.E.*, and *Hogan's Heroes*). She had the talent to do more than just look good, though usually that's all she was asked to do. During the decade she studied art at UCLA, practiced as a jazz and ballet dancer, wrote songs, and played the guitar (she finally showed off her musical skills by singing a Spanish folk song in a '66 episode of *The Big Valley*).

Her biggest break came in '67, when the screen exposure led to *Playboy* exposure. Over the next ten years she got more than a dozen plays in the magazine, with the touchdowns coming in September '67 as Playmate of the Month and the following spring when she was the Playmate of the Year for '68. For all of these *Playboy* appearances she was billed as Angela Dorian, a stage moniker playing on the name of the doomed Italian liner, the *Andrea Doria*.

In '68 more screen time came her way, notably a role as the belly-dancing Florence of Arabia on *Batman* and as a victim in *Rosemary's Baby*. In the latter, billed as Angela Dorian and playing a character named Terry, she entered the movie after thirteen minutes and had a three-minute scene with Mia Farrow that included this curious exchange:

> Mia: "I'm sorry, I thought you were Victoria Vetri, the actress."
> Angela: "S'all right, a lot of people think I'm Victoria. I don't see any resemblance."
> Mia: "Do you know her?"
> Angela: "No."

Two minutes later, Angela's character lay dead outside the Dakota building in Manhattan. A year later, filming began on *When Dinosaurs Ruled the Earth*. This stop-motion epic was a clear attempt by Hammer Films to jump on the bikini bandwagon of their earlier hit, *One Million Years B.C.*, which helped make a half-dressed Raquel Welch an international sex symbol. Using her real name in the credits and playing a sexy blonde cavegirl called Sanna, Victoria (and the other characters) spoke a primitive twenty-seven-word vocabulary in service to the Oscar-nominated special visual effects. Victoria looked amazing, as usual.

The '70s brought some B movies (including a real "bee" movie, '73's *Invasion of the Bee Girls*) plus some TV appearances (*Mission Impossible*, *The Smothers Brothers*, *Run for Your Life*, two guest shots on *The Tonight Show*, and commercials for Mercury Cougar

and Groom 'n' Clean). According to reports, in the '80s Victoria worked as a waitress in a popular watering hole near UCLA, hoping to save enough money to produce a movie.

HER '60s LOOK:
Sultry, passionate, earthy—she was an Italian goddess who could give the iconic Raquel Welch a run for her money in a battle of cavegirl bikinis. Her incredible figure was the Playmate ideal: Her stats in '68 were given as 36-21-35, with a fighting weight of 109 lbs and a height of 5' 5". Interestingly, in '69 a Warner Bros. press release for *When Dinosaurs Ruled the Earth* increased her bust size to 37 and her weight to 115. Either way, she was quite a contrast to the wispy little hippie chicks of the late '60s, and she certainly didn't cater to the "mod" look that was swirling around her. According to Leonard Maltin's review of *When Dinosaurs Ruled the Earth*, "Vetri…seems to have ordered her wardrobe from Frederick's of Bedrock."

BEHIND THE SCENES:
Details are sketchy about her personal life, but supposedly she was married in '67 to an interior design consultant, and then two more times after that, with possibly one son born in '64. Sadly, there's a story that she was the victim of a brutal attack in her Hollywood home in '80, suffering a broken nose and broken ribs. The two assailants were supposedly never caught.

BONUS SWINGABILITY:
Her exotic birthplace—San Francisco, California … Victoria may have made a major career gaffe when she rejected the part of Lolita in Kubrick's famous '61 film, which was a break for young Sue Lyon … Playmate lore: during one of the *Playboy* photo sessions, the hammock in which Victoria was reclining gave way and she suffered two broken ribs … in her first guest shot on *The Tonight Show* Victoria was introduced as Angela Dorian, then for her second appearance two years later she was introduced as Victoria Vetri … she offered up this lifestyle information for *Playboy*: turn-ons included men, sports cars, and cats; among turn-offs were women who wear hair curlers in public; the person she admired most was Audrey Hepburn … according to movie legend, her screen test for *When Dinosaurs Ruled the Earth* was shot by budding director Francis Ford Coppola … supposedly several nude scenes with Victoria were filmed for *When Dinosaurs Ruled the Earth*, but they didn't make it into the final version released in the U.S. (though some fans say that they are in rare U.K. versions of the film) … in '68 Victoria was filmed as a guest star in the pilot episode of *The Courtship of Eddie's Father*, though the episode wasn't shown until the fall of '69 … it's said that Victoria has always loved fast cars and car racing, and in her time she's owned a Porsche, a Sprite, and the pink AMX she won as Playmate of the Year in '68 … in addition to *One Million Years B.C.* and *When Dinosaurs Ruled the Earth*, several other movies have pitted scantily-clad prehistorians against special-effects dinosaurs, among them *Dinosaur Island* (with a dozen actresses credited as "Cave Girls") in '94, and *Dinosaur Valley Girls* (with Karen Black) in '96 … Victoria's co-star in '72's *Group Marriage* was Claudia Jennings. While working as a Playboy receptionist in Chicago, Claudia was named one of the decade's last Playmates of the Month (November '69), and she won the Playmate of the Year title seven months later. In the '70s this vivacious redhead was known as the "Queen of the B's" for her many drive-in movies (including *Truck Stop Women* in '74, *'Gator Bait* in '76, and *Moonshine County Express* in '77). Sadly, in '79 29-year-old Claudia died in a car accident on the Pacific Coast Highway in Malibu, California.

A DATE WITH VICTORIA

September 26, 1944	Victoria Vetri is born
December 20, 1949	Claudia Jennings is born
December 3, 1962	Victoria (as Angela) debuts on *Cheyenne*
February 22, 1968	Victoria (as Angela) appears on *Batman*
June 12, 1968	*Rosemary's Baby* is released
September 17, 1969	Victoria appears on *The Courtship of Eddie's Father*
October 25, 1970	*When Dinosaurs Ruled the Earth* is released in the U.K.
October 3, 1979	Claudia Jennings dies in a car accident

MARY QUANT

SWINGIN' '60s CREDENTIALS:

If you ever wore a miniskirt, or admired someone who did, thank Mary Quant. She's the designer who made the mini the decade's defining fashion statement.

WORKIN' IT:

Fab and fun, the flamboyant fashions of the '60s were the products of a determined revolution. The revolution's catalyst was Mary Quant. She was the hippest designer in the hippest city in the world, the unrivaled Queen of Swingin' London. Wrote London's *Sunday Times*, "It is given to a fortunate few to be born at the right time, in the right place, with the right talents. In recent fashion, there are three: Chanel, Dior and Mary Quant."

After graduating in '55 from Goldsmiths College of Art in London, 21-year-old Mary opened Bazaar, a stylish clothing shop in Chelsea. Catering to urban youth, she filled the shop (and a second one, opened in Knightsbridge in '57) with the exciting clothes being worn by rock 'n' rollers— bell bottoms, bright patterns, and thigh-climbing skirts. When she couldn't find the creative clothes she wanted, she designed them herself. Some sources credit French designer Andre Courreges with actually inventing the miniskirt ahead of Mary; that may or may not be true, but Mary's the one who brought the style to the masses by keeping prices affordable (J.C. Penney carried her designs as early as '62) and the look whimsical. Brigitte Bardot and Nancy Sinatra were just two of her famous customers; when George Harrison married model Pattie Boyd in the winter of '66, they were both wearing Quant's clothes. Mary also designed the costumes for several popular films, including the Oscar-nominated *Georgy Girl* ('66) and Audrey Hepburn's *Two for the Road* ('67).

Sparked by her design innovations, '60s fashions exploded in bursts of crazy new colors, prints, and fabrics. Mary dropped another bombshell into the fashion world in '69—hot pants, which did for shorts what her minis did for skirts. How fun! How creative! How '60s! Later she brought her touch to hosiery, linens, and home furnishings. She also wrote several books, among them her autobiography, *Quant by Quant*, in '66, followed by *Color by Quant*, *The Ultimate Make-up and Beauty Book*, *Classic Make-up and Beauty*, and *Mary Quant's Daisy Chain of Things to Make and Do*. Today her Colour Concepts boutiques, which showcase her color-saturated make-up, are located in world capitals like Paris, New York, and Tokyo. Mary is still working in London, with jewelry and umbrellas and bags and socks among her latest creations. The '60s may be over, but the revolution lives on!

HER '60s LOOK:

Unlike fashion designers of previous decades who were much older than the models who wore their clothes, Mary Quant was of the same generation as her clientele. This meant that Mary, who was petite and pretty, could convincingly sport the hip new fashions she created. Though she's best known for the mini, her legacy is more than a single garment—it's an entire style known as the "London Look," which by mid-decade meant clothes with simple lines, short/shorter/shortest skirts, bold colors, flat shoes, and strong, colorful eye make-up. Photos of Mary in the '60s show her with the same precision Sassoon haircut, short skirts, and tights, boots, blouses, and eye shadow as any of her marvelous models.

BEHIND THE SCENES:

When Mary opened Bazaar in '55, her partners were Alexander Plunket-Greene and Archie McNair. Mary married Plunket-Greene and together they have one son.

BONUS SWINGABILITY:

Her exotic birthplace—Kent, England … her logo—a simple daisy … when the Queen awarded Mary the Order of the British Empire (O.B.E.) in '66, Mary accepted while wearing a miniskirt … other awards she's won include Italy's *Piavolo d'Oro* in '66, the Royal Society of Arts Annual Design Medal in '67, and the Hall of Fame Award from the British Fashion Council in '69 … the quotable Mary: "a woman," Mary once said, "is as young as her knees" … two direct results of Mary's mini-revolution: the inventions of pantyhose and the maxi coat (to keep suddenly exposed legs warm) … Mary knows a good revolution when she sees one: She's got a stylish Web site at http://www.maryquant.com.

A DATE WITH MARY

February 11, 1934	Mary Quant is born.
June 10, 1966	Mary is awarded the O.B.E.
October 17, 1966	*Georgy Girl* is released
April 27, 1967	*Two for the Road* is released

THE MOVIE STARS:
THE ALL-AMERICANS

Complementing the luminous '50s stars who continued to shine in the '60s (legends like Ava Gardner, Rita Hayworth, and Kim Novak), some glittering new screen stars, including the following, emerged in the '60s, bringing new attitudes and fresh looks to Hollywood. On screen, women were stronger, and more sexual, in the '60s than they'd ever been since the pre-code '30s. Revolution was not just in the air, it was on the silver screen.

CARROLL BAKER

Anita Ekberg, Ursula Andress, and Brigitte Bardot never did—an Oscar nomination as Best Actress. Carroll's came for her second movie, *Baby Doll*, the sensational '56 film that cast her as a 19-year-old, thumb-sucking nymphet who slept in a crib. Her terrific acting, and the subsequent controversy over the movie's "indecency," catapulted her to stardom at age 25. Soon followed *The Big Country* ('58) and *How the West Was Won* ('62), with a variety of challenging roles and prominent Westerns in between. It was *The Carpetbaggers* ('64) that made her a goddess. Paramount's highest-grossing movie that year, it presented her as a sexually aggressive bombshell and led to her platinum glamour-queen role in *Harlow* ('65). The studios would have been happy to typecast her as a Marilyn-style sex symbol for the rest of her career, but Carroll wanted more diversity. ("I was always a rebel that way," she boasted to *Biography* magazine in '99.) She fled to Europe to make twenty-seven foreign films in twenty years.

Returning to Hollywood in the '80s, she appeared in another two dozen movies, including *Star 80* ('83), *Ironweed* ('87), *Kindergarten Cop* ('90), and *The Game* ('97). A talented writer (she won a national award for her writing while she was in high school), she wrote her autobiography, *Baby Doll*, in '83, a sizzling tell-all that the *New York Times* praised: "Carroll Baker's behind-the-scenes anecdotes are the freshest, the wildest, the funniest ... howlingly candid!"

Encouraged by the reception, she wrote two more books, a personal romantic adventure called *To Africa with Love* and a novel called *A Roman Tale*. Throughout her long career she's been recognized with many prominent awards, including the Best Actress award from the Foreign Press Club in '57, the

SWINGIN' '60s CREDENTIALS: This beautiful blonde sex symbol springboarded from the scandalous *Baby Doll* in '56 to more than a dozen '60s movies, including *The Carpetbaggers* and *Harlow*, establishing herself as one of the decade's memorable screen sirens.

WORKIN' IT: Although she was compared to other screen goddesses of the '50s and '60s, Carroll Baker earned something that Marilyn Monroe, Jayne Mansfield, Kim Novak, Gina Lollobrigida,

'58 Woman of the Year award from Harvard's Hasty Pudding Club, and a "Golden Boot" award in honor of her starring roles in such great Westerns as *The Big Country* and *Cheyenne Autumn* ('64). She was made a Kentucky Colonel in '62 and named an Honorary Member of the Cheyenne Indian Tribe in '64. Still busy and beautiful, now with over sixty films to her credit, Carroll Baker is that rarest Hollywood goddess: one whose own life story will have a happy ending.

HER '60s LOOK: Carroll's is a natural beauty suitable for a strong frontier woman, a role she often played. But it's the glamour most people remember. At her peak she was a platinum throwback to '50s screen sirens à la Marilyn and Jayne. Her lovely face was framed by the white-gold hair deemed necessary by the studios for sexy roles, and her vivacious figure was packed into the requisite sequin gowns of classic Hollywood. The most famous was Balmain's transparent sequined sensation that she wore to the Hollywood premiere of *The Carpetbaggers*, a dress that Marlene Dietrich helped her find in Paris. Carroll steamed up *Playboy* in August '68, and she also made the magazine's '99 list of "The 100 Sexiest Stars of the Century," coming in at #94, right behind another blonde sex goddess, Fay Wray.

BEHIND THE SCENES: Close friendships with Elizabeth Taylor, Robert Mitchum, Steve McQueen and Debbie Reynolds, studio antics with Jerry Lewis, dances with Gene Kelly, motorcycle rides with James Dean—Carroll's '50's and '60s were filled with the stuff that fanzine dreams are made of. For most of this era, Carroll was a married woman. She had a brief marriage in the early '50s, then she remarried happily in '55 to writer/director Jack Garfein (*Something Wild*, '61). They had a daughter in '56 and a son in '58, but the marriage broke up at the end of the '60s. She married the British actor and writer Donald Burton in '82 and now lives with him in Southern California.

BONUS SWINGABILITY: Her exotic birthplace—Johnstown, Pennsylvania ... before she was famous, Carroll once worked as a magician's assistant ... there were two movies called *Harlow* in '65; the other one, starring Carol Lynley, came out on May 14th, while Carroll's came out on June 23rd ... her role in Andy Warhol's *Bad* ('77) was supposedly intended for Shelley Winters, who turned it down ... Herschel Garfein, Carroll's son, is a composer and theatrical director ... Blanche Baker, Carroll's daughter, was in *Sixteen Candles* ('84) as Molly Ringwald's about-to-be-married sister, and starred on Broadway in *Lolita*, opposite Donald Sutherland. She now works as a sculptress ... Carroll's autobiography, *Baby Doll*, is available at http://www.backinprint.com ... Carroll has her own official Web site—http://www.carrollbaker.com.

A DATE WITH CARROLL

May 28, 1931	Carroll Baker is born
February 20, 1963	*How the West Was Won* is released
April 9, 1964	*The Carpetbaggers* is released
June 23, 1965	*Harlow* is released

DYAN CANNON

SWINGIN' '60s CREDENTIALS: An alluring actress with a sexy charm, Dyan Cannon had a limited screen output during the '60s, but she had one starring role that brought her international fame: she was married to Cary Grant, who was over thirty years her senior, from '65 to '68.

WORKIN' IT: Dyan's screen career began in the early '50s when she appeared on *Playhouse 90* and in several TV Westerns at the end of the '50s. In the early '60s she was in a few minor movies (*The Rise and Fall of Legs Diamond* and *This Rebel Breed*, both in '60) and a TV series (*Full Circle*, '60–'61).

However, by '62 she was already seeing Grant, and her screen appearances came to a screeching halt as of '64. After their bitter '68 divorce, she made a huge Hollywood splash in '69 as the Alice in the controversial *Bob & Carol & Ted & Alice* (Natalie Wood was the Carol). The role of the dignified wife brought her Oscar and Golden Globe nominations, positioning her for a long run as a memorable screen actress. She capitalized quickly on her sudden momentum with four movies in '71 alone and three dozen more by the end of the century. Highlights include *The Love Machine* ('71), another Golden Globe nomination for *Such Good Friends* ('71), *The Last of Sheila* ('73), another Oscar nomination for *Heaven Can Wait* ('78), *Deathtrap* ('82), and *Christmas in Connecticut* ('92). Proving herself to be a versatile talent, she's also written, produced, and directed her own projects, including the Oscar-nominated short *Number One* in '76 and the full-length autobiographical drama *The End of Innocence* in '91. A hard-workin' actress, she's continued to make movies (six in '97, including *Out to Sea* and *That Darn Cat*), and she's become a regular on TV's *Ally McBeal*.

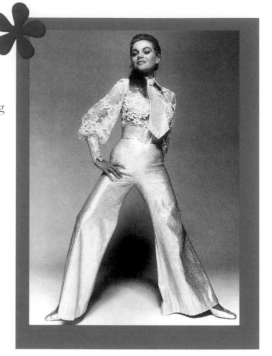

HER '60s LOOK: Dyan's disheveled sultriness made her look like one of the decade's wild things, with long blonde movie-star hair giving her a recklessly sexy style. She also flashed a great bare midriff, revealing herself to be an honors graduate of the Navel Academy. She still got nervous, however, about the famous bedroom scene in *Bob & Carol & Ted & Alice*, according to an August '99 *L.A. Times* interview: "The day we had to do the scene where we all got in bed together, we were all a wreck. Elliott Gould was on a diet, but he started stuffing food in his mouth. Bob Culp was so nervous that he talked a mile a minute. And Natalie Wood—at first she wouldn't even come out of her trailer. It was my first big movie, and I was panicked about having to take my bra off. I kept thinking, 'People are going to see me without my clothes on this really big screen.'" As she got older, her blonde hair went wonderfully curly and the young sexpot transformed into a mature, radiant beauty.

BEHIND THE SCENES: She was born in 1937 (according to most sources, though dates vary between '36 and '39); Cary Grant was born in 1904. Thus was the fascination with their marriage, which, aside from Frank and Mia's, was the most-discussed of the decade. They started seeing each other in '62, but Dyan, aware of Cary's rep for having disastrous relationships, often broke their dates. She must have kept enough of them, as she was pregnant with Cary's child when they were married in '65 at the Desert Inn in Vegas. Daughter Jennifer was born seven months later, but for Dyan and Cary problems and differences already existed. The union would last only 32 months. "I lost my individuality completely after I married Cary," she would say later. He countered with, "Dyan is strong. That's why I married her. I chose her for her strength, but instead of joining her strength with mine, she has used it against me. Emotionally, she's a child." Unfortunately, he would spank her and beat her "with his fists," as she charged in their divorce hearing, for reasons as insignificant as her wearing of a miniskirt. For years they continued to tangle over their daughter, and it took primal therapy for Dyan to recover

from the marriage. Long after they were divorced, she said, "If I'd stayed in that marriage I'd be dead today, dead, dead, dead, dead, really dead, in a grave, dead." Dyan married again in '85, but that ended in divorce in '91.

In a departure from her screen career, two Saturdays a month Dyan has hosted a Christian-fellowship meeting in Studio City, California. Called God's Party with Dyan Cannon and You, the evening of prayer and celebration is open to the general public. As she told Sandy Engel in an interview, "We praise and we worship and I teach, and all kinds of wonderful things happen. The Holy Spirit does healings, and it's just amazing. And people who have never, ever known the Lord, or thought about it, are being drawn in. God put it on my heart about five years ago to start a Bible study that started in my house, and we started with five people and it grew to several hundred. And then recently I was led to start this GPDC&U [God's Party with Dyan Cannon and You], and it's been placed right in the middle of the CBS lot, and it's not just for the people in the movie industry or the television industry—it's for anyone."

BONUS SWINGABILITY: She uses a stage moniker—her real name is Samile Diane Friesen. She has sometimes been billed as "Diane Friesen," and her high school nickname was "Frosty" ... her stage name was given to her by producer Jerry Wald, who was impressed by her looks and supposedly said, "You need a name that's explosive—Boom! Bang! Cannon!" ... her exotic birthplace—Tacoma, Washington ... Dyan's daughter Jennifer is also an actress and had the regular role of Celeste on *Beverly Hills 90210* ... when Dyan and Cary went on an ocean voyage to England, she took thirty-six suitcases and fifty pairs of shoes ... Dyan was one of the 100 invited guests to the July '99 wedding of Raquel Welch and restaurateur Richard Palmer ... Dyan's deeply involved with Operation Lookout, an organization that helps locate kidnapped children ... according to oxygen.com, Dyan bounces on a trampoline at night to help get to sleep, and she gives these words of romantic wisdom: "There's no age and there's no color—you're attracted to someone's soul or you're not" ... there's one other regular role Dyan plays on TV, though this one is in real life: she's the second-most-visible L.A. Laker fan after smilin' Jack Nicholson ... the Engel interview quoted above is shown at http://www.geocities.com/Heartland/Bluffs/1125/Tv_and_Movies/Dyan_Cannon.html.

A DATE WITH DYAN

January 18, 1904	Cary Grant is born
January 4, 1937	Dyan Cannon is born
November 5, 1959	Dyan debuts on *Zane Grey Theater*
July 22, 1965	Dyan and Cary get married
February 26, 1966	Dyan gives birth to daughter Jennifer Grant
March 21, 1968	Dyan and Cary divorce
September 18, 1969	*Bob & Carol & Ted & Alice* is released

mericans

ANGIE DICKINSON

SWINGIN' '60s CREDENTIALS: There's no doubting the swingability of this strong, reliable sex symbol—in a TV biography, the first line used to describe her was "She was a swingin' party chick." Combining brains and beauty, style and independence, she's always managed to convey both sexiness and strength in her movies, among which are several '60s classics.

WORKIN' IT: Always popular and always working, Angie Dickinson made an average of two movies a year through the '60s. Born in '31, she began her career by entering TV's *Beauty Parade* in '53,

winning the weekly, monthly, and yearly competitions. That success led to a part on the *Colgate Comedy Hour* and secretary-type parts in minor movies in the '50s. She was also doing lots of Westerns back then. *Rio Bravo* in '59 made her a star and confirmed her strengths as a beautiful, self-assured woman with enough moxie to stand up to a cast fulla tough guys. After the stylin' Rat Packer *Ocean's Eleven* ('60), she won a Golden Globe as the Most Promising Newcomer (some Newcomer—she'd already been in a half dozen movies). She signed a seven-year deal with Universal in '63, but there was no percentage in the kind of routine roles she was getting, so she wrangled out of it after two years in hopes of scoring bigger and better parts. Among her sixteen '60s flix were *Jessica* (the title role) in '62, *Captain Newman, M.D.* in '63, *The Killers* in '64, *The Art of Love* (alongside Elke Sommer) in '65, *The Chase* (with Marlon

Brando, Robert Redford, and Jane Fonda) in '66, *Cast a Giant Shadow* (with boyfriend Frank Sinatra) in '66, the hardboiled cult classic *Point Blank* (her character got to beat up Lee Marvin's) in '67, and Burt Reynolds's *Sam Whiskey* in '69.

From the '70s to the '90s she had some great credits, including the sexy-but-respected lead in *Big Bad Mama* in '74, then her own *Police Woman* TV series, the erotic *Dressed to Kill* in '80, and memorable supporting roles in *Wild Palms*, *Sabrina*, and *Even Cowgirls Get the Blues*. She turned down the role of Krystle Carrington in *Dynasty*, the role that went to Linda Evans. Angie also rejected an offer from *Playboy* to be featured in a photo spread, which came when she was over 50 years old. Although she got Emmy nominations every year from '75-'77, Angie's won only one major acting award, the 1975 Golden Globe as Best Actress for *Police Woman*. But you don't have a career of over seventy-five big-screen and TV movies without being able to please the studios who pay and the audiences that continue to come. Isn't she due for some kind of lifetime achievement award by now?

HER '60s LOOK: In the '60s, Angie's wonderful face conveyed an amiable sweetness that combined vulnerability with experience, as if she'd been in some sad relationships but still had romantic hopes. This dual image came out in her film roles: early in *The Sins of Rachel Cade* ('61), she's described as "very American, very pretty," and "insatiably virtuous." Yet when the Rat Pack needed a fulsome femme to play Frank's wife for a little hey-hey in *Ocean's Eleven*, they knew who to call. And how's this for a testament to her looks: in '63 Universal Studios had her legs insured for a million clams. Two decades later, those same legs were spotlighted in a memorable billboard for California Avocados. When *Playboy* published its list of

the all-ar

the "100 Sexiest Stars of the Century" in January '99, the magazine ranked Angie in the top fifty, putting her at #42, between the legends Clara Bow and Hedy Lamarr.

BEHIND THE SCENES: She married semi-pro football player Gene Dickinson in '51. As she got more involved with her career, they split up amicably in '55 and divorced in '60. Angie's been linked romantically to many cultural icons—JFK, Sinatra, and Johnny Carson, to name a few. There's a JFK rumor that's especially titillating—supposedly he celebrated his 1960 presidential nomination by skinny-dipping with Angie. Another oft-told story has him giving her an autographed photo that tells her she was the only woman he ever loved. She herself once said that her liaison with JFK was "the most remarkable sixty seconds of my life." More significant was her on-again/off-again ten years with Sinatra, which continued even though they were at times married to other people. She explained his appeal in the book *The Way You Wear Your Hat*: "He has a way, a magical way. It's not just the blue eyes and their very color, but the way they look at you. You feel very, very comfortable. And he doesn't ignore you when he's in the company of others. A lot of men abandon the woman they come to a party with. But he still stays connected to you, without coddling." She married a swingin' composer, Burt Bacharach, in '65. They tied the knot in Vegas after a whirlwind three-month romance, but they split up in the late

birthplace—Kulm, North Dakota ... as a young girl her dad, a small-town newspaper man, ran the local movie house once a week, so she saw all the latest flix and was dreaming early of stardom ... she's often played screen characters with great names, including Lucky Legs, Feathers, Ruby, Pepper, and Lindy ... in 61's *The Sins of Rachel Cade*, she shares above-the-title billing with a future Bond, Roger Moore ... in the mid-'60s she and husband Burt Bacharach appeared in suave commercials for Martini & Rossi ...
wearing a slinky black pants outfit, she once crooned "I'll Never Fall in Love Again" on *The Dean Martin Show* ... she has frequent poker games with Barbara Sinatra, Gregory Peck, and Dom DeLuise ... Angie has campaigned for Alzheimer's research, and she's spoken before Congress on worker's rights ... in a TV bio she said, "I think most people would think, Gee, I would like to have led her life" ... coyly, she has also said, "I dress for women, and undress for men."

'70s when her schedule got too chaotic with *Police Woman*. After they divorced in '80, he turned around and married singer/songwriter Carole Bayer Sager, while Angie went on to date Larry King, Billy Vera, Julio Iglesias, and Harry Reasoner. As of 2000 she has still not remarried.

BONUS SWINGABILITY:
Her moniker at birth—Angeline Brown ... her exotic

A DATE WITH ANGIE

September 30, 1931	Angie Dickinson is born
June 2, 1951	Angie marries Gene Dickinson
April 4, 1959	*Rio Bravo* is released in the U.S.
August 10, 1960	*Ocean's Eleven* is released in the U.S.
May 15, 1965	Angie marries Burt Bacharach
August 30, 1967	*Point Blank* is released in the U.S.
September 13, 1974	*Police Woman* debuts
September 11, 1977	Three-time nominee Angie co-hosts the Emmy Awards with Robert Blake

nericans

FAYE DUNAWAY ✱

SWINGIN' '60s CREDENTIALS: This sleek high-cheekboned dramatic actress became an international star with one of the decade's most famous films, *Bonnie and Clyde*. She also teamed with cool-guy Steve McQueen in *The Thomas Crown Affair* before really hitting her stride as an Oscar-winning superstar in the '70s.

WORKIN' IT: A runner-up in the Miss University of Florida contest of '59, Faye Dunaway was a stage actress who didn't start appearing on screen until the mid-'60s. With only a few TV and movie credits behind her (*The Trials of O'Brien* in '66, *Hurry*

Sundown in '67) but five years of prominent New York theatre work on her résumé, she landed the choice role of Bonnie Parker in the landmark *Bonnie and Clyde* ('67). Supposedly Carol Lynley, Natalie Wood, Tuesday Weld, and Shirley MacLaine had also been considered as potential Bonnies, but 28-year-old Faye turned out to be the perfect fit. Of the character she later wrote, "Never have I felt so close to a character as I felt to Bonnie....There was a real kind of fierceness I'd seen in Bonnie that I recognized in myself as well." It was a remarkable performance. She made the gun-toting killer a sympathetic three-dimensional character complicated by inner torments and desires. The role brought her the first of many Oscar and Golden Globe nominations, as well as landing her on the covers of *Newsweek, Look,* and *Life* magazines within a year of the movie's release.

Suddenly one of Hollywood's hottest actresses, she went glamorous for *The Thomas Crown Affair* a year later, Western for *Little Big Man* in '70, and royal for *The Three Musketeers* in '73. For Faye the '70s were filled with memorable movies, especially the classic *Chinatown* in '74 and *Network* in '76; the former brought her another Oscar nomination, the latter an Oscar win. Her busy '80s swung from the campy *Mommie Dearest* in '81 (earning her a Razzie for the year's worst performance) to the risky role of the downtrodden Wanda in *Barfly* in '87. She suffered a TV debacle when her attempt at a sit-com in '93 quickly bombed, followed by a Broadway debacle when she was rejected for the lead role in *Sunset Boulevard* after she said she was given the lead by Andrew Lloyd Webber himself. Ever resilient, she starred in, and got glowing notices for, the remake of *The Thomas Crown Affair* in '99, and her film credits now number over seventy roles. She's got an Emmy on her mantel for a '93 *Columbo* TV movie, and a '95 autobiography, *Looking for Gatsby*, on her bookshelf. Her impact on film history is undeniable. On the American Film Institute's list of the "100 Greatest American Movies," three of the hundred starred Faye Dunaway: #19 *Chinatown*, #27 *Bonnie and Clyde*, #66 *Network*.

HER '60s LOOK: She had the look and the confidence of an established star—which she wasn't yet—for *Bonnie and Clyde*. Ironically, while audiences everywhere saw her Bonnie as a tall, slender, distinctive beauty with a model's sense of poise and movement, she thought she looked ugly and tried not to throw up when she first saw the film. Her gun-moll look dramatically influenced international fashions, with Faye's beret, blonde 'do, and sleek styles sparking a retro-'30s trend that made the midi-skirt and maxi-skirt into fashion phenoms for the last years of the decade. As she explained in her autobiography, "the Bonnie look became the rage because women saw it and felt they could pull it off. It was glamorized, but real." And she still looks good. As she discussed with *W* magazine in the fall of '99: "A lot of actresses at my age are fat ... I could be, but somehow I've found a way of living that keeps me fit and looking good."

BEHIND THE SCENES: "Sex isn't everything," Faye once said. "Love isn't everything. Nothing can be everything." True, but sex and love can be *something*. Faye has found something with some of the most famous names in Hollywood. She was reputedly romanced by many great stars of the '50s, '60s and '70s—Marlon Brando, Michael Caine, Steve McQueen, Jack Nicholson, even Lenny Bruce, not to mention a long tempestuous affair with Marcello Mastroianni. She married Peter Wolf, the lead singer of the J. Geils Band, in 1974, divorcing him in '79. She was married to Terry O'Neill from '83 to '87; together they have a son who's now a model.

BONUS SWINGABILITY: Her full moniker—Dorothy Faye Dunaway ... her exotic birthplace—Bascom, Florida ... supposedly Jane Fonda was seriously considered for the Evelyn Mulwray role in *Chinatown* that eventually went to Faye ... in her autobiography she writes about Steve McQueen: "Steve I loved. He was darling. He was daunting....He was a chauvinist ... but a chivalrous one to me ... in later years Steve would say again and again that *Thomas Crown* was his favorite movie and that I was the best actress he had ever worked with" ... the important lesson she learned from the driven Warren Beatty: "If you have a

vision, the only way to protect it is to fight body and soul, to go to the mat time and again. You have to deal with all your wits and everything that you are. It's to go through brick walls. It's intense determination" ... Faye was quoted by syndicated columnist Liz Smith in July '99: "The whole era when I was busy being a big movie star was terribly disconcerting. I was cared for and cosseted, and yet I was totally dependent. I didn't know where the corn flakes were kept. I didn't know how to turn on the washing machine. That might sound very chic, but I'm telling you: when you don't know how your own life works, you get disconnected."

A DATE WITH FAYE

January 14, 1941	Faye Dunaway is born
January 14, 1966	Faye debuts on *The Trials of O'Brien*
August 13, 1967	*Bonnie and Clyde* is released
June 19, 1968	*The Thomas Crown Affair* is released
March 28, 1977	Faye wins the Best Actress Oscar (*Network*)

MIA FARROW

her first major screen credit and her first major accolade: "Mia Farrow Lights Up Screen," headlined the *Hollywood Reporter*. She won the 1965 Golden Globe as Most Promising Newcomer, but she was ambitious for more. According to Kitty Kelly's *My Way*, Mia said, "I want a big career, a big man, and a big life. You have to think big—that's the only way to get it." She got the biggest, Frank, but her career stalled during their '65-'68 relationship.

She came back strong in '68 with the horror classic *Rosemary's Baby*, followed a year later by *John and Mary* (which brought her another Golden Globe nomination). She made some conspicuous movies in the '70s (*The Great Gatsby* in '74, *Death on the Nile* in '79), but it was her work in Woody Allen's films throughout the '80s and early '90s that brought her the most recognition and acclaim (though she'd now probably hate to admit it). The thirteen she made with him included *A Midsummer Night's Sex Comedy* in '82, *Broadway Danny Rose* in '84, *The Purple Rose of Cairo* in '85, and *Hannah and Her Sisters* in '86. She averaged a movie a year during the '90s, ranging from starring roles to interesting supporting parts and cameos. Her '97 memoir, *What Falls Away*, discussed her loves, related stories about chums like Liza Minnelli, Yul Brynner, Michael Caine, Thornton Wilder, and Salvador Dali, and described her lifelong pursuit of that which is truly meaningful.

HER '60s LOOK: Her cute shorn-waif '60s hair—as first cut by Vidal Sassoon—really caught on and was a nice counterbalance to the elaborate 'dos of the era (Frank supposedly loved her look, and according to *The Way You Wear Your Hat*, he bought her a T-bird the same color as her pale yellow hair). Like Audrey Hepburn, the ultimate gamine, Mia might've been a top fashion model had she not made movies. (Magazines have always appreciated her appeal—she made the cover of *Vogue* in August '67, and she was on the cover of the first *People*.) The

SWINGIN' '60s CREDENTIALS: This ethereal young actress made the quantum leap from a sullen supporting role on TV's *Peyton Place* to a world-famous marriage with Frank Sinatra, travels to India with the Beatles, and starring roles in several prominent late-'60s movies.

WORKIN' IT: Mia Farrow was born for stardom. Her godfather was Hollywood legend George Cukor, her godmother was famous columnist Louella Parsons, her mother, Maureen O'Sullivan, co-starred in early *Tarzan* movies, and her father, John Farrow, wrote and directed dozens of movies from the '20s to the '50s. After overcoming polio as a child, the teenage Mia had bit parts in a few '50s movies, including her dad's *John Paul Jones* ('59). Her big break came in '64 with the part of Allison Mackenzie on TV's *Peyton Place*, gentle-hippie style she affected suited her and the times, though not everybody thought she was sexy: Ava Gardner once said, "I always knew Frank would end up in bed with a little boy." Supposedly Mia jokingly told Frank that the measurements of her 98-pound body were 20-20-20, but later, when she heard the Ava quote, Mia retorted, "I can match bottoms with anyone in Hollywood!"

BEHIND THE SCENES:

Mia was Frank's third wife, and a pal of the Beatles—could it get any better in the '60s? It's possible she also

had relationships with singer Eddie Fisher, director Roman Polanski, British actor Peter Sellers, and John Phillips of the Mamas and the Papas. "Men had an instinctive desire to protect Mia," said her mother in *My Way*. On *Late Night with David Letterman* in '99 she described her first meeting with Frank, to whom she was instantly attracted despite the 30-year age difference. She said that she was so nervous in his presence, she dropped her handbag right in front of him. He helped her scoop up the spilled contents, which embarrassingly included bubble gum, an old donut, and her retainer. She was 20 years old at the time.

He soon layed a nine-carat $85K rock on her, and they were married at the Sands in Vegas in mid-July of '66, with honeymoons first in New York, then London. Meanwhile, back home the pairing generated instant material to wits everywhere: "I've got Scotch older than Mia" joked pal Dean Martin; "Frank didn't have to buy Mia a diamond ring, he gave her a teething ring," guffawed singer Eddie Fisher; and "At his age, he should marry me!" declared Mia's surprised mom. Unfortunately, her desire to act in the late '60s broke up the marriage. He confronted her on the set of *Rosemary's Baby* and demanded that she leave the film to be with him, but she chose her career. He immediately served her with divorce papers. To get away from the turmoil, in the spring of '68 she went to India, seeking enlightenment and purpose at Maharishi Mahesh Yogi's ashram. The Beatles and their women showed up soon after. Mia became friends with all of them, especially John, who made her laugh,

George, who she later wrote was "gentle and kind, with a radiant spiritual quality," and Paul's girlfriend, Jane Asher, who was "not noticeably serious about meditating" and so helped lighten the mood. That summer she and Frank got a quick-but-amiable Mexican divorce. Her later relationships received almost as much attention. After a scandalous pursuit of married conductor Andre Previn, she was married to him through most of the '70s (inspiring Previn's ex-wife Dory to write the song "Beware of Young Girls"). Mia was then the unmarried romantic partner of Woody Allen from the '80s until their acrimonious tabloid-covered split in '92. From these post-Frank relationships she had given birth to, and adopted, a total of fourteen children by the turn of the millennium.

BONUS SWINGABILITY: Her full moniker is Maria de Lourdes Villiers Farrow, and her nickname growing up was Mouse ... her exotic birthplace—L.A., California ... Mia's younger sister Tisa appeared in a dozen films in the '70s and '80s ... Mia's nickname for Frank: Charlie Brown; his for her: Angel Face, Baby Face, Doll Face, and sometimes, affectionately, "my little boy" ... according to *My Way*, at Frank's first Vegas concert after the wedding, he startled the audience by introducing Mia and adding, "I finally found a broad I can cheat on" ... supposedly director Roman Polanski originally wanted Tuesday Weld to star in *Rosemary's Baby*, but Paramount pushed for Mia, who was "hotter" because of her marriage to Frank ... so popular was *Rosemary's Baby*, Mia recorded its gentle lullaby as a single, which briefly lit onto the *Billboard* charts in the summer of '68 ... while Mia was in India with the Beatles, the group created several songs that later appeared on their *White Album*: "Dear Prudence" was about Mia's sister Prudence, who secluded herself in meditation, and "The Continuing Story of Bungalow Bill" was about a character who left the ashram to go tiger hunting ... when Frank finally bought the big casino in '98, Mia and his daughter Nancy slipped a bottle of Jack Daniel's into his casket because, as she told Letterman in '99, "he never wanted to go far without it, sort of one for the road."

A DATE WITH MIA

December 12, 1915	Frank Sinatra is born
April 6, 1929	Andre Previn is born
December 1, 1935	Woody Allen is born
February 9, 1945	Mia Farrow is born
September 15, 1964	*Peyton Place* debuts
July 19, 1966	Mia marries Frank
June 12, 1968	*Rosemary's Baby* is released
August 19, 1968	Mia and Frank divorce
December 14, 1969	*John and Mary* is released

JANE FONDA

SWINGIN' '60s CREDENTIALS: The '60s version of a '50s blonde bombshell, sex kitten Fonda was smart, aggressive, liberated, risqué, an acclaimed actress, and the star of numerous classic '60s films including *Cat Ballou* and *Barbarella*.

WORKIN' IT: Born in '37 to prominent parents (dad Henry was a screen legend, mom Frances was a leading New York socialite), Jane came from a successful career on Broadway to become one of the top international film stars of the '60s. She

averaged almost two movies a year throughout the decade, starting in '60 with *Tall Story*, in which Jane recreated her Broadway role of a cheery college student opposite gangly Tony Perkins. *Period of Adjustment* (in which she went blonde) and *Walk on the Wild Side* (with Jane as the young temptress Kitty Twist) came in '62 (along with a Golden Globe as Most Promising Newcomer), with *Sunday in New York* following a year later. Critics were quickly impressed with her: in '62 *Newsday* called her "the loveliest and most gifted of all our new young actresses." Jane's big-screen breakthrough, of course, was *Cat Ballou* ('65), in which she played the sweet title role that had been offered to Ann-Margret but rejected. The rootin'-tootin' Western got five Oscar nominations, was one of the year's top-ten moneymakers, and made her a star at age 28.

After *Any Wednesday* in '66 and *Barefoot in the Park* (with Robert Redford) in '67 came the dazzling *Barbarella* in '68, which sent her sexpot image into orbit. By contrast, the grim *They Shoot Horses, Don't They?* ('69) showcased her serious acting talent, bringing her the first of seven Oscar nominations. Her momentum, and her reputation as an acclaimed actress, increased in the '70s as she starred in some of the decade's most significant films, including *Klute* in '71 (her first Oscar win), *Coming Home* in '78 (her second Oscar), and *The China Syndrome* in '79. In addition to making more successful films in the '80s (*Nine to Five* in '80, *On Golden Pond* in '81, *The Morning After* in '86), Jane won an Emmy in '84 for *The Dollmaker*. In the meantime she was reinventing herself as a health guru, setting up the Jane Fonda Workout studio in Beverly Hills and creating best-selling books and tapes. As with everything else she's ever done, she pursued these passions with gusto and commitment.

HER '60s LOOK: In the '60s Jane Fonda had a face at once innocent and knowing, able to convey both sensuality and strength—in *They Shoot Horses, Don't They?* you only have to see her face to know she's the only dancer with the smarts and the guts to win. But her looks were versatile enough to take her from the cartoony sci-fi of *Barbarella* to the harrowing Depression-era drama of *They Shoot Horses*. Did we say versatile? She once said, "My husband said he wanted to have a relationship with a redhead, so I dyed my hair red." Figure-atively speaking, she was perhaps the most voluptuous young American actress of the mid-to-late '60s, an image enhanced by her nearly nude appearance in *La Ronde* in '64 (making her one of the first American starlets to appear semi-naked in a major film). Her Barbarella—with costumes and corsets that were painful to wear—is one of the decade's most memorable characters, and the costumes, which theoretically anticipate the forty-first century, are among those most clearly connected to the sensibilities of the '60s ("Barbarella psychedella" went the chorus's refrain in the movie). Back on Earth, she was featured in *Playboy* in August '66, again in March, April, and July '68, and then in January and December '69 (she also made the cover of *Life* magazine in '68). So strong was her impact and image, in '99 *Playboy* ranked her #28 on its list of the "100 Sexiest Stars of the Century," right between Stella Stevens and Mamie Van Doren.

BEHIND THE SCENES: Of long-term relationships, Jane Fonda once said, "For two people to be able to live together for the rest of their lives is almost unnatural." She has had three husbands: director Roger Vadim, politician Tom Hayden, and tomahawk-choppin' media mogul Ted Turner. She married Vadim in '65 in a room at the Dunes in Vegas. They lived on a farm in France through the '60s and had a daughter, Vanessa (named after Vanessa Redgrave) in '68. Divorced from Vadim and pregnant with Hayden's child, she married Tom Hayden in an informal ceremony at her L.A. home in early '73. Their son was born that summer. The marriage ended in '89, and Jane married Turner in '91. They announced their separation in January 2000. True to her image in the '60s and '70s as a liberated modern woman, stories and rumors through the years have placed her with Warren Beatty, Donald Sutherland, Alain Delon, and Huey Newton, among others. Her most controversial choices have come in the political arena. In '70 the F.B.I dubbed her an anarchist and with the C.I.A. kept a voluminous record of her speeches and travels. An outspoken critic of America's

involvement in the Vietnam War, she earned the derisive nickname "Hanoi Jane" when she flew to North Vietnam in '72. Many vets have still never forgiven the smiling photographs taken of her while she was sitting atop a North Vietnamese anti-aircraft gun used to shoot down American planes.

BONUS SWINGABILITY: Her nickname— "Lady Jane" ... her

exotic birthplace— New York City ... brother Peter starred in the seminal '60s film *Easy Rider* ... she traveled to Russia in '64 and was welcomed warmly by people who knew of her father's career ... she visited Warhol's Factory in '66 ... about her '71 Oscar triumph her father Henry said: "How in hell would you like to have been in this business as long as I and have one of your kids win an Oscar before you do" ... early in her career she was extremely critical of her father, but in 1980 she bought the rights to the play *On Golden Pond* so that he could star in it, hopefully to get the Oscar he'd never won ... he did ... on her sixtieth birthday Ted Turner gave her $10 million so she could start her own foundation ... Turner confided to the *New York Post* that he made love to Jane thrice daily ... director Roger Vadim once said about her: "She cannot relax. Always there is something to do," adding, "There is also in Jane a basic wish to carry things to the limit."

 A DATE WITH JANE

January 26, 1928	Roger Vadim is born
December 21, 1937	Jane Fonda is born
June 24, 1965	*Cat Ballou* is released
August 14, 1965	Jane marries Roger Vadim
March 29, 1968	Jane makes the cover of *Life* magazine
October 10, 1968	*Barbarella* is released
December 10, 1969	*They Shoot Horses, Don't They?* is released
April 10, 1972	Jane wins the Best Actress Oscar (*Klute*)

nericans

LINDA HARRISON

SWINGIN' '60s CREDENTIALS: This tanned beauty, a contestant in the '65 Miss American pageant, played the sexy, athletic, loin-clothed Nova in *Planet of the Apes*.

WORKIN' IT: Linda was one of the loveliest actresses of the '60s. Competing as Miss Maryland, 20-year-old Linda was the first runner-up in the '65 Miss American pageant. Though she didn't win, she did get noticed by a Hollywood agent, who put her in front of the camera. She did two *Batman* episodes in '66 and had small roles in films, most notably five minutes as the jaw-droppingly sexy Miss Stardust in *A Guide for the Married Man*, '67.

Then came Nova, the part that has kept her signing autographs for thirty-plus years. *Planet of the Apes* was perfect for a young actress still learning her craft. As the sexy silent love interest for stogie-chompin' Charlton Heston, Linda just had to look frightened, fascinated, and fabulous as the action unfolded around her. On a '99 TV special about the '68 movie, she explained the motivations of her mute character: "I think I went instinctively with her. I thought about animal instincts: the way she would move and the way she would react would be the way an animal would react, from fear." The movie made $26 million and was nominated for Best Score and Best Costume Oscars, winning a special Oscar for the ape make-up. Linda graduated to a role on the TV series *Bracken's World* in '69, and in '70 she reprised Nova for *Beneath the Planet of the Apes* (this time she did get a line—a word, actually—"Taylor!").

After a brief retirement, she reemerged in the mid-'70s with some screen time in the high-profile *Airport '75*, but there was a bigger movie she supposedly got aced out of. As the story's told, her husband, producer Richard Zanuck, wanted her for the plum role of Ellen Brody in *Jaws*, but Sid Sheinberg, who was the head of Universal and Zanuck's boss, decided to give his own wife, Lorraine Gary, the part of the police chief's wife. (Maybe it's just as well—with Linda waiting at home, Roy Scheider never would've gone off to fight the shark.) The '80s brought her roles in two *Cocoon* movies ('85 and '88), and the '90s have kept her busy with travels and appearances at film conventions.

HER '60s LOOK: Whether she was on a planet of apes or a planet of humans, luscious Linda was always the prettiest girl in town. Great tan, long black hair, huge brown eyes, big smile, and strong white teeth — no wonder she won beauty contests. In *A Guide for the Married Man*, she went blonde, playfully and spectacularly. She first appeared walking down the street in a sparkly bikini, her waist a concave wonder. Her lean loincloth action alongside Heston on the monkey planet was enough to make any guy go ape. And as additional testimony to her sleek, modern beauty, she was the gorgeous cover girl on the January '70 *Cosmopolitan*, the issue that was on newsstands as the '60s ended and America looked ahead to a new decade.

BEHIND THE SCENES: She married producer Richard Zanuck, ten years her senior and the son of studio kingpin Darryl Zanuck, in '69. They have two sons, with Helen Gurley Brown and her husband David as godparents. Divorced in '78, Linda and Richard are still close friends. Linda currently lives in Maryland and plans to write her autobiography.

BONUS SWINGABILITY: Her fake moniker—she briefly changed her name in '74 to Augusta Summerland, and in *Airport 1975* that's how she's billed ... her exotic birthplace—Berlin, Maryland, where she was Miss Berlin in '63 ... in a test made for the *Planet of the Apes*, Linda wore ape make-up and played the part of Zira ... there was an additional scene filmed for *Planet of the Apes* that revealed Nova's pregnancy, but the scene was cut from the final film ... Linda's got her own official Web site—http://www.lindaharrison.com.

A DATE WITH LINDA

December 13, 1934	Richard Zanuck is born
July 26, 1945	Linda Harrison is born
March 2, 1966	Linda appears on *Batman*
May 25, 1967	*A Guide for the Married Man* is released
February 8, 1968	*Planet of the Apes* is released
September 19, 1969	*Bracken's World* debuts

the all-am

TIPPI HEDREN

SWINGIN' '60s CREDENTIALS: This cool blonde model got her screen career off to a quick start in the early '60s with starring roles in two Alfred Hitchcock movies.

WORKIN' IT: In 1963 Tippi Hedren was working as a New York fashion model when Alfred Hitchcock spotted her doing a commercial on *The Today Show*. Hitchcock had cast elegant blonde actresses in most of his movies—including Grace Kelly, Kim Novak, and Eva Marie Saint—and the lovely, sophisticated Tippi suited his cinematic style perfectly. He cast her alongside 3,200 birds in his big-budget thriller, *The Birds*. The film was an instant success. So was Tippi, who won the Golden Globe in '64 as the Most Promising Newcomer (an award she shared with two other beautiful newcomers, Ursula Andress and Elke Sommer). Hitchcock, dazzled by her subtle talent, which he said was "like a dormant volcano we know one day is going to erupt," starred her in his next movie, the psychological thriller *Marnie* ('64). Critics are divided over these two Hitchcock films— some consider them under-appreciated classics, others rank them as two of the master's lesser achievements. Either way, they spring-boarded Tippi to stardom, and she continued to make movies for the rest of the decade. The most notable was Charlie Chaplin's last film, *A Countess from Hong Kong*, in '67.

Pursuing an eclectic mix of screen projects, her post-'60s appearances have ranged from the insubstantial (the TV movies *Return to Green Acres* in '90 and *Birds II* in '94) to the memorable (*The Harrad Experiment* in '73 and *Pacific Heights* in '90, both with daughter Melanie Griffith, plus *Citizen Ruth* in '96). She produced a movie—*Roar*, about saving African animals—in '80, and from that has sprung two decades of work dedicated to saving big cats. Founder and President of the Roar Foundation, Tippi now oversees (and lives on) a wildlife preserve north of L.A. called Shambala. There she cares for over fifty lions, cheetahs, and other big cats that have been cast off from movie productions, circuses, and zoos. She wrote a heart-wrenching book about the experience, *The Cats of Shambala* ('85). Other humanitarian endeavors include global travels to help feed the hungry and appearances before Congress on behalf of Asian refugees.

HER '60s LOOK: Sleek, modern, and regal, Tippi has most often been compared to the legendary Grace Kelly. Her perfect features, crowned by upswept hair, give her a sophisticated urban look that was ideal for Hitchcock's intelligent film-making. Conservative suits and dresses adorned her slender frame, effecting a smart, classic style that carried her from the early '60s to the '90s.

BEHIND THE SCENES: Tippi was married to actor Peter Griffith until '61, then she married actor/producer Noel Marshall in '64, followed by a third husband in '85. With Griffith she had a daughter in '57, actress Melanie. (Melanie, by the way, was also the name of Tippi's character in *The Birds*.) Of morbid curiosity to film fans and psychologists are Alfred Hitchcock's alleged bizarre practices. In *Hollywood Babylon II*, Kenneth Anger said Hitchcock "developed a powerful romantic and sexual obsession for Hedren" who "paid dearly for piquing his passions," and so he terrorized her in *The Birds* with actual birds, not the mechanical birds she was expecting. According to Anger, Tippi's resulting wounds were bad enough to shut down the production for a week. Anger also writes that while making *Marnie* Hitchcock gave Tippi's daughter Melanie "a custom-made portrait doll of her mother, dressed and coiffed as the character she portrayed in *The Birds*—and enclosed in a small pine coffin."

BONUS SWINGABILITY: She uses a stage moniker—her real name is Nathalie Hedrin ... her exotic birthplace—New Ulm, Minnesota ... supposedly *Marnie* was going to be Grace Kelly's comeback movie after living for six years as a royal in Monaco, but scheduling problems and disapproval from her subjects caused her to back out ... one of Tippi's most distinctive features is her sexy voice ... Tippi has her own Web site filled with information about the Roar Foundation—http://www.shambala.org.

A DATE WITH TIPPI

January 19, 1935	Tippi Hedren is born
August 9, 1957	Tippi gives birth to daughter Melanie
March 28, 1963	*The Birds* is released
Julie 22, 1964	*Marnie* is released

GOLDIE HAWN ✳

SWINGIN' '60s CREDENTIALS: This giggly go-go dancer regularly stole the show on TV's *Rowan & Martin's Laugh-In*, then won an Oscar for Best Supporting Actress in her first major movie.

WORKIN' IT: Goldie Hawn established the lasting archetype of the teen ding-a-ling, and she could've cruised on that persona—what she has called her "zany/ditsy/dingy shtick"—for years, but to her credit she established herself as a talented actress and eventually as a serious film producer.

Though she's best known for her comedy roles, she has formal training as a dancer, having taken ballet and tap lessons from the age of 3. Her early-'60s jobs included working as a 19-year-old cancan dancer at New York's '64 World's Fair, a go-go dancer in Jersey, and a chorus girl at the Desert Inn in Vegas. In '67 she played a dingbat neighbor on the quickly canceled *Good Morning, World*; then came *Laugh-In*. With its psychedelic design and rapid-fire jokes, this hour-long laff-fest was an instant hit when it debuted as a '67 special, and it only got more popular when it became a weekly show the following January. The show and the stars—including Goldie—received many Emmy and Golden Globe nominations, but of everyone in the original cast, Goldie was the most popular and got the most fanmail. Part of her popularity was due to her great comic timing, part to her adorable looks, and part to the sweet naiveté she displayed as chaos swirled around her. This naiveté wasn't an act: as a dyslexic, she really *did* have trouble reading cue cards, but her resulting befuddlement only amplified the comic return.

In '68 she got her first major role in her first big movie, *Cactus Flower*, and at a mere 24, she won the Oscar as that year's Best Supporting Actress (an award that Raquel Welch accepted for her because, as Goldie explained later, she forgot to go to the ceremony). After the '60s she became a major Hollywood player, both starring in and/or producing numerous hits. $ with Warren Beatty ('72), *Butterflies Are Free* ('72), Steven Spielberg's *The Sugarland Express* ('74), *Shampoo* with Beatty and Julie Christie ('75), *The Duchess and the Dirtwater Fox* ('76), *Foul Play* with Chevy Chase ('78), *Private Benjamin* ('80), *Best Friends* with Burt Reynolds ('82), *Housesitter* with Steve Martin ('92), *Death Becomes Her* with Meryl Streep and Bruce Willis ('92), and *The First Wives Club* with Diane Keaton and Bette Midler ('96) are just some of the movies that have made her one of Hollywood's most durable, and powerful, stars. "I know who I am, and I'm very proud of what I've accomplished," she said at the end of Marc Shapiro's '98 bio, *Pure Goldie*. "Now my focus is moving on to the next stage of my life. And that is about who I want to be at sixty, who I want to be at seventy, and who I want to be at eighty. I still have a lot to do."

HER '60s LOOK: The golden bob, the koo-koo smile, those huge eye sockets—she is a '60s icon, one of the most memorable faces of the decade. As revealed when she danced on *Laugh-In*, her lean, lithe figure expressed a wonderful formula for '60s memories: bikinis + tattoos = nutty! Incredibly, while pregnant in '76, her

the all-am

weight swelled from 119 pounds to 170, according to Marc Shapiro's '98 bio *Pure Goldie*. But she got back her slim shape and was a comely covergirl, flaunting her long, fish-net-stockinged dancer's legs for the January '85 issue of *Playboy*. Today she's still got the youthful, energetic look she had thirty years ago, which *Parade* magazine explained in October '98: "The secret of her youthfulness is a positive attitude. She gets up each morning looking forward to the day ahead. After meditating, she does dance exercises in the gym…Goldie also says she eats low-fat foods and avoids bread products because of the carbohydrates. And she keeps busy with projects she enjoys."

BEHIND THE SCENES: "Marriage is a form of ownership," she once declared. "You lose personal power." Goldie has had three husbands, and three divorces: director Gus Trikonis (married in '69), actor Bruno Wintzell ('73), and entertainer Bill Hudson ('76). With Hudson she had two kids, Oliver and Katie (both of whom have appeared in movies). Goldie has said that these marriages broke up because the men couldn't handle her fame. Since '84 she's lived with actor Kurt Russell, whom she first met in '68 when they both had roles in *The One and Only Genuine Original Family Band*. They started dating when they co-starred in *Swing Shift* ('84); later they also co-starred in *Overboard* ('87).

Together they have a son, Wyatt.

BONUS SWINGABILITY: She uses a stage moniker—her real name is Goldie Studlendgehawn— her first name is in honor of a great-aunt … her exotic birthplace— Washington, D.C. … one of her ancestors was Edward Rutledge, the youngest person to sign the Declaration of Independence … as something fun

to do between film projects, in '72 she recorded an album of country-western songs called *Goldie* … when Woody Allen directed her in his charming musical *Everyone Says I Love You* ('96), he had to caution Goldie to rein in her dancing talent during her musical numbers. Because of her earlier training, she was clearly much better than the other actors in the movie; this was especially evident when she was paired with Allen himself for the final glorious dance sequence along the Seine in Paris … in '96 she made *People* magazine's list of the 25 Most Intriguing People … of her giggly *Laugh-In* dimbulb she once said, "I'm like her only in small ways" … of herself: "I have a light personality and a deep-thinking brain."

A DATE WITH GOLDIE

November 21, 1945	Goldie Hawn is born
March 17, 1951	Kurt Russell is born
September 5, 1967	*Good Morning, World* debuts
September 9, 1967	*Rowan & Martin's Laugh-In* debuts as a one-hour special
January 22, 1968	*Laugh-In* reappears as a weekly show
December 16, 1969	*Cactus Flower* is released
April 7, 1970	Goldie wins the Best Supporting Actress Oscar (*Cactus Flower*)

nericans

JANET LEIGH

SWINGIN' '60s CREDENTIALS: This interesting, versatile dramatic actress had an impressive '60s career, and she'll forever be remembered as the human pegboard in one of the most terrifying scenes in movie history—the bloody shower sequence in Hitchcock's *Psycho*.

WORKIN' IT: Had Janet Leigh done nothing besides *Psycho*, she would still be venerated by film fans. As it is, way before she stepped into that Bates Motel shower, she had a successful career making dramas, adventure flix, comedies, and film noir mysteries in the '40s and '50s. Among her thirty pre-'60s films were *Little Women* ('49), *Scaramouche* ('52), *Houdini* ('53), *Prince Valiant* ('54), *Pete Kelly's Blues* ('55), and the great *Touch of Evil* ('58). In '60, *Psycho* catapulted her to true stardom, even though she was killed off only 45 minutes into the film. But what a 45 minutes. Her complex evolution from guilt-ridden criminal to helpless victim brought her an Oscar nomination, a Golden Globe trophy, and lasting fame. Riding the momentum, she landed starring roles in diverse films with some of the decade's most prominent stars: the political thriller *The Manchurian Candidate* with Frank Sinatra ('62), the musical *Bye Bye Birdie* with Ann-Margret ('63), the detective story *Harper*

with Paul Newman ('66), and the comic *Three on a Couch* with Jerry Lewis ('66).

Guest spots on programs like *The Andy Williams Show* and *The Man from U.N.C.L.E.* only added to her rep as a versatile, appealing presence. From the '70s onward she made a dozen TV movies, but writing was her main focus. She's written three books: one in '84, the autobiography *There Really Was a Hollywood*, and two in the mid-'90s, *Psycho: Behind the Scenes of the Classic Chiller* and the novel *House of Destiny*. Another novel is purportedly in the works. In tribute to her long, remarkable career, in '99 she received the highest honor the French government can bestow on an artist, the *Commandeur des Arts et des Lettres*.

HER '60s LOOK: She has an intense and interesting appeal, combining beauty with sincerity and intelligence, which makes her a good photographic subject—twice she was on the cover of *Life*, and countless times on the covers of movie magazines. Blonde for much of her career, Janet was a beautiful brunette in *Bye Bye Birdie*. In the '60s she had a fab figure (with measurements of 35-23-35, according to '63's *Movie Life Yearbook*) that made the most of sophisticated business suits, casual clothes, or glamorous gowns.

BEHIND THE SCENES: Janet married two times in the '40s. The first marriage, when she was only 14, was annulled; the second ended late in the decade. In the '50s rumors placed her in the company of billionaire Howard Hughes

the all-ar

and later the Rat Pack. But her main relationship through that decade was with movie idol Tony Curtis. Their romance was closely watched in all the fan mags, and in '51 they married, becoming one of Hollywood's most glamorous couples. (Interestingly, Janet herself got more glamorous once they were married, wearing her hair blonder and her clothes tighter.) She and Tony co-starred in five films and co-produced two daughters, actresses Jamie Lee Curtis and Kelly Lee Curtis. They divorced in '61, and a year later Janet married her current husband, director Robert Brandt.

BONUS SWINGABILITY: Her moniker at birth was Jeanette Helen Morrison ... her exotic birthplace—Merced, California ... a good student, she skipped several grades and graduated high school at only 15 ... Janet was "discovered" when actress Norma Shearer saw her photo at the ski lodge run by Janet's dad; Norma took the

photo back to Hollywood with her and Janet soon had a screen test at MGM ... in *Two Tickets to Broadway* in '51, Janet didn't just sing, dance, and act—she also twirled a mean baton ... Janet broke her wrist during the filming of *Touch of Evil*, but she refused to stop production and filming continued ... supposedly Martha Hyer, Shirley Jones, Hope Lange, Piper Laurie, Eva Marie-Saint, and Lana Turner were considered for the role of Marion Crane in *Psycho* ... the *Psycho* shower scene took seven days to film ... in September '98 the *San Francisco Chronicle* pointed out some striking similarities between her *Touch of Evil* role for director Orson Welles and

Psycho for Hitch: "[in *Touch of Evil*] Susan goes to an out-of-the-way motel where she is the only guest. The night manager, played by Dennis Weaver, is every bit as creepy as Anthony Perkins' Norman Bates character in *Psycho*. In both films, Leigh strips down to her slip and awful things happen to her. 'I never thought about that when I was making the movies,' she said. 'In my mind, they were so different, it didn't even dawn on me. But then later, much later, people would say to me, 'What is it with you and motels and strange motel managers?'"

A DATE WITH JANET

June 3, 1925	Tony Curtis is born
July 6, 1927	Janet Leigh is born
June 17, 1956	Janet gives birth to daughter Kelly Curtis
November 22, 1958	Janet gives birth to daughter Jamie Lee Curtis
March 8, 1960	*Psycho* is released
October 24, 1962	*The Manchurian Candidate* is released
April 4, 1963	*Bye Bye Birdie* is released
February 23, 1966	*Harper* is released

SHIRLEY MACLAINE ✿

Hollywood to be true, she got her big break in '54 when the star of Broadway's *The Pajama Game*, Carol Haney, hurt her ankle. Unknown understudy Shirley MacLaine stepped in, was spotted by a Hollywood producer who happened to be in the audience that night, and the rest, as they say, is motion-picture history.

Shirley built considerable momentum during the '50s with movies like *Artists and Models* and *The Trouble with Harry* in '55, *Around the World in 80 Days* in '56, and her Oscar-nominated role as the ring-a-ding flooz in *Some Came Running* in '58. In '60 her dazzlin' dancin' got her into the *Can-Can* line; hangin' with Frank and the Rat Packers landed her a hilarious cameo as a guest who's had a few too many martoonies in *Ocean's Eleven*; and her wonderful performance as the funny, vulnerable mistress in *The Apartment* brought her a second Oscar nomination. At the dawn of the decade she was an established star with a famously nutty screen presence ("a kook, but very warm," Frank called her). She continued with a dozen more '60s films, including *My Geisha* ('62), *Irma la Douce* ('63, her third Oscar nomination), *The Yellow Rolls-Royce* ('65), *Woman Times Seven* ('67, with Shirley playing seven different characters), and the Bob Fosse musical *Sweet Charity* ('69). After a failed TV series, *Shirley's World*, in '71, and a self-imposed five-year break from the

big screen, her film career regained the momentum in the late '70s with *The Turning Point* in '77 and *Being There* in '79, followed by her Oscar-winning Aurora in *Terms of Endearment* in '83 and *Steel Magnolias* in '89.

Busybusybusy, she kept going through the '90s with *Postcards from the Edge* in '90, *Guarding Tess* in '94, *Mrs. Winterbourne* in '96, and more, pushing her total number of films well past fifty. As if that weren't enough, she's had a long career of live stage performances (her one-woman

SWINGIN' '60s CREDENTIALS: Always working and always reliable, this adorable actress, dancin' dynamo, and Rat Pack mascot flourished in the '60s with almost two movies a year, including several that are now considered classics.

WORKIN' IT: Shirley MacLaine is show biz like nobody's biz—acting, singing, dancing, doing comedy or drama, and playing roles as diverse as a hooker, a nun, or a Japanese geisha. You name it, she could do it. Need proof? She won a special Golden Globe in '59 as the industry's Most Versatile Actress. In a moment almost too

the all-ar

musical special, *Gypsy in My Soul,* won an Emmy in '76), she's written movies (*Out on a Limb* in '87), she's directed movies (*Bruno* in '99), she's produced movies (*The Other Half of the Sky* in '75), and she's been a mainstay on bestseller lists with various books about her own current life, her past lives, and

various New Agey experiences like channeling and reincarnation. "Vigorously original," hailed *Look* magazine when describing her in '59; the words are as appropriate now as they were then.

HER '60s LOOK: Shirley's look was nothing if not versatile, making her capable of playing everything from sweet to sexy to prim to glamorous or anything else she wanted. A vivacious part-time model when she was just starting out, Shirley had an impish style in the '50s and '60s that was playful and charming. She helped make ultra-short hair popular, presaging the boyish cuts that would later adorn Twiggy, Mia Farrow, and others. On stage or on screen, her 5' 6" 122-pound frame (according to the stats in '63's *Movie Life Yearbook*) moved with the grace and energy of an exuberant cheer-leader. And she had gams for days.

BEHIND THE SCENES: Like everything else in Shirley's life, her marriage to Steve Parker was truly unique. As she herself has described, on the night they wed in '54 they used their bed for jumping up and down, then they went their separate ways. For the next decade or so he lived in Japan, while she traveled and pursued her career. They got together infrequently, though they did manage to conceive a daughter, Sachi, who was born in '56. Late in the '50s and into the '60s she was a steady pal of Frank, Dino, and the rest of the Rat Pack (experiences she wrote about in her '95 book

My Lucky Stars). Others she's been linked to include Robert Mitchum, Danny Kaye, Yves Montand, writer Pete Hamill, and a politician or two. Supposedly she was introduced to JFK in the back of Frank's limo in '61, and when the prez made a handsy move on her, she bolted the car while it was still moving and took a few scrapes. Classy doll that she is, she later dismissed the incident by saying, "I would rather have a president who does it to a woman than a president who does it to his country."

BONUS SWINGABILITY: Her moniker at birth was Shirley MacLean Beaty (with one "t," but her younger bro' Henry Warren Beaty spells his last name Beatty) ... she was named after 6-year-old Shirley Temple, whose birthday comes one day before MacLaine's ... her exotic birthplace—Richmond, Virginia ... of her famous brother, she once said: "I'd like to do a love scene with him just to see what all the yelling is about" ... her great line in *The Apartment*: "Some people take, some people get took" ... a global traveler, she has had eight homes around the world ... "I deserve this," she said when she won her Oscar for *Terms of Endearment* ... actor Yves Montand once said about her: "Shirley MacLaine—who does she think she isn't?" ... Shirley has her own official Web site—http://www.shirleymaclaine.com, where she writes: "For me the search for Truth is paramount…the truth of a character I'm playing, the truth of the subject matter I write about or the truth of why we are alive and how it relates to our destiny. I see life as a creation each of us paints for ourselves. We do create our own reality in order to be aligned with our destiny. The search then becomes a search for self. It is the most important journey we will ever take."

 A DATE WITH SHIRLEY

April 24, 1934	Shirley MacLaine is born
March 30, 1937	Warren Beatty is born
September 1, 1956	Shirley gives birth to daughter Sachi
March 9, 1960	*Can-Can* is released
June 15, 1960	*The Apartment* is released
August 10, 1960	*Ocean's Eleven* is released
June 5, 1963	*Irma la Douce* is released
May 12, 1964	*What a Way to Go!* is released
May 13, 1965	*The Yellow Rolls-Royce* is released
April 1, 1969	*Sweet Charity* is released

JAYNE MANSFIELD

SWINGIN' '60s CREDENTIALS: One of Hollywood's most popular cleavage queens used a slight film career and an ample publicity campaign to challenge Marilyn's title as reigning sex goddess of the late '50s and early '60s.

WORKIN' IT: It's amazing how far Jayne Mansfield got, considering how limited her acting range was. She usually played on-screen the person she was off-screen, parlaying her breathy voice and voluptuous looks into a twelve-year career. But then again, Jayne Mansfield wasn't famous as an actress—she was famous for being Jayne Mansfield. A Texas collegian who won several minor beauty contests (Miss Photoflash, Miss Fire Prevention Week) in the early '50s, Jayne headed west in '54 to fulfill the Hollywood dreams she had had since she was a young girl plastering movie photos all over her room. Bit parts in mid-'50s movies led to TV game shows,

Broadway, scene-stealing roles in *The Girl Can't Help It* in '56 and *Will Success Spoil Rock Hunter?* in '57, and a Golden Globe as the Most Promising Newcomer of '57.

Though it's easy to dismiss her performances as a series of come-hither squeaks and percolating giggles (Bette Davis once said of Jayne, "dramatic art in her opinion is knowing how to fill a sweater"), to her credit she tried to convey a sympathetic vulnerability unexpressed by most other bombshells of the era. Unfortunately, audiences never accepted her as the serious actress she wanted to be, so she was locked into her dumb-blonde role. She was great at it, though, and she managed to sustain a career of B-movie roles into the '60s. Most prominent were her scandalous near-nude appearance in *Promises, Promises* in '63 and a memorable cameo in *A Guide for the Married Man* in '67. Unfortunately, when Jayne's friend Marilyn died in '62, the classic platinum-blonde, sex-siren look died with her. Jayne's roles became more and more cartoonish, and her movies slipped down the alphabet from B titles to C and worse. By mid-decade her movie career was downright embarrassing (she starred in *The Las Vegas Hillbillys* in '66, for example). Not to be denied an audience, Jayne performed in one fashion or another all decade long, right up until her sudden death in '67. She had her own Vegas show in the early '60s, toured military bases with Bob Hope, released a live album called *Jayne Mansfield Busts Up Las Vegas*, traveled the nightclub circuit, and when all else failed made personal appearances for any organization or supermarket that would have her. Sadly, for some of these appearances she wasn't even paid in cash—to show up at a meat-packing plant, she once received 250 pounds of meat. She even tried reverting to her naturally dark hair color, as if that might spark some interest.

Still working as best she could in '67, 34-year-old Jayne Mansfield died tragically on the way to yet another nightclub appearance when her car slammed into the back of a truck on a fog-shrouded highway near New Orleans, Louisiana. She was killed instantly, as was lawyer Sam Brody, a 20-year-old driver, and two pet dogs. Her three kids, asleep in the back, all survived. (In contrast to grisly rumors, it was a wig, not Jayne's decapitated head, that flew out of the car). When she was buried in her Pennsylvania hometown, thousands of fans came to pay respects—Jayne was then, as she remains today, one of Hollywood's most popular legends, a symbol of a time long gone but fondly recalled.

HER '60s LOOK: Jayne explained it all in the book *Jayne Mansfield and the American Fifties*: To her, sex appeal was "just knowing what to do and then doing it with a lot of naiveté.... If a girl has curviness, exciting lips and a certain breathlessness, it helps, and it won't do a bit of harm if she has a kittenish, soft cuddly quality.

the all-ar

Men want women to be pink, helpless, and do a lot of deep breathing." Jayne exemplified all these qualities, of course, but it was her figure, representing the most dramatic curves this side of a Swiss road, that was her biggest asset. At the time of her death, her measurements were reported to be an awe-inspiring 40-21-35.5, and in her prime her waist size was said to be an incredible 18 inches (that's four inches smaller than Twiggy's!). The stuff of *Playboy* legend, natch, she was

a Playmate in February '55, she made appearances in '58 and '63 that were the magazine's biggest-selling issues to date, and every February from '57 to '64 she was the magazine's "Valentine girl." Add the platinum hair (a natural brunette, she started bleaching in '52), the heavy make-up, the sexy pout, and she, along with Marilyn Monroe, pretty much defined the lusty busty sex goddess look that has been imitated ever since. In January '99 *Playboy* published its list of "The 100 Sexiest Stars of the Century," and Jayne came in second, right between two other film icons—Marilyn and Raquel.

BEHIND THE SCENES:

"Men are those creatures with two legs and eight hands," Jayne once said. In an interview she claimed that she started dating at 11, but other sources say she was considered a wallflower into her high school years at Highland Park High in Dallas. Sixteen years old in January of 1950, she eloped with 24-year-old Paul Mansfield; they had a daughter, Jayne Marie, the following November. The couple divorced in '58, but Jayne kept his last name. Five days after the divorce, Jayne married Mickey Hargitay, a former Mr. Universe dubbed by the authoritative Mae West as "the most perfectly built man in the world." Mickey gave Jayne a ten-carat diamond, and they married in Palos Verdes, California, with Jayne in a pink lace gown. Together they built the massive "pink palace" on Sunset Boulevard and decorated it all in—what else?—pink. The mansion had a fountain spurting champagne, pink fur on the floor of

the bathrooms, a pink heart-shaped bathtub, a pink heart-shaped pool that piped underwater music, and a bed surrounded by pink fluorescent lights, with a heart-shaped canopy and marble cupids above the bedstead. To this they added a veritable zoo with thirty dogs, an elephant, monkeys, donkeys, ocelots, and dozens of cats. They also added three kids, though the third, Mariska, was rumored to be the daughter of actor Nelson Sardelli. Jayne divorced Hargitay in '64, married director Matt Cimber a month later, and had his son in '65. However, a year later she was reputedly chronically unhappy and alcohol-dependent, and she and Cimber separated in the summer of '66. During her life Jayne may have also had affairs with JFK, novelist Henry Miller, director Nicholas Ray, actor Richard Egan, and fashion designer Oleg Cassini, all of them older men, in some cases much older (Miller wasn't even born in the same century). When she died in '67, she was driving with a new lover, lawyer Sam Brody, who died in the car crash with her.

BONUS SWINGABILITY: She used a fake moniker—her real name was Vera Jane Palmer ... her exotic birthplace—Bryn Mawr, Pennsylvania ... her childhood idol was Shirley Temple ... some bios credit her with an IQ of 163, though she wasn't a great student ... another hidden talent was her ability to play the violin ... she once released an album of Shakespeare sonnets read to orchestral accompaniment ... supposedly when Jayne first hit Hollywood, she brazenly called Paramount Studios and said she wanted to be a movie star— the operator said, "We already have a movie star" ... the Hollywood story goes that she got her first TV job by slipping a note to a producer that read "36, 22, 34" ... Jayne reputedly turned down a role that was created with her in mind—Ginger on *Gilligan's Island* (Tina Louise got the part) ... Jayne was arrested for indecent exposure during her nightclub act in Burlington, Vermont in '63 ... daughter Jayne Marie appeared in *Playboy* in '76 ... daughter Mariska played a hooker in *Leaving Las Vegas* ('95) ... Jayne's grave in a rural Pennsylvania cemetery is marked by a heart-shaped, pink-tinged stone.

A DATE WITH JAYNE

April 19, 1933	Jayne Mansfield is born
October 12, 1955	*Will Success Spoil Rock Hunter?* opens on Broadway
January 13, 1958	Jayne marries Mickey Hargitay
August 5, 1962	Marilyn Monroe dies
August 26, 1964	Jayne and Mickey divorce
September 24, 1964	Jane marries Matt Cimber
May 25, 1967	*A Guide for the Married Man* is released
June 29, 1967	Jayne is killed in a car crash

mericans

MARILYN MONROE

Norma Jean Baker, was married in '42 at only 16 years old. She was working as a model in the mid-'40s, getting small movie parts in the late '40s, appearing as a centerfold in the first issue of *Playboy* (December '53), and becoming a star by '53. Highlighting her memorable movie career were such hits as *Gentlemen Prefer Blondes* and *How to Marry a Millionaire* in '53, *The Seven Year Itch* in '55, and the classic *Some Like It Hot* in '59. Discussions about her talent still generate controversy. Some people dismiss her as having played herself onscreen; others, though, believe that the Marilyn we saw on and off screen was a character she expertly created. Lee Strasberg, her acclaimed acting teacher, said, "There are only two actors of our time; the first is Marlon Brando and the second is Marilyn Monroe." And even if she didn't earn a single Oscar nomination—which may have had more to do with studio politics than with Marilyn's ability— she did win other acting awards, including the Henrietta Award as 1951's Most Promising Personality of the Year, Golden Globes as the World's Film Favorite in '53 and '62, the Italian and French versions of the Oscar in '59, and a Golden Globe as Best Actress in '60. Assessing her own image, she once said, "To put it bluntly, I seem to be a whole superstructure with no foundation. But I'm working on the foundation."

In the '60s she finished only two movies (*Let's Make Love* in '60, *The Misfits* in '61); she'd been fired from a third, *Something's Got to Give*, in '62, but she'd been rehired and filming would have continued had she not died. Sadly, after bouts with alcohol and pills, she died in her Brentwood bedroom of an overdose of forty-seven Nembutal and chloral hydrate pills on August 5, 1962, at the age of 36. L.A.'s chief medical examiner ruled it an accidental suicide, but her death is still shrouded in mystery. Her plain wall crypt, for decades decorated by Joe DiMaggio's fresh roses, is in Westwood Memorial Park, Westwood, California, the same cemetery where Natalie Wood is buried.

In '99 she ranked high on several significant end-of-millennium lists: *People* magazine named her the century's sexiest woman, the American Film Institute placed her number six among the "50 Greatest Screen Legends" (right below Greta Garbo), and *Playboy* put her atop its list of the "100 Sexiest Stars of the Century."

SWINGIN' '60s CREDENTIALS: The very definition of a sizzling superstar, beautiful Marilyn defined Hollywood glamour and tragedy with her dramatic life on and off screen. Perhaps the most famous actress ever, she completed only two '60s films—*Let's Make Love* and *The Misfits*—but her legacy lives on, built more on her roller-coaster life than on any movie she ever made.

WORKIN' IT: She's one of the few women known everywhere by a single name—say "Marilyn," and not only will everybody know who you mean, they'll know something about her. Like Liz Taylor, who was probably the only other '60s actress to command truly global attention, Marilyn Monroe couldn't go to the mailbox without generating international headlines. As large as her legend looms, her Hollywood career was tragically short, lasting little more than a decade.

Raised in a foster home after her Danish father disappeared and her mother had a nervous breakdown, Norma Jean Mortenson, then

HER '60s LOOK: The woman who once said that "no one ever called me pretty when I was a little girl" came to symbolize what it meant to be beautiful in the twentieth century. Certain images of her—standing over the subway grate in *The Seven Year Itch*, for instance—have been absorbed into the public's collective subconscious, like a universally shared dream that always brings a smile. Eternally photogenic, the "Stradivarius of sex" according to Norman Mailer, she made the cover of *Life* magazine five times during the '60s. To some people her platinum sex appeal was starting to diminish in the '60s (she turned 34 in 1960), and she appeared to be looking older and rundown. But Marilyn's "older and rundown" was still amazing. To her credit and the world's delight, she revitalized herself in '62 to such a degree that many fans consider the months before her death the peak of her beauty. Her figure, of course, was the stuff of legend. Her measurements in her prime were given as 37-23-35, numbers describing a geometry that has overwhelmed any transitory notion of what's stylish or alluring. Her assets were shown off to stunning effect on the famous spring night in '62 when she was stitched into a $12,000 rhinestone-encrusted handmade Jean Louis gown so she could sing the sultriest, breathiest version of "Happy Birthday" ever heard to President John F. Kennedy at his Madison Square Garden "Birthday Salute." In '99 that dress was auctioned off by Christie's for almost $1,300,000, the world's record for the highest price ever paid at auction for a woman's garment. Fashions come and go, styles change hourly, but Marilyn is eternal.

BEHIND THE SCENES: During her life Marilyn had many relationships, some rumored, some factual, and all part of the legend that has made her one of the most-discussed, most-written-about, most-desired women in history. She was married and divorced three times: to factory worker James Dougherty from '42 to '45, to baseball star Joe DiMaggio from January to October of '54, and to playwright Arthur Miller from '56 to '61. Names that frequently come up in

published discussions of her other relationships include Frank Sinatra, Marlon Brando, Yves Montand, Dean Martin, Tony Curtis, Sammy Davis, Jr., Yul Brynner, Milton Berle, Robert Mitchum, Mickey Rooney, George Sanders, Mel Torme, Orson Welles, Walter Winchell, Darryl Zanuck, plus at least one of those Kennedy boys (some published sources claim that she was such a regular caller to JFK, she had her own private phone line with the White House). The most romantic of all these relationships was the passionate love she shared with Joe DiMaggio, himself a storied symbol of American pride. They were married on January 14, 1954, with Marilyn telling the *S.F. Chronicle*, "marriage is my main career now."

But their interests—his in sports and hangin' at home with the guys, hers in theatre and nightlife—were too different. Theirs became what the *L.A. Times* called "America's most famous terrible marriage," and within nine months they were divorced. In the early '60s he would rally to her support, emotionally, and financially, and it was he who made the arrangements for, and cried throughout, her funeral.

BONUS SWINGABILITY: She used fake monikers—her real name was Norma Jean (sometimes seen spelled as Norma Jeane) Mortenson, she later used Norma Jean Baker, then Marilyn Monroe as of '46, and even Zelda Zonk as an occasional *nom d'hotel* ... her exotic birthplace—L.A., California ... some biographies report that she had minor plastic surgery on her nose and some electrolysis on her hairline to remove her widow's peak ... she was the only actress of the early '60s to have her own production company ... she claimed that her idea of a sexy man was Albert Einstein ... a gift from Frank was a poodle named Jewel, who outlived her ... quotable Marilyn: She once said, "I've been on a calendar, but never on time" ... once when she was asked what she wore to bed, she replied "Chanel No. 5" ... when asked what she had on when she posed for *Playboy*, she answered "the radio" ... and finally, a Marilyn for the ages: "I knew I belonged to the public and to the world, not because I was talented or even beautiful, but because I never had belonged to anything or anyone else."

✳ A DATE WITH MARILYN ✳

November 25, 1914	Joe DiMaggio is born
May 29, 1917	John F. Kennedy is born
June 1, 1926	Marilyn Monroe is born
November 5, 1953	*How to Marry a Millionaire* is released
January 14, 1954	Marilyn marries Joe DiMaggio
October 27, 1954	Marilyn and Joe divorce
June 3, 1955	*The Seven Year Itch* is released
August 15, 1960	Marilyn makes the cover of *Life* magazine
February 1, 1961	*The Misfits* is released
May 19, 1962	Marilyn sings "Happy Birthday" to JFK
June 22, 1962	Marilyn makes the cover of *Life* magazine
August 5, 1962	Marilyn Monroe is found dead
August 17, 1962	Marilyn makes the cover of *Life* magazine
November 22, 1963	John F. Kennedy is assassinated
August 8, 1964	Marilyn makes the cover of *Life* magazine
December 22, 1969	Marilyn makes the cover of *Life* magazine
March 8, 1999	Joe DiMaggio dies
October 27, 1999	Marilyn's "Happy Birthday" dress sells at auction for $1.3 million

KATHARINE ROSS

SWINGIN' '60s CREDENTIALS: This dark-eyed intelligent beauty played the love interest in two of the decade's biggest films, *The Graduate* ('67) and *Butch Cassidy and the Sundance Kid* ('69).

WORKIN' IT: Combining brains and beauty with sensitivity and subtle sexuality, Katharine Ross was an icon for young actresses of the late '60s. Her impact on Hollywood was swift and strong. In her early twenties she was a busy TV actress, usually appearing in Westerns like *The Virginian, Gunsmoke,* and *The Wild, Wild West.* After a couple of minor movies in the mid-'60s, she made a major break-through when she played Elaine in *The Graduate.* The sly comedy was one of the greatest movies of that or any decade, and Katharine was one of the hottest actresses of the year. The exposure brought her the '68 Golden Globe as the Most Promising Newcomer and an Oscar nomination as Best Supporting Actress. In '68, when Twentieth Century Fox could've cast anyone it wanted for the high-profile *Butch Cassidy and the Sundance Kid,* the studio chose Katharine. Smart and sexy, she was a perfect match for the handsome, witty leads, Paul Newman and Robert Redford.

More Westerns carried her into the '70s and beyond: Redford's *Tell Them Willie Boy Is Here* ('69), and the TV movies *Wanted: The Sundance Woman* ('76), *The Shadow Riders* ('83), *Red-Headed Stranger* ('86), and *Conagher* ('91, which she co-wrote). Other notable post-60s credits include *The Stepford Wives* ('75), *Voyage of the Damned* ('76, bringing her a second Golden Globe), Irwin Allen's *The Swarm* ('78), *The Final Countdown* ('80), and the part of Francesca on *The Colbys* ('85-'87). As testament to her career, when the American Film Insitute ranked the "100 Greatest American Movies" Katharine Ross had starred in two of them: *The Graduate* (#7) and *Butch Cassidy* (#50).

HER '60s LOOK: With her unique cleft chin, those big brown eyes, that great smile, and that long, lustrous hair, she was one of the most appealing young actresses of the late '60s. Hers was a natural, youthful beauty, but it also radiated intelligence. She was a believable college student in *The Graduate,* and a worthy foil for Newman's quick-witted Butch Cassidy. (Note that she teaches the boys Spanish, and she and Butch try to reign in the impulsive Sundance, who calls her his "teacher lady.") Her no-nonsense manner made her a believable pioneer woman in her many Westerns. She could make even a traditional farm dress look sexy, as evidenced by the long slow disrobing scene in *Butch Cassidy* that makes Sundance a hardened criminal indeed.

BEHIND THE SCENES: Since '84 Katharine has been married to actor Sam Elliott, the mustachioed star of *Mask* ('85) and *Tombstone* ('93). They met on the set of *Butch Cassidy,* where he had a small part as one of the card players in the sepia-toned opening sequence. Besides *Butch Cassidy,* he and Katharine have been in six movies together including *Conagher* ('91) on which they both got writing credits. Together they have a daughter, Chloe, and live in Mailbu. Said Katharine: "Somehow, working [together] has always worked well for us. It's life that has its ups and downs."

BONUS SWINGABILITY: Like the great Katharine Hepburn, she spells her first name with two A's ... her exotic birthplace—Hollywood, California ... in *The Graduate,* Katharine played the daughter of Anne Bancroft's character—when the movie came out Katharine was 25 and Anne was 36 ... a photogenic pair, she and Sam Elliott were on the cover of *Playgirl* in October of '79.

A DATE WITH KATHARINE

January 29, 1942	Katharine Ross is born
August 9, 1944	Sam Elliott is born
December 21, 1967	*The Graduate* is released
September 23, 1969	*Butch Cassidy and the Sundance Kid* is released

the all-an

STELLA STEVENS

SWINGIN' '60s CREDENTIALS: The decade's first *Playboy* Playmate, this beautiful blonde siren made fifteen movies during the '60s, among them some of the decade's swingin'est.

WORKIN' IT: Stella Stevens packed more living into her first quarter-century than most people do into a full lifetime. Married at 15, she was a mother at 16 and divorced at 17. At 23, in the first month of the first year of the '60s, she was a *Playboy* Playmate ("bella Stella," the magazine called her). The *Playboy* connection continued with later features in May '65 and January '68. But it was on the silver screen where her stunning beauty made its greatest impact. After winning a 1960 Golden Globe as the Most Promising Newcomer for her debut as Appassionata von Climax in *Li'l Abner*, she was one of the title females in Elvis' *Girls! Girls! Girls!* in '62, the wide-eyed innocent Stella Purdy in Jerry Lewis's *The Nutty Professor* in '63, and she adeptly played it for laughs in Dino's *The Silencers* in '66. Her awesome screen appeal kept her busy in a wide variety of roles, from college co-ed to scheming seductress to drug addict, and even a nun in *Where Angels Go, Trouble Follows* ('68).

In '70 she got one of her richest roles in the Sam Peckinpah Western *The Ballad of Cable Hogue*, and two years later she played the doomed hooker married to Ernest Borgnine in *The Poseidon Adventure*. She's never *not* worked ever since, building an amazing résumé that pushes her big- and small-screen appearances into triple digits, with four projects in '77, five in '79, five more in '90, four in '94, and on into the new millennium with a role on TV's *General Hospital*. As if all that weren't enough to keep a star busy, in the '90s she appeared as characters in computer games, she's done stage work, twice tried her hand at film directing, co-wrote a novel called *Razzle Dazzle* in '99, and is working on an autobiography. She even launched her own fragrance company. (Appropriately enough, Stella's scents are called Sexy, with Gold Label for women and Black Label for men.) Stars may come and go, centuries may pass, but Stella Stevens is eternal.

HER '60s LOOK: Stella Stevens is living proof that beautiful blondes with glamorous make-up, alluring eyes, and full lips never go out of style. In the tradition of the great screen goddesses, her naive, sweet expressions (exhibit A: *The Nutty Professor*) only added to her highly erotic appeal. As a *Playboy* centerfold she had 37-22-36 measurements, almost identical to those of the iconic Raquel Welch. Her costume changes in *Girls! Girls! Girls!* put her in gowns and a sleek bare-midriff ensemble while she knocks out her three bluesy songs. Watch the costume montage in *The Nutty Professor*, where young Stella goes from evening gowns to tennis togs, and you'll know why her professor went nutty. No wonder director Henry Hathaway supposedly said "Stella Stevens was born to be in movies ... and to drive men crazy!"

BEHIND THE SCENES: A smitten Jerry Lewis wrote to her in 1962: "You are the reason men can't live without the pride and thrill of direction." Stella's the mother of actor/director/producer Andrew Stevens. Since '84, she has been living in Beverly Hills with record producer Bob Kulick, former lead guitarist for Alice Cooper and Meatloaf.

BONUS SWINGABILITY: Her moniker at birth was Estelle Eggleston, which she changed to Stella Stevens at 18 ... her exotic birthplace—Yazoo City, Mississippi ... before she hit it big, she attended Memphis State, ... after being named a *Playboy* Playmate in '60, Stella later provided the requisite Playmate data: her turn-ons included eating fresh strawberries for breakfast in bed, her hobbies were writing, reading, and collecting records, and her favorite sports were horseback riding and skin diving ... Stella has her own Web site—http://www.stellastevens.com.

 A DATE WITH STELLA

October 1, 1938	Stella Stevens is born
June 10, 1955	Andrew Stevens is born
November 21, 1962	*Girls! Girls! Girls!* is released
June 4, 1963	*The Nutty Professor* is released
February 18, 1966	*The Silencers* is released
December 12, 1972	*The Poseidon Adventure* is released

SHARON TATE

SWINGIN' '60s CREDENTIALS: This big-eyed, perfect-featured, well-endowed, slim-bodied stunner starred in the camp classic *Valley of the Dolls*, but sadly it took the gruesome Manson Family to make her a household name in '69.

WORKIN' IT: "Few actresses have her kind of vulnerability, she's got a great future," said the director of *Valley of the Dolls*, Mark Robson. We'll never know how big a star Sharon Tate might've become. Daughter of an army officer, Sharon was a well-traveled beauty-contest winner and prom queen at an American high school in Verona, Italy, when she started getting bit parts in Italian movies. Heading to Hollywood, she spent the '60s steadily building a screen career, first with TV commercials, then as bank secretary Janet Trego on fourteen episodes of the wildly popular *The Beverly Hillbillies* from '63 to '65. She also auditioned for the part of Billie Jo on *Petticoat Junction* but reportedly was rejected because she had posed for *Playboy*. It didn't matter, though, because the movies came calling, most notably the parts of doomed pill-popping Jennifer in *Valley of the Dolls* ('67), the naïve innkeeper's daughter in Roman Polanski's *The Fearless Vampire Killers* ('67), and the koo-koo accomplice for Dino's Matt Helm in *The Wrecking Crew* ('68).

August 9, 1969. On that hot summer night, in a rented house on Cielo Drive in Beverly Hills, 26-year-old Sharon Tate was horribly butchered, a tragic, senseless killing engineered by the brutal Charles Manson ("the villain of our time," *Rolling Stone* called him)

and executed by his blindly allegiant drug-ravaged followers. Sharon was eight and a half months pregnant at the time. Her death, and the savage slayings of the four others at the house with her, will forever be remembered as one of the most awful, sadistic events in L.A. County history. And one of the grisliest: wearing only her undergarments, Sharon died with sixteen knife wounds in her body and a rope around her neck, her blood used to write "Pig" on the door. Four days later she was buried wearing a Pucci mini, with such stars as Yul Brynner, Steve McQueen, Warren Beatty, Kirk Douglas, and Peter Sellers in attendance. It took a year for Manson's motivations to be revealed. The intended victim that night had been Doris Day's son, Terry Melcher, who Manson felt had reneged on a promise to help Manson get his songs published. (The Beach Boys did record one of his songs, "Cease to Exist," which they retitled "Never Learn Not to Love" on the album *20/20* in '69.) But Melcher was no longer living there, so Manson's clan killed anyone else who happened to be in the house. More celebrity murders would've followed: the Manson Family had a "death list" of Hollywood stars to be targeted, among them McQueen, Frank, Liz and Dick, and Tom Jones. "Love," commented Polanski later, "carries in it the seed of tragedy."

HER '60s LOOK: Sharon was regarded as one of Hollywood's most beautiful actresses. She's said to have looked much younger than she really was, and supposedly many people who met her thought she was in her mid-teens, not her mid-twenties. Her hair color varied with her roles, ranging from blonde to brunette to red. And she was slink city, baby, all taut lines and awesome curvage,

the all-am

innocent, lovable human being. She was kindness itself to everybody and everything around her—people, animals, everything. She just didn't have a bad bone in her body....She was just utterly good, the kindest human being I've ever met." When they married, the bride wore an off-white mini made of taffeta, the reception was held at London's Playboy Club, and the honeymoon was spent skiing in the Swiss Alps. For Sharon and Roman, their life together was a whirlwind of travel and Hollywood parties. They counted among their friends Sean Connery, Peter Sellers, Rudolf Nureyev, Warren Beatty, Prince and Princess Radziwill, Vidal Sassoon, and Rolling Stones Brian Jones and Keith Richards, all of whom attended their wedding reception. Oh, and one other famous person Sharon probably met during her life, though he wasn't famous at the time: Manson himself, who in March '69 came to her door and supposedly spoke to Sharon while looking for either Terry Melcher or the owner of the house.

capable of playing athletic roles like the one in *Don't Make Waves* ('67) where she bounced on a trampoline and played a skydiver named Malibu. *Playboy* loved her, of course, publishing in March '67 a "Tate Gallery" of erotic photos that Polanski took before they were married.

BEHIND THE SCENES: "My whole life has been decided by fate," she once said. "I've never planned anything that happened to me." Fate decided that she would have some famous boyfriends and an intense marriage. After relationships with hairdresser Jay Sebring and actors Richard Beymer and Steve McQueen, Sharon married Roman Polanski, who had directed and starred in *The Fearless Vampire Killers* in '68. In a December '71 *Playboy* interview Polanski remembered her as "the sweetest, most

BONUS SWINGABILITY: Her exotic birthplace—Dallas, Texas ... other actresses rumored to have been considered for the three main roles in *Valley of the Dolls* were Candice Bergen, Petula Clark, Raquel Welch, Ann-Margret, and Jill Ireland; the roles eventually went to Sharon, Patty Duke, and Barbara Parkins ... after Sharon's death, many celebrities claimed they had been invited to the house on the night of the murders, but something prevented them from making it; among these near-misses was Steve McQueen, who said that he was headed to her house for dinner that night, but he picked up another woman and spent the night with her instead ... Polanski dedicated his 1979 film *Tess* to Sharon.

 A DATE WITH SHARON

August 18, 1933	Roman Polanski is born
November 12, 1934	Charles Manson is born
January 24, 1943	Sharon Tate is born
October 16, 1963	Sharon first appears on *The Beverly Hillbillies*
December 15, 1967	*Valley of the Dolls* is released
January 20, 1968	Sharon marries Roman Polanski
March 23, 1969	The likely date when Sharon comes face to face with Manson
August 9, 1969	Sharon is murdered
August 13, 1969	Sharon is buried
December 9, 1969	Charles Manson is formally charged
January 25, 1971	Charles Manson is convicted of first-degree murder

ericans

MAMIE VAN DOREN

SWINGIN' '60s CREDENTIALS: When informed that she was going to be profiled in a book called *Swingin' Chicks of the '60s*, Mamie's response was, "In the '60s, there was nobody more swingin' than me!" We're inclined to believe her. More than just a movie star or live entertainer, Mamie Van Doren is a sexual icon on the level of the other famous "M's" she's usually compared to—Monroe and Mansfield. To her credit, and everybody's delight, Mamie has outlasted 'em all.

WORKIN' IT: Acting has been Mamie Van Doren's main career, but acting talent has never been her greatest claim to fame. As she wrote in her autobiography, "Fun, I believe, was where I excelled." After a childhood spent on a South Dakota farm, Mamie got her first job at 13 as an usherette at Hollywood's Pantages Theatre, and a

year later she landed her first acting gig, a bit part on an early TV talk show. Soon she was winning local beauty pageants (at age 15 she was Miss Palm Springs), working as a band singer, and appearing in movies for Howard Hughes's RKO Studios. *Forbidden* in '53 got her a contract with Universal and the official name-change to Mamie Van Doren. She made some rockin' records in the mid-'50s, did another dozen '50s movies including *Untamed Youth* ('57), *High School Confidential* and *Teacher's Pet* (both in '58), and became identified with the energetic rock and roll revolution.

Her most memorable '60s movies came early in the decade: the campy but entertaining *Sex Kittens Go to College* in '60 and *The Private Lives of Adam and Eve* in '61. Throughout the '60s, Mamie was in eleven more movies; granted, these weren't major award-winning epics, and among her '60s flix were such minor works as *The Navy vs. the Night Monsters* and *The Las Vegas Hillbillys*, both in '66. To Mamie's credit, when the movie roles dried up toward the end of the decade, she hit Broadway in *Gentlemen Prefer Blondes*, performed in nightclubs and in Vegas showrooms, appeared in men's magazines, and even made two tours of Vietnam and Southeast Asia in '68 and '71 to entertain the troops. After the '60s, she's stayed in the spotlight and kept busy with constant projects, including the movie *Free Ride* in '86, a highly entertaining, highly revealing autobiography called *Playing the Field* in '87, and continued night-club appearances. For over forty years now, she's been stealing the spotlight—always working, always visible, always being Mamie.

HER '60s LOOK: Not surprisingly, Mamie's childhood idol was Jean Harlow. Like Jean, Marilyn Monroe, and Jayne Mansfield, Mamie has always had that goddess look workin' to perfection, with a lush crown of blonde hair topping a knock-out body. (Nobody does that look anymore, do they? Besides Mamie, that is? Anna Nicole Smith tried to resurrect it, but she just tramped-up the whole sex-symbol concept, dagnabbit. Anyway, back to Mamie...) She's always had the curves and swerves, in your finest sex-symbol tradition. What's more, she's accentuated her figure with a classic "bullet bra" and revealing clothes that have kept her a fave of magazine editors throughout her career. Here's a great item on her résumé that few other actresses have: At 18 years old she posed for Alberto Vargas, the painter of the glamorous "Varga Girls," and his rendition of her made the July '51 cover of *Esquire*. Two years later, while filming a *Yankee Pasha* fight scene with Rhonda Fleming, Rhonda accidentally slugged Mamie in the mouth and dislocated her jaw. Not to be deterred, Mamie bounced back and ultimately made an impact so strong that when *Playboy* ranked the "100 Sexiest Stars of the Century" in January '99, the magazine put her at #29, right behind Jane Fonda.

BEHIND THE SCENES: There's no doubting Mamie's active lifestyle—and the beauty part is that she herself has talked and written about it at length, often in fascinating detail and with memorable quotes. ("It is possible," she once said, "that blondes prefer gentlemen.") Among the famous names she's been linked with are boxer Jack Dempsey, singer Eddie Fisher, baseball star Bo Belinsky, football hero Joe Namath, cool guy Steve McQueen, TV-star Johnny Carson, pretty-boy Tony Curtis, singer Johnny Rivers, mustachioed machoman Burt Reynolds, producer Robert Evans, and playboy Nicky Hilton, plus an infamous liaison with actor Rock Hudson in January of '53, when Mamie and Rock rolled around on her mother's kitchen floor. Even more impressive is the list of men Mamie rejected. According to her book, Mamie turned down earnest romantic overtures from Howard Hughes, Burt Lancaster, Warren Beatty, Frank Sinatra, James Dean, Prince Axel of Denmark, Cary Grant, Henry Kissinger, and Elvis. Mamie's got lots of stories about all of 'em: Cary Grant tried unsuccessfully to get Mamie to take LSD with him, Johnny Carson first asked her for a date during a commercial break on *The Tonight Show*, Burt Reynolds called out his ex-wife's name (Judy Carne) during their brief moment of ecstasy, and Henry K. took her on a private tour of the White House in '73 and let Mamie sit in the president's Oval Office chair. When she wasn't dating, Mamie was marrying, and to date she's had five husbands. At age 17 she eloped to Santa Barbara with sportswear manufacturer Jack Newman, but he proved to be abusive and she soon got out of the marriage. Two months pregnant in '55, she married bandleader Ray Anthony and in early '56 gave birth to her son, Perry. Baseball player Lee Meyers was briefly her third husband, and businessman Ross McClintock was briefly her fourth. Happily, for over twenty years now, Mamie's been securely married to actor and video producer Thomas Dixon. Still the life of any party, Mamie's a regular guest at Hef's soirees at the Playboy Mansion.

BONUS SWINGABILITY: She uses a fake moniker—her real name is Joan Lucille Olander, named after Joan Crawford ... Universal gave her a new name when she signed her seven-year deal in '53—the surname came from the studio's belief that she looked Dutch, while the name Mamie was borrowed from Eisenhower's wife (Ike was inaugurated the same day she inked the contract) ... her exotic birthplace—Rowena, South Dakota ... at 17 Mamie used her Vegas showgirl money to buy her first car—the MG roadster formerly owned by Humphrey Bogart ... "I don't wear panties anymore," Mamie once said. "This startles the Hollywood wolves so much, they don't know what to pull at, so they leave me alone" ... in '64, Mamie flew to Paris in search of dresses to wear in an upcoming Aqua Velva commercial; Coco Chanel herself met with Mamie and made the arrangements for Mamie's black dress ... also in '64, Mamie was

at the Whisky-a-Go-Go in L.A. when the Beatles were there, and a drunk George Harrison accidentally flung his drink on her (he was trying to throw it on some predatory journalists) ... you can read some of Mamie's insider stories about Hollywood at her remarkable Web site, where "the first authentic sex-kitten in cyberspace" gives one of the most intimate looks at a celebrity's personal life as you'll find on the Internet (plus humorous advice about "size," truly emotional excerpts from her Vietnam journals, touching memories of her close friends, lots of photos and autographs for sale, paper dolls, and more)—http://www.mamievandoren.com.

 A DATE WITH MAMIE

February 6, 1933	Mamie Van Doren is born
January 20, 1953	Mamie inks the deal with Universal
August 29, 1955	Mamie marries Ray Anthony in Toledo, Ohio
March 18, 1956	Mamie gives birth to her son, Perry
October 2, 1957	Mamie opens at the Riviera Hotel in Vegas
April 1, 1963	Bo Belinsky proposes

RAQUEL WELCH

SWINGIN' '60s CREDENTIALS: This fiery Amazonian actress with the fantastic figure took a *Fantastic Voyage* from struggling single mom to international fame as one of the decade's dominant sex symbols.

WORKIN' IT: "My career started ass-backwards," she once joked; whether Raquel Welch started out ass-forwards or -backwards, by the mid-'60s she was one of the world's most famous actresses. As a little girl, Raquel escaped from the conflicts between her parents by going to the movies, where her favorite film was the ballet classic *The Red Shoes*. A veteran of dance classes and beauty contests, at 18 she enrolled at San Diego State University. A year later she was married, and a year after that she had a daughter. In '64, struggling as a divorced single mom with two kids, she landed a job as the "billboard girl" on TV's *Hollywood Palace* variety show. Her stunning figure and photogenic appeal quickly led to auditions, a studio contract, bit parts on TV shows like *McHale's Navy*, *The Virginian*, and *Bewitched*, and even a brief appearance in Elvis' *Roustabout* ('64), where in the very first scene she delivered a single line at a swingin' club called Mother's Tea House: "Uh, how come they call this place a tea house, dear?" In '65 she shook 'n' shimmied while she sang "I'm Ready to Groove" in the beachy *A Swingin' Summer*. Then came her two back-to-back hits in '66 and '67, and suddenly the whole world knew who Raquel Welch was. *Fantastic Voyage* was the landmark sci-fi film that put her in a clingy scuba suit; *One Million Years B.C.* was the landmark caveman-film that put her in an animal-skin bikini.

Late-'60s highlights for her included starring roles in the spy flick *Fathom* ('67), Sinatra's *Tony Rome* sequel, *Lady in Cement* ('68), and the Jim Brown Western, *100 Rifles* ('69). Her busy '70s began with the notoriously catastrophic *Myra Breckenridge* ('70), but she bounced back—and won a Golden Globe as Best Actress—with *The Three Musketeers* in '74. (When she made her acceptance speech she cried and said she'd been waiting for this "since one million years B.C.") Showing the wide range of her talent, through the '70s she headlined shows in Vegas and New York, in the '80s and '90s she starred in two big Broadway musicals, *Woman of the Year* and *Victor/Victoria*, and she got rave reviews for her acclaimed TV movies (*The Legend of Walks Far Woman* in '82, *Right to Die* in '87).

Ever diversifying, she wrote a best-selling fitness book (emphasizing yoga and nutrition, not bodybuilding), she became a major activist for women's rights and health issues (meeting with President Ford in '74 at the White House to raise awareness in the fight against cancer), and she created her own lines of wigs and beauty products. Just to keep her hand in, she turned up on some pretty hip TV comedies of the '90s—a couple of *Spin City* episodes, *Lois & Clark*, and a self-parodying cameo on 1990's *Seinfeld* episode called "The Summer of George" where, spoofing her rep, she beats up both Elaine and Kramer!

HER '60s LOOK: In the mid-'60s, only a real clyde could've ignored ravishing Raquel. Actor Edward G. Robinson once said about her, "I pity any actor who gets second billing to Raquel Welch; he's really getting third billing to her breasts!" As a teenager Raquel developed quickly, and by the time she was a voluptuous 15 she was already winning California beauty pageants such as Miss Contour, Miss La Jolla, Miss Photogenic Teen, and Miss San Diego. By '68, when Dudley Moore and Peter Cook were looking for someone to play Lust in their film *Bedazzled*, they knew who to call. Raquel's 5' 6", 118-pounds frame and 37-22-35 measurements were the ultimate in passionate, voracious sexuality. (Interestingly, ads for *Fathom* in '67 touted her measurements as an even more voluptuous 39-22-33.) Scuba gear never looked so good, as validated by several *Playboy* appearances (including January, November, and December '69). According to a TV bio about her, Hef has always considered her one of his favorites, describing her as being "magical." In the January '99 *Playboy* list of "The 100 Sexiest Stars of the Century," magical Raquel finished at #3, right between two other '60s icons—Jayne Mansfield and Brigitte Bardot. Still stunning, in '97 Raquel made *Shape* magazine's list of the ten sexiest women in the world.

BEHIND THE SCENES: While her image in the '60s was that of a torrid sexpot, Raquel's private life seems to have been very different: "What I do on the screen is not to be equated with what I do in my private life," she once said. "Privately, I am understated and dislike any hoopla." She likes to be married, though. Raquel married James Welch, her high school sweetheart, in '59; they divorced in '64 after having two kids. (One of them, Tahnee, is an actress in her own right—see the two *Cocoon* movies, '85 and '88.) Late in the '60s she married publicist Patrick Curtis in Paris (he had played Olivia de

Havilland's baby in *Gone With the Wind*), but they divorced five years later. In the early '70s she had a relationship with fashion designer Ron Talsky after he designed the dazzling dress she wore to the '71 Oscars. (He said she "was the best fringe benefit I ever got from my service as an Oscar designer.") The '80s were spent married to writer Andre Weinfeld, then after a '90 divorce she mar-

ried again in July 1999, this time to restaurateur Richard Palmer. The wedding was held at their Beverly Hills mansion, with Dyan Cannon among the 100 invited guests. True to her image, Raquel's spectacular tight-fitting wedding gown was cut low, low, low in front and back.

BONUS SWINGABILITY: Her real name is Jo Raquel Tejada ... her exotic birthplace—Chicago ... in '72 she broke her wrist while skating in the roller derby flick *Kansas City Bomber* ... at times she's had the reputation for being difficult on the set, and on that subject a critical James Mason once said he "would spank her from here to Aswan" ... however, when she sued the producers of 1982's *Cannery Row* for firing her amidst claims that she was "unprofessional," Burt Reynolds testified in her behalf that she "was always on time, well prepared, and thoroughly professional"; she eventually won over $5 million from MGM ... supposedly she came close to being a Bond girl—it's said that Raquel was signed to do *Thunderball* in '65, but Twentieth Century Fox got her out of her contract so she could star in *Fantastic Voyage* (Claudine Auger got the part of Domino in *Thunderball*) ... allegedly Raquel also turned down one of the three starring roles in *Valley of the Dolls*.

 A DATE WITH RAQUEL

September 5, 1940	Raquel Welch is born
December 26, 1961	Raquel gives birth to daughter Tahnee Welch
November 11, 1964	*Roustabout* is released
November 12, 1964	Raquel appears on *Bewitched*
August 24, 1966	*Fantastic Voyage* is released
February 21, 1967	*One Million Years B.C.* is released

nericans

TUESDAY WELD

SWINGIN' '60s CREDENTIALS: Tuesday Weld, "one of the finest actresses ever to have a name comprised of a day of the week and an industrial verb" (according to Greg Altenberger at his glorious " Elvis' Women" Web site). In the '60s Tuesday was a beautiful but tragic figure whose youthful appeal brought her prominent movie parts but not the true superstardom that she might've attained and that loyal fans had hoped for.

WORKIN' IT: "No actress was ever so good in so many bad films," decided Roddy McDowell, one of her '60s co-stars (*Lord Love a Duck*, '66). That assessment perhaps was a little harsh, because Tuesday Weld has starred in some fine films in her long career. The bad ones did indeed cause her to retire briefly on a few different occasions, but she always managed to bounce back to good notices. Her father died when Tuesday was 3 years old, and she worked as a catalog model to help support her struggling family. Modeling led to TV commercials, then as a teen Tuesday became an understudy in Broadway's *The Dark at the Top of the Stairs* in '57. By decade's end she had appeared as a supporting actress in four films (including *Rally 'Round the Flag, Boys!* in '58), and as the delectable-but-just-out-of-reach Thalia Menninger for the '59–'60 season of *The Many Loves of Dobie Gillis*. In the latter, her

Thalia tried to inspire poor Dobie to improve himself: "If he had a girl like me with expensive tastes, why then he'd have to make a success, wouldn't he? You show me a financial tycoon and I'll show you right behind him a girl like Thalia Menninger. It's girls like me who open up their vistas. We broaden their horizons! We make things happen! Dobie is the clay and I am the sculptor."

Her momentum building rapidly, in '60 she shared the Golden Globe for Most Promising Newcomer with Angie Dickinson, Janet Munro, and Stella Stevens, and from '60–'61 she made seven movies. Projecting both vulnerable innocence and erotic allure, youthful beauty and wild experience, throughout the decade she starred alongside some of the screen's biggest names, highlighted by *High Time* with Der Bingle ('60), *Wild in the Country* with Elvis ('61), *The Cincinnati Kid* with Steve McQueen ('65), and *I'll Take Sweden* with Bob Hope ('65). She was in lots of dramatic TV shows, too, including *Route 66*, *The Fugitive*, and *Naked City*. Her best moments came as the energetic all-American girl-turned-killer opposite Tony Perkins in *Pretty Poison* ('68), something of a cult classic. Paired with Perkins once more, she got her second Golden Globe nomination for her work in the gut-wrenching *Play It As It Lays* ('72). Post-'60s work was balanced between major and minor movies, the best being *Looking for Mr. Goodbar* ('77, with a Best Supporting Actress Oscar nomination), *Who'll Stop the Rain* ('78), *Thief* ('81), *Author! Author!* ('82), *Once Upon a Time in America* ('84), *Falling Down* ('93), and *Feeling Minnesota* ('96).

HER '60s LOOK: As an ingénue she had an early flower-child appeal. Danny Peary compliments her in his acclaimed book *Cult Movies* by saying, "She is sexy, but it has less to do with her body than her manner. Her sexiness lies in a cherubic face with eyes that sparkle with wickedness." It was a look appealing enough to get her onto the cover of *Life* magazine in '63. Always a nubile young thang, she had a slender figure that looked great in a simple dress, conveying both innocence and desire. *Movie Life Yearbook* of '63 gave her stats as 5' 3" and 112 pounds, with a remarkable 36-19-35 figure. Man, a 19-year-old girl can get into a whole messa trouble with numbers like those. In fact, rock star Alice Cooper always maintained that the greatest turn-on he could imagine was Tuesday "in a dirty slip, drinking a can of beer."

the all-am

BEHIND THE SCENES: Tuesday herself once said that she doesn't remember much of what she did as a young girl, because "as a teenager, I was a wreck. I drank so much I can't remember anything." Distressingly, reports are that she was only 9 when she had her first nervous breakdown, was a serious drinker by the time she was 10, and had attempted suicide before she turned 12. All that was before she'd made her first movie, *Rock, Rock, Rock*, at 13. "Tuesday is 15 going on 27," mused Danny Kaye. During the '60s and '70s she reputedly was a hard-livin' lover of many '50s-'60s icons, including Elvis, Frank, Ryan O'Neal, Dennis Hopper, Gary Lockwood from *2001: A Space Odyssey*, Al Pacino, Fabian, Edd "Kookie" Byrnes, Sal Mineo, Ray Anthony, John Ireland, and Dudley Moore. After getting pregnant by Dud, she married him and gave birth to his son, Patrick, in '76. Unfortunately, the marriage was rocky, marked by arguments, reconciliations, and his infidelities. By May '78 Tuesday and Dudley were separated and living on opposite coasts. Tuesday later married classical violinist Pinchas Zukerman, but in November '98 it was reported in national newspapers that they were headed for divorce. One affectionately imagines the results if she'd married composer Gavin Friday, actor Walter Sunday, and then baseball star Rick Monday—her name would've been Tuesday Friday Sunday Monday. Or imagine if she married the son of golfer Don January, she'd be Tuesday January the Second. Or imagine if there were this French guy named Pierre D'Livery, see, and they got married…actually, at this point please imagine that Tuesday and her lawyers don't mind these gentle jests with her unique and memorable name.

BONUS SWINGABILITY:

She uses a stage moniker—her real name is Susan Ker Weld, her childhood nickname was "Tu-Tu" … her exotic birthplace—New York City … the one

season she was on *Dobie Gillis* was the same single season that then-unknown Warren Beatty was on the show, playing a rival for her affections … collectors say that around 1960 Tuesday recorded a now-hard-to-find 45 of the song "Are You a Boy?" … allegedly Tuesday turned down *Lolita*, the role that ultimately went to Sue Lyon; "I didn't have to play it," said Tuesday to an interviewer, "I *was* Lolita" … when *Bonnie and Clyde* was first being discussed mid-decade, she was seriously considered for the role of Bonnie, as were Carol Lynley, Natalie Wood, and Shirley MacLaine, but they all lost out to her Fayeness … other movies she supposedly rejected were *Rosemary's Baby* ('68), *Bob & Carol & Ted & Alice* ('69) and *True Grit* ('70) … one of Tuesday's biggest fans was Steve McQueen, who starred with her in *The Cincinnati Kid* in '65; he later said she was "the best actress I'd worked with up to that point" …she inspired the song "Tuesday Weld" by Walter Egan, and a Texas band called Tuesday Weld came out with an album in '96 called *Sting of the Pimp Slap* … her comment about her life: "It seems the brighter you are, the deeper the hole you get into" … the Elvis' Women Web site mentioned on the previous page is at http://greggers.granitecity.com/elvis/women/.

A DATE WITH TUESDAY

August 27, 1943	Tuesday Weld is born
September 29, 1959	*Dobie Gillis* debuts
June 15, 1961	*Wild in the Country* is released
July 26, 1963	Tuesday makes the cover of *Life* magazine
October 15, 1965	*The Cincinnati Kid* is released

ericans

NATALIE WOOD

SWINGIN' '60s CREDENTIALS: This petite, dark beauty rode '50s success to a rare stardom through the entire '60s, taking her from a singin' senorita at the beginning of the decade to a swingin' suburbanite at the end.

WORKIN' IT: Natalie Wood was a major star who looked and lived the part. Born to Russian immigrants, she began her legendary career as a child star in the '40s, most notably in the Christmas classic *Miracle on 34th Street* in '47. Without skipping a beat, her stardom continued through her teen years, and she made two films per year during the '50s, including *Rebel Without a Cause* in '55 (her first Oscar nomination), *The Searchers*

in '56 (leading to a Golden Globe in '57 as the Most Promising Newcomer), and *Marjorie Morningstar* in '58. So busy and popular was Natalie that by the time she was 20 she'd already been in thirty movies.

The '60s for her were filled with more hits—great movies that put her in romantic, comedic, dramatic, and musical roles, often as a sexy, strong-minded young woman. She starred in the classic *West Side Story* and *Splendor in the Grass* in '61 (the latter bringing her a second Oscar nomination), *Gypsy* in '62, *Love with the Proper Stranger* in '63 (her third Oscar nomination), *Sex and the Single Girl* in '64, and *Inside Daisy Clover* and *The Great Race* in '65, all before she was 30.

After *Bob & Carol & Ted & Alice* in '69, the '70s and '80s saw a dwindling number, and a dwindling significance, of her films. Starring roles in Olivier's TV presentation of *Cat on a Hot Tin Roof* ('76), *Meteor* ('79), and *Brainstorm* ('83) stand as the best-known of the last works in a career that came to a sad, sudden end. Throughout her life Natalie had an intense fear of water, and ironically, at the age of 43, she tragically drowned off Catalina Island. Today she's buried at Westwood Memorial Park in Westwood, California, the same cemetery where Marilyn Monroe is interred. And though she was a star who knew fame in every decade from the '40s to the '80s, her tombstone is a tribute to Natalie, the person: "Beloved daughter, sister, wife, mother & friend," with the words "More than love" an adoring coda to her memory.

HER '60s LOOK: Glamorously beautiful with great coloring, Natalie was one of Hollywood's true beauties and one of the most popular queens of movie magazines (*Life* named her Screen Personality of the Year in '63). Her dark features enabled her to play ethnic roles, as in *West Side Story*, but also to play a traditional Hollywood siren in *The Great Race*. Early in her career she would wear six-inch high heels to add some loft to her 5' 3" height, but movie audiences rarely noticed her height as her stunning beauty and knockout figure developed. One physical characteristic that's rarely noticed: Bios refer to her slightly deformed left wrist, which she hid with bracelets, long sleeves, and proper camera angles.

BEHIND THE SCENES: As a young actress Natalie supposedly dated much older men such as Robert Vaughn, Raymond Burr, and John Ireland. She also dated Elvis briefly: "Elvis was so square, we'd go … for hot fudge sundaes," she once said. "He didn't drink, he didn't swear, he didn't even smoke. It was like having the date that I never had in high school." She even flew to Memphis to meet the family, but the relationship didn't last. She was also linked with such luminaries as James Dean, Warren Beatty, Tab Hunter, Dennis Hopper, Robert Evans, Steve McQueen, Frank Sinatra, and pre-governor Jerry Brown. The Beatty break-up is infamous: the legend is that he got up from their restaurant table to use the phone and instead left with the hat-

check girl. Natalie had three marriages, but only two husbands. The first husband was suave Robert Wagner, whom she married in '57 (a formal wedding in Arizona) and divorced in '62. Late in the decade she was married to producer Richard Gregson for two years, and then in '72 she remarried Wagner (a more casual wedding in L.A.), who was her husband until her death. She had daughters with both Gregson and Wagner. Of relationships, she once said, "The only time a woman really succeeds in changing a man is when he's a baby."

BONUS SWINGABILITY: She used a stage moniker—her real name was Natasha Gurdin, she was given the name Wood by a studio exec … her exotic birthplace—San Francisco, California … her sister is an awesomely constructed Bond girl of the '70s, Lana Wood, who played Plenty O'Toole in *Diamonds Are Forever* … supposedly the studio nudged Natalie into a relationship with Warren Beatty while *Splendor in the Grass* was shooting, figuring the personal chemistry would add to the picture … in *West Side Story* Natalie's singing was dubbed by Marni Nixon, the same woman who later dubbed Audrey Hepburn in *My Fair Lady* (but Natalie really did sing in *Gypsy*) … some stories say she beat out Ann-Margret for the starring role in *Gypsy*, the movie in which she shed her sweet image to play the role of a sexy stripper … supposedly Warren Beatty begged her to co-star in *Bonnie and Clyde*, but she refused, not wanting to go on location in Texas without her therapist for three months … Natalie put in a cameo on Robert Wagner's *Hart to Hart* in '79; she and Wagner were also in *All the Fine Young Cannibals* ('62) and the TV movies *The Affair* ('73) and *Cat on a Hot Tin Roof* ('76) together … after Natalie was gone, bereaved husband Robert Wagner said, "She worked so hard all her life. Natalie had some tough times, being put out there to work at 4 years old, being pushed…working very hard on her life, on her talent, and then bang! Gone! And it's terrible….Natalie lived more than most of us live. She felt more. She experienced more. She did more and gave more. She created a lot of light in her life. She caught her rainbows."

A DATE WITH NATALIE

February 10, 1930	Robert Wagner is born
July 20, 1938	Natalie Wood is born
March 1, 1946	Lana Wood is born
May 2, 1947	*Miracle on 34th Street* is released
October 27, 1955	*Rebel Without a Cause* is released
December 28, 1957	Natalie marries Robert Wagner
October 10, 1961	*Splendor in the Grass* is released
October 18, 1961	*West Side Story* is released
April 27, 1962	Natalie and Robert Wagner divorce
November 1, 1962	*Gypsy* is released
December 25, 1964	*Sex and the Single Girl* is released
July 1, 1965	*The Great Race* is released
September 18, 1969	*Bob & Carol & Ted & Alice* is released
June 16, 1972	Natalie remarries Robert Wagner
November 29, 1981	Natalie Wood drowns

JILL ST. JOHN

SWINGIN' '60s CREDENTIALS: This red-headed, hour-glass figured knockout blazed across the big screen in lightweight comedy, adventure, and thriller flix alongside some of the decade's most famous leading men.

WORKIN' IT: Jill St. John has lived, looked, and played like a true Hollywood star. She hasn't had a stellar movie career, but she's sure stolen some scenes in her time. A stage actress at the age of 5, Jill was in four '50s flix as a teen, including *Summer Love* in '58, and she starred in Irwin Allen's *The Lost World* ('60) at only 20 years old. High-profile movies filled her '60s, including Jerry Lewis's *Who's Minding the Store?* ('63), *The Liquidator* with Rod Taylor ('65), and *Tony Rome* with Frank ('67). Unappreciated by film critics, some sources say she was only brought into *Tony Rome* because she was Frank's girl. (He did get parts for all his gang in that movie, including his lawyer Mickey Rudin, pals Shecky Greene, Jilly Rizzo, and Mike Romanoff, plus a couple of other playmates, Deana Lund and Tiffany Bolling.) Still, she has always been a memorable presence on screen, and she has the distinction of being the first American-born Bond Beauty. The sparkling role of Tiffany Case in the penultimate Connery Bond flick, *Diamonds Are Forever* in '71, showed her off at her sexiest and propelled her onward to many more screen appearances, including a half dozen TV movies, cooking demos on *Good Morning America*, lots of Bob Hope specials, and even a *Seinfeld* episode in '97. A food columnist for the *USA Weekend* newspaper, she wrote *The Jill St. John Cookbook* in '87.

HER '60s LOOK: With that stunning face, sexy red hair, and 36-24-36 figure (according to the '63 *Movie Life Yearbook*), she was one of those actresses so dang attractive it didn't matter if she was a great actress or not. Sometimes there just for set decoration, she had enough sex appeal to resonate long after many of her movies were forgotten. She's still got it, too, as evidenced by her appearance with other Bond girls in the November '99 issue of *Vanity Fair*. Most of the other '60s actresses were conservatively covered up, but not Jill—she was flashing plenty of seductive leg, as sexy as ever.

BEHIND THE SCENES: She's alleged to have once said that "the longest period of celibacy for Jill St. John is the shortest distance between two lovers." She's had at least three husbands, one of whom was playboy Lance Reventlow (the son of Woolworth heiress Barbara Hutton). She had some hey-hey with Frank Sinatra and something undefined with Henry Kissinger. Of the latter, Jill found his intellect to be his most admirable feature and a good match for her own high I.Q., which is said to be 162. (This would make Jill a terrific actress, because she can play such a convincing dingaling.) Since 1990 she's been married to Natalie Wood's ex-husband, Robert Wagner. She and Wagner worked together on the TV movie *How I Spent My Summer Vacation* in '66. They were reintroduced in '82, after Natalie tragically drowned off Catalina Island. They now have homes in Aspen, Colorado, and Pacific Palisades, California, where Jill keeps a number of horses.

BONUS SWINGABILITY: She uses a stage moniker—her real name is Jill Oppenheim ... her exotic birthplace—L.A., California ... ... supposedly Jill beat out Raquel Welch, Faye Dunaway, and Jane Fonda for the Tiffany Case role in *Diamonds Are Forever* ... the name Tiffany Case is explained as the result of the character having being born on the first floor of Tiffany's jewelry store while her mom shopped for a wedding ring ... Jill and Robert Wagner have been in several screen projects together, including the *Around the World in 80 Days* miniseries ('89), *The Player* ('92), and *Something to Believe In* ('98); they've also toured together with A.R. Gurney's play *Love Letters*.

 A DATE WITH JILL

August 19, 1940	Jill St. John is born
June 5, 1963	*Come Blow Your Horn* is released
November 28, 1963	*Who's Minding the Store?* is released
January 12, 1966	Jill appears on *Batman*
April 26, 1967	*Eight on the Lam* is released
November 19, 1967	*Tony Rome* is released
December 17, 1971	*Diamonds Are Forever* is released

the all-ar

THE MOVIE STARS:
THE BRITISH INVASION

In the '60s, various locations arose as capitals of style and significance. New York, propelled by Pop Art, Warhol's Factory, the Velvet Underground, and Edie Sedgwick, was the focus for urban hipness; San Francisco, grooving with wild colors, long hair, Love-Ins, the Dead and the Airplane, could rightly claim to be the world's psychedelic "head"quarters; and Los Angeles, all sunshine and surf and Beach Boys and Disney Girls, was, early on, anyway, like a national playground for California Dreamin'. But as distinct and memorable as they were, these and all other worlds orbited around London, the true center of the '60s universe. In April of '66 a *Time* magazine cover story joyously crowned London the city of the decade. In the '60s all things English were all things swingin'. The Beatles, the Stones, miniskirts, models, hairstyles, James Bond movies, the '66 World Cup champions, Grand Prix winners, new vocabulary words, and the actresses profiled here all burst from the British Isles in exciting, exuberant explosions of color and creativity. Like Roger Miller once sang, "Eng-a-land swings!"

JANE ASHER

SWINGIN' '60s CREDENTIALS: A stylish upper-class sweetheart to Paul McCartney in the mid-'60s, for a while Lady Jane was everyone's favorite answer to the question of whom the world's most eligible bachelor would marry. Away from Paul she appeared in a half-dozen '60s flix and did some significant stage work; her onscreen highlight was her prominent role as a hard-workin' homebody for Michael Caine in *Alfie*.

WORKIN' IT: Overshadowed by her famous Beatle, Jane Asher had talent that didn't generate the recognition it deserved. Jane was a child actress who graduated from kid roles in the '50s to grown-up co-starring parts in the '60s. Key roles included a featured part in the Vincent Price thriller *The Masque of the Red Death* ('64), the Caine-ing in *Alfie* ('66), and Perdita in Shakespeare's *The Winter's Tale* ('69). But her real impact was on young girls of the '60s who

copied her look, envied her privileged life, and read about her in articles with titles like "The Truth About Paul McCartney's Marriage." Her '60s fame peaked during the five years she was rumored to be the first Mrs. Paul. As early as '64 she was the subject of printed gossip and commentary, and his songs were analyzed for personal revelations about their relationship. Critics have surmised that some of his best-loved ballads, such as "And I Love Her" and "Here, There, and Everywhere" (said by Paul to be one of his faves) were likely about her, as well as "All My Loving," "You Won't See Me," "For No One," "Things We Said Today," "I'm Looking Through You," and "We Can Work It Out." Toward the end of the decade she established herself as a serious stage actress with the Bristol Old Vic, a company that toured the U.S. during the height of her popularity.

Continuing to work steadily for the next three decades, Jane joined the National Theatre in '76, and she's made dozens of appearances on popular British TV shows, including "Rumpole of the Bailey," "Brideshead Revisited," and "Absolutely Fabulous." Displaying her wide-ranging talent, she has also written a dozen books, most notably a best-selling novel in '96 called *The Longing*, followed up two years later by *The Question*. (She's finishing another novel, *Trying to Get Out*, aimed for a 2001 release.) Today she's considered the British equivalent of Martha Stewart for her helpful magazine articles, her TV show *Good Living*, and her lifestyle book *The Best of Good Living*. Since '90 she's run a catering business called Jane Asher Party Cakes, which makes decorative cakes (including a birthday cake for Prince Charles) and helps locals lead the good life in London.

HER '60s LOOK: Jane had the classic London look workin' for her—the sweet face, the long bangs, the straight reddish/auburn hair. It was a look similar to that of Mick Jagger's girl, Marianne Faithfull,

the british

who was another stylin' scene maker during the decade. So influential was Jane's hair, she did commercials for Breck in the '60s, and young girls would iron their hair to emulate her style.

BEHIND THE SCENES: Jane was the steady date of the cutest Beatle from '63 to '68, so one can only imagine what that was like as the Beatlemania tidal wave swept around the world. Jane and Paul first met in April of 1963 after a Beatles concert at London's Royal Albert Hall. Working for the BBC's *Jukebox Jury* show, Jane interviewed the group, and though her original favorite was supposedly George, she and Paul quickly got together. According to Hunter Davies' book *The Beatles*, Paul knew right away that "this was the girl for me. I hadn't tried to grab her or make her. I told her, 'it appears you're a nice girl.'" Wrote Cynthia Lennon, in *A Twist of Lennon*, "Paul fell like a ton of bricks for Jane. The first time I was introduced to her was at her home and she was sitting on Paul's knee. My first impression of Jane was how beautiful and finely featured she was. Her mass of Titian-colored hair cascaded around her face and shoulders, her pale complexion contrasting strongly with dark clothes and shining hair. Paul was obviously as proud as a peacock with his new lady. For Paul, Jane Asher was a great prize." Paul soon moved into her parents' London home, and it was on the piano there that he and John composed "I Want to Hold Your Hand." (Paul may have also composed "Yesterday" in that house.) In '66 Paul and Jane moved into a London Victorian home of their own, plus he bought a fixer-upper farm in Scotland as their retreat. (This farm was the subject of Paul's "Fixing a Hole.") They traveled together (she accompanied him on the Beatles' famous trip to India in '68), she hung out with his band mates (when model Pattie Boyd married George Harrison in Surrey on January 21, 1966, Jane and Paul both attended, Paul as one of two "best men"), and she even sang in the chorus of "All

You Need Is Love." But would they marry? Jane addressed the topic in an interview: "I am not Paul's wife—but yes, we are going to get married. We won't be married for a while yet, but when it happens we've got a family planned. First we want a boy and then—come what may.... I shan't give up my career unless it interferes with our being together...I love Paul. I love him deeply, and he feels the same. I don't think either of us has looked at anyone else since we first met.... I want to get married probably this year and have lots and lots of babies. I certainly would be surprised indeed if I married anyone but Paul." On Christmas Day in '67 Paul finally announced their engagement, presenting her with a diamond and emerald ring. However, he evidently continued the wandering ways he was known for, and seven months later, after she allegedly caught him in bed with an Apple employee, Jane announced that the engagement was off. He married Linda Eastman in '69. Jane married artist Gerald Scarfe (he did the animations for '82's *Pink Floyd The Wall*), and today they have three children: Kate, Alexander, and Rory.

BONUS SWINGABILITY: Her exotic birthplace—the swingin'est, London, England ... everyone in Jane's immediate family has had successful careers: her father as a doctor, her mother as a music professor, her younger sister as an actress (and now a teacher), and her brother as a pop star and record producer. (He was the Peter in Peter and Gordon, the guys who sang "Lady Godiva." Paul wrote "A World Without Love," a top-ten hit for Peter and Gordon in '64) ... she made her stage debut at age 12 as Alice in *Alice in Wonderland*, and when she was 14 she played Wendy in *Peter Pan*, making her at the time the youngest actress to play the role on the London stage ... today Jane is president of the National Autistic Society and vice-president of the Child Accident Prevention Trust ... Jane has her own official Web site— http://www.jane-asher.co.uk/.

A DATE WITH JANE	
April 5, 1946	Jane Asher is born
April 18, 1963	Jane meets Paul after a Beatles' concert at London's Royal Albert Hall
January 18, 1964	For the first time a Beatles' song ("I Want to Hold Your Hand") appears on the *Billboard* music charts
August 24, 1966	*Alfie* is released
December 25, 1967	Paul announces his engagement to Jane
July 20, 1968	Jane announces that the engagement is off
March 12, 1969	Paul marries Linda

invasion

JULIE CHRISTIE

and intelligence, is to see the incarnation of the '60s mod ideal. "She is marvelous, absolutely adorable, enchanting, sexy, alive, vibrant, astute, clever and knowledgeable," praised Laurence Harvey, her *Darling* co-star. As a 20-year-old she first got noticed as the title character in the British TV sci-fi drama *A Is for Andromeda*. She then appeared in several minor films, making a strong impression in John Schlesinger's *Billy Liar* ('63). *Darling* ('65) catapulted her to fame. Her character, Diana Scott, was described in the movie as someone who thinks sexual fidelity means "not having more than one man in bed at the same time." Julie's portrayal brought her an Oscar as Best Actress—surprising because she was still considered to be a newcomer on the scene. Rocketing her stardom to even greater heights, later that same year came the much-coveted role of the luminous Lara in David Lean's much-loved *Doctor Zhivago*.

Truffaut's fascinating *Fahrenheit 451* ('66), Schlesinger's underrated *Far from the Madding Crowd* ('67), and Richard Lester's masterful *Petulia* ('68) set her up for the triumphs that would come in the '70s. She got a second Oscar nomination for *McCabe and Mrs. Miller* ('72), while *Don't Look Now* ('73), *Shampoo* ('75), and *Heaven Can Wait* ('78) confirmed her stature as one of the most beautiful and appealing actresses in the world. She's worked continuously ever since, often in films that focus on political issues. The most popular of her recent efforts are *Dragonheart* and *Hamlet* (both in '96) and *Afterglow* ('97), which brought her another Oscar nomination and reaffirmed her place among the world's cinematic treasures.

HER '60s LOOK: In the '60s she was a sad-eyed, refined beauty, but she was also totally believable when conveying raw sexuality and mental torment. At 5' 4" and 112 pounds in her prime, she looked natural and beautiful no matter what she wore, whether it was a peasant dress or a swingin' mini. However, she did lose the *Dr. No* role that eventually went to Ursula Andress, supposedly because the producers didn't think Julie was endowed enough for the bikini action. How did a '60s icon go clothes shopping back then? Here's what she told *Vogue*: "In London I go to all the boutiques at least once a week. I know everything they have."

SWINGIN' '60s CREDENTIALS: The trendsetting star of several significant '60s movies, Julie Christie, "the most poetic of actresses," according to Al Pacino, is lionized today as one of the great symbols of the Swingin' '60s.

WORKIN' IT: Does any actress represent the '60s as well as lovely Julie Christie? So perfectly does *Darling* capture the decade's zeitgeist, watching that landmark film is like watching a documentary that explains what the Swingin' '60s were all about. And to see 24-year-old Julie Christie at her best, all youthful beauty and style

BEHIND THE SCENES: Julie's tried to keep her private life away from prying eyes: "I'm not a myth or a legend," she once said, "just somebody who works in films. I don't do anything in public. I try to live a private life when I'm not working." Unfortunately, when you're that beautiful and that famous, you *will* get noticed, so here's the skinny: For the first half of the '60s she had a steady boyfriend, an artist named Don Bessert, whom she met (the story goes) when he was working as a part-time mailman and delivered her a letter.

the british

Once fame came knocking mid-decade, here's how she spent her free time, according to a '65 interview she did with *Cosmo*: "I love modern jazz-pop music—and I love dancing so I go to clubs like the Ad Lib and the Flamingo, but most of the time I muck around with my friends." Among those she mucked around with later in the '60s were some of the decade's most eligible bachelors, including Omar Sharif, Terence Stamp, and Warren Beatty, all of whom were co-stars. Sharif, of course, was the Doctor in *Zhivago*. When she was dating Terence Stamp, his roommate was Michael Caine. "It was like being with two blond gods of London," she told *Premiere* in '98. "They were taller than anyone else, they were blonder than anyone else, they had such a lot of confidence, they just sort of shone." She and Stamp were in *Far From the Madding Crowd* ('67) together. Beatty, whom she met in the summer of '67, was her co-star in *McCabe and Mrs. Miller, Shampoo*, and *Heaven Can Wait*. Later she was linked romantically to techno-musician Brian Eno. More recently she's reportedly been living with journalist Duncan Campbell on a Welsh farm. "I'd rather talk to my ducks than some of the freaks I met in Hollywood," she once said. And still she's never married; "men don't want any responsibility," she commented, "and neither do I."

Head unwittingly let her slip by and Oscar fashions never looked back ... in '65, Julie remarked to *Cosmopolitan* magazine (while on the set of *Doctor Zhivago*): "I hate all this work. I resent it immensely because it takes me away from London and Don. I get so furious when work mucks up my life" ... as further proof that the British had truly invaded, two of the other Best Actress nominees in '66 were also British (Samantha Eggar, *The Collector*, and Julie Andrews, *The Sound of Music*), as were two of the five Best Actor nominees, and half of the ten Best Supporting Actor/Actress nominees.

BONUS SWINGABILITY: Her nickname as a child—"Bugs" ... her exotic birthplace—Assam, India, where she grew up on her father's tea plantation ... the '66 Academy Awards ceremony was the first one broadcast in color. That night Julie made a stunning appearance on the show: she wore a gold mini from Carnaby Street, even though minis had been officially banned by the academy. Show costumer Edith

A DATE WITH JULIE

April 14, 1941	Julie Christie is born
August 3, 1965	*Darling* is released
December 22, 1965	*Doctor Zhivago* premieres in New York
April 16, 1966	Julie wins the Best Actress Oscar (*Darling*)
April 29, 1966	Julie makes the cover of *Life* magazine
September 16, 1966	*Fahrenheit 451* is released in the U.K.
October 18, 1967	*Far from the Madding Crowd* is released

invasion

VANESSA REDGRAVE

SWINGIN' '60s CREDENTIALS: This dignified, complex, and controversial British actress didn't usually make movies, she made *films*, bringing her famous family heritage to key productions in the second half of the decade and establishing herself as one of modern cinema's foremost actresses.

WORKIN' IT: Vanessa Redgrave was never a superstar, but she has always been a highly respected talent, "the greatest actress of our time," according to Tennessee Williams. Dignified and elegant, she performed in dramas, romances, even musicals, and she handled them all skillfully. Born in '37 into a family of actors, she has been surrounded by prominent performers all her life. Her sterling theatrical relations include her father, actor Sir Michael Redgrave; her mother, actress Rachel Kempson; younger sis and fellow Oscar-nominee Lynn Redgrave; her brother, actor Corin Redgrave; her husband, director Tony Richardson; her daughters, both actresses, Natasha and Joely; and her niece, actress Jemma Richardson. A drama and ballet student in the '50s, Vanessa was an actress with the Royal Shakespeare Company in the early '60s. She made a sensational screen splash in '66 with three memorable films: the cult classic *Morgan!* (her first Oscar nomination), the Oscar-dominator *A Man for All Seasons*, in the role of Anne Boleyn, and in Michelangelo Antonioni's influential *Blowup* as the mysterious Londoner. Continuing a habit of starring in movies set in different eras, a year later she starred as a free-thinking 1920s dancer in *Isadora* (her second Oscar nomination),

and in '68 she sang, danced, and tolerated scenery-chewer Richard Harris in the majestic medieval musical *Camelot*.

Her subsequent career has been filled with interesting, challenging, sometimes eccentric projects, among them *Mary, Queen of Scots* in '71 (her third Oscar nomination), *Murder on the Orient Express* in '74, *Julia* in '77 (her first Oscar), *Agatha* and *Yanks* in '79, *The Bostonians* in '84 (another Oscar nomination), *Howard's End* in '92 (yet one more Oscar nomination), *A Month by the Lake* in '95, *Mission: Impossible* in '96, *Mrs. Dalloway* in '97, *Deep Impact* in '98, and *The Cradle Will Rock* in '99, with lots of prominent stage work filling the gaps between her films.

Inseparable from Vanessa's working career are her politics. She traveled to Cuba in '62 and became sympathetic to Castro's revolution. In '67 she organized a full-page ad in *The Times* of London to protest America's continued bombing of North Vietnam, in '73 she joined the Socialist Labor League, and in '74 she gave lectures in Hollywood on Marxism to raise funds for a Marxist school in Britain. When she won the Oscar in '77, she made a defiant, controversial political speech: "My dear colleagues, I thank you very, very much for this tribute to my work. I think that Jane Fonda and I have done the best work of our lives, and I salute you and I pay tribute to you, and I think you should be very proud that in the last few weeks you have stood firm and you have refused to be intimidated by the threats of a small bunch of Zionist hoodlums whose behavior is an insult to the stature of Jews all over the world and to their great and heroic record of struggle against fascism and oppression. And I pledge to you that I will continue to fight against anti-Semitism and fascism. Thank you." Screenwriter Paddy Chayefsky, the next speaker at the podium, immediately chastised her before making his Oscar presentation. Later Vanessa claimed she was the target of protests by Jewish groups after she appeared in a TV movie about concentration camps, *Playing for Time*, a role that brought her an Emmy in '81. She's supported the Worker's Revolutionary Party and has demonstrated against the bomb. Less well known is that she has established a trust for disadvantaged children and built a nursery school in one of London's poorest neighborhoods. Throughout her career she's held her head high, even though she has been burned in effigy, received bomb threats, and been accused of being a terrorist. She discussed her busy life and controversial stances in the poignant, articulate *Vanessa Redgrave: An Autobiography* in '94. If the '60s were about revolution and fighting for important causes, then Vanessa Redgrave may be the most archetypal '60s actress of all.

HER '60s LOOK: Her elegant facial features have always enabled her to display a regal dignity and a sharp intelligence. Slender and mobile, she had graceful, queenly moves in *Camelot*, and though she wasn't voluptuous, she still had a lithe sexual appeal in *Blowup*.

BEHIND THE SCENES: From '62 to '67 Vanessa was married to Tony Richardson, the Oscar-winning director of *Tom Jones* ('63) and the father of her two daughters. Richardson directed Vanessa in three movies: *The Sailor from Gibraltor* and *Red and Blue* (both in '67) and *The Charge of the Light Brigade* ('68). In the late-'60s and early-'70s she had a relationship and a son with actor Franco

Nero, her *Camelot* co-star. Rumors have also put her alongside Warren Beatty and even Cuban cigar-chomper Fidel Castro. Her private life, like her career choices, has sometimes generated controversy: In '97 she said she was targeted by the fascist group Combat 18 because of her rumored relationship with an African-American actor.

BONUS SWINGABILITY: Her exotic birthplace—the swingin'est, London, England … sister Lynn got an Oscar nomination for *Georgy Girl* ('66). She and Vanessa were in a TV remake of *Whatever Happened to Baby Jane?* in '91 … in addition to being directed by Vanessa's husband, Tony Richardson, *The Charge of the Light Brigade* in '68 featured Vanessa, brother Corin, mother Rachel, and daughter Joely … director Tony Richardson once said about her: "Vanessa Redgrave is controversial; her enemies hate her, and her friends dislike her."

A DATE WITH VANESSA	
June 5, 1928	Tony Richardson is born
January 30, 1937	Vanessa Redgrave is born
November 23, 1941	Franco Nero is born
March 8, 1943	Lynn Redgrave is born
May 11, 1963	Vanessa gives birth to Natasha Richardson
January 9, 1965	Vanessa gives birth to Joely Richardson
December 12, 1966	*A Man for All Seasons* is released
December 18, 1966	*Blowup* is released
October 25, 1967	*Camelot* is released

invasion

ELIZABETH TAYLOR

SWINGIN' '60s CREDENTIALS: This violet-eyed, awards-laden dramatic actress was elevated to royal status in the '60s with important Oscar-winning films and a passionate diamond-studded romance with actor Richard Burton.

WORKIN' IT: Elizabeth Taylor couldn't cough in the '60s without the international papers printing a picture or writing a story. She was to the decade what Lady Di was to the '90s: photogenic royalty, the ultimate celebrity. Her long film career started with twenty-nine films in the '40s and '50s, beginning when she was 9 years old in the B-movie *There's One Born Every Minute* ('42). At 12 she made *National Velvet* ('44), her breakthrough to stardom. Quickly maturing, at 15 she was dubbed "the most beautiful woman in America" by Hedda Hopper, and a few years later she was co-starring in *Giant* ('56) alongside the doomed James Dean. Then came a remarkable streak in which she was nominated for a Best Actress Oscar every

year for the next four years, thanks to a series of powerful dramas and equally powerful performances: *Raintree County* ('57), *Cat on a Hot Tin Roof* ('58), *Suddenly, Last Summer* ('59), and the movie that brought her the first of two Oscars, *Butterfield 8* ('60). She had made the leap to global fame; *Cleopatra* would take her to global legend. In '63 *Cleopatra* was by far the most expensive movie ever made. It was also the most publicized film to date. Unfortunately, by costing the most, being delayed the most, and raising expectations the most, *Cleopatra* also flopped the most, collapsing under the sheer weight of the hype and bloated production. Elizabeth went on to *The Sandpiper* ('65), won a second Oscar for the masterful *Who's Afraid of Virginia Woolf?* ('66), and teamed again with Richard Burton in *Taming of the Shrew* ('67). During the decade she also made playful guest appearances on TV (*The Sammy Davis, Jr. Show* in '66, *Here's Lucy* in '68), fun little exercises she would continue into the '90s.

Her post-'60s films commanded attention but not respect from audiences or critics, and she ended up doing a lot of TV as her film roles dwindled. With fewer movie appearances, her most glamorous roles in the '80s and '90s came in commercials for her perfumes, Passion and White Diamonds. She also made TV history by appearing on four network shows on one night in '96, each show continuing a story line about her lost gems. Nothing in recent years—not divorces or frail health or a shorn skull—has diminished her stature as a Hollywood goddess and one of the last links to Hollywood's Golden Age. When the American Film Institute released its distinguished list of the "100 Greatest American Movies" in '99, she had starred in two of them (A *Place in the Sun* and *Giant*). When AFI announced the "50 Greatest Screen Legends" in June '99, Liz was #7 among the actresses, sandwiched between Marilyn and Judy Garland. At the turn of the millennium, she became Dame Elizabeth Taylor, a prestigious British title bestowed by one Queen Elizabeth to another.

HER '60s LOOK: "I hate to see myself on the screen," she once said. The world begged to differ. Just 5' 4" (some sources say only 5' 1"), but with a voluptuous figure, a flawless face, and legendary violet eyes, La Liz was acclaimed as the world's greatest beauty at the start of the '60s. And perhaps the sexiest, too. According to Richard Burton—and he oughta know—"her breasts would topple empires before they withered." Courageously she let herself be shown as an alcohol-ravaged harpie for *Virginia Woolf* in '66, which was both great acting and a sad foreshadowing of what the '70s and '80s held in store when her weight problems overtook weight solutions.

BEHIND THE SCENES: Rock Hudson once said about her, "Elizabeth Taylor likes men around her...with men around, she can have the illusion that it's romantic, but without the hassles." But hassles there have been. In the '60s she was the center-third of the legendary love triangle that led to her divorce from singer Eddie Fisher and her front-page marriage to the talented, tormented Welsh actor Richard Burton. But her love story began a decade before. Eighteen years old in 1950, she wore the studio's wedding gown when she married her first husband, hotel heir Nicky Hilton, a bad boy of international repute. On their *Queen Mary* honeymoon he abandoned her to go drinking and gambling, and they separated within a few months. Her next marriage was to English actor Michael Wilding in '52—he was 39, she was 20. Two kids later, they divorced in '56. A day after the divorce, Liz married swaggering producer Mike Todd, with Todd's best friend Eddie Fisher and his wife Debbie Reynolds in the wedding party. With Todd, Liz had a daughter named Liza, and it looked like she had her true love at last, until tragedy struck. Todd's plane *The Lucky Liz* crashed in New Mexico and killed him, in '58. Six months later she took up with Fisher, who left wife Debbie in what was Hollywood's biggest scandal of the '50s. On the same day Eddie and Debbie were divorced in '59, Eddie and Liz got married. While on their honeymoon in Europe she got a telegram inviting her to star in *Cleopatra*. It was during the filming of *Cleo* that she and the already-married Burton began what she called *le scandale*. The director, Joseph Mankiewicz, said that their love scenes in the movie were so intense he felt like a stranger on his own set. Off the set, Liz and Dick quickly paired up, even though her husband Eddie was very much around. Astonishingly, as the affair gained momentum, the Vatican published a statement denouncing her "erotic vagrancy." Liz herself said "it was probably the most chaotic time of my life…it was fun and it was dark—oceans of tears, but there were some good times, too." And some good ice: she owned some of the world's grandest gems, thanks to Burton's profligate generosity. When they married in '64, she pronounced "this marriage will last forever"; however, drinking, brawling, and affairs led to several separations and finally a divorce in '74. Burton won her back a year later, they married in Botswana, and divorced for good in '76. Her last two marriages were a six-year union with politician John Warner, who called her "my little heifer," and then for four-plus years to construction worker Larry Fortensky, whom she met in group therapy at the Betty Ford Clinic. In addition to her seven husbands, she's alleged to have had relationships with Howard Hughes, Frank Sinatra, Peter Lawford, Victor Mature, George Hamilton, director Stanley Donen, Rod Steiger, and possibly a Kennedy. Of her many men, she once said, "What do you expect me to do? Sleep alone?"

BONUS SWINGABILITY: Her exotic birthplace—the swingin'est, London, England … her father was an art dealer, her mother a Broadway actress … when she was hired by MGM as a child, the

studio arranged for everything throughout her adolescence, including her first "boyfriend"—football hero Glenn Davis … Liz wore a $10,000 Halston gown to the '72 Oscars, at the time the most expensive dress ever worn to that event … addicted at different times to pills and alcohol, she was the first celebrity to acknowledge a stay in the Betty Ford Clinic … she's bounced back from repeated illnesses and injuries throughout her life–here's a partial list: back injury when she fell off a horse in '44, emergency tracheotomy in '61, rehab at Betty Ford Clinic in '83 and '88, respiratory problems in '90, a hip replacement and two more hip surgeries since '95, an irregular heartbeat in '96, and something like three-dozen surgeries overall … to her credit she was an early and major AIDS fundraiser, efforts that brought her the Jean Hersholt Humanitarian

Award in '93 … if you wrote out her full name, including her middle name and all her husbands, it would be Elizabeth Rosemond Taylor Hilton Wilding Todd Fisher Burton Burton Warner Fortensky. "I've been through it all," she once said, "I'm Mother Courage."

A DATE WITH ELIZABETH	
November 10, 1925	Richard Burton is born
February 27, 1932	Elizabeth Taylor is born
December 14, 1944	*National Velvet* is released
April 17, 1961	Liz wins the Best Actress Oscar (*Butterfield 8*)
June 12, 1963	*Cleopatra* is released
March 15, 1964	Liz marries Richard Burton
April 10, 1967	Liz wins the Best Actress Oscar (*Virginia Woolf*)
August 1, 1976	Liz remarries Richard Burton
August 5, 1984	Richard Burton dies
March 29, 1993	Liz is given the Jean Hersholt Humanitarian Award at the Oscars
February 26, 1996	Liz plays "Herself" on four network TV shows

THE MOVIE STARS: LES INTERNATIONALES

In the '50s and '60s, the collapse of the traditional Hollywood studio system and the new generation's increasing rejection of all things conservative invited an exciting new wave of foreign directors to American movie screens. Thus the great European *auteurs*—legendary filmmakers like Fellini, de Sica, Truffaut, Bergman, and Vadim—swept into theatres. Along with these men came their preferred actresses—Vadim's Brigitte Bardot, de Sica's Sophia Loren, Bergman's Bibi Andersson, *et al*. The stories they told on film were often more artistic—and more daring—than what Hollywood was churning out, and the women were often more sensual—and less dressed—than their American counterparts. With the new popularity came new respect: for the first and only time, an actress in a foreign-language film (Sophia Loren in *Two Women*, '62) won the Oscar as Best Actress. Following their precedent, Hollywood's own *auteurs* would later thrust their own favorite actresses forward—Warren Beatty and Julie Christie, Woody Allen and Diane Keaton, Mel Brooks and Madeline Kahn, John Cassevetes and Gena Rowlands, Blake Edwards and Julie Andrews. In the same way the decade impacted TV and music, the '60s was the compass pointing the way for future cinematic achievement.

BRIGITTE BARDOT

SWINGIN' '60s CREDENTIALS: The very definition of an erotic French sex kitten, and perhaps the most famous French actress ever, this archetypal nymphet throbbed her way through two foreign films a year during the '60s, released breathy record albums, and generated international news with her independent lifestyle and uninhibited sexuality.

WORKIN' IT: Like Marilyn and Cher and Aphrodite, Brigitte Bardot is known throughout the world by just a single name. At age 18 a brunette Bardot became famous when she strutted in front of photographers at the '53 Cannes Film Festival. At 22 she became the very symbol of sexual temptation when the world saw her nude and lying on her stomach in the first thirty seconds of *And God Created Woman* ('56). That shot, the movie's later undressing scenes, and the erotic five minutes of dancing at the climax thrust Bardot into two decades of sexy films and three decades of scandalous news stories. Ironically, her own country didn't immediately accept her—the French censors branded *And God Created Woman* as being immoral and demanded edits before it could be shown. The movie got terrible reviews in France and lost money. Internationally, however, her career spurted to new heights. In '57 English and American reviewers praised *And God Created Woman*, and for months audiences flocked to see it. "Since the Statue of Liberty," wrote *Life*, "no French girl has ever shone quite as much light on the United States." To American audiences her near-mythic status as the embodiment of steamy sexual desire eventually would be attributable more to her liberated lifestyle than to her movies—her real talent has always been for attracting men, photographers, and headlines. Even so, for the next few years Bardot was responsible

for bringing new attention to the French cinema, and if not a great actress, she was always riveting, able to seduce audiences with both untrammeled sexuality and an appealing naiveté.

Her '60s movies included *The Truth* in '60 (the movie she thinks represents her best work), *A Very Private Affair* in '61 (based on experiences from her own life), *Contempt* in '63 (one of her most versatile performances, directed by Jean-Luc Godard), *Dear Brigitte* in '65 (the English-language Jimmy Stewart comedy in which she had a single scene at the end), *Viva Maria!* in '65 (directed by Louis Malle), *Masculine-Feminine* in '66 (more great Godard), *Tales of Mystery and Imagination* in '68 (three directors created a Poe anthology), and *Shalako* in '68 (a Sean Connery western). Meanwhile, from '60 to '68 she released five French record albums and dozens of singles. In '73 she retired from the movies, though she has continued to speak in public and appear in documentaries to promote animal rights (a major animal-rights advocate, she fills her home with pets). She's also written two volumes of memoirs: the first, *Initiales BB* in '96, takes her from birth to her last movie, and the second, *Le Carre de Pluton* in '99, focuses on her campaigns for animal rights and her efforts to "erase the Bardot legend." In '84 she was officially recognized as a French institution with the prestigious *Legion d'honneur award*. For many people, she will always be the truest definition of the twentieth-century woman. Simply, and eternally, Bardot.

HER '60s LOOK: A beauty even as a young girl, at 15 Bardot worked as a model and appeared on the cover of *Elle* in May '49. Ex-husband Vadim wrote about her at that ripe age: "When I met Brigitte for the first time I was immediately struck by her posture, her bearing and her curved waist. She held her head like a queen." Naturally, in the '60s she appeared in *Playboy* (June '64, April '69), the magazine that never met a sex symbol it didn't like. Three decades later, *Playboy* ranked her at #4, between Raquel Welch and Cindy Crawford, on its list of the "100 Sexiest Stars of the Century." Other *fin-de-siècle* kudos came from *Time* magazine, which described her as "the princess of pout, the countess of come hither" while naming her one of the twentieth century's twenty most beautiful stars. Little wonder that Bardot could draw such raves. The wild honey-colored hair, the pouty lips, the big eyes, the casualness of her sexuality—*enchanté*! And while she was adept at costumed roles, her best outfit was usually just a towel or a sheet, a look enhanced by her smooth tan (like Liz Taylor she advanced the concept of tanning to heights hitherto unexplored). With 35-23-35 measurements, the *courbes d'triomphe* on her 5' 7" frame were legendary. Brigitte was fully aware of their appeal. Said actor Stephen Boyd, her co-star in *The Night Heaven Fell*: "All I can say is that when I'm trying to play serious love scenes with her, she's postioning her bottom for the best-angle shots."

BEHIND THE SCENES: She's had four marriages: director Roger Vadim, '52–'57 (he later married Jane Fonda); actor Jacques Charrier, '59–'62 (with whom she had a son, Nicholas); playboy Gunter Sachs, '66–'69; and politician Bernard d'Ormale in '92. When she wasn't allowed to marry older guy Roger Vadim at 15, she tried to asphyxiate herself; she was allowed to marry him at 18. Vadim is the one who liberated her on-screen image, told her to pout, and put her in tight jeans and bikinis. She made a total of nine films that he either wrote or directed. Vadim called her "the last of the sex symbols," but said she had "anguish, fears, and a talent for unhappiness that often took her to the edge of tragedy." It's believed that she attempted suicide at least four times, including a foiled attempt to slash her wrists on her 26th birthday. "I really wanted to die at certain periods in my life," she has said. "Death was like love, a romantic escape. I took pills because I didn't want to throw myself off my balcony and know people would photograph me lying dead below." Living in real life the kind of uninhibited roles she played on screeen, she had well-publicized relationships with many of the '60's most eligible men, a veritable all-star team of celebrities—Brando, Beatty, Jagger, Connery, Belmondo, and many more. The press stalked her capricious movements, the public watched in fascination, and the sexual revolution thumped on. On the subject of infidelity, Vadim wrote that "though she had a gift for infidelity, she always suffered if she had an affair with more than one man at a time," while Bardot herself said that "it is better to be unfaithful than to be faithful without wanting to be." Of her fondness for younger men as she's gotten older, she said, "I have always adored beautiful young men; just because I grow older my taste doesn't change, so if I can still have them, why not?"

BONUS SWINGABILITY: Her moniker—though her real name is Brigitte Bardot, some bios insist that she was born Camille Javal, which was her character's name in one of her biggest films, *Contempt* ... her nickname: "BB" ... her exotic birthplace—Paris, France ... before Bardot was a model she was a dancer-in-training from the age of 5, and at 13 she studied alongside future dance legend Leslie Caron ... a journalist asked her what was the best day of her life; her reply—"a night," a line Fellini later gave to Anita Ekberg in *La Dolce Vita* ... and whom does she admire most? "Sir Isaac Newton—he discovered that bodies attract each other" ... of her own life: "I believe I have certainly been more honest and frank than most people. I could have lived my life the way other people wanted me to. But I think we should live the way we want to and not worry about living the way we're told to" ... her foundation has its own French/English Web site for animal-rights info: www.fondationbrigittebardot.fr.

A DATE WITH BRIGITTE

January 26, 1928	Roger Vadim is born
September 28, 1934	Brigitte Bardot is born
December 20, 1952	Brigitte marries Roger Vadim
November 28, 1956	*And God Created Woman* is released in France
December 6, 1957	Brigitte divorces Roger Vadim
June 18, 1959	Brigitte marries Jacques Charrier
November 20, 1962	Brigitte divorces Jacques Charrier
December 20, 1963	*Contempt* is released in France
December 22, 1965	*Viva Maria!* is released in France
March 22, 1966	*Masculine-Feminine* is released in France
July 14, 1966	Brigitte marries Gunter Sachs
October 1, 1969	Brigitte divorces Gunter Sachs

CAPUCINE

SWINGIN' '60s CREDENTIALS: This exotic, regal French beauty rose from the modeling ranks to star with some of Hollywood's top leading men in the first half of the '60s before meeting a sad end.

WORKIN' IT: As an actress, Capucine was usually someone to watch rather than hear, and the film industry usually asked her to look her parts rather than act them. Using a stage name taken from the French word for a nasturtium, Capucine (pronounced CAP-oo-seen) made her film debut when she was only 16 in the French flick *Rendezvous de Juillet* ('49). At 24 she was a fashion model in Paris for Givenchy, and in '57 she was spotted by a Hollywood director, who brought her west. She made her Hollywood debut in the Oscar-winning biopic about composer Franz Lizst, *Song Without End* ('60). Her role as a princess set a royal precedent that would repeat several times in her career. She played Princess Dominique in *The Honey Pot* in '67, and Lady Litton in two *Pink Panther* sequels, *Trail of* in '82 and *Curse of* in '83. Among her '60s highlights were the John Wayne western *North to Alaska* in '60, the William Holden African melodrama *The Lion* in '62, the Laurence Harvey/Jane Fonda bordello curiosity

Walk on the Wild Side in '62 (in which Capucine was romantically pursued by Barbara Stanwyck), the Peter Sellers comedy *The Pink Panther* in '63 and the Woody Allen-scripted *What's New, Pussycat?* in '65.

Despite this early promise, her career never really took off in Hollywood, and by the late '60s she was making foreign-language films almost exclu-

sively and with less frequency. Of her later work, only Fellini's *Satyricon* in '69, the two Sellers-less *Pink Panther* sequels in the early '80s, and the *Sins* TV mini-series with Joan Collins in '86 will stand out for most Americans. Capucine moved to Switzerland in '62, and that's where she died, broke and chronically depressed, throwing herself out of an eighth-floor window in Lausanne, Switzerland, in 1990.

HER '60s LOOK: According to *Cosmo* editor Helen Gurley Brown, Capucine "had a face that was caressed by angels, created by the gods." Her high cheekbones, inviting oval eyes, and full lips made her almost like an early, dark-haired version of Faye Dunaway. Her height was 5' 7" and her build was slender, hence the early modeling career and the roles as a royal sophisticate.

BEHIND THE SCENES: Much about Capucine's life remains a mystery. One story has her being married for just seven months while in her late teens. Whatever happened, she never married again. In the early '60s she had a passionate two-year affair with Hollywood legend William Holden, who was a dozen years her senior. At the time Holden had been married for two decades to actress Brenda Marshall. Later cryptic quotes from Capucine—"I used to think I needed a man to define myself; no more"—led to all kinds of speculations about her private life, including one persistent rumor that she was a transsexual. The truth wasn't quite that extreme—Capucine's lifestyle was confirmed in Boze Hadleigh's '94 book *Hollywood Lesbians*.

BONUS SWINGABILITY: She used a fake moniker—her real name was Germain Lefebvre ... the nasturtiam, *Tropaeolum majus*, is an edible plant found on mountain slopes and valleys in Peru and Ecuador. It's thought to be an anaphrodisiac, thus decreasing the sex drive ... Capucine is also the name of a creamy liqueur ... her exotic birthplace—Toulon, France ... in '52 she worked for two weeks doing fashion shows on board a French cruise ship; her cabinmate was 17-year-old Brigitte Bardot, who was working on the ship as a dancer ... in his will, William Holden left Capucine $50,000.

 A DATE WITH CAPUCINE

April 17, 1918	William Holden is born
January 6, 1933	Capucine is born
November 7, 1960	*North to Alaska* is released
February 21, 1962	*Walk on the Wild Side* is released
March 20, 1964	*The Pink Panther* is released
June 22, 1965	*What's New, Pussycat?* is released
March 17, 1990	Capucine commits suicide

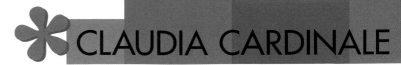

SWINGIN' '60s CREDENTIALS: The Italian version of Brigitte Bardot, this sexy pantheress gained international stardom in two-dozen '60s movies including *8½*, *The Pink Panther*, and *Once Upon a Time in the West*.

WORKIN' IT: While she's not a household name in most American homes, Claudia Cardinale has enjoyed a forty-year career that includes over ninety films with some of the world's greatest directors, including Luchino Visconti, Abel Gance, Federico Fellini, Philippe de Broca, and Sergio Leone. Unfortunately, most American moviegoers probably couldn't pronounce most of the titles of her movies. When she was voted the Most Beautiful Girl in Tunisia in '57, she won a trip to the Venice Film Festival, and acting became her life. She made ten Italian movies in the late '50s, then ten more from '59–'60.

Her American breakthrough came with her role as the fantasy girl in Fellini's *8½* in '63, with Visconti's *The Leopard* that same year and Blake Edwards' *The Pink Panther* in '64 establishing her rep as a rising talent with international appeal. To Americans she might've been too similar to other well-tanned European hourglasses such as Gina Lollabrigida and Sophia Loren to distinguish herself, but to international audiences she was one of the most popular actresses in the world, as verified by the awards she won in the first half of the decade: Italy's David di Donatello Award in '62, the Grolla d'Oro in '64, the European Prix Orange for popularity in '64, the Victorie of French Cinema as the Best Foreign Actress in '64 and '65, and the Nastro d'Argento in '65. In the second half of the decade she made some marvelous English-language films—two rugged adventures, *Lost Command* and *The Professionals* in '66, the Tony Curtis comedy *Don't Make Waves* in '67, and Leone's epic western *Once Upon a Time in the West* in '69—that cemented her image stateside as a stunning star with a smoldering beauty. Dozens of sultry Italian flix followed in later decades, punctuated by *Escape to Athena* ('79), Werner Herzog's artsy *Fitzcarraldo* ('82), and the feeble *Son of the Pink Panther* ('93). None of her post-'60s films was classic by itself, but taken together with her '60s work they add up to an impressive *oeuvre*, and in '99 Italy presented her with its Rudolph Valentino Lifetime Achievement Award.

HER '60s LOOK: Almost 5'7" tall, and with a 37-22-36 figure (according to '63's *Movie Life Yearbook*), Claudia had the classic contours of other magnificent Mediterraneans like Loren and Lollobrigida. For elegant roles she would wear her long hair up (as in *8½*, where she was a sultry vision in white), for some of her movies her hair was cut short, and then for playful or rugged movies she would let it wrangle and tangle so it looked like she'd just rolled out of bed. No matter what movie she was in, Claudia's dark sultry sexiness translated into any language. So universal was her appeal that

since '58 she's graced almost *900* magazine covers around the world. Over half of those covers appeared in the '60s.

BEHIND THE SCENES: At 19 Claudia had a son, Patrick, but because the child was the product of a rape, the father was never named. For years Claudia presented Patrick as her younger brother. Early in her career she was guided by producer Franco Cristaldi, who was fifteen years her senior. Cristaldi reshaped Claudia's image and took her from a novice actress to a major international sex symbol. They married in '66, divorced in '75, and he died in '92. After the divorce she took up with, but didn't marry, Italian film director Pasquale Squitieri, and had a daughter, Claudia, with him in '79.

BONUS SWINGABILITY: She uses a fake moniker—her real name is Claude Josephine Rose Cardin ... her exotic birthplace—Tunis, Tunisia ... in '66 she appeared in the first edition of Bob Dylan's classic *Blonde on Blonde* record album... Claudia made waves in the '60s when she wore a miniskirt for a meeting with the Pope! Now THAT'S swingin'!

A DATE WITH CLAUDIA

April 15, 1939	Claudia Cardinale is born
June 25, 1963	*8½* is released
March 20, 1964	*The Pink Panther* is released
July 8, 1966	Claudia makes the cover of *Life* magazine
November 2, 1966	*The Professionals* is released
May 28, 1969	*Once Upon a Time in the West* is released

CATHERINE DENEUVE

Roger Vadim. By '64 she was an international star when her offbeat *The Umbrellas of Cherbourg* became the triumphant hit of the Cannes Film Festival. And by now she's been in over ninety films, a remarkable cinematic output that has made her one of France's most prestigious and prominent global exports.

Like Grace Kelly's in the '50s, her cinematic rep has usually been that of an elegant ice queen, beneath whose beautiful, cold exterior lurks a passionate sexuality. Busy all through the '60s (she made five movies in '65 alone), she explored a range of themes, from the terror of Roman Polanski's *Repulsion* ('65) to the fascinating mystery of Luis Bunuel's *Belle de Jour* ('67) to the cheery romance of the *Umbrellas* sequel, *The Young Girls of Rochefort* ('68). Though an entertaining musical in which her singing was dubbed, *The Young Girls of Rochefort* was anything but lightweight, and Catherine brought to it the same depth audiences found in her more serious films. She went on to star in over fifty more films, few of them Hollywood productions. The most notable were Bunuel's serene *Tristana* ('70), the wild *A Slightly Pregnant Man* with boyfriend Marcello Mastroianni ('73), the Burt Reynolds crime-stoppin' *Hustle* ('75), Truffaut's interesting *The Last Metro* ('80), the David Bowie blood-luster *The Hunger* ('83), the wonderful *Indochine* ('92, bringing her an Oscar nomination), and *Les Voleurs* ('96, showing her fifty-something body in a discreet nude scene).

While she was averaging two movies a year during the '70s, she also did popular perfume commercials for Chanel, and a decade later she launched her own perfume, Deneuve. But Catherine Deneuve's true impact has always been as more than just an actress or a celebrity. Burt Reynolds testified as much in his autobiography: "Catherine took my breath away.…Women and men were fascinated by Catherine. Without carrying a banner, she lived very independently. She'd had two children without marrying, long before that sort of thing was done. She had a career. She set styles and conducted herself with true elegance and class."

SWINGIN' '60s CREDENTIALS: A classic French beauty with the bearing of a queen, she starred in over two dozen films in the '60s, including Roman Polanski's macabre *Repulsion* and Luis Bunuel's enigmatic *Belle de Jour*.

WORKIN' IT: Unlike many other beautiful actresses, Catherine Deneuve didn't play gumsmackers in cheesy flix that exploited her incredible looks for audience attention. She was usually in serious French films with artistic intentions, which means the mass American audience hasn't appreciated her in the same way international audiences have. By the time she was 17, Catherine was a leading lady in French films, thanks to her early-'60s work with

HER '60s LOOK: Only one other '60s actress can claim what Catherine can: in '85 her image was chosen to succeed Brigitte Bardot's as "Marianne," the very symbol of the French Republic. So exquisite are Catherine's looks, it's possible that she's been underrated by most movie-goers, who are usually awed by her beauty. In her prime (which was like, what, forty years long?), she had one of the world's most exquisite faces, a face born to be photographed, a face often heralded by the '60s press as the most beautiful in the world. Wrote Reynolds: "There was nothing not to love about Catherine. She looked more spectacular in person than on film." Not just spectacular, but sexy: watch her in *Belle de Jour*, where she

changes from sheer night-gowns to adorable tennis whites to a "precocious schoolgirl" uniform—she is never less than ravishing (quite an accomplishment considering that in one scene she took a bullet in the face). No less an expert than legendary ladies' man Roger Vadim, the director whose relationship résumé includes Brigitte Bardot and Jane Fonda, wrote that when he first went to bed with her—she was only 17 at the time, he was 32— "her body was very white, rather fragile, and as delicate as the features on her face. I remember thinking I'd never seen such beautiful breasts." Paying attention was *Playboy*, which featured her in October '65 in a pictorial called "France's Deneuve Wave," with sexy photos by David Bailey. A quarter-century later, *Playboy* positioned her at #45, right behind a cinematic legend of another era, Mae West, on its '99 list of the "100 Sexiest Stars of the Century."

BEHIND THE SCENES: In the middle of the '60s Catherine married—and when the '60s were over she divorced—the decade's most famous fashion photographer, David Bailey, who was also closely allied with Jean Shrimpton. Catherine also took up with, but didn't marry, two of the decade's top celebs, director Roger Vadim (pre-Bailey) and actor Marcello Mastroianni (post-Bailey) and had love children by both. She was also linked romantically to Dean Martin, Omar Sharif, Roman Polanski, Michael Des Barres, and Burt Reynolds, though in his book Reynolds claims they didn't have an affair. Vadim was the one who kissed and told: "She was intelligent, she was capable of scathing humor…and she was very passionate under her rather cold exterior. Being both sensual and intellectual, she showed a great deal of imagination in what are discreetly called intimate moments."

BONUS SWINGABILITY: She uses a fake moniker—her real name is Catherine Dorléac. Deneuve is her mother's maiden name, which Catherine started using as a teen … her exotic birthplace—

Paris, France … her father is French actor Maurice Teynac, her sister was French actress Francoise Dorléac, who was killed in a car wreck soon after she starred with Catherine in *The Young Girls of Rochefort* in '68 … when she married David Bailey, Mick Jagger was the best man, and the bride wore black (a little Yves St. Laurent number) … she has said that she still goes out salsa dancing with her daughter … she told Liz Smith in '98 that she considers herself a "middle-aged gardener" and jokingly added, "that's all I want to do; I love my garden…. I don't want the *Legion d'Honneur*, though it's been offered; I would prefer the Order of Merit for Agriculture" … of herself she's said: "I don't try to charm. I have quite strong and straight relations with people" … from the *San Francisco Chronicle*, September '98: "When asked how she might like to be

remembered, Ms. Deneuve turns away from a photographer who is taking her portrait. Still seated, she throws her arms open and with a warm, engagingly mischievous smile, practically shouts, 'Like an aloof icon!'"

 A DATE WITH CATHERINE

September 28, 1924	Marcello Mastroianni is born
January 26, 1928	Roger Vadim is born
January 2, 1938	David Bailey is born
October 22, 1943	Catherine Deneuve is born
June 18, 1963	Catherine gives birth to son Christian Vadim
February 19, 1964	*The Umbrellas of Cherbourg* is released in France
May 28, 1972	Catherine gives birth to daughter Chiara Mastroianni

ANITA EKBERG

SWINGIN' '60s CREDENTIALS: An immensely endowed Swedish sexpot, Anita Ekberg decorated two movies a year during the '60s, including the Rat Packy *4 for Texas*.

WORKIN' IT: Even though she was never the star of her movies, Anita Ekberg had a huge impact on anyone who saw her or had to squeeze through a doorway alongside her. As a 19-year-old Miss Sweden in 1950, she competed in the Miss Universe pageant, which led to her first screen credit. In '53 she and a handful of other pageant winners were cast as scenery in *Abbott and Costello Go to Mars*. For Anita, another twenty movies followed in the '50s, including *Artists and Models* with Jerry and Dean in '55, the Duke's *Blood Alley* in '55, the film-noir classic *Screaming Mimi* in '58, and *The Man Inside*, also in '58.

The '60s got off to a great start with Fellini's *La Dolce Vita* in '60, the memorable movie that had her cavorting in a low-cut black dress and a shimmering Trevi Fountain. She was described in that movie as "the first woman on the first day of Creation…mother, sister, friend, angel, devil, home!" Other '60s films included *Boccaccio '70* in '62 (also featuring Sophia Loren); *4 for Texas* in '63 (Frank, Dino, and Ursula Andress were the other three); *The Alphabet Murders* and *Way…Way Out*, both in '66 (the latter introduced young Linda Harrison); *Woman Times Seven* in '67 (with Shirley MacLaine); and a small role in *If It's Tuesday, This Must Be Belgium* in '69. After the '60s she made a dozen more movies that took her through the '90s (including one more with Fellini, *Intervista* in '87).

Throughout a career that has lasted almost forty years, she did win one major acting award, a Golden Globe in '56 as the Most Promising Newcomer, but acting wasn't this actress's forte. "Anita Ekberg might not have been much of an actress," wrote Roger Ebert, "but she was the only person who could play herself."

HER '60s LOOK: With big curves and big blonde hair, she was more of a '50s goddess than a '60s mod, which explains why her helium-chested impact got lighter as the decade got later. Still, she always had remarkable physical assets—the hair like spun sugar, the pneumatic pecs—that assured her attention in any setting, in any costume, in any company. Applauded singer Ethel Merman: "Anita Ekberg is the thinking man's dunce cap—two of them." Naturally she made a considerable impact on *Playboy*, which in August '56 showed her posing nude for sculptor Sepy Dobronyi. She also made the November '61 issue and was later ranked #14, right behind the great Ann-Margret, on the magazine's January '99 list of the "100 Sexiest Stars of the Century."

BEHIND THE SCENES: As you'd guess of a statuesque Swedish beauty queen, she was pretty popular. She was married to two different actors, Anthony Steele from '56 to '59 and Rik Van Nutter from '63 to '75, and as one of the endowed crowd she allegedly had affairs with Frank, Gary Cooper, and Marcello Mastroianni. She currently lives in Italy, the setting for her most famous movie. "I like three things," her character said in *La Dolce Vita*, "love, love, and love."

BONUS SWINGABILITY: Her real name is Kerstin Anita Marianne Ekberg … her exotic birthplace—Malmo, Sweden … Sandra Bernhard used Anita's "love, love, and love" line as the title of her '93 book … Bob Dylan included her name in the song "I Shall Be Free" on his '61 album *Freewheelin' Bob Dylan*; other celebrities named in that song include President Kennedy, Brigitte Bardot, Sophia Loren, Willie Mays, Yul Brynner, Charles de Gaulle, Elizabeth Taylor, Richard Burton, and fictional characters Little Bo Peep and Mr. Clean … in January of 2000 documentary filmmakers presented her with the *Playboy* list of the century's sexiest stars, which had her at #14; about #6, Cindy Crawford, Anita said, "Who is that? I never heard of her" … she also believed that she should've been rated ahead of Sophia Loren.

A DATE WITH ANITA

September 29, 1931	Anita Ekberg is born
January 16, 1956	Anita makes the cover of *Life* magazine
June 26, 1962	*Boccaccio '70* is released
December 25, 1963	*4 for Texas* is released

SWINGIN' '60s CREDENTIALS: This straight-haired, full-bodied Argentine teen queen won instant international acclaim as the doomed Capulet in Franco Zeffirelli's stylish *Romeo and Juliet*.

WORKIN' IT: Born in Argentina, Olivia Hussey moved to England as a child and began studying to become an actress. She had supporting roles in minor British TV and film productions until she was spotted in a West End play at age 15. The spotter was director Franco Zeffirelli, who selected her out of 800 girls to be in his lavish production of *Romeo and Juliet*. Released in '68, the movie was an internationally acclaimed Oscar-nominated hit, and young Olivia was a star. To many youths who saw the film in the late-'60s and early-'70s, she represented the teen ideal of romantic love. Though she was given the Golden Globe as the Most Promising Newcomer, by her next role she was back to minor British films. She made another two-dozen flix after the '60s, half of them overseas. She overcame the lost potential of *Lost Horizon* ('73), in which she both sang and danced, to star in the creepy *Black Christmas* ('74), then she was part of the all-star cast of *Death on the Nile* ('78). Seen on screen all through the '90s in various projects, most notably as Norma Bates in *Psycho IV* ('91), she also did a voice for a popular *Star Wars* video game.

HER '60s LOOK: Her long dark hair and exotic oval face perfectly captured Juliet's teenage ideal, all poetry and innocence and devotion. So pure-looking was she, a decade later she played the Virgin Mary in Zeffirelli's '77 TV mini-series, *Jesus of Nazareth*. This was despite the bosomy fullness she displayed in *Romeo and Juliet*, when those velvety high-waisted empire gowns pushed forward from her 5' 3" 100-pound frame a bounteous bounty of ripe creamy-white *décolletage*. *Romeo and Juliet* was intentionally made more sensual than previous Shakespeare films, in hopes of arousing the interests of a younger, hipper audience. Thus there was partial nudity, and the shot of Juliet hittin' the sheets with Romeo was used in the movie's ads.

BEHIND THE SCENES: There are conflicting reports about the dates of her marriage to Dino's son, Dean Paul Martin; either way, they divorced in '78. "Being married to Olivia Hussey," he said, "isn't exactly a Romeo and Juliet thing." She then married a British pop star, Paul Ryan, whom she'd briefly been engaged to ten years before. After that marriage and divorce, she was married to another singer, Akira Fuse, from '80 to '87, and then again in '91, this time to hard-rocker David Eisley of the group Dirty White Boy. She has three kids—sons by Martin and Fuse, and a daughter by Eisley.

BONUS SWINGABILITY: She uses a fake moniker—she was born Olivia Osuna, but after her parents' divorce when she was 2, she adopted her mother's maiden name ... her exotic birthplace—Buenos Aires, Argentina ... her Juliet represented one of the first times that a teenager actually played this teenage role ... in '98 *Cosmo* rated *Romeo and Juliet* one of the ten most romantic films ever, calling it "the sexiest, most action-packed retelling of the Veronese love story so far" ... the film's theme song, "A Time for Us," became a #1 hit for Henry Mancini ... at the Royal Command Performance of the movie, Olivia was presented to the Queen of England, Prince Philip, and Prince Charles ... before Len Whiting got the role of Romeo, it was reportedly offered to Paul McCartney.

 A DATE WITH OLIVIA

April 17, 1951	Olivia Hussey is born
October 8, 1968	*Romeo and Juliet* is released

AUDREY HEPBURN

SWINGIN' '6Os CREDENTIALS: This beloved international sweetheart was a '50s screen star and a '60s legend, thanks to classy films like *Breakfast at Tiffany's* and *My Fair Lady* that made her Queen of the Early-'60s Cinema.

WORKIN' IT: With a career that stretched for over forty years, Audrey Hepburn is one of the most-admired actresses of all time. She starred in only twenty-two major films, but among them are some of Hollywood's best-loved movies of the '50s and '60s. Today she's still spoken of reverentially, and she regularly turns up on prominent movie lists. In June '99 the American Film Institute named the "50 Greatest Screen Legends," and Audrey was #3 among the actresses (between Bette Davis and Ingrid Bergman).

She was born to wealthy parents in Belgium, but her father walked out on the family when she was only 6, a defining trauma from which Audrey never fully recovered. Audrey grew up in London, attended private schools, and at 10 was evacuated to neutral Holland when World War II broke out. Holland became occupied by the Nazis and in her early teens Audrey worked for the Resistance by helping to raise funds and passing out anti-Nazi leaflets. During these war years she was taking ballet lessons at the Arnhem Conservatory of Music, which became an idyllic refuge for her. By '44 food was scarce—Audrey later confessed to eating flower bulbs out of desperation.

After the war she and her mother relocated to Amsterdam, where Audrey intensified her dance training. When they moved to London in '48, Audrey's grace and beauty started to bring her modeling and acting jobs. A meeting with the writer Colette, and Colette's urgent recommendation to the producers, put 22-year-old Audrey on Broadway as the title character in *Gigi*. The show was a smash, and Audrey was a star. Days after the show closed in May of '52, she flew to Rome to film *Roman Holiday*, the movie that would bring her an Oscar as Best Actress in '54. Audrey followed that stunning success with some of the most acclaimed and popular films of the '50s: *Sabrina* ('54), *Funny Face* ('57), and *The Nun's Story* ('59).

Breakfast at Tiffany's in '61 brought 32-year-old Audrey one of her defining roles, spirited Holly Golightly, and her fourth Oscar nomination. It also showed off her singing, as she performed "Moon River" (a song that composer Henry Mancini said was inspired by Audrey) in the movie and on the soundtrack. *Charade* in '63 successfully teamed her with another Hollywood legend, Cary Grant. The following year, *My Fair Lady* charmed audiences and critics around the world. Controversy ensued when her performance as Eliza Doolittle wasn't nominated for an Oscar, probably in response to the news that her singing voice was dubbed. Studio chief Jack Warner downplayed the move, saying "We've been doing it for years. We even dubbed the barking of Rin Tin Tin." After '67's underrated *Two for the Road* and the creepy *Wait Until Dark* (her fifth Oscar nomination), Audrey retired to concentrate on her personal life and have a baby.

The romantic *Robin and Marian* with Sean Connery was her wonderful comeback film in '76. Her film output was sporadic after that, capped by Steven Spielberg's *Always* in '89, in which she played, appropriately enough, an angel. Sadly, the irreplaceable Audrey Hepburn died of cancer in '93. Later that year the Academy of Motion Picture Arts and Sciences gave her the Jean Hersholt Humanitarian Award in recognition of her years of tireless charity work for UNICEF. More than just a magnificent star, Audrey was a magnificent inspiration.

HER '60s LOOK: Those expressive oval eyes, that graceful swan's neck, that sweet beguiling smile—only Grace Kelly could match Audrey for sheer beauty. At a time when big brassy blondes like Marilyn Monroe and Jayne Mansfield were dominating the fan mags, Audrey's distinctive ethereal elegance was thrown into high relief. Had she not been an actress, she could've been a top fashion model, and in fact she made the cover of *Vogue* in November '64. She was also on nine *Life* covers in the '50s and one more in the '60s. Her eternally slender figure may have been the result of the malnutrition she suffered as a pre-teen during World War II. In her teens she stood 5' 6" but weighed only 90 pounds; as an adult she added an inch and twenty pounds. Her exquisite grace and poise derived from her background in dance (she held her own alongside Fred Astaire in *Funny Face*, remember). Onscreen, she had one of the most famous collaborations with a designer in movie history, wearing Hubert de Givency's designs in *Sabrina, Funny Face, Love in the Afternoon, Breakfast at Tiffany's, Charade, Paris When It Sizzles,* and *How to Steal a Million*. Late in the '60s she went mod with Mary Quant fashions for *Two for the Road*.

BEHIND THE SCENES: When her father abandoned Audrey and her mother in May of '35, Audrey's emotional life was forever changed. She later admitted to being ever insecure in relationships, as she told Phil Donahue in '80: "When I fell in love and got married, I lived in constant fear of being left." In the '50s Audrey was romantic with William Holden, her *Sabrina* co-star. Other names she has been tenuously linked to include actors Ben Gazzara, Peter O'Toole, Albert Finney, and John F. Kennedy. She was married to actor Mel Ferrer for most of the '50s and through to '68, giving him a son, filmmaker Sean, in '60. After divorcing Ferrer, she married a psychiatrist, Dr. Andrea Dotti, in '69, and she had his son, Luca, three years later, but in the late '70s that marriage also broke up. Her last and most serene relationship was with actor Robert Wolders, widower of Merle Oberon. Audrey and Wolders met in '80, and for the last dozen years of her life he was her live-in companion.

BONUS SWINGABILITY: She used a fake moniker—her real name was Edda Kathleen van Heemstra Hepburn-Ruston ... her exotic birthplace—Brussels, Belgium ... multilingual, Audrey could speak English, Flemish, Dutch, and French from childhood ... in '54 Audrey won an Oscar and a Tony (for the play *Ondine*); at the time she was one of only two actresses (Shirley Booth was the other) to win both awards in the same year ... in *Hollywood Babylon II* author Kenneth Anger says Audrey begged out of Hitchcock's *No Bail for the Judge* because she didn't want to perform the graphic rape scene, especially after her recent role in *The Nun's Story*;

Hitchcock's film was abandoned and he made *Psycho* instead ... Audrey's co-star in *Breakfast at Tiffany's* was almost Steve McQueen. He was offered the part that went to George Peppard, but he couldn't get out of his contract for the TV show *Wanted: Dead or Alive* ... a curious personal foible—supposedly whenever Audrey traveled, she took with her as many personal belongings from home as she could. She'd unpack all the dozens of trunks and suitcases filled with things like picture frames and mementos from her home, set them all up in whatever hotel she was staying, then repack them all and take them with her to the next destination ... in a TV bio, Richard Dreyfuss, her *Always* co-star, called her "perfectly charming, perfectly loving…the best that we can hope to be" ... Audrey herself told you all you need to know: "The most important thing is to enjoy your life—to be happy—it's all that matters" ... her estate has its own official Web site—http://www.audreyhepburn.com.

A DATE WITH AUDREY

May 4, 1929	Audrey Hepburn is born
November 24, 1951	*Gigi*, starring Audrey, opens on Broadway
March 25, 1954	Audrey wins the Best Actress Oscar (*Roman Holiday*)
September 25, 1954	Audrey marries Mel Ferrer
October 5, 1961	*Breakfast at Tiffany's* is released
April 20, 1962	Audrey makes the cover of *Life* magazine
December 5, 1963	*Charade* is released
October 22, 1964	*My Fair Lady* is released
April 27, 1967	*Two for the Road* is released
October 26, 1967	*Wait Until Dark* is released
December 5, 1968	Audrey divorces Mel Ferrer
January 18, 1969	Audrey marries Dr. Andrea Dotti
December 22, 1989	*Always* is released
January 20, 1993	Audrey dies in Switzerland
March 29, 1993	Audrey is given the Jean Hersholt Humanitarian Award at the Oscars

SOPHIA LOREN

SWINGIN' '60s CREDENTIALS: This statuesque Italian thrill-ride made two movies a year through the '60s, picking up several Oscar nominations along the way.

WORKIN' IT: Many European actresses got famous in the '60s, but almost none of them have on their shelves what Sophia Loren has on hers: an Oscar. Far more than just a sex symbol with a Himalayan topography, Sophia earned critical praise in the '60s that made her one of the most popular, and respected, actresses in the world. Three different times during the '60s she was anointed with the Golden Globe as the World's Favorite Film Actress. It was astonishing acclaim for the girl who had lived a true rags-to-riches story.

Born in the charity ward of a hospital for unwed mothers, she grew up in a town that was bombed in WWII. Living in poverty, as a child Sophia was nicknamed "the toothpick" because of her skinny, under-nourished body. Debuting as a 15-year-old extra in 1950, she filled out to become decorative scenery in dozens of Italian films until *Gold of Naples* in '55. That movie made her Italy's top star, supplanting Gina Lollobrigida as the country's leading box-office attraction. The impressed Italian press dubbed '55 the Year of Sophia.

Her Hollywood breakthrough came at age 21 in her first two English-language films, the Alan Ladd treasure-huntin' yarn *Boy on a Dolphin* and the Sinatra/Grant war drama *The Pride and the Passion* (both in '57). Her critical breakthrough came at age 26 in the Vittorio De Sica war-time drama *Two Women* ('61). She was rewarded with a Best Actress Oscar, the first ever given to a woman in a foreign-language film. Showing her range, she followed with some high-profile epics, *El Cid* ('61) and *The Fall of the Roman Empire* ('64); the sexy bedroom striptease of *Yesterday, Today and Tomorrow* ('63); a contemporary comedy, *Marriage Italian Style* ('64), which brought her another Oscar nomination; an explosive adventure, *Operation Crossbow* ('65); the period comedy *Lady L*, with Sophia as the L ('65); the Gregory Peck spy thriller *Arabesque* ('66); and Chaplin's directorial swan song *A Countess from Hong Kong* ('67).

She crawled out of the crater left when *Man of La Mancha* bombed in '72 to make two dozen more movies that took her into the '90s and attracted a new generation of fans. Late in the '90s she got rave reviews for *Soleil* which, according to the *L.A. Times*, packed "an emotional wallop, thanks to Loren's enduring, formidable presence and beautifully understated performance."

After fifty years of performing, she's received a shelf-full of lifetime-achievement honors. One came in '91, when she was given an Honorary Academy Award by the Academy of Motion Picture Arts and Sciences "for a career rich with memorable performances that has added permanent luster to our art form." And in June '99, on the American Film Institute's distinguished list of the "50 Greatest Screen Legends," Sophia was # 21 among the actresses (between Lauren Bacall and Jean Harlow). She's also written a cookbook—*Sophia Loren's Recipes and Memories* in '98—and pitched her own eyewear and perfume. Sophia Loren—more than a film legend, a lifestyle.

HER '60s LOOK: To the comfort of pasta lovers everywhere, she has said of her famous 5' 8" figure that "everything you see, I owe to spaghetti," consistently maintaining that she's never had any cosmetic surgery. "Sex appeal is 50 percent what you've got," she once explained, "and 50 percent what people think you've got." A 38-inch bust is what's she got, supplemented by enchanting eyes the color of cocktail olives and lips that are inviting and full. The irony is that this glamorous bombshell has been at her most memorable when playing an earthy working-class woman. But *Playboy* saw the riches beneath the rags. An August '60 pictorial lensed Loren and lavished praise on

her "unforgettably opulent figure," alliterating her as a "superlatively sensuous" and "classically curvaceous creature." And on the magazine's '99 list of the "100 Sexiest Stars of the Century," Sophia stands at #6, one step ahead of another goddess of the '50s and '60s, Liz Taylor.

BEHIND THE SCENES:

Amazingly, she didn't have much impact on Cary Grant when they first met. Supposedly, at their introduction in '57, he said, "How do you do, Miss Lolloloren, or is it Lorenigida? I can never get these Italian actresses' names straight." Quickly smitten, Cary romantically wined and dined her as *The Pride and the Passion* was being filmed in Spain, but each was encumbered by other attachments. She said, "I was fascinated with him and his warmth, affection, intelligence, and his wonderfully dry, mischievous sense of humor." He sent her roses every day and finally did propose to her, even though he was already married to Betsy Drake, who happened to be in Spain with him as he was courting Sophia. *Cary Grant: The Lonely Heart* by Charles Higham and Roy Mosely had Drake returning to New York—or at least, most of the way to New York—on the *Andrea Doria*, which collided with another ship before it arrived. Meanwhile, Sophia turned down Cary's proposal and instead married producer Carlo Ponti, whom she had met in the early '50s when he judged teenage Sophia in a beauty contest. However, five years after the wedding, with rumors of affairs on both sides and problems with the legality of the marriage in Italy, Sophia divorced Ponti in '62, then remarried him in France in '66. While she's been linked to several prominent names—including JFK, Gary Cooper, Peter Sellers, Omar Sharif, Gig Young, and Marcello Mastroianni—one star she supposedly sent packin' for Scramsville was Frank Sinatra. Ol' Blue Eyes tried to make nice with her on the set of *The Pride and the Passion* by teach-

ing her English phrases that she didn't know were obscene. Sophia eventually gave Frank the brush for keeps. Despite all this famous, even infamous, attention, she has managed to emerge as a devoted family-woman, something she acknowledged when she accepted Oscar's honorary award in '91. "I will share this eventful evening with three men in my life—my husband Carlo Ponti, without whom I wouldn't be the person I am today, and my sons Carlo Jr. and Eduardo, that taught me to conjugate the verb *to love*."

BONUS SWINGABILITY: She uses a fake moniker—she was born Sofia Scicolone, got early billing as Sofia Lazzaro, then changed it in '52 to Sophia Loren ... her exotic birthplace—Rome, Italy ... in one of the most famous photos in Hollywood history, Sophia sat next to Jayne Mansfield at Romanoff's and stared incredulously as Jayne popped out of her low-cut top ... Sophia reportedly was going to play the love interest in Hitchcock's classic *North by Northwest*, but contractual problems kept her out and she was replaced by Eva Marie Saint ... incredibly, Italy put her in the Big House in '82, when Sophia served about half of her husband's thirty-day sentence for tax evasion ... she claims she still cuts and dyes her hair herself ... in the TV movie *Sophia Loren: Her Own Story*, she played both herself and her own mother ... director Vittorio De Sica once said about her: "I never forget the Sophia Loren of the early days, in Italy. But as she has grown into more of a lady, she is less of a comedienne. What a pity" ... "I have no regrets," she once said, "regret only makes wrinkles" ...she has her own official Web site: http://www.cmgww.com/stars/loren/intro.html.

A DATE WITH SOPHIA

December 11, 1912	Carlo Ponti is born
September 20, 1934	Sophia Loren is born
July 25, 1956	The Swedish liner *Stockholm* rams the Italian liner *Andrea Doria*
May 9, 1961	*Two Women* is released
December 14, 1961	*El Cid* is released
April 9, 1962	Sophia wins the Best Actress Oscar (*Two Women*)
March 26, 1964	*The Fall of the Roman Empire* is released
December 20, 1964	*Marriage Italian Style* is released
April 1, 1965	*Operation Crossbow* is released
April 1, 1966	Sophia makes the cover of *Life* magazine
May 5, 1966	*Arabesque* is released
September 16, 1966	Sophia makes the cover of *Life* magazine
March 25, 1991	Sophia is given an honorary award by the Oscar academy

ELKE SOMMER

SWINGIN' '60s CREDENTIALS: This busy blonde *fräulein* averaged almost *four* movies a year through the '60s, most of them foreign, many of them comedies. Among her '60s work was *A Shot in the Dark*, perhaps the best of the *Pink Panther* movies.

WORKIN' IT: In the '60s Elke Sommer was a honey-blonde sex symbol who proved herself to have a gift for light comedy. Born into one of the oldest families in Germany, 18-year-old Elke was discovered by director Vittorio De Sica while she was vacationing in Italy. She began making films in Europe in the late '50s, got some key exposure in *The Victors* ('63), and came to California in '63 for her first Hollywood film, *The Prize* with Paul Newman. After winning the 1964 Golden Globe as the Most Promising Newcomer, she made movies nearly every year of the decade, and after mastering seven languages, she made movies in many different countries, including Germany, Italy, France, and England. By now the total number of her films is over eighty.

American audiences have often seen her as a beautiful innocent in comedies, especially in the '60s when she was in such nutty farces as *A Shot in the Dark* with Peter Sellers ('64), *The Art of Love* with Angie Dickinson ('65), *Boy, Did I Get a Wrong Number!* with Bob Hope ('67), and *The Wrecking Crew* with Dino ('69). Her post-'60s movies declined in prominence and number, though she did get starring roles in the adventure flick *Zeppelin* ('71), in the swashbuckler *The Prisoner of Zenda* ('79), and in the TV movie *Anastasia: The Mystery of Anna* ('86), among others. She also played herself on *Forever Fernwood* in '77 and on *The Muppet Show* in '78. Diversifying as a performer, she's enjoyed a long stage career, she's a great guest on international talk shows (thanks to those language skills), and in her movie-makin' prime she released a record album called *Elke Sommer: Love in Any Language* ('65). What's more, she's established herself as a serious painter. A budding artist even as a child, she had her first gallery exhibition in '65, and she has since had her work shown in over three dozen one-woman shows around the world. She even hosted the instructional PBS series *Painting with Elke*. In fact, at her Web site she says, "I'd rather be known as a painter who acts than as an actress who paints."

HER '60s LOOK: In the '60s Elke combined a pretty face with a sweet, come-hither smile, making her the perfect alluring victim in *A Shot in the Dark*. Though she wasn't the most endowed of the '60s goddesses, she always made her clothes look sexy, as if she was one gentle tug away from the bedroom—think of her wearing just the man's shirt in *Boy, Did I Get a Wrong Number!*, or skip the shirt and think of the hilarious nudist camp scenes in *A Shot in the Dark*. When *Playboy* devoted a pictorial tribute to her in September '70, her husband at the time, Joe Hyams, wrote that "Elke is the perfect wife—inexpensive to dress." Dressed or undressed, Elke's shapely figure impressed *Playboy* enough to get ranked #31 (just ahead of another teutonic temptress, Marlene Dietrich) on the magazine's '99 list of the "100 Sexiest Stars of the Century."

BEHIND THE SCENES: Married in the mid-'60s to journalist Joe Hyams, in August '93 she married her current husband, hotelier Wolf Walther.

BONUS SWINGABILITY: She uses a stage moniker—her real name is Elke Schletz ... her exotic birthplace—Berlin, Germany ... according to her Web site, her lineage entitles her to be called Baroness, but she's never used the title ... also appearing with Elke in *The Wrecking Crew* was Sharon Tate—it was her last movie to be released while she was alive ... an avid racecar driver, Elke hosted a syndicated TV show called *The World of Speed and Beauty* ... legend has it that Elke's house, located in Benedict Canyon above Beverly Hills, is haunted. It's listed among homes that experience paranormal activity ... learn more about Elke and purchase her original art at her official Web site—http://members.aol.com/elkesommer.

A DATE WITH ELKE

November 5, 1940	Elke Sommer is born
June 23, 1964	*A Shot in the Dark* is released
June 23, 1965	*The Art of Love* is released
June 8, 1966	*Boy, Did I Get a Wrong Number!* is released

THE SONGBIRDS

The music of the '60s was as varied as the fashions, and just as revolutionary. In the same way that '60s clothing designers rebelled against '50s conventions, so too did '60s songwriters and singers revolt against '50s musical tastes. Elvis, Jerry Lee Lewis, Little Richard and other giants of the '50s were leading the charge into new territory, but the charts were still peppered with bland teen idols and copycat vocal groups singing mild, two-minute love songs. The '60s redefined the form and function of popular music. Folksingers inspired with new politics, Motown challenged with new freedoms, British singers dazzled with a new sound, and rock music electrified with a new energy. The decade that gave us Dylan and Hendrix and Beatles and Beach Boys also gave us remarkable female artists. They took us Downtown, gave us Somebody to Love, and taught us that, even As Tears Go By, the Beat Goes On...

CHER

She also became an actress, getting her start alongside Sonny in '65's *Wild on the Beach*. When the duo's popularity was at its peak, Sonny and Cher starred as themselves in the spoofy *Good Times* ('67). Unfortunately, the good times were temporarily squelched at the end of the decade when the two seemed to lose touch with fans who were demanding music that was harder, louder, and more socially relevant. According to some reports, Sonny and Cher seemed so outdated they were hooted off the stage at the Newport Folk Festival in '68. To reinvent themselves, they hocked the furniture in their Bel Air mansion so that Sonny could write and produce a '69 movie, *Chastity*, intended to spark Cher's movie career.

Hollywood waited until the '80s to accept her as a movie star. But the town soon embraced her as a solo artist and a TV star. Cher enjoyed admirable success in the '70s, recording three more #1 songs—"Gypsys, Tramps and Thieves" in '71, "Half-Breed" in '73, and "Dark Lady" in '74—and starring in an Emmy-nominated TV variety show with husband Sonny from '71 to '74. After breaking away from Sonny, she starred in her own show, *Cher*, in '75. Now completely out on her own, she did a flamboyant Vegas act at the end of the '70s that brought her $350K a week and the disco hit "Take Me Home."

Reinventing herself once again, Cher found Broadway success in '82 with *Come Back to the 5 and Dime, Jimmy Dean, Jimmy Dean*, which led to a lengthy film career highlighted by her Oscar-winning performance in *Moonstruck* ('87). Her other notable movies included *Silkwood* ('83, her first Oscar nomination), *Mask* ('85), and *Mermaids* ('90), with six Golden Globe nominations or wins during this time. Cher continued to branch out, going into the perfume/skin lotion business in the late '80s and early '90s with her Uninhibited line. After losing some fans with appearances on infomercials in the early '90s she resurrected her career yet again in the late '90s with another hit album, *Believe*, and an energetic dance song, "Strong Enough." Still touring, still putting on an energetic, dazzling show, she has proved herself to be an incredible survivor. After decades of Sonny and Cher success, Hollywood glamour, tabloid scandals, defeat, and triumph, she has reinvented herself one last time—as a mature, though playful, entertainer able to laugh at herself and her mistakes. "I answer to two people, myself and God" she declared in an interview. When she did win her Oscar at last in '88, she gave a gracious, respectful acceptance speech, bestowing praise on the other nominated actresses, and ending with a humble summary: "I don't think this means I AM somebody, but I guess I'm on my way."

SWINGIN' '60s CREDENTIALS: Before she was a TV star and an Oscar-winning actress, Cher was the lanky good-singing, good-looking half of the wildly dressed husband-and-wife team Sonny and Cher, scoring major chart success and starring in two movies in the '60s.

WORKIN' IT: Cher wasn't always Cher. In '64, she began her singing career as Bonnie Jo Mason, releasing the little-heard songs "Ringo, I Love You" and "Beatle Blues." She then teamed up with producer/songwriter Sonny Bono to make a go as the duo Caesar and Cleo (Sonny chose the names to capitalize on all the hoopla surrounding Liz and Dick's *Cleopatra* film). Not until they changed their names in '65 to Sonny and Cher did they get a hit and become one of the most popular acts of the decade. Ironically, when Sonny first sang a work-in-progress called "I Got You Babe" to her, Cher told him, "I don't think it's your best work." Three million record-buying fans disagreed, and the single soared to #1. A dozen other top-40 hits followed, including "The Beat Goes On" ('67) and "You Better Sit Down Kids" ('67). Though the material was lightweight, Cher proved that she had the pipes to command attention. Though severe stage fright almost kept her from performing, as the '60s progressed she became a more confident, passionate singer.

HER '60s LOOK: Cher once said, "The square people think I'm too hip and the hip people think I'm too square." Square or hip, Cher is nothing if not versatile. Just look at her hairstyles over the years.

She's gone from the long, straight, black-bangs-to-the-eyes look of the '60s to the wildly curly and creative multi-colored sculptures she experimented with in the '70s and beyond. Always long and lean, she dazzled the '60s with psychedelic colors and fabrics, often flaunting fur vests and two of the widest bell bottoms in the biz. Later, during her most glamorous era, she added excitement and surprise to the Oscars. For the '86 ceremony she wore a $12,000 Bob Mackie gown, at the time the most expensive dress ever worn to that event. When she has gone over the top with her fashions, she's aware of the commotion she's caused, especially at events like the Oscars. To her credit, she offers no apologies, just the occasional self-deprecating joke, such as this comment she made at a live show in '99 about her costume of boots, a cape, and red hair: "It's my *Braveheart* meets Bozo the Clown look." While she's always had music's biggest eyes and best cheekbones, she also admits to having had repeated plastic surgeries. She's also had at least six tattoos, her first—a butterfly with a flower—landing on her butt when she was 27. However, in August, '98 she told *Newsday* that she was having all the tattoos removed, explaining that "We all have to move on." True, but what the ever-surprising Cher is moving on *to* is anybody's guess.

BEHIND THE SCENES: One of Cher's best talents—and what helped endear her to TV audiences in the '70s—is her quick wit, usually sharpened by her deadpan delivery. But she wasn't quipping when she first set her eyeballs on Sonny. In her '99 book *The First Time*, she described her thoughts at their first encounter: "I actually thought to myself, *Something is different now. You're never going to be the same.*" The year was '62; she was 16; he was 27. She unofficially married him two years later in the bathroom of their Hollywood Hills house. Cher officially married Sonny in '69 when their daughter Chastity was born. They stayed married into '75, at which point her tabloid life began in earnest. (She scolded the tabloid reporters who hounded her: "You go through my garbage and hide in my plants—it's not what grown-ups should do for a living.") Within three

days of her divorce from Sonny, Cher married heroin-addled musician Gregg Allman in Vegas and then filed for dissolution less than two weeks later. "I wasn't fully aware of what I was getting into," she said later. She eventually had his son, Elijah Blue, and the marriage officially ended within three years. She's also been linked with rocker Gene Simmons, media mogul David Geffen, actors Warren Beatty, Val Kilmer, and possibly even Tom Cruise. Supposedly on her 40th birthday she saw hunky 22-year-old bagel-boy and future boyfriend Rob Camilletti for the first time and said, "Have him washed and brought to my tent." "A girl can wait for the right man to come along," she's explained, "but in the meantime that still doesn't mean she can't have a wonderful time with all the wrong ones."

BONUS SWINGABILITY: Her moniker at birth was Cherilyn Sarkisian ... her exotic birthplace—El Centro, California ... her mother was married at least eight, possibly ten times, supposedly three times to Cher's father ... Cher's daughter Chastity is now a prominent activist in the lesbian community ... in the mid-'90s on David Letterman's *Late Night* show she had a moving, tearful reunion with Sonny; they sang "I Got You Babe" together for the first time in decades ... After Sonny died in '98 from a skiing accident, she delivered an eloquent, heartfelt eulogy at his funeral, describing him as "the most unforgettable character I've ever met" ... and finally, in a TV interview: "After a nuclear holocaust there'll be cockroaches and there'll be Cher—I think that pretty much sums it up" ... Cher has her own official Web site—http://www.cher.com.

A DATE WITH CHER

February 16, 1935	Sonny Bono is born
May 20, 1946	Cher is born
June 12, 1965	Sonny and Cher make their first TV appearance (*American Bandstand*)
July 31, 1965	Sonny and Cher's "I Got You Babe" enters the *Billboard* charts (it will reach #1)
August 25, 1965	*Wild on the Beach* is released
January 28, 1967	"The Beat Goes On" enters the *Billboard* charts (it will reach #6)
March 4, 1969	Cher gives birth to daughter Chastity
August 1, 1971	*The Sonny and Cher Comedy Hour* debuts
February 20, 1975	Cher files for divorce from Sonny
June 26, 1975	Sonny and Cher divorce
June 28, 1975	Cher marries Gregg Allman
April 11, 1988	Cher wins the Best Actress Oscar (*Moonstruck*)
January 5, 1998	Sonny dies skiing

PETULA CLARK

SWINGIN' '60s CREDENTIALS: A cheerful clear-voiced British belter who went from child star in the '40s to pop star in the '60s, Pet had mid-decade smashes, such as "Downtown," "I Know a Place," and "A Sign of the Times," plus starring roles in two big movie musicals.

WORKIN' IT: When people think of the British Invasion, they usually think of the Beatles, the Stones, and other "boy bands." But Petula Clark was right there with them at the vanguard of a musical revolution. "Downtown" in '64 made her the first British female singer to hit #1 on the American charts, and it brought Petula her first Grammy Award in the same year the Fab Four won their first Grammy. That was just one more highlight for her in a long career already filled with them.

Petula Clark was a star from childhood. Before she was 10 she was being paid to sing and was appearing regularly on British radio programs. Before she was 12 she was entertaining the troops and had her own BBC show, *Pet's Parlour*. She started appearing in movies as a teen, making dozens in the '40s and '50s and becoming so well known that her life was the subject of a popular comic strip. Her first '60s hit was "Sailor," which hit #1 in the UK in February '61. Within a year, 30-year-old Petula had million-selling songs in England, France, and Germany.

Her U.S. breakthrough, of course, came when she went "Downtown." Energetic and polished, it had "a great sound and a great feeling," she later told *People* magazine. Additional well-rated numbers—"I Know a Place" (bringing her a second Grammy), "My Love," "A Sign of the Times," "I Couldn't Live Without Your

Love," "Colour My World," "This Is My Song," and "Don't Sleep in the Subway"—quickly followed, giving her eight top-20 hits in the U.S. between '64 and '67. A major concert draw, she gave appealing performances that translated well to TV, so she was on lots of music shows during the decade, including *Ed Sullivan*, *Shindig*, and *Hullabaloo*. On her own '68 special she made a controversial gesture for racial equality: while singing "On the Path of Glory" with Harry Belafonte, she touched his hand. Despite NBC's efforts to cut the image, she made them keep the shot in when the show aired.

Late in the decade she had starring roles in two big-budget musicals, *Finian's Rainbow* (which brought her a Golden Globe nomination as Best Actress) and *Goodbye, Mr. Chips*. While neither one thrived at the box office, they did establish Petula as one of the few music stars popular and talented enough to make the transition from the recording studio to the big screen.

She's continued to make music ever since, and even though she's had no more glittering U.S. hits to match the rich vein of gold she tapped into in the mid-'60s, she's still a major global star. By now she's sold somewhere in the neighborhood of seventy million albums around the world, and with over a thousand recorded songs in five languages (English, French, German, Italian, and Spanish) to her credit, she's the most popular British female singer in history. She still performs benefit concerts, and in '96 she made it to Broadway with *Blood Brothers*. Late in the century she toured the U.S. as Norma Desmond in *Sunset Boulevard*. Currently she's writing songs and working on an autobiographical one-woman show full of stories and songs from her wonderful career. In recognition of her longevity and accomplishments, in '97 the Queen bestowed the title Commander of the British Empire upon her. "I've lived in many different places," she said in the *L.A. Times* in July '99, "I've seen things I never would have seen otherwise, and I'm still enjoying it."

HER '60s LOOK: Pleasantly attractive, Petula had a kicky strawberry blonde 'do that perfectly suited the times. She told *People* that she "used to do Carnaby Street, I seemed to be wearing lots of mauve" in the swingin' '60s. However, she also had a timeless quality that would've easily translated to a previous decade: witness the film *Goodbye Mr. Chips*, where she blended in naturally with the early-twentieth-century milieu.

BEHIND THE SCENES: Being a child star, she acknowledged to the *Daily Mail* in a '98 interview, wasn't easy: "Because of the circles I mixed in, professionally, I knew about things that children in those days were shielded from. Yet, at the same time, I was still very young in my own experiences of life. It was all rather peculiar and confusing. It caused so many problems for me in my teens that I was on the verge of a breakdown. So I shut myself in a room and gave myself a good talking to. It wasn't always an enjoyable experience but it was character building. I wouldn't say I had a normal childhood, but then what is normal?" In '61 Petula married a French PR man named Claude Wolff, who later became her manager. She told the *Daily Mail* about her life before they met: "He wasn't the first person I'd been involved with. I'd spent the previous few months making up for all the lost time when I'd been living at home. I remember one particularly wild night with Sean Connery when we ended up under a piano drinking gin and cider cocktails. Very strange. But when I first met Claude, it was love at first sight, though it took him a little longer to fall in love with me. We were married a year later." They're still

married, have three kids, and now divide their time between a Swiss estate and a French chalet. As conventional as her private life seems, she did get into the spirit of the '60s a little. Here's what she told *Choice* magazine in April '98 about the making of

Finian's Rainbow: It "was the most fun I ever had making a movie. It was totally mad because we did it on the back lot at Warner Brothers studios. It was 1968 so there were beards, long hair, motorbikes, flower power and a bit of marijuana thrown in, too, of course."

BONUS SWINGABILITY: Her full moniker: Petula Sally Olwen Clark ... her nickname—Pet. She was dubbed "The English Shirley Temple" as a child ... her exotic birthplace—Ewell, England ... in '98 she told *Yours* magazine about a meeting with Elvis: "I met Elvis when I was appearing in Las Vegas and like most people, I wanted to see him on stage. I met him after his performance and he was very flirtatious. Some years later I saw him again and he was not a happy sight. He was so overweight, he was hardly able to sing and hardly able to move. Since he knew I was there, I felt I had to go backstage. He didn't come out of his inner sanctum for a long while and his Memphis Mafia were saying how brilliant he was. I couldn't get out of there fast enough" ... she has claimed her favorite singer is Peggy Lee ... to *People* in August '99 she said, "You can't minimize the '60s by saying it was just about fashion and music. Nothing was the same after the '60s."

A DATE WITH PETULA

November 15, 1932	Petula Clark is born
January 2, 1965	"Downtown" enters the *Billboard* charts (it will reach #1)
April 3, 1965	"I Know a Place" enters the *Billboard* charts (it will reach #3)
January 15, 1966	"My Love" enters the *Billboard* charts (it will reach #7)
July 30, 1966	"I Couldn't Live Without Your Love" enters the *Billboard* charts (it will reach #9)
June 17, 1967	"Don't Sleep in the Subway" enters the *Billboard* charts (it will reach #5)
October 9, 1968	*Finian's Rainbow* is released

MARIANNE FAITHFULL

SWINGIN' '60s CREDENTIALS: The angel-faced singer who hit the charts with "As Tears Go By" was also a minor film and stage actress during the '60s, but she's best known as the girlfriend to Mick Jagger and one of the decade's most infamous drug casualties.

WORKIN' IT: Marianne Faithfull had it all: looks, talent, connections, and inner strength. Several times in her life she has come close to losing it all because of a terrible drug dependency. In some ways she was England's Edie Sedgwick—another carefree celebrity who was beautiful, charismatic, and aristocratic but who ended the decade as a drugged-out symbol of the era's worst excesses.

The daughter of a baroness and a British Intelligence officer, Marianne was sickly and tubercular as a child. After her parents' divorce she lived in a convent school, but by her mid-teens she was singing in London coffee houses. At 17 she went to a party attended by several Beatles and Rolling Stones, and her life changed forever. Stones' manager Andrew Loog Oldham met her at the party and, overwhelmed by her angelic beauty, declared his intentions to make her a singing star. He ordered Mick Jagger and Keith Richards to write a song for her, which they did overnight—"As Tears Go By," their first co-writing credit. Within six months Marianne's gentle rendition of the sweet song was a top-10 hit in the U.K. More

delicate, well-crafted hits—"This Little Bird" and "Summer Nights"—quickly followed.

Taking up with Jagger in '66 (he had been with Chrissie Shrimpton, Jean's sister, before Marianne), she started living the indulgent life of a rock star, with days and nights full of partying and performing, drugs and decadence. For a while there in the mid-'60s, her mythical image, ability to handle the lifestyle, and famous friends made her the epitome of London at its swingin'est. Her fame and face made her a natural for the big screen, so in the late '60s she made several films: *I'll Never Forget What's 'is Name* ('67), *Don't Look Back* ('67), and *Girl on a Motorcycle* ('68).

Unfortunately, "being the kept sort of plaything of the great rock star wasn't my destiny," as she later said. Use became abuse as drugs overtook her in the late '60s, a situation she described in her lyrics for the Stones' song "Sister Morphine." As a stage actress in '69 she performed in *Hamlet*, and she displayed a manic intensity that often left her exhausted—once she even collapsed onstage. Sadly, by this time Marianne was shooting heroin during the intermissions. Breaking off with Jagger in '70, her career destroyed, she punched her ticket to junkieville and floundered onto the London streets, crashing in abandoned buildings alongside other hopeless addicts.

With some help she was able to pull herself together enough to record an album, *Rich Kid's Blues* in '71, and from that came the money and strength to enter rehab for eight months. Gradually rebuilding her career, she re-established herself as a solo artist with the bold, wrenching album *Broken English* in '79. By then her raw-edged voice had become a raspy croak that added emotive power to her intense songs. However, a painfully revealing appearance on *Saturday Night Live* in February 1980, in which Marianne lost her weary voice during a song and staggered to finish it on live TV, strongly suggested she was using drugs again. By the mid-'80s she had totally relapsed, so addicted to heroin that she intentionally tried to overdose in order to end her miserable life.

After another rehab, one that finally seemed to take, she continued to make music with autobiographical lyrics that confronted her troubles. New audiences discovered her in the '90s, thanks to her searing '94 autobiography, *Faithfull,* her startling appearance in a '96 Metallica video for the song "The Memory Remains," and a deeply introspective '99 album, *Vagabond Ways*. That Marianne Faithfull is still alive and still recording is something of a minor miracle.

HER '60s LOOK: Until drugs wasted her youth and beauty, Marianne had the classic London look: thick, straight hair with bountiful bangs, a sweet smile, and what everyone described as one of the best bodies in rock music. She started her career singing in old-fashioned peasant dresses that emphasized her ample bosom, but as the '60s progressed she moved to various great styles—mod, rocker, hippie, Carnaby Street. You name it, she epitomized it, always with sexy stylishness. Few could rival her in her prime. Take it from someone who knew her, Stones' associate Tony Sanchez, writing in *Up and Down with the Rolling Stones*: "Marianne Faithfull was as blithe and pure as a midsummer's day…. Her body was slender, frail as a blade of grass. But it was the woman's face that was singular—it was the face of an angel, with its big, blue, innocent eyes, soft, pouting lips, and a frame of blonde hair that glowed like the sun with youth and health. It was a face that stopped all talk whenever she entered any gathering of people—a face that subjugated all men to her will." So alluring was she in the mid-'60s, Marianne was able to coax Roy Orbison to take off his trademark sunglasses, a remarkable accomplishment noted by *Biography* magazine in January 2000.

BEHIND THE SCENES: Married in '65 to art student John Dunbar, Marianne was a mother when she gave some Satisfaction to the ultimate '60s rock icon, Mick Jagger, in '66. "I left everything for Mick," she later said. Within months she was living with the Stones' singer, and their movements were being covered in the papers. During this time of being a favored courtier among rock's royalty, she had affairs with many other swingin' Londoners, including Brian Jones, Keith Richards, and even Keith's girl, Anita Pallenberg (open to experimentation, she was found in bed with another woman on several occasions by Jagger). But her drug lifestyle was what made her infamous. In February of '67, she was rounded up in a drug raid at Redlands, the country manor owned by Keith and the site of a well-attended weekend party. Whereas others emerged from the ordeal with their reputations as outlaws enhanced, Marianne emerged with her "feminine self…completely besmirched," as she later described. She had been found at the party nude save for a fur rug she'd hastily wrapped around herself. What was a lark to others, or a milestone in the Stone's history as anti-establishment rebels, was devastating for Marianne. She summarized the continued gossip and unrelenting accusations as "a particularly vicious piece of character assassination," adding that "I came out of it diminished, demeaned, trampled in the mud." Her career sliding at a rate inversely proportional to her drug intake, in '68 she and Mick were arrested again, she miscarried Mick's baby, and she was plummeting into the abyss. Supposedly the first words Jagger said to her when she pulled out of one drug-induced coma in '68 were "wild horses couldn't drag me away," a phrase he turned into a Stones classic. To rid herself of him and their life in '70, she overdosed on…not drugs, but fatty food! She was hoping to put on some tonnage, knowing the sudden change would repulse him. It worked, and they soon split for good. Much later, Jagger's '90s paramour, Jerry Hall, read a boxful of Mick and

Marianne's love letters and concluded, "of all the girlfriends he's had, he loved her the most." Perhaps, but here's the tally from her three-plus years with Jagger: a nervous breakdown, an addiction to heroin, a miscarriage, two arrests, a career-wrecking scandal, and a suicide attempt. For the next few decades, as she conducted an on-off affair with heroin, she did try marriage twice more. Unapologetic about her choices, in a televised interview she said, "I have lived my life as an adventure, and it's been rather wonderful and I really wouldn't change much about it."

BONUS SWINGABILITY: Her exotic birthplace— Hampstead, England … she was the first person to ever use the f-word in a movie (*I'll Never Forget What's 'is Name*) … in her autobiography Marianne speculates on the true love of Mick's life—she says it's Keith Richards … in October '98 she told the *S.F. Chronicle* about what her life would've been like if she could start over again at 18: "I'd leave out the narcotics, but the rest of it I wouldn't leave out. I don't think I could change anything. I'm not a conventional person, I'm an adventuress, and as an adventuress my life has been a blinding success…. Like anybody who's worth having, I've got my difficult side, but I'm great fun to be with…. The difficult stuff is made up for by the good stuff."

A DATE WITH MARIANNE

December 19, 1946	Marianne Faithfull is born
December 19, 1964	Marianne's version of "As Tears Go By" peaks at #22 on the U.S. charts
June 26, 1965	"This Little Bird" enters the *Billboard* charts (it will reach #32)
September 4, 1965	"Summer Nights" enters the *Billboard* charts (it will reach #24)
February 12, 1967	Marianne, the fur rug, and the infamous Redlands raid
May 24, 1968	Marianne and Mick are busted for drugs in their London home
February 9, 1980	Marianne self-destructs on *Saturday Night Live*

JOEY HEATHERTON

SWINGIN' '60s CREDENTIALS: For many men and boys who saw her in the '60s, this scintillating sex kitten is one of their best, most formative memories. Never a major recording or film star, sizzling Joey Heatherton still managed to leave an indelible impression as the wriggly, jiggly, go-go dancin' scene-stealer on many a TV variety show.

WORKIN' IT: Born to the biz, Joey Heatherton grew up on Long Island as the daughter of a mother who was a Broadway dancer and a father, Ray Heatherton, who was TV's "Merry Mailman" on a local kids' show. According to a '63 profile of Joey in *TV Guide*, her parents met while they were both performing in a Broadway production of *Babes in Arms*.

After studying dance throughout her childhood years, Joey got her big break in '59 when, at 15, she was put in the Broadway cast of

The Sound of Music. She released her first single ("That's How It Goes"/"I'll Be Seeing You") that same year, with three more 45s to come in the mid-'60s ("My Blood Runs Cold"/"Hullabaloo" in '64, "Tomorrow Is Another Day"/"But He's Not Mine" in '65, and "When You Call Me Baby"/"Live and Learn" in '66). None of them made much impact, however—Joey's appeal was more visual than aural.

In the early '60s she started making what would be dozens of TV appearances on everything from westerns (*The Virginians*) to dramas (*Route 66*, *The Nurses*) to comedies (*I Spy*) to teen dance shows (*Hullabaloo*) to grown-up variety shows (*The Steve Lawrence Show*, *Hollywood Palace*, *The Mike Douglas Show*, *The Jackie Gleason Show*) and more. Of all these, the variety shows proved to be her launching pad to stardom, because they showcased her, not as a costumed character, but as what she truly was: one of the hottest live performers on TV. Singing and dancing energetically in fringy mini-outfits, with the gams and curves to make 'em really swing, sexy Joey was stoppin' shows and heartbeats in living rooms across the country for most of the decade. *Dean Martin Presents The Golddiggers* in '68 gave her regular exposure and her best chances to cut loose as a whirling sex goddess. In a '66 *Look* magazine story called "Joey Heatherton: Heavenly Body Entering Orbit," choreographer Jaime Rogers said that her "tremendous vitality and her energy make her very sensual. She gets her motor going, and it just flows out naturally." Unfortunately, her talents didn't translate so well to the big screen, though she took her shot at Hollywood: Her first starring role was opposite Richard Chamberlain in '63's *Twilight of Honor*, she played a murderous teen in the '64 Susan Hayward/Bette Davis/Mike Connors potboiler *Where Love Has Gone*, and a year later she had the female lead in the Troy Donahue movie, *My Blood Runs Cold*. But the live stage was where she sparkled, so between big-time TV gigs she took her brilliant wattage to the darkest corners of Vietnam, touring several times—and always to riotous acclaim—with Bob Hope's USO shows.

In '72 she released an album (*The Joey Heatherton Album*) and three singles ("Gone"/"The Road I Took to You," "I'm Sorry"/"Someone to Watch Over Me," and "Crazy"/"God Only Knows"). She also headlined Vegas during the '70s and continued to put in TV appearances on various variety shows, including *The Glen Campbell Goodtime Hour* in '70, *Sonny & Cher* in '72, a Bob Hope special in '73, *Circus of the Stars* in '77, and several Jerry Lewis telethons. She did get a crack at her own sitcom, *Joey and Dad*, but it came and went in '75. And she made more films, most notably *Bluebeard* in '72 and *The Happy Hooker Goes to Washington* in '77. Always a magazine fave (she was on the cover of *Esquire* in December '65), in April '97 she was featured in *Playboy* in an array of sexy poses at the age of 53! Today she puts in occasional screen appearances (John Waters' *Cry-Baby* in '90) and appears at autograph shows, still titillating those who first saw her over thirty years ago.

HER '60s LOOK: Barry Williams of *The Brady Bunch* fame briefly described her in his book *Growing Up Brady: I Was a Teenage Greg*. While shooting an episode of *It Takes a Thief* together, he thought she was a "white-hot, vaguely slutty-looking sex goddess." With her shag 'do, heavy make-up, pouty lips, and perfectly curved 5' 3" body, Joey was the complete package. She also sported the swingin'est styles, but don't take our word for it: when *TV Guide* put her on the cover of its November 13–19 issue in '65, the coverlines read, SWINGING GIRL—

SWINGING FASHIONS. Fans looking for further exposure might seek out the brief nude scene she did in '72's *Bluebeard*.

BEHIND THE SCENES: "I want men, not marriage!" boasted Joey on the cover of *Silver Screen* magazine in August '65. Sadly, when she did want marriage, she ended up suffering through one of the most agonizing unions of the early '70s. In '69 she married glamorous Dallas Cowboy wide receiver Lance Rentzel, and for a year or so they were the toast of the town, appearing together at events and on TV. Unfortunately that marriage ended in '71 after he was arrested for indecent exposure in front of a young girl (an episode he wrote about in his '72 book *When All the Laughter Died in Sorrow*). Though she stayed with him for a while, they eventually split up. The notoriety seemed to take the spark out of her career. Unfortunately, when her career was in decline, she was arrested for cocaine possession and causing a disturbance in an airport. Her career, and her rep, led People Magazine Online to name a trophy after her, to be given for the "best blonde bimbo performance of the year." But that doesn't shake the conviction for many males that Joey Heatherton is still one of the best things to remember about the '60s.

BONUS SWINGABILITY: She uses a stage moniker—her real name is Davenie Johanna Heatherton ... she was on the very first *Dean Martin Show* in '65; also on the show with her were Frank Sinatra, Bob Newhart, Danny Thomas, and Diahann Carroll ... Catherine O'Hara did wicked parodies of Joey with her Lola Heatherton character on *SCTV* in the '80s ... Joey turned up on one of David Letterman's Top 10 lists in '88, as described in his *Book of Top Ten Lists* ('90): "Top Ten Fears of Snuggles the Fabric Softener Bear, #5—First wife Joey Heatherton will write book claiming he beat her regularly" ... Joey has her own official Web site http://joeyheatherton.net.

 A DATE WITH JOEY

September 14, 1944	Joey Heatherton is born
November 2, 1964	*Where Love Has Gone* is released
January 12, 1965	Joey first hosts *Hullabaloo*
January 18, 1967	Joey guest stars on a Bob Hope special
June 20, 1968	*Dean Martin Presents the Golddiggers* debuts
February 19, 1969	Joey and Lance Rentzel get engaged
April 12, 1969	Joey and Lance get married
July 15, 1972	"Gone" enters the *Billboard* charts (it will reach #24)
July 6, 1975	The show *Joey and Dad* debuts

JANIS JOPLIN

Collins. "Every secret was laid bare." There was simply no white singer in the '60s like Janis. Nobody could match her super-charged voice full of carnality and adrenaline and Southern Comfort, for one thing. Singer Ethel Merman once said about her, "That girl has problems; bein' heard ain't one of 'em. Like me, she gives an audience their money's worth." And nobody could match Janis's pain, either, the result of trying to cram a full life into twenty-seven short years.

Born in conservative east Texas in '43 as the eldest of three kids, Janis was a lonely, troubled outcast as a child. "There was nobody like me in Port Arthur," she once lamented. She split from home at 17. For a few years she attended Lamar State and the University of Texas, she hitchhiked randomly around the country, and she sang folk songs in coffeehouses from Texas to California.

In '66 she jumped into the burgeoning San Francisco scene and joined an already-established local band, Big Brother and the Holding Company. Hooked in deep to the free-love/free-drugs atmosphere of the Haight-Ashbury, Janis started gaining recognition for her gut-wrenching live performances with Big Brother, especially a show-stopping turn at the Monterey Pop Festival in '67. Their chart-topping *Cheap Thrills* album in September of '68 showcased her powerful vocals with such signature songs as "Ball and Chain" and "Piece of My Heart." Lured by the promise of solo stardom, later that year she quit Big Brother to form the Kozmic Blues Band. With them came the masterful "Try" and another successful rock festival, Woodstock. Finally, working in '70 with a new group called the Full-Tilt Boogie Band, she recorded *Pearl*, though this classic album (and the only #1 song of her career, "Me and Bobby McGee") wasn't released until after her death in '71.

Her sad heroin overdose in a Hollywood motel precluded the future success she might've had. But the music community has never forgotten her impact. In '90 *Rolling Stone* voted *Pearl* the #11 album of all time, in '95 she was posthumously inducted into the Rock and Roll Hall of Fame, and in '99 VH1 put her third (behind Aretha and Tina) on its list of "The 100 Greatest Women of Rock and Roll." Many of the Swingin' Chicks of the '60s were great; Janis was legend.

SWINGIN' '60s CREDENTIALS: A growly whisky-swiggin' belter of bluesy rock songs, free-wheelin' Janis Joplin fronted Big Brother and the Holding Company in the late '60s and gained rock immortality with soul-baring songs, passionate live performances, and a sad premature death.

WORKIN' IT: Singers know. "Her performance was so in your face and electrifying that it really put you right there in the moment," wrote Chrissie Hynde of the Pretenders. "There you were living your nice little life in the suburbs and suddenly there was this train wreck, and it was Janis." "She shouted her story and spilled it out into the world with an abandon that had genius in it," added Judy

HER '60s LOOK: Unkempt and ungroomed, Janis in some ways embodied the classic hippy chick image, that of someone who looked like she'd spent the night bongin' in a van outside a Grateful Dead concert. Her soft shape was masked by funky vintage wear—she could wear anything and make it look amiably, nostalgically trashy, often by adding an array of colorful jewels and feather boas. Interestingly, weeks after Barbra Streisand wore her controversial "see-through" black pajamas at the Oscars, Janis wore a copy of the

exact same outfit at a San Francisco concert. But one always had the feeling with Janis that eventually looks didn't really matter to her. The child who was the ugly duckling became the adult grappling with issues much deeper than mere fashion or appearance.

BEHIND THE SCENES:

Rumor has it that in the last five or six years of her life Janis squeezed lots of celebrities onto her dance card, men with last names like Clapton, Morrison, Hendrix, Kristofferson, Cavett (!), Namath, plus assorted bandmates, roadies, and even other women. If true, it's an amazing list for someone who died so young, and for someone who was once nominated as the U of T's "Ugliest Man on Campus." Never married, she was engaged to a rich Berkeley student in the last months of her life. She knew she was living a reckless, dangerous lifestyle: when she heard that Jimi Hendrix had died in September of '70, she said, "Dammit! He beat me to it!" Three weeks later, she too was gone, her ashes scattered from a plane over the coastline of Marin County, California. Hers was one of the deaths—along with Jimi Hendrix, Jim Morrison, and Brian Jones—that signaled the spiritual end of the '60s. "Yeah, life's groovy," she once told an interviewer, "sometimes it ain't groovy enough."

BONUS SWINGABILITY:
Her nickname—"Pearl" ... her exotic birthplace—Port Arthur, Texas, the same area that gave the world the Big Bopper, George Jones, and ZZ Top ... singer David Crosby wrote in his autobiography about the night Janis met an obnoxious Jim Morrison: "Jim tells Janis she can't sing the blues, which does not make her happy. Her first reaction was to run out of the room,

crying. Then…Janis picked up a bottle of Jim Beam bourbon and, instead of taking a drink, took the bottle back into the room with Morrison, where she broke it on his forehead" ... according to the book *They Went That-A-Way*, the Southern Comfort distillery gave her a fur coat in gratitude for all the free publicity Janis gave them by drinking their brand onstage ... the liner notes for *Box of Pearls: The Janis Joplin Collection* included tributes written by famous fans who named Janis as an inspiration:

Chrissie Hynde, Joan Jett, Stevie Nicks, Meredith Brooks, Deborah Harry, Amy Ray (Indigo Girls), and Ann Wilson (Heart) ... after Janis's death, Mimi Farina composed, and her sister Joan Baez recorded, the song "In the Quiet Morning" in her memory ... the '79 Bette Midler film *The Rose* was a loose retelling of Janis's life ... Janis explained it all for us: "Don't compromise yourself, you're all you've got."

A DATE WITH JANIS

January 19, 1943	Janis Joplin is born
June 17, 1967	Janis performs at the Monterey Pop Festival
September 28, 1968	"Piece of My Heart" enters the *Billboard* charts (it will reach #12)
July 3, 1969	Brian Jones drowns
August 16, 1969	Janis performs at Woodstock
August 12, 1970	Janis's last live performance (Harvard Stadium)
September 18, 1970	Jimi Hendrix dies of a drug overdose
October 4, 1970	Janis dies of a drug overdose
March 20, 1971	"Me & Bobby McGee" enters the *Billboard* charts (it will reach #1)
July 3, 1971	Jim Morrison dies of a heart attack

NICO

SWINGIN' '60s CREDENTIALS: The marvelously macabre Nico rode a modeling career and small film roles to legendary cult status in the late '60s as a key scene maker at Andy Warhol's Factory and as the headlining chanteuse for the seminal avant-garde rock band Velvet Underground.

WORKIN' IT: Never a big movie star or a major seller as a singer, Nico was still one of the most influential personalities of the '60s. As proof, here's a partial list of men and the songs they wrote for or about her: Gordon Lightfoot ("I'm Not Sayin'," her first European single); Jimmy Page ("The Last Mile"); Lou Reed ("I'll Be Your Mirror"); Jackson Browne ("These Days"); Bob Dylan ("I'll Keep It With Mine"); Iggy Pop ("We Will Fall"); and Leonard Cohen ("Take This Longing"). The inspiration for these songs had been a child of war. Born in Germany in '38, less than a year before the start of World War II, Nico was evacuated and her father was killed during the war. She was raised by an aunt who described her as quiet, shy, and "always smartly dressed, like a princess."

At 16 Nico moved to Paris, where her striking beauty and magnificent height (she stood about six feet tall) landed her modeling gigs for *Vogue*, commercials for Terry liqueur, and a brief appearance as a nutty, deep-voiced girl in Fellini's '60 classic *La Dolce Vita* (she wore a knight's metal helmet in most of her scenes).

Unhappy with modeling, and hoping to reunite with Bob Dylan (whom she'd met in Paris in '64), Nico moved to New York. She soon fell in with pop artist Andy Warhol. At the time, Andy was managing a band, the dark, poetic Velvet Underground. Far ahead of their time, the Velvets would have profound influences on groups as

disparate as R.E.M., the Sex Pistols, the Talking Heads, and U2. Recognizing her as a compelling image of exquisite indifference, Warhol immediately grabbed Nico to be the headlining singer for the Velvets. As a singer, she could barely carry a tune, and her monotonous, flat voice sounded like a sonorous foghorn echoing under cold, black water. Her deadpan delivery sharply divided listeners—what was eerily gothic to some was painfully off-key to others. Image was all to Warhol, however, and he captured Nico on film, first in an experimental documentary called *The Velvet Underground and Nico* in '66, and then in one of his bizarre underground movies, *Chelsea Girls* in '67. That same year, Nico and the Velvet Underground released the record album that is now considered a rock landmark. Warhol himself designed the cover, a bright yellow banana peel. At the time the album was deemed insignificant—*Rolling Stone* magazine didn't even review it, and the highest chart position it achieved was #179. Ultimately, however, it would be the foundation upon which the Velvets' lofty rep was built, a rep that got them into the Rock and Roll Hall of Fame in '96. Nico sang only three songs on the album and so, feeling underutilized, she left the group in '68.

Out on her own, she had a hard time getting her career to take off, despite two impressive '60s albums— *Chelsea Girl* in '68 and the remarkable *The Marble Index* in '69. For the next two decades she struggled to sustain her sagging career, write bleak songs, and perfect her minimalist sound, even as prolonged drug use started to take its toll. She made a half-dozen obscure foreign films in the '70s while living in Paris, but she released only a few albums after '72. *Drama of Exile* in '81 and *Camera Obscura* in '85 were the best of an impenetrable lot. She did continue to perform live, however, and did close to a thousand concerts in her last two decades.

Sadly, she continued to sink into heroin addiction and seemed to lose interest in life as the '90s loomed ahead; in fact her manager in the '80s, Alan Wise, said "life was a bore to her...she used to say she was only two minutes from death." Death did come for her in '88 when, at the age of 49, she was killed in a bicycling accident in Spain. At the time, she was working on an autobiography called *Moving Target*.

HER '60s LOOK: Warhol described her as someone who looked like she could have come to America "right at the front of a Viking ship." Tall, imposing, almost regal, Nico had dazzling blue-green eyes and the highest, best-defined cheekbones this side of Cher. She herself thought her eyes were her best feature. Right at the end of the '60s she cut her blonde hair and dyed it dark red, because she'd heard rocker Jim Morrison preferred redheads: "I was so in love with him that I made my hair red after a while. I wanted to please his taste. It was silly, wasn't it, like a teenager." Later she dyed her hair black, presaging the stark gothic look that would become all the rage.

BEHIND THE SCENES: "I'm a nihilist," Nico once said, "so I like destruction." And destruction she got. From '59–'61 Nico lived with a filmmaker/nightclub owner. She then met French actor Alain Delon and had his son, Ari, who was raised by Delon's mother. In '64 it's likely that Nico had relationships with Brian Jones and Bob Dylan, both of whom she met in Europe. Within two years Nico was a Warhol Factory regular, hanging with Edie Sedgwick and New York's "in" crowd. Nico was probably having affairs with musicians Iggy Pop, John Cale, and Lou Reed at the time. About Reed, Nico said he "was very soft and lovely. Not aggressive at all. You could just cuddle him like a sweet person when I first met him, and he always

stayed that way. I used to make pancakes for him." In '67 she met Jim Morrison in L.A., and they had a brief, intense relationship. Obsessed with Jim, she called him her "soul brother." All of this was happening, remember, while Nico was a mother. For one period during the '60s she went three years without seeing her young son once. When she finally reunited with him she brought him a gift—a single orange. Her own heroin use spiraled out of control in the '70s and '80s, so that she was traveling to her concerts with bags of heroin and syringes. In the '80s heroin even snared her son, who lapsed into a drug-induced coma and was put on a life-support machine. Nico showed up at the hospital to tape the beeping sounds of the machine for an album.

BONUS SWINGABILITY: She used a fake moniker—her real name was Christa Päffgen, and she was sometimes billed as the Moon Goddess ... she was sometimes credited in her movies as Krista Nico or Nico Otzak (the latter for *La Dolce Vita*) ... her name is a traditional Greek male name, given to her by one of her first photographers. She took it because she hated "Christa," saying "it's so GERMAN!" ... her exotic birthplace—Cologne, Germany ... she credited Jim Morrison as being the one who told her to write songs. She sang one of his, the apocalyptic "The End" ... she was the subject of a remarkable documentary movie called *Nico Icon* in '95; in it Nico said, "My only regret—I was born a woman instead of a man."

A DATE WITH NICO

August 6, 1928	Andy Warhol is born
November 8, 1935	Alain Delon is born
October 16, 1938	Nico is born
February 22, 1987	Andy Warhol dies after a gall-bladder operation
June 6, 1988	Nico performs her final concert
July 18, 1988	Nico dies in a bicycling accident

MICHELLE PHILLIPS

SWINGIN' '60s CREDENTIALS: Young Michelle was the sweet-faced free-livin' harmonizer on such classic Mamas and Papas songs as "California Dreamin'," "Monday, Monday," and "I Call Your Name."

WORKIN' IT: Michelle was born in 1944, making her only sweet 16 when the '60s started and only 21 when "California Dreamin'" hit it big for the Mamas and the Papas in '65—barely of legal age, and she was singin' hit songs and touring overseas! Though the group only lasted from '65 to '68, the Mamas and the Papas had a significant impact on the history of rock 'n' roll. They came to symbolize the sophisticated folk-rock sound that was coming out of Southern California in the mid-'60s. Songs by the Mamas and the Papas were always well-crafted productions à la the Beatles, with intricate harmonies à la the Beach Boys, but ultimately they had a sound that was all their own. When the group was really cooking, the two-men-two-women lineup had a unique, timeless appeal that

resulted in thirteen hit singles and earned them a position in the Rock and Roll Hall of Fame.

While she was a key part of the group's image and sound, Michelle was not the vocalist that powerful Cass Elliot was. There's only one great M & P song on which Michelle sings lead—"Dedicated to the One I Love" on the '67 album *Deliver*. But Michelle's sweet voice, "the purest soprano in popdom," declared *Time* magazine, perfectly complemented Cass's brassy, jazzy vocals. As a vocal quartet the group was matchless. Furthermore, Michelle was more than just a singer—she was an inspiration. John Phillips wrote many of the group's hits about her, including "Go Where You Wanna Go," "Words of Love," and "I Saw Her Again." And Michelle even co-wrote some of their best songs, including "California Dreamin'," "Creeque Alley," and "Trip Stumble and Fall." Michelle's moment on the national music stage lasted as long as the group did, peaking in June of '67 with the Monterey Pop Festival and ending two months later with their final concert at the Hollywood Bowl.

However, Michelle was talented, beautiful, and well-connected, so it wasn't long before she established a successful career in Hollywood. Her career in front of the camera had begun in '66 when the group made the rounds of all the music-variety shows (*Ed Sullivan*, *Hollywood Palace*, etc.); she also appeared with the Mamas and the Papas in the documentary film about the Monterey Pop Festival. With her first major movie, *Dillinger* in '73, she was nominated for a Golden Globe as the Most Promising Newcomer. Michelle's long list of screen credits includes several regular roles on prominent TV shows—including *Beverly Hills 90210*, *Knots Landing*, *Hotel*, *Second Chances*, and *Malibu Shores*—plus over a dozen TV movies—including *The California Kid* in '74, *Secrets of a Married Man* with William Shatner in '84, *Assault and Matrimony* in '87, *Pretty Poison* in '96, and *Sweetwater* in '99. Along the way Michelle recorded a solo album, *Victim of Romance*, in '76, and wrote an entertaining book, *California Dreamin': The True Story of the Mamas and the Papas*, in '86. She's also executive producer on a new Twentieth Century Fox movie about the Mamas and the Papas, due to be released in the early 2000s. But most of all, unlike some of her famous friends, Michelle managed to make it to the twenty-first century, her beauty and talent and *joie de vivre* intact.

HER '60s LOOK: During the decade Michelle had an angelic, lovely visage, as beautiful as any woman in rock. Her long hair, pretty features, and natural appeal sans make-up gave her an ethereal quality that made her the late-'60s hippie ideal. One of the favorite pictures of her is a photo of Michelle walking in Bel Air, wearing a Girl Scout uniform and a Girl Scout beret, smoking a hand-rolled something. It's her insouciant stylishness, the confident ease with which she pulls the look off, that makes it such an archetypal '60s moment. Concert pictures show her looking great in big floral prints, elaborate silks, and bell bottoms. With her figure and looks, she could've been a top fashion model if she

hadn't gone into pop music. Today, still living in L.A., she radiates happiness and looks more beautiful than ever.

BEHIND THE SCENES: "It was…a time for youth to be itself," Michelle wrote in *California Dreamin'*. "Youth was all. To be young was everything. Drugs were young, music was young, freedom was young." Michelle Gilliam was young, too. A 17-year-old model in San Francisco, she met and quickly fell for folk-singer John Phillips, who was nine years her senior, in the summer of '61. She married Phillips at the end of '62. They were living in New York when they and John's friend, Denny Doherty, took an extended vacation to the Virgin Islands in '65. Singer Cass Elliot, who was sweet on Denny, joined the trio there, and they practiced as a quartet while living in tents on the beach. They relocated to L.A. in '65 and at the end of the year recorded "California Dreamin'." The song was an instant smash, and almost immediately Michelle was speeding down the rock 'n' roll highway—tours, concerts, recording sessions, celebrity parties, travel by Lear jet, an ocean voyage to Europe, impulsive trips to Acapulco and Morocco, shopping sprees (she and John had two Jags and three Rolls-Royces), and the obligatory drug excesses (marijuana and LSD were the narcotics of choice). The main speedbumps during this time were the affairs Michelle had with Denny and Gene Clark of the Byrds while she was married to John. As tensions rose, John, with Denny and Cass taking his side, expelled Michelle from the group in '66. Another singer, Jill Gibson, was brought in for several concerts, a time Michelle later called "the most desperate, painful, hysterical months of my life." After Michelle begged to get back in, Jill was excused and the reformed Mamas and the Papas continued for another year. In '68 Michelle had a daughter, Chynna, who herself became a popular singer in

the '90s. But by the end of '68 Michelle and John had broken up for good.

Michelle then took up with actor Dennis Hopper, a relationship that culminated in a disturbing eight-day marriage in '70. With the group finally disbanded, her Hollywood life took over, resulting in romantic links with Warren Beatty, Jack Nicholson, and Roman Polanski. She gave birth to a son, Austin Hines, in '82, and adopted another son, Aron Wilson, in '88, both of whom are now in college. In March of 2000 Michelle married plastic surgeon Steven Zax, whom she'd known for twenty-eight years, in Mexico.

BONUS SWINGABILITY: Her full moniker at birth was Holly Michelle Gilliam … her exotic birthplace—Long Beach, California … the name Mamas and the Papas was created by Mama Cass, who heard a motorcycle gang calling their women their "mamas" … Michelle's mentioned by name three times in the great "Creeque Alley" … when Michelle and John were trying to name their daughter, Michelle suggested the name India, but John replied, "You might as well call it North Vietnam or China—ah, China, that's nice"; Michelle concurred … Chynna later got famous as the "Phillips" in the group Wilson Phillips in the early '90s … the "Wilsons" were Wendy and Carnie, daughters of Beach Boy Brian … Michelle is the stepmother of Mackenzie Phillips, who played the spirited youngster in the classic *American Graffiti* in '73 and co-starred on the show *One Day at a Time* … in a TV bio, Michelle fondly recalled the brief flash of glory enjoyed by the Mamas and the Papas: "Most wonderful things are not meant to last forever, they're special, they're unique…and that's what the Mamas and the Papas were."

✳ A DATE WITH MICHELLE ✳

August 30, 1935	John Phillips is born
June 4, 1944	Michelle Phillips is born
December 31, 1962	Michelle marries John Phillips
February 5, 1966	"California Dreamin'" enters the *Billboard* charts (it will reach #4)
May 7, 1966	"Monday, Monday" enters the *Billboard* charts (it will reach #1)
June 28, 1966	Michelle is kicked out of the band for two months
March 4, 1967	"Dedicated to the One I Love" enters the *Billboard* charts (it will reach #2)
June 18, 1967	The Mamas and the Papas perform at the Monterey Pop Festival
February 12, 1968	Michelle gives birth to daughter Chynna
July 29, 1974	Cass Elliot dies of a heart attack at the age of 32

NANCY SINATRA

SWINGIN' '60s CREDENTIALS: This hip, hot, happenin' songstress scored major mid-'60s success with hit movies like *Elvis' Speedway* and hit songs like "These Boots Are Made for Walkin'," "Sugar Town," and the smooth "Somethin' Stupid" with dad Frank.

WORKIN' IT: The eldest child of the legendary Frank Sinatra, Nancy Sinatra established herself in the '60s as one of the decade's pre-eminent teen rebels. She was born in Jersey in '40, and by the end of '44 everybody knew her name because of her dad's song, "Nancy with the Laughin' Face." Nancy's first major showcase was on Frank's '59 TV show, where she sang as part of a vocal group called the Tri-Tones. A year later she was on his celebrated TV special, the one with Elvis as a guest star. Within a few years she was appearing in teen-oriented movies like *Get Yourself a College Girl* and *For Those Who Think Young* (both in '64), but her singing, while popular in other countries, was still mired in saccharine puddles of soft pop and novelty tunes.

A radical remake of her image mid-decade positioned her as a tough, no-nonsense alternative to gentle vocalists such as Annette Funicello and Shelley Fabares. In '66 she hit the top of the charts with her assertive anthem, "These Boots Are Made for Walkin'." "Summer Wine," "Sugar Town," "Love Eyes," and "Somethin' Stupid" quickly followed, giving her a total of ten top-40 hits in a three-year period. Her voice wasn't the equal of classic divas like Janis Joplin, but she did convey the right attitude at a time when there was revolution in the air. In April '99 she confessed as much to the *San Francisco Chronicle*: "What little success I have can be directly attributed to the songs," she said, and she credited singer Lee Hazlewood with creating her distinctive sound—"part spaghetti Western and part Los Angeles pop, liberally sprinkled with strange lyric twists," according to the *Chron*.

The hits fortified her movie career. A starring role alongside Peter Fonda in *The Wild Angels* ('66) was followed by a starring role alongside Elvis in *Speedway* ('68). In the latter she belted out "Your Groovy Self," one of the few times an actress was allowed to solo in an Elvis movie. Her popularity helped the movie do boffo box-office biz. During this time she had her own innovative TV special, *Movin' with Nancy*, which brought her a Golden Globe nomination as Best TV Star. In '67 she also joined a select group of vocalists who sang a theme song for a James Bond movie (*You Only Live Twice*). In '67 and '68 she performed in Vietnam for the troops, and in '69 she headlined in Vegas. (Some kind of record was set during her stint, because her dad and brother were also performing in separate hotels at the same time.)

Nancy spent the next two decades concentrating on her family, with only sporadic recording. In the '90s she made a comeback that included a popular *Playboy* spread in May '95; to her credit, at 55 she still looked remarkably good (though her dad was only coolly accepting of the exposure). Late in the '90s she returned to the concert stage with a series of well-received concerts at some of the country's hippest venues, proving that she is still one of the most durable and popular stars to emerge from the '60s.

HER '60s LOOK: The big hair and bold make-up—or is it the bold hair and big make-up?—that Nancy perfected and popularized in the mid-'60s had its roots in the glamorous styles of movie queens from an earlier era. The look fell out of favor as the more natural hippie styles gained favor at the

end of the decade, but for a while there Nancy and her colorful fashions were the apotheosis of hip. She helped make go-go boots a fashion staple, of course. In the April '99 *San Francisco Chronicle* article she proudly stated, "I traveled, and I brought back fashions that hadn't yet been seen here, like [designer] Mary Quant. I had the good fortune of going to Carnaby Street in the early '60s. Of course, when I came back here, my friends would ask me where I was gonna go play tennis, because they'd never seen a miniskirt! Of course, the boots were an absolute necessity because of the song."

BEHIND THE SCENES: In '60, 20-year-old Nancy married pop singer Tommy Sands, who would star with Annette in *Babes in Toyland* a year later. Nancy and Tommy divorced in '65. Later stories linked her with both Bobby Darin and Elvis. Whatever her brief relationship was with Elvis, it allegedly broke off when his wife, Priscilla Presley, announced she was pregnant. Nancy then threw Priscilla a baby shower. Early in the '70s Nancy remarried, to Hugh Lambert, and gave birth to two girls. Meanwhile, resolutely and tenaciously loyal to her family, Nancy has written two books about her famous dad, *Frank Sinatra, My Father* and *Frank Sinatra: An American Legend*, and she's worked hard to preserve his legacy and defend his reputation when she's felt it has been unfairly attacked. "People deserve to be treated fairly, whether they are doctors, secretaries, teachers, crossing-guards, presidents, homemakers or legends," she writes at her family's Web site. "Nobody in this country should ever be made to feel like a second-class citizen—including, and especially not, Frank Sinatra. He is the one who has fought all his life for fair play and equal rights for all people."

BONUS SWINGABILITY: Her dad's nickname for her—Chicken ... her exotic birthplace—Jersey City, New Jersey ... she's the sister of Tina and Frank, Jr. ... "Nancy with the Laughing Face" was written by Phil Silvers and Jimmy Van Heusen to commemorate her fourth birthday ... when she appeared on an episode of *The Man from U.N.C.L.E.* called "The Take Me to Your Leader Affair," she played a character named Coco Cool and sang a duet— "Trouble"—with Illya Kuryakin, played by David McCallum ... Nancy today is comfortable with her music legacy; she told the *San Francisco Chronicle* in '99, "I'm not going to go down as one of the world's greatest singers. I don't have a shot at that. But I still have people say they always know it's me when they hear a record of mine, even if they don't recognize the song. I guess that's something"... Nancy has her own Web site—http://www.sinatrafamily.com/nancy.html.

A DATE WITH NANCY

December 12, 1915	Frank Sinatra is born
August 27, 1937	Tommy Sands is born
June 8, 1940	Nancy Sinatra is born
September 11, 1960	Nancy marries Tommy
May 12, 1960	Frank's TV special with Elvis and Nancy
February 5, 1966	"These Boots Are Made for Walkin'" enters the *Billboard* chart (it will reach #1)
July 20, 1966	*The Wild Angels* is released
December 19, 1966	"Sugar Town" enters the *Billboard* chart (it will reach #5)
March 25, 1967	"Somethin' Stupid" enters the *Billboard* chart (it will reach #1)
December 11, 1967	*Movin' with Nancy* is aired
June 12, 1968	*Speedway* is released
December 12, 1970	Nancy marries Hugh Lambert
May 14, 1998	Frank Sinatra dies

GRACE SLICK

elsewhere for her ticket to stardom. Fortunately, Jefferson Airplane was now boarding. This S.F. band had made one minor album in '65 when its lead singer, Signe Anderson, left to raise a family. In '66 Grace, now 21, replaced her, and Airplane took off. Not only did Grace bring a distinctive, forceful vocal style and hypnotic looks to the band, she brought two songs with her from her Great Society days: "White Rabbit" (written by Grace) and "Somebody to Love" (written by her brother-in-law). The Airplane soared in '67 with the release of these two top-10 hits and *Surrealistic Pillow*, a majestic rock album that became (along with *Sgt. Pepper* and *The Doors*) one of the three seminal albums of the Summer of Love. At its peak, the Airplane was both vital and popular, showing its psychedelic stuff at all three major rock festivals of the late '60s (the Monterey Pop Festival in '67, Woodstock in August '69, and Altamont in December '69). Grace was the band's centerpiece, commanding attention with her riveting beauty and a fearless onstage presence that made her capable of doing anything at anytime, from lifting up her skirt onstage to improvising monologues to dressing as a nun to flashing her breasts to photographers. It was quite a contrast to the more traditional styles of contemporaries like Petula Clark and Dionne Warwick.

Unfortunately, Jefferson Airplane's flight was relatively short. Within two years the tensions among the band members and consecutive commercial failures brought the group crashing back to earth. While Jefferson Airplane continued to produce albums after the '60s, relevance and hits were harder to come by. Renamed Jefferson Starship, the band released a huge hit, "Miracles" in '75, but by '78 Grace had quit to make a couple of solo albums. She came back on board in the mid-'80s, and with another name, Starship, the group had enough fuel for a few more hits—"We Built This City" in '85, "Sara" in '86, and "Nothing's Gonna Stop Us Now" in '87—before Grace left the band for good in '88. The '90s brought induction in the Rock and Roll Hall of Fame, Grace's autobiography (*Somebody to Love?* in '98), and a Marin County exhibition of her mixed-media drawings of rock stars (some of the profits from the sales went to welfare and animal-rights organizations), but an end, it seemed, to performing. "I don't like old people on a rock 'n' roll stage," she said, "including myself."

SWINGIN' '60s CREDENTIALS: The formidable dark-eyed diva of San Francisco's Jefferson Airplane sang "White Rabbit," "Somebody to Love," and other hits that established this band as a strong force at the end of the decade.

WORKIN' IT: "Apart from lifting heavy furniture, it never occurred to me that I couldn't do anything I wanted to," Grace explained to the *San Francisco Chronicle* in '98. "It just depended upon my own level of desire and talent. I stick to what I'm good at." What's she's good at is survival. Raised comfortably in an affluent suburb of San Francisco, Grace was married and modeling when she and family members formed a band called the Great Society. The band never garnered more than mild local interest, so Grace looked

HER '60s LOOK: She's got striking blue eyes, a pretty face framed by black bangs, and long black hair, yet there's a toughness to her look—a balance between psychedelic hippie chick and rockin' biker chic. Always prepared to be outrageous, she once appeared on the Smothers Brothers' TV show in blackface. She embraced all the fashions of the late '60s—soft 'n' lacy, tough 'n' leathery, psychedelic 'n' swirly—and made them her own. She listed these outfits among those she wore onstage: a Nazi stormtrooper uniform, a samurai outfit, a Girl Scout uniform, Indian caftans, and an L.A.P.D. shirt. Once, she claims, she even went topless during an outdoor show because she didn't want the rain to ruin her silk blouse. Here's her own description of a famous outfit she wore: "When all else failed, I got two extra-large paisley-printed towels, sewed them together at the top corners, stuck my head through the opening, and belted the front and back at the waist with an enormous five-inch-wide black rubber tire tread. No more couturier department for Grace. To this day, you can still see me in that towel outfit on some VH1 'Flashback' programs. Lucky you."

BEHIND THE SCENES: Grace Slick is admirably unapologetic about her affairs with: A) most drugs known to man; and B) most men known to drugs. "I was just doing whatever felt good at the time," she said in a TV bio. Grace readily confesses to trying every narcotic except heroin (heroin is "too much work," she said). Among her drug stories is one involving an invitation she received from First Daughter Tricia Nixon to visit the White House in the early '70s. Grace showed up with Yippie leader Abbie Hoffman as her "bodyguard" and 600 micromilligrams of LSD that she hoped to slip into the president's drink, but she and the notorious rabble-rousing Hoffman were escorted out before they could get close. Unfortunately, her wanton drug use resulted in several DUI's and bouts with rehab. Grace also admits to sleeping with almost every bandmember in the original Airplane lineup, as well as a barely coherent Jim Morrison. All the while, Grace was a married woman. Her cool last name came from Jerry Slick, "the boy next door" whom she'd married in '61; she left him when she left the Great Society, but they didn't divorce until the early '70s.

In '71 she had a daughter, China Wing Kantner, by Airplane cohort Paul Kantner. Motherhood didn't slow her down much—she still kept her defiant attitude and was shown breastfeeding her baby in a national magazine. In '76 she married lighting director Skip Johnson, who was approximately thirteen years her junior. But trouble still lurked ahead. In an event tinged with irony, her Marin County house burned down in '93 when it was ignited by sparks from nearby workers. They were welding a sign that read "Danger: Fire Area." A year later, after drunkenly brandishing an unloaded shotgun at the fuzz, Grace had to be forcibly taken down and disarmed. Her marriage broken, Grace now lives in Malibu. The key word is "lives." Unlike others who sped through the reckless, indulgent '60s, Grace Slick has managed not to die. And she's managed not to conform, either. Her goal, she once said, was to be hanging out in bars at the age of 75.

BONUS SWINGABILITY: Her moniker at birth was Grace Wing ... her exotic birthplace—Chicago, Illinois ... her idol while growing up: Betty Grable ... her idol in the '60s: Mick Jagger ... daughter China Kantner is an actress who's appeared in several '90s films like *Grace of My Heart* and *The Evening Star*, played a recurring character, Willow, on *Home Improvement*, and worked as a VJ for MTV ... in '92 *Life* asked her if she missed anything about the '60s: "No, not really. I did it. It's like asking, Do you miss the fourth grade? I loved the fourth grade when I was in it, but I don't want to do it again."

A DATE WITH GRACE

October 30, 1939	Grace Slick is born
August 26, 1961	Grace marries Jerry Slick
October 14, 1966	Grace's first concert with Jefferson Airplane
January 14, 1967	The Airplane performs at the first "Be-In" in San Francisco
May 6, 1967	"Somebody to Love" enters the *Billboard* charts (it will reach #5)
June 17, 1967	Jefferson Airplane performs at the Monterey Pop Festival
July 1, 1967	"White Rabbit" enters the *Billboard* charts (it will reach #8)
August 17, 1969	Jefferson Airplane performs at Woodstock
December 6, 1969	Jefferson Airplane performs at Altamont
January 25, 1971	Grace gives birth to daughter China

DUSTY SPRINGFIELD

SWINGIN' '60s CREDENTIALS: This husky-voiced, blonde pop-rocker charted big with such top-10 hits as "I Only Want to Be with You," "Wishin' and Hopin'," and "Son of a Preacher Man," the latter off her great *Dusty in Memphis* LP.

WORKIN' IT: A spearhead of the British Invasion that swept across America in the mid-'60s, Dusty Springfield was one of the decade's most prominent and distinctive singers. She was born and raised in London, where, in her late teens and early twenties, she sang with two groups, the Lana Sisters and the Springfields, a folk group that also included her brother. Changing her style to emulate the Motown sound she loved, she hit the British charts in '63 with the peppy "I Only Want to Be with You," which jumped across the Atlantic concurrently with the first Beatles songs to become an American hit in '64. Three years of steady airplay followed for Dusty, highlighted by "Wishin' and Hopin'," "Stay Awhile," "All I See Is You," and "You Don't Have to Say You Love Me." During the decade she toured, appeared on *Ready, Steady, Go!* and *The Ed Sullivan Show*, and even hosted her own music-variety show on the BBC (among her guests were Jimi Hendrix, Tina Turner, and Woody Allen). It was her voice that people loved, a raw, intensely soulful sound that conveyed powerful emotions but also unspoken vulnerability. "The Queen of Soul," some called her. Burt Bacharach wrote after she died, "You could hear just three notes and you knew it was Dusty. It was such a rare and beautiful voice." *Rolling Stone* magazine called her the best pop singer ever to come out of Britain.

She also had a good sense of what to record. According to the *San Francisco Chronicle*, "She sang with exquisite longing and had a discriminating ear for orchestrated pop-soul gems. She was among the first to cover material by Burt Bacharach, Randy Newman, Jimmy Webb, Carole King and other young songwriters."

Surprisingly, she never scored a #1 hit, but she did release a landmark album, the powerful *Dusty in Memphis* in '69 with its classic cut, "Son of a Preacher Man." She explained in the liner notes why this album eclipsed her earlier work: "For five years, since I started recording, I had been coming into studios and finding everything all done beforehand…in Memphis, I was a little intimidated at first because I'd never worked the way they do…trying out different approaches until we eventually came to some agreement between everybody, myself included. Being used to working in a different way, I felt very tight about it, almost entirely on my own and exposed all of a sudden, but I sort of grew up as the album progressed, became less inhibited." Critics instantly hailed the album as her masterpiece.

Sadly, at age 30, she had reached the pinnacle of her career, and she began a long, depressing slump. Her late-'70s attempt at a comeback got only a lukewarm reception, but she did have a few more milestones left in her: She sang with the Pet Shop Boys on "What Have I Done to Deserve This?," a #2 hit in '88, "Son of a Preacher Man" made it onto the soundtrack for the film *Pulp Fiction* in '94, and she had two anthology albums released in '97 and '98. After recording her last album, *A Very Fine Love*, in '94, Dusty was diagnosed with breast cancer. She later told a London newspaper her reaction when she found out about the disease: "I shed about three tears in the hallway and then said, 'let's have lunch…' I had a really good time—don't know why, that's the spirit of my family, as if to say, 'oh to hell with it.'" Five years later, she died in her home at the age of 59. Her death came a day before she was to be honored at Buckingham Palace and eleven days before her induction into the Rock and Roll Hall of Fame. Even the Queen of England said she was "saddened" by Dusty's demise. At her funeral, another great British singer from the '60s, Lulu, addressed the congregation: "Dusty was the first one to demonstrate girl power. She was a real powerful force but yet she was shy. She was very vulnerable. She drew me close to her. She had tremendous courage and she bared her soul to the whole world. I say now that she and her gift have returned to Heaven. She had such a great spirit that it will never die and will never disappear."

HER '60s LOOK: When it came to classic physical beauty, Dusty had a really great voice. Even she admitted that she wasn't a looker: She once said that she never shook off the feeling of being an "awful fat, ugly middle-class kid." She told a London newspaper that her appearance inspired her to sing. At the age of 16 she looked at her reflection in the mirror and told herself, "be miserable or become someone else," which she attempted with a blonde beehive hairdo and dark, smudgy "panda" make-up around her eyes. Not one for wild costumes or the popular hippy fashions, she dressed glamorously in glitzy gowns when she was onstage, part of her effort to metamorphose herself from the ugly-duckling kid into a beautiful entertainer. Just before she died she colored her hair one last time— "I'm going out blonde," she reportedly declared to friends.

BEHIND THE SCENES: When the hits stopped coming in the early '70s, Dusty claimed she was "bored with Britain" and moved to L.A., dropping out of show biz for most of the decade. During the L.A. years Dusty lived alone and was the topic of wild rumors concerning her bisexuality, which she neither admitted to nor denied. What she did admit to was living a life of drugged debauchery. While in L.A., she suffered through a prolonged depression and even attempted suicide. After fifteen years in California Dusty moved to Amsterdam and then back to her homeland. She lived the last few years of her life in Henley-on-Thames, about thirty miles outside of London, England.

BONUS SWINGABILITY: She used a fake moniker—her real name was Mary Isabel Catherine Bernadette O'Brien ... the British press had a nickname for her—"the white Negress," because of her soulful style ... her exotic birthplace—the swingin'est, London, England ... one of the early critics of apartheid, she was deported from South Africa in '64 after performing for a racially mixed audience ... Dusty was known as a perfectionist in the studio, which

brought her a rep as being "difficult" to work with, but she knew what she wanted, and she was usually right ... according to Neil Tennant and Chris Lowe of the Pet Shop Boys, "Dusty was a tender, exhilarating and soulful singer, incredibly intelligent at phrasing a song, painstakingly building it up to a thrilling climax" ... here's the *L.A. Times'* report on her funeral, held on March 12, 1999: "To the sounds of Dusty Springfield's greatest hit, 'You Don't Have to Say You Love Me,' a crowd of well-wishers and fans gathered in the rain Friday for the funeral of the 1960s pop star, and watched as a horse-drawn carriage brought her coffin to a church in the riverside town of Henley-on-Thames, west of London. Pop singers Elvis Costello and Neil Tennant, lead singer with the Pet Shop Boys, spoke at the service. 'She sang with her whole heart,' a mourner told Sky Television."

A DATE WITH DUSTY

April 16, 1939	Dusty Springfield is born
January 25, 1964	"I Only Want to Be with You" enters the *Billboard* charts (it will hit #12)
March 28, 1964	"Stay Awhile" enters the *Billboard* charts (it will hit #38)
June 20, 1964	"Wishin' and Hopin'" enters the *Billboard* charts (it will hit #6)
May 21, 1966	"You Don't Have to Say You Love Me" enters the *Billboard* charts (it will hit #4)
September 17, 1966	"All I See Is You" enters the *Billboard* charts (it will hit #20)
November 30, 1968	"Son of a Preacher Man" enters the *Billboard* charts (it will hit #10)
March 2, 1999	Dusty dies of cancer

TINA TURNER ✳

SWINGIN' '60s CREDENTIALS: The hardest-workin' woman in show biz sang, sweated, and sizzled her way to fame as lead singer of the Ike and Tina Revue; only later was it revealed that she'd been through hell during the decade.

WORKIN' IT: Elton John has said that Tina Turner was the first real woman singer in rock and roll. While many other performers sang their songs while standing still or swaying a little (think of the Supremes), Tina was all kinetic energy and white-hot sexuality. It was a style, she said later, that was based on the performances she saw in a Pentecostal church as a kid growing up in Nutbush, Tennessee.

After her mother moved out when Tina was 10 years old and her father split three years later, Tina was raised by cousins and a sister in St. Louis. Sixteen years old in early '56, she met 24-year-old Ike Turner. An experienced session musician, Ike was leading a band called the Kings of Rhythm at Club Manhattan, a popular St. Louis nightclub that Tina frequented. The story goes that Tina badgered him to let her sing, and when he refused, she jumped up onstage one night during intermission, grabbed the microphone, and let it rip. Ike quickly hired her to sing backup, and by the turn of the decade she was the undeniable star of the dynamic Ike and Tina Turner Revue. In '60 their raw, earthy "A Fool in Love," broke through to #2 on the R&B charts. More chart successes followed through the '60s: "I'm Blue," "Poor Fool," "I Can't Believe What You Say," "It's Gonna Work Out Fine," "I Idolize You," and Phil Spector's majestic "River Deep, Mountain High" (which Tina recorded without Ike). Tina's singing, however, was best appreciated live, where she put her entire body into her performances. "I don't just sing my songs, I act them," she

said. The Ike and Tina Turner Revue toured successfully throughout the decade. Sometimes they would perform a half-dozen shows in a single night. In '69 the group landed the prime position as one of the much-noticed opening acts for the Rolling Stones on their fabled '69 tour of the states.

The '70s began with more Ike and Tina hits: "Come Together," "I Want to Take You Higher," "Proud Mary" (which brought Tina her first Grammy Award), and Tina's autobiographical "Nutbush City Limits." Tina ventured into films with a show-stopping debut as the frenzied Acid Queen in *Tommy* ('75), followed by the *Sgt. Pepper's Lonely Hearts Club Band* debacle in '78, the villainous Aunty Entity role in *Mad Max Beyond Thunderdome* in '85, and *The Last Action Hero* in '93. On her own as of the mid-'70s, Tina revived her slumping singing career in '84 with the triumphant album *Private Dancer*, which brought her three Grammy awards and ushered in a new era of hits, record-breaking tours, and popular music videos. Her most well-known songs during this time were "Better Be Good to Me," "Private Dancer," "What's Love Got to Do With It," "We Don't Need Another Hero (Thunderdome)," and "Typical Male." In '86 her autobiography, *I, Tina*, revealed the dark side of her years with Ike and her struggle to stardom. Her albums (*Wildest Dreams* in '96 and *Twenty Four Seven* in '99) were both released to wild acclaim, adding to her stature as one of the biggest-selling singers in music history. Touring one more time in 2000, she might be the most electrifying 60-year-old in the world.

HER '60s LOOK: Tina's got an intensely passionate and expressive face, with enormous teeth and a smile you could read by. Unfortunately, when she bleached her hair in late '60, the treatment was done incorrectly and all of her hair fell out. She's worn wigs ever since. After Ike broke her nose enough times, she finally had to get doctors to not just fix it, but reconstruct it. Few noticed, though, because she's always had the fastest-moving legs in the biz. In fact, whenever she appeared on *Late Night with David Letterman* in the '90s, he introduced her as having "the best legs on the planet," an opinion confirmed by ads she did for Hanes Resilience Hosiery when she was in her late fifties. "I was raised on pork," she wrote in her autobiography, "and believe me, I'm healthy."

BEHIND THE SCENES: "I wasn't as smart then as I am now," Tina wrote in *I, Tina*, "but who is?" At 16 Tina got a close-up view of Ike Turner and thought, "God, he's ugly." But, she admitted, "I kept listening and looking. I almost went into a trance just watching him." At 19 she first went to bed with Ike and thought, "God, this is horrible." But, she wrote later, soon she had fallen in love and "become addicted to it." Almost 21 in the fall of '60, Tina gave birth to Ike's baby, her second son (the first, fathered by one of the Kings of Rhythm with sax appeal, had been born in '58). At 22 Tina married 30-year-old Ike in Tijuana, Mexico. While touring and recording throughout the '60s, Tina had housekeepers to help with her sons and two of Ike's from a previous relationship. Her private life throughout the decade was hell, lowlighted by Ike's continuous physical and emotional abuse that allegedly got so bad he burned her with cigarettes, hit her with phones, and broke her ribs. Completely dispirited by the violence and Ike's constant womanizing, Tina attempted suicide in '68. In the '70s she took to carrying a gun, so fearful was she of Ike's drug-fueled rampages. During these difficult years she pursued inner peace by studying Buddhism. Finally, she walked away from Ike in '76, though she was broke and had little hope of solo success. Her stunning turnaround in the '80s is almost too fantastic to be true.

Since '86 she's been living with a German recording executive who is sixteen years her junior; she divides her time between estates in Switzerland and in the south of France. Might she marry again? "Marriage is important when you're afraid, insecure, or need something," she told an interviewer in early 2000. Comfortable with her present and future, she seems to have put her turbulent past well behind her. "One

shouldn't have time for bitterness when you're trying to be successful," she has said. "Work towards what you want, that's my attitude."

BONUS SWINGABILITY: She uses a fake moniker—her real name is Annie Mae Bullock. The name Tina was given to her by Ike, who was playing on the name of one of his favorite fictional characters, Sheena, Queen of the Jungle ... her exotic birthplace—Brownsville, Tennessee ... Tina recorded her first hit, "A Fool in Love," when the regularly scheduled singer failed to show up at the studio ... supposedly Tina taught Mick Jagger the dance moves he displayed in his '60s concerts ... Sammy Davis, Jr.'s appreciative gift to her when she appeared with him in a 1970 TV show—a new white Jaguar XJ6 ... Tina's life was depicted in the '93 film *What's Love Got to Do With It*, starring Angela Bassett ... arrested numerous times after Tina left, Ike was in prison on a drug conviction when the couple was inducted into the Rock and Roll Hall of Fame in '91 ... in February of 2000 she told *Vanity Fair* that her greatest fears are spiders and snakes, the person she admires most is Oprah Winfrey, and her personal motto is "Put my right foot forward" ... keep up with Tina at her Web site—http://www.tina-turner.com.

 A DATE WITH TINA

November 15, 1931	Ike Turner is born
November 26, 1939	Tina Turner is born
October 3, 1960	"A Fool in Love" enters the *Billboard* charts (it will hit #27)
October 27, 1960	Tina gives birth to Ike's son Ronald
September 4, 1961	"It's Gonna Work Out Fine" enters the *Billboard* charts (it will hit #14)
January 13, 1962	"Poor Fool" enters the *Billboard* charts (it will hit #38)
November 8, 1969	The first concert, held in the L.A. Forum, of the Stones' U.S. tour
February 13, 1971	"Proud Mary" enters the *Billboard* charts (it will hit #4)
July 2, 1976	Tina walks out on Ike
March 29, 1978	Tina's divorce is final

LULU

SWINGIN' '60s CREDENTIALS: This big-voiced carrot-topped Scot took the world "from crayons to perfume" with "To Sir With Love" in '67.

WORKIN' IT: Like Petula Clark, Lulu was a child star in the U.K. who became an international sensation in the mid '60s. Born in Scotland, Lulu knew poverty and hard work as a child growing up in a tough part of Glasgow. However, even at a young age she was a noteworthy singer—she was performing in public at age 9 and singing in clubs with a group called the Gleneagles while barely in her teens.

Spotted in '63 by a talent scout (who became her manager), in '64, 15-year-old Lulu and her newly renamed back-up band, the Luvvers, made it into the top-10 of the U.K. charts with a raucous remake of the Isley Brothers' song "Shout." By '65 she was a solo act, recording two more minor hits, "Leave a Little Love" and "Try to Understand." During this time she also started getting film work, making her debut in a bizarre British sci-fi/puppet movie called *Gonks Go Beat* ('64).

Her biggest movie came in '67, the year the Lulupalooza phenomenon finally jumped across the pond. Not only did Lulu have a prominent role as a precocious London schoolgirl in *To Sir with Love*, but she sang the movie's lush theme, pumping heartache into the provocative plea, "What can I give you in return?" It would become her signature song. The movie was a smash, the song quickly leaped to #1 in the U.S., and Lulu was an international star. She followed up with several more popular songs in the U.K. (notably "Boom Bang-a-Bang" in '69), though none of them approached the international success of "To Sir with Love." She did, however, host her own BBC variety show, *It's Lulu*, which cemented her stature in the U.K.

Modestly successful with records in the '70s, she did have one song that hit number 007: the theme to the Bond flick *The Man with the Golden Gun* ('74). She had another hit in '81, the top-20 "I Could Never Miss You (More Than I Do)," followed by new albums and more U.K hits in the '80s and '90s, including a re-recording of "Shout" in '86 and the dancy "I'm Back for More" in '93.

Expanding her skills, she wrote her autobiography in '85 and co-wrote Tina Turner's Grammy-nominated hit "I Don't Wanna Fight" in '94. In recent years she's had a recurring role on the British comedy series *Absolutely Fabulous*, sung with Soul Asylum on *MTV Unplugged*, once again played Barbara Pegg for the TV-movie *To Sir with Love 2* in '96, and started hosting a music show called *Red Alert* in '99. Her album, *Where The Poor Boys Dance*, came out in 2000.

HER '60s LOOK: Photographer David Bailey described her to Britain's *Daily Express*: "She was this cute young thing. Tiny with the most enormous eyes. Everyone fell in love with her." What was not to love about Lulu? A short, swingin' flame-colored 'do, a big sweet smile that burst from underneath cheery cheeks, and expressive blue eyes added up to a fab '60s look. Though it looked like she was wearing the same baggy clothes all through *To Sir with Love*, she's really got terrific fashion sense and has always stayed au courant. Today, with her hair dyed blonde, she looks as hip and radiant as ever.

BEHIND THE SCENES: Twenty years old in '69, Lulu married a Bee Gee, Maurice Gibb, with another Gibb brother, Robin, standing as the best man. Lulu divorced her Gibb in '74, married a hairdresser that same year, had a son in '78, and had a divorce in '92.

BONUS SWINGABILITY: She uses a fake moniker—her real name is Marie McDonald McLaughlin Lawrie ... the name Lulu was supposedly invented by her first manager as a short, peppy alternative to her full name ... her exotic birthplace—Glasgow, Scotland ... on *To Sir with Love*, one of the arrangers was John Paul Jones, who would later play bass for Led Zeppelin ... "I'm a fighter, always have been," she told the *Daily Express*, "I like a challenge. The bigger, the better."

 A DATE WITH LULU

November 3, 1948	Lulu is born
December 22, 1949	Maurice Gibb is born
June 14, 1967	*To Sir with Love* (the film) is released
September 23, 1967	"To Sir with Love" (the song) enters the *Billboard* charts (it will reach #1)

THE TV STARS

The '50s are usually referred to as the Golden Age of television. And rightfully so: Almost fifty years later, there's still not much that's any better than *I Love Lucy* or *The Honeymooners*. Though the '60s didn't surpass the '50s in television excellence (well, maybe a case could be made for *The Dick Van Dyke Show*), at least the '60s were pushing TV's boundaries. *Julia* proved that a minority could be the focus of a successful series, that girl in *That Girl* was portrayed as more than a '50s housewife, *Laugh-In* broke all the rules of traditional TV comedy, and audiences suspended their disbelief for fantasy shows like *I Dream of Jeannie* and *Bewitched*. These '60s hits paved the way for the even more daring and creative shows (*The Jeffersons*, *Maude*, *The Flip Wilson Show*, *The Six Million Dollar Man*) of the '70s. The TV actresses profiled here were trailblazers, bringing new kinds of characters to the airwaves and helping us see television in brand new ways.

JUDY CARNE

SWINGIN' '60s CREDENTIALS: This talent-light accent-heavy short-haired free-loving drug-taking British bird clowned around as the resilient "sock it to me" girl on *Rowan & Martin's Laugh-In*, but she's probably better known for her role as Burt Reynold's wife in a tempestuous two-year marriage.

WORKIN' IT: Judy Carne had a gimmick. Her "sock it to me" bit on *Rowan & Martin's Laugh-In* ('68-'70) involved the cast trying to trick the 29-year-old comedienne into saying "sock it to me," then as soon she did they'd

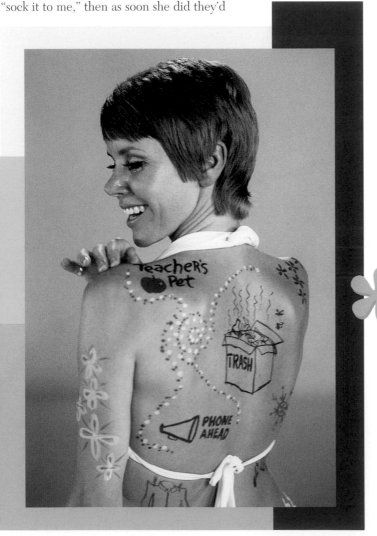

bombard her with water or drop her through a trapdoor or do something equally slapsticky. Here's the kind of simple exchange that caused wacky hijinks to ensue:

> Dan Rowan: "Read any good books lately, Judy?"
> Judy: "Well, right now I'm reading that old Greek saga,
> *The Odyssey.*"
> Dan: "You mean Homer's epic?"
> Judy: "It may be an epic to you, but it's a saga to me."

Saga to me = sock it to me = madcap merriment. Sometimes Judy didn't even have to say the line to get pummeled:

> Judy: "The audience is getting bored"
> Dan Rowan: "What did you say, Judy?"
> Judy: "They're getting bored, you know, bored?"
> Dan: "Board?"
> Judy: "Yes!" (a board hits her in the head)
> Judy: "Cute, fellas, cute, well at least it wasn't water"
> (two buckets dump water on her)
> Judy: "Oh, I get it, it was all just a trap" (she falls through a
> trap door)

Milking her British accent for all it was worth (at a time when British accents were the hippest fashion accessory), she got famous for the routine, the show became a huge, influential hit, and her phrase became part of the popular lexicon (even Richard Nixon was coaxed into saying it on the show). Up till then, her résumé had included four obscure '60s movies (a role as the Nameless Broad in *The Americanization of Emily*, '64) and various '60s TV shows like *The Man from U.N.C.L.E.*, *The Big Valley*, and *I Dream of Jeannie*. After her *Laugh-In* years, Judy had a date with obscurity. The marijuana and mescaline she experimented with in the '60s turned into a heroin addiction in the '70s, and her downward-spiraling career eventually disintegrated altogether. Early in the decade she did a few TV movies, performed a musical act in Vegas, and got some notoriety for her talk-show appearances, but by the mid-'70s there was nothing really significant in her career. (At one point she did her act in a Juarez, Mexico, nightclub on a stage where the blood from the opening act—a cockfight—had to be mopped up before she could go on.) Regrettably, she was busted for quaaludes in '77 and for heroin in '78, and though she eventually won acquittals on both charges, by then her career and her money were gone. Compounding her problems, she suffered a broken neck in a '78 car crash, forcing her to wear an ungainly 65-pound "cage" with a steel "halo" screwed into her skull for support. She wrote her

bittersweet autobiography, *Laughing on the Outside, Crying on the Inside: The Bittersweet Saga of the Sock-It-To-Me Girl*, in '85. In it she seemed to find some meaning to her roller-coaster life: "I think I'm being saved for something," she wrote after her '78 accident. "Sometimes life's tragedies are the very things that help us survive."

HER '60s LOOK:

Her short kicky haircut came courtesy of Vidal Sassoon himself. With her big smile and ninety-pound frame, she had features 'n' figure made for cute comedy. She might've seemed cuter 'n' perkier if adorable Goldie Hawn hadn't been taking the whole cute 'n' perky image to starry new heights on *Laugh-In*. Reynolds once said that she dressed like Peter Pan, and Judy admitted in her book that throughout her life she's "been drawn to wearing boyish things."

BEHIND THE SCENES: During the '60s Judy had relationships with hairboy Vidal Sassoon, racer Stirling Moss, actors Steve McQueen and Anthony Newley, and photographer Dean Goodhill. In her book, Judy also described a love affair she had in the mid-'60s with a woman named Ashley. Nervous TV execs warned her of the bad publicity that might result, and they arranged carefully chosen escorts for her when she attended public events. Judy left Ashley for actor Peter Deuel in '66. But her most famous relationship of all began when she happened to share a flight to Miami with actor Burt Reynolds in '62. After a meeting that she said was "magical," they "were immediately in love." They soon rented a house together in the L.A. hills and were married in a North Hollywood church in the summer of '63. In their Studio City home they entertained friends like Clint Eastwood and Ryan O'Neal. But in '65, Judy and Burt divorced, bitterly. Both of them wrote about the break-up in their autobiographies. Burt claimed he couldn't stand her drug use and low-life friends. She claimed that he was threateningly jealous of her past loves, was very domineering, and was insecure about his hair

loss. She claimed that he once chainsawed the legs and sides off their big TV to make it fit into a hole he had sledgehammered into the wall. More distressingly, she also claimed that he slapped her around and threw plates at the walls. Burt defended himself against these charges by writing that she was an outrageous flirt, she used profanity in almost every sentence, and "she was game for anything from moose hunting to car racing, dinner in Europe, whatever anyone suggested." Still, she has stuck to her story. She wrote, "I left Burt Reynolds the day he threw me against our fireplace and cracked my skull," to which he countered, "She sometimes claims that I beat her, other times she says I was a saint. Both are entirely untrue." Both acknowledge that he gave her money when she was engulfed in drug and financial problems in the '70s. Five years after divorcing Burt, Judy had a one-year marriage to TV producer Robert Bergmann.

BONUS SWINGABILITY: She uses a stage moniker—her real name is Joyce Botterill ... her exotic birthplace—Northampton, England ... she had a nose job, "a bob," she called it, early in her career ... on New Year's Eve in '68 she and boyfriend Goodhill threw a Hollywood party attended by such entertainment luminaries as Jim Morrison, Harry Nilsson, Flip Wilson, and members of the Mamas and the Papas and Three Dog Night ... when she appeared on *The Ed Sullivan Show* in '69, Ed introduced her as Judy Crane, but she carried on with a live musical tribute to the Apollo 11 moonwalk ... Judy was on *The Kraft Music Hall* TV show in '69 that featured a number from an unlikely singer: New York Mets' pitching sensation Tom Seaver ... in '71, she appeared on *The Tonight Show* on a night that ex-husband Reynolds was hosting; they apologized to each other and joked comfortably ... Judy wrote that she was there the night Cher met Gregg Allman in a Hollywood nightclub in '75; later that night, Judy invited them back to her place, where Cher and Gregg were able to talk quietly for the first time ... Judy turned down a *Penthouse* magazine offer to pose with other naked women for $50,000—she thought it would be a career killer.

A DATE WITH JUDY

February 11, 1936	Burt Reynolds is born
April 27, 1939	Judy Carne is born
June 28, 1963	Judy marries Burt Reynolds
September 9, 1967	*Rowan & Martin's Laugh-In* debuts as a one-hour special
January 22, 1968	*Laugh-In* debuts as a weekly show
July 20, 1969	Judy sings on *The Ed Sullivan Show*

DIAHANN CARROLL

SWINGIN' '60s CREDENTIALS: This classy actress/singer dazzled the Broadway critics and then won the prestigious title role on the ground-breaking TV sitcom *Julia*.

WORKIN' IT: Before she was Julia, Diahann Carroll was a musical star. A student first at New York's distinguished High School of Music and Art, and then at NYU, she was working as a part-time model and nightclub singer when she made her movie debut as one of Dorothy Dandridge's sidekicks in the Otto Preminger-directed musical *Carmen Jones* ('54). After earning a Tony nomination for *House of Flowers* in '54, Diahann returned to Hollywood and in '59 made another operatic movie directed by Preminger, *Porgy and Bess*, followed in '61 by the jazzy *Paris Blues* (the great music was by

Duke Ellington). In '62 she went back to Broadway and won a Tony Award for the musical *No Doubt*. An Emmy nomination for a '63 appearance on *Naked City* and a couple of solid movie dramas—Preminger's *Hurry Sundown* in '67 and the crime caper *The Split* in '68—set her up for *Julia* ('68–'71).

The first show to star an African-American actress, the gentle comedy/drama injected reality into the otherwise lightweight prime-time network TV shows. The top-40 Nielsen-rated shows of the '68–'69 season included such nutty comedies as the fantasy-based *Bewitched* and *I Dream of Jeannie*, *The Beverly Hillbillies*, *Green Acres*, *Petticoat Junction*, *Gomer Pyle*, *Here's Lucy*, and *Hogan's Heroes*. *Julia* countered all this slapstick with the story of a nurse and single mom whose husband had been killed in 'Nam.

Nothing especially powerful happened on the show (Diahann herself said it was only "slightly controversial"), but it was pleasing and polished, and it finished in the top-10 of the '68–'69 ratings. Diahann won a Golden Globe and an Emmy nomination as Best Actress, with another Golden Globe nomination coming in '70. What's more, her character was popular enough to generate a line of dolls in her image, Mattel's Talking Julia.

During this time Diahann continued to pursue her musical career with several big Vegas engagements. After *Julia* left the air in '71, Diahann returned to films and starred in the reality-based *Claudine* ('74), earning an Oscar nomination for her portrayal of a welfare mom with six kids. *The Diahann Carroll Show* ran for one season in '76, and she starred in *I Know Why the Caged Bird Sings* in '79. The '80s and '90s brought lots of TV shows and TV movies, among them a glamorous three years on *Dynasty* in the late '80s, an Emmy-nominated guest appearance on *A Different World* in '89, and *Lonesome Dove: The Series* in '92. She also found time to write an honest, insightful autobiography, *Diahann!*, which was published in '86. Still making music, she has now released over a dozen albums (most recently *The Time of My Life* in '97 and *Side by Side* in '99); still making musicals, in the mid '90s she played Norma Desmond in the lavish *Sunset Boulevard*; and still blazing trails, in '97 she became the first African-American woman with her own line of wigs, clothes, lingerie and accessories.

Happily, in '97 she won a much-publicized fight against breast cancer, yet another triumph that would inspire others. "When a young person comes up to me and says they pursued something because of something I did—that I had an influence on their thinking," she once told an interviewer, "that's a very nice feeling."

HER '60s LOOK: Let Sidney Poitier describe her, which he did in his autobiography *This Life*: "Great, great, great face with its fantastic cheekbones and dark mysterious eyes…She had perfect teeth, and skin whose brown was somewhat deeper than the color of a peach…In short, she was hard to ignore." She was especially hard to ignore in the late '60s, when Diahann dressed glamorously, made several "best-dressed" lists, and was a much-photographed target of the paparrazi. Unfortunately, the stress of shooting *Julia* took a toll on her, causing her weight to drop below a hundred pounds and twice sending her to the hospital. But she bounced back more glamorous and beautiful than ever. More from Sidney: "She was unique. She carried herself with admirable flair and style. She was beautiful—thin, but well defined—she moved with a rhythm and at a pace that tantalized. She seemed both confident and inviting."

BEHIND THE SCENES:

"I'm always getting involved in the wrong relationship," Diahann said in a TV bio. "I do that very well." In '59, while they were both making *Porgy and Bess*, Diahann and Sidney Poitier, who was approximately eight years her senior, fell in love. In her book she described their first encounter: "The door opened. He

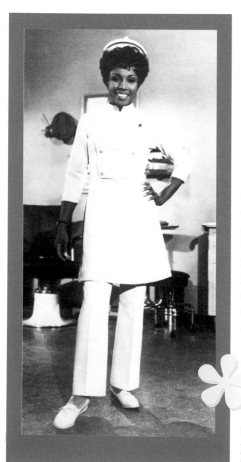

stepped inside. My life changed." Both of them were married at the time, she since '56 to Broadway casting director Monte Kay. In the fall of '60 Kay and Diahann had a daughter, Suzanne. But Diahann and Sidney still stayed in contact and still pursued their feelings for each other. In '61 Diahann and Poitier each told their spouses of their relationship, and by '64 Diahann and Sidney were divorced from them and engaged to each other. They stayed together for almost four more years without marrying, and then they broke up. Poitier tried to explain the inexplicable: "Strange, isn't it, how love sometimes fights its way through the dangerous uncharted forest of life to the edge of the clearing, only to wither in the first light of success. Were we afraid to win?" Diahann wrote in her autobiography that the split represented her maturation into a strong adult: "I understood that I was actually growing up.…There was some sadness in the recognition, yet there was also a fantastic feeling of relief. For the first time in nine years I was breathing clean air. I felt eleven feet tall. I finally had a handle on the two of us." Diahann got engaged to TV-interviewer David Frost in November '72 but called it off the following February. Within two weeks, Diahann married a Vegas businessman, then divorced him that summer. She married again in '75, this time to a man who was about fifteen years younger than she was. Their troubled union ended two years later when he was killed in a car accident. Late in the '80s Diahann married singer Vic Damone, and together they performed a stage act. They divorced in '96.

BONUS SWINGABILITY:

She uses a fake moniker—her real name is Carol Diahann Johnson; she changed it to Diahann Carroll at 16 when she successfully auditioned for *Arthur Godfrey's Talent Scouts* ... her exotic birthplace—the Bronx, New York ... early in her career, she was at a party where Marlon Brando slapped her on the butt—she turned around and whacked him in the face; he called her the next day with career advice and gave her books on acting ... 7-year-old Jodie Foster appeared in an episode of *Julia* in '69 ... Sidney continued with more description of her: "Diahann was beautiful, intelligent, witty, sophisticated, and feminine…an independent woman who shifted emotional gears quickly. From getting angry quickly or hurt deeply, she would always come bouncing back a little wiser and a little stronger" ... "All I ever wanted to do was sing," wrote Diahann in her book. "What happened was more."

A DATE WITH DIAHANN

February 20, 1927	Sidney Poitier is born
July 17, 1935	Diahann Carroll is born
October 28, 1954	*Carmen Jones* is released
March 15, 1962	*No Strings* opens on Broadway
November 21, 1962	Diahann appears on *Naked City*
February 9, 1967	*Hurry Sundown* is released
September 17, 1968	*Julia* debuts
May 25, 1971	*Julia* concludes its three-season run in primetime

DONNA DOUGLAS

SWINGIN' '60s CREDENTIALS: This likable Southerner played "Frankie" in Elvis' *Frankie and Johnny* and the curvaceous Elly Mae Clampett on *The Beverly Hillbillies*.

WORKIN' IT: Of '60s TV actresses, Donna Douglas was one of those who was probably the closest in real life to the role she played on TV. A Loozeeana-born farm-raised critter-lovin' tomboy, she got her start in beauty pageants in the '50s, winning the 1957 Miss New Orleans title while in her early twenties. (Sources vary on her birthyear, but 1933 seems to be the most common.) The exposure led to bit parts—as a "letter girl" on *The Perry Como Show,* and in the '59 *Li'l Abner* movie (alongside two other Swingin' Chicks of the '60s, Julie Newmar and Stella Stevens). The new decade brought her a small role in the 1960 Rock Hudson/Doris Day comedy *Lover Come Back,* two appearances on *Mister Ed,* and a couple of *Twilight Zone* episodes (including the great "The Eye of the Beholder" offering, in which she was deemed "ugly" in a society populated by disfigured people). Her career was made, of course, when she landed the part of Elly Mae on *The Beverly Hillbillies*.

The most-watched show of the '60s, the homey hillbilly comedy debuted on her birthday in the fall of '62 and within three months was #1 in the Nielsen ratings, a position it maintained until '65. So popular was *The Beverly Hillbillies*, it set ratings records that lasted for decades, it inspired another hit, *Green Acres*, and its theme song, written by the show's creator Paul Henning and recorded by the country duo Flatt and Scruggs, hit #44 on the pop charts. On the

show, young Elly had an undemanding role that was pretty much limited to looking attractive, out-wrasslin' Jethro, and bringing home whatever animals she found (among her many critters were a bear, bobcat, buzzard, chimpanzee, eagle, lion, ostrich, and skunk). Elly's confrontations with the high-falutin' locals, as in the episodes "Elly's First Date" and "Elly Starts School," occasionally allowed her to shine in the spotlight, but the other Clampetts usually got more airtime. For a while Elly had a movie-star boyfriend named Dash Riprock (played by Larry Pennell; "Dash" was only the character's stage name, his given name on the show was Homer Noodleman).

For the last couple of seasons Elly had a boyfriend named Shorty (played by Shug Fisher) and another named Mark Templeton (Roger Torrey). A master of the exaggerated hill-billy accent, she made one other memorable, if minor, contribution to the show: She delivered the enthusiastic "This has been a Filmways presentation!" coda at the end of each episode. Even as a supporting character, Elly Mae was popular enough for Kellogg's to offer an 11" Elly doll on its cereal boxes (she came wearing either a skirt or jeans, both tied with a rope belt).

While the show was in its peak years, Donna landed the title role of Frankie, paramour to the riverboat-gambler Johnny, in one of Elvis' most energetic and most entertaining flix, *Frankie and Johnny* ('66). Though Donna has a fine singing voice, her vocals were dubbed in the duet she did with Elvis, "Petunia, the Gardener's Daughter." Back on TV, the Clampetts moved from the hills of Beverly to the hills of syndicationland in '71. Donna put in a couple more TV appearances (a *Night Gallery* in '72 and a *Love American Style* in '73), and her last TV hurrah came with the slight TV movie *The Return of the Beverly Hillbillies* ('81). From the mid-'70s into the '80s she sold real estate.

Donna has spent recent years performing, not in front of a camera, but in front of a microphone as a gospel singer. She's also listed on the current board of the Country Legends Association. And unlike other actresses who prefer to forget their earlier roles, Donna has embraced hers, and today she occasionally makes public appearances dressed in her Elly Mae duds.

HER '60s LOOK: She was cute 'n' all on *The Beverly Hillbillies*, but who was her competition—Granny? Miss Jane? Mrs. Drysdale? Her big smile, big eyes, and big blonde piled-up curls put her closer to a '50s siren than a '60s mod. Usually she wore tight-fitting jeans and tomboyish shirts, an outfit the studio must've loved because it could be put together for less than a sawbuck. Stephen Cox offered the following *TV Guide* quote in his comprehensive '93 book, *The Beverly Hillbillies*: "Donna Douglas did more for blue jeans in seven months than cowboys did in 110 years." Once in a while she got to wear a gown (accompanied by smooth background music), and in the "Cool School Is Out" episode she went beatnik. As noted in Cox's book, one clothing item that Elly was unfamiliar with was a bra—she thought it was a weapon, and so did Jed, who called it "a store-bought, lace-trimmed, double-barreled slingshot." Welllll doggies! Anyway, no matter what she wore, Donna revealed a shapely figure that made you want to tug her gently by the rope belt all the way back to the cee-ment pond. *Movie Life Yearbook* of '63 listed her stats as a robust 5' 6" and 118 pounds, 36.5-21-36.

BEHIND THE SCENES: Cox's *The Beverly Hillbillies* claimed that Donna got married in '49 while still in high school and had a son and a divorce five years later. Despite a few weak rumors that she and

Elvis got a little more than friendly during *Frankie and Johnny*, it's more likely that their relationship was limited to discussions about their shared religious beliefs and their favorite spiritual readings (all sources confirm her life as a devout Christian). She married and divorced Bob Leeds, one of the directors of *The Beverly Hillbillies*, in the last half of the '70s.

BONUS SWINGABILITY: She uses a fake moniker—her real name is Doris Smith, and she was sometimes credited as Donna Douglass ... her exotic birthplace—Baywood, Louisiana ... Sharon Tate played the role of bank-secretary Janet Trego for over a dozen episodes of *The Beverly Hillbillies* ... the show ran for 274 episodes, 106 in black and white, switching to color in '65 ... the episode called "The Giant Jackrabbit" (referring to a kangaroo) is still the highest-rated half-hour program since Nielsen began its rating system in 1960 ... originally the Clampetts had $25 million from their oil discovery, but by the end of the show's long run they had $95 million ... in the '93 film starring Jim Varney, Erika Eleniak played the role of Elly Mae ... the city of Beverly Hills honored the show with an official "Possum Day" in '65.

 A DATE WITH DONNA

September 26, 1933	Donna Douglas is born
November 11, 1960	Donna appears in "The Eye of the Beholder" episode of *The Twilight Zone*
September 26, 1962	*The Beverly Hillbillies* debuts
October 20, 1965	"Possum Day" in Beverly Hills
March 31, 1966	*Frankie and Johnny* is released
September 7, 1971	*The Beverly Hillbillies* concludes its nine-season run in primetime

PATTY DUKE

SWINGIN' '60s CREDENTIALS: This award-winning multi-talented teen star wowed Broadway and movie audiences with her landmark role in *The Miracle Worker*, then she landed her own popular TV sitcom, sang hit pop songs, and descended into the *Valley of the Dolls*.

WORKIN' IT: How many other actresses had a twelve-inch doll of themselves in the '60s? Patty did, and it shows how strong her impact was on the decade. Not only was she a major star from the get-go, she was a role model. During the '60s Milton Bradley had a board game called the Patty Duke Game (filled with teenage dilemmas such as balancing homework with parties), plus there were paper-doll books, storybooks, and coloring books that cashed in on her fame. All this while she was still just a teenager.

She had started working as a child, making commercials and getting her first speaking role on TV at age 9 in an *Armstrong Circle Theatre* drama. A dozen more '50s TV appearances led up to her stunning Broadway debut as the young Helen Keller in *The Miracle Worker* in '59. Only 12, she was a Broadway star. After two years on the stage, she reprised the role for the '62 film. Her prodigious talent was recognized with her first major award: an Oscar for Best Supporting Actress. At the time she was the youngest actress ever to win an Academy Award (a record not broken until a decade later when 10-year-old Tatum O'Neal won in the same category for *Paper Moon*). That same year, Patty also won a Golden Globe as '63's Best Newcomer. In '64 she got her own eponymous TV show, which again broke ground. At 18, she was the youngest actress ever to have her own show.

Patty's dual roles as the identical cousins Cathy (who, according to the theme song, "adores a minuet") and Patty ("a hot dog makes her lose control") brought her the first of nine Emmy nominations. Firmly entrenched as one of the most popular and talented teens in America, she started making music, and from '65–'67 United Artists released four hit albums—*Don't Just Stand There*, *TV's Teen Star*, *Patty*, and *Patty Duke's Greatest Hits*.

When *The Patty Duke Show* left primetime in '66, Patty returned to the big screen with several strong roles, including the pilled-up Neely O'Hara in the '67 camp classic *Valley of the Dolls* (*Valley of the Dreck*, she called it) and the touching lead in the sensitive *Me, Natalie*, bringing her a second Golden Globe in '70. After the '60s she became one of the queens of the TV movie, and her Emmy Awards piled up with wins or nominations for *My Sweet Charlie* ('70), *Captains and the Kings* ('76), *A Family Upside Down* and *Having Babies III* (both in '78), *The Miracle Worker* remake with Patty in the Annie Sullivan role and Melissa Gilbert as Helen ('79), *The Women's Room* ('80), and *George Washington* ('84). Recent TV movies include *A Christmas Memory* ('97) and a '99 revival of her "identical cousins" for *The Patty Duke Show: Still Rockin' in Brooklyn Heights* (featuring the same cast as the '60s TV show). *Hail to the Chief* ('87) was just one of the three TV sitcoms she starred in during the '80s and '90s.

Signifying her long contributions to the medium, in '99 *TV Guide* ranked her #40 on its list of the Top Fifty TV Stars ever. More than just a popular star, however, she has become a bright light in the dark, misunderstood world of manic-depression, thanks to *Call Me Anna* ('87) and *A Brilliant Madness* ('92), her two best-selling books that illuminated her struggles with the mental disorder. "I've survived," she wrote at the end of *Call Me Anna*, "…and on some days, on most days, that feels like a miracle."

HER '60s LOOK: "Younger than springtime, and twice as exciting," read Neely's headline in *Valley of the Dolls*. With her ready smile and all-American appeal, teenage Patty looked how most parents wanted their kids to look—pretty, wholesome, well-groomed, and stylish. But by the end of the decade she had a harder look born of painful experience. What sex appeal she had as a five-foot-tall cutie was almost wiped out by raging substance abuse and anorexia. She dropped from 105 pounds to a scant 76 (!). She later tried to explain her motivations in her writing: "I know now that one of the explanations for anorexia is the refusal to grow up: You starve yourself to get smaller, you attempt to physically match how small you feel mentally, and I think that's what I was doing."

BEHIND THE SCENES:
As she later wrote, Patty's "childhood was one of outward glory and inner torment." Her father was a handyman and an alcoholic who left the family when Patty was 6. Her mother was given to bouts of severe depression. Born Anna, Patty received her name from her managers, whom she called "tyrannical" and "obsessed with fame" in *Call Me Anna*. "Anna Marie is dead, you're Patty now," they told her with no explanation. She moved in with her managers when she was 16, and according to her they controlled her life, giving her pills and liquor, subjecting her to sexual abuse, and wreaking psychological damage that later resulted in depression, fits of rage, substance abuse, and suicide attempts. Her first beau was Frank Sinatra, Jr., whom she met in '64 and who has remained a loyal friend. In November '65 she married Harry Falk, Jr., who was fourteen years her senior and an assistant director on *The Patty Duke Show*. It would be the first of four marriages. Spiraling into a morass of drugs and alcohol, she experienced hallucinations and displayed bizarre, impulsive behavior, which included marrying someone she had known for mere days. Their turbulent marriage lasted only thirteen days in the summer of '70 and ended with an annulment. In that same year a budding romance between 24-year-old Patty and 17-year-old Desi Arnaz, Jr. was ix-nayed, Patty later wrote, by a forceful Lucille Ball. In early '71 Patty gave birth to Sean, son of actor John Astin, who is best remembered for playing Gomez on *The Addams*

Family. (Sean has gone on to a Hollywood career of over two-dozen movies, including *The Goonies* in '85, *Memphis Belle* in '90, and *Rudy*, '93.) Patty and John married in '72, and another son, Mackenzie (later a regular on *Facts of Life*), was born in '73. "We never lived a day—not a day—in our relationship without real stress," Patty wrote. In '85 she and John divorced. That fall she met her fourth husband, a married drill-sergeant named Michael Pearce, while training at Georgia's Fort Benning for the TV movie *A Time to Triumph*. They married in March of '86 and he left the service to become her manager. All of these topics and more she has courageously discussed in her books because, as she wrote, "there must be many others who feel as I felt, and there might be a little relief for them in reading." Now living in Idaho, she has emerged in the twenty-first century as a successful writer, a TV legend, and one of Hollywood's most honest, candid stars.

BONUS SWINGABILITY: She uses a fake moniker—her real name is Anna Marie Duke, and as an adult she has been credited as Patty Duke Astin and Anna Duke-Pearce... Patty's exotic birthplace—New York City ... like another Swingin' Chick of the '60s, Barbara Feldon, Patty won TV's *$64,000 Challenge*. When news leaked that the quiz show was rigged, Patty testified to the investigating committee that she had been fed the answers ... in *Valley of the Dolls*, after she belted out a number at the telethon, Joey Bishop announced "Tell Frank, Dean and Sam they'll have to wait" ... respected by her peers, Patty was for a time the president of the Screen Actors Guild, the first woman to hold that position ... she has also crusaded for women's rights, famine relief, AIDS research, and nuclear disarmament ... many of the facts presented here come from Patty's own attractive and thorough Web page, which is one of the best "official" celebrity sites—http://pattyduke.net.

A DATE WITH PATTY	
March 30, 1930	John Astin is born
December 14, 1946	Patty Duke is born
October 19, 1959	*The Miracle Worker* opens on Broadway
April 8, 1963	Patty wins the Best Supporting Actress Oscar (*The Miracle Worker*)
September 18, 1963	*The Patty Duke Show* debuts
July 17, 1965	"Don't Just Stand There" enters the *Billboard* charts (it will reach #8)
August 31, 1966	*The Patty Duke Show* concludes its three-season run
October 30, 1965	"Say Something Funny" enters the *Billboard* charts (it will reach #22)
December 15, 1967	*Valley of the Dolls* is released

stars

BARBARA EDEN

SWINGIN' '60s CREDENTIALS: This small-waisted big-curved ever-smilin' dreamgirl was a happy, welcome sight in over a dozen '60s movies, including Elvis' *Flaming Star*; status as a TV legend came when she played the bare-midriffed wish-granter in the classic series *I Dream of Jeannie*.

WORKIN' IT:

Always fun and always watchable, Barbara Eden has stolen every scene she's ever been in. Born in Arizona but raised in San Francisco, she moved to Hollywood as a teen to try to break into show biz. Within a few years she had her first movie role, *Will Success Spoil Rock Hunter?* ('57). That year, she was also on one of the last episodes of *I Love Lucy*. In '58 she became a TV sitcom star, playing Loco Jones, the glasses-wearing-Monroe-style-bombshell,

on *How to Marry a Millionaire*. One of the best Elvis movies, the song-light tension-heavy *Flaming Star*, followed in '60, with lots more swingin' movies close behind, among them *Voyage to the Bottom of the Sea* ('61), *Five Weeks in a Balloon* ('62), *Ride the Wild Surf* ('64), *The 7 Faces of Dr. Lao* ('64), and *The Brass Bottle* (also '64). The latter was notable as a retelling of the classic "genie in a bottle" story, but in this one the troubled master was Tony Randall and the genie was Burl Ives, not exactly a genie with a cute bare midriff. That job was Barbara's.

I Dream of Jeannie debuted in '65, lasted five years, covered 139 episodes, brought Barbara a Golden Globe nomination as Best Actress, and made her one of the most popular TV stars ever. Yet she wasn't even close to being the studio's first choice, as she disclosed to *People* magazine. The creators "had tested every brunette in town, every Miss Greece, Miss Italy, Miss Israel had been interviewed," but once the show debuted with 31-year-old Barbara starring as the 2000-year-old genie Jeannie, the results were magical. Cute 'n' giggly 'n' subservient to her "master," she appealed to every teenage boy in America; smart 'n' sassy 'n' confident, she was popular with women, too, as she engaged in a playful battle of the sexes with the male lead (Larry Hagman). So successful was the show, it became one of the first to have a complete merchandising program, including a board game, dolls, and books. Throughout the show's five-year run, Barbara and the creators would playfully experiment with the characters, costumes, and situations. Barbara sometimes played Jeannie's wicked sister (the fun "wicked sister" strategy was also used by Elizabeth Montgomery on *Bewitched*), and in '69 Jeannie married Cap'n Tony. (Q: What does a genie wear to her wedding? A: A white pantsuit.)

In the '70s Barbara made a TV movie almost every year, and she had a big-screen hit with the surprisingly successful *Harper Valley P.T.A.* ('78). Her '80s featured a sitcom version of that film and more TV, especially *I Dream of Jeannie: 15 Years Later* in '85 (Wayne Rogers played Tony because Larry Hagman was busy doin' *Dallas*). *Dallas* in '90–'91, another Jeannie TV movie (*I Still Dream of Jeannie* in '91), and some memorable Old Navy and Lexus commercials in the late '90s proved that she was a perennial public-pleaser. She has occasionally performed a terrific nightclub act in Vegas, Tahoe, and Atlantic City, surprising everyone with her great singing voice. Here it is the twenty-first century, and we're all still dreamin' of Jeannie.

HER '60s LOOK: What a great cheerleader she'd make. Or a great beauty contest winner (actually, she *was* a beauty contest winner, taking the Miss San Francisco title in '50). The coloring, the shape, the pretty smile—in the '60s hers was an all-American kind of beauty with just a touch of the exotic behind her eyes. Speaking of those eyes, she has said that she wore glasses from the first grade on, but we believe the only time she wore them onscreen was in the '57 TV series *How to Marry a Millionaire*. Directors knew how to use her well-developed 5' 3" frame to get attention—in *Voyage to the Bottom of the Sea*, she was introduced twenty minutes into the movie via an aft-view closeup as she danced wildly in a tight dress, with Frankie Avalon a-wailin' on the trumpet. Kids at the matinees of *The 7 Faces of Dr. Lao*, an otherwise gentle fantasy story, must've flipped their ids at the sight of auburn-haired Barbara in her knickers, or in later scenes where she worked up a sweat with a lascivious Pan. Though her shapely legs later made her an ideal spokesperson for L'Eggs pantyhose, in the '60s it was her bare midriff that hatched debates among the network censors. Contrary to the common perception, Barbara didn't show her bellybutton on *I Dream of Jeannie* until the '91 TV movie. Before then it was covered by fabric or a jewel to satisfy overanxious advertisers. The navel battle didn't matter to *Playboy*—in January '99 the magazine ranked her #58 (ahead of supermodel Claudia Schiffer) on its list of the "100 Sexiest Stars of the Century."

BEHIND THE SCENES: Though she was in an Elvis movie, Barbara has maintained that she and the King never had an affair. She told *People* in '97 that Elvis was "a real gentleman. I never saw him use drugs and I never had an affair with him. I used to work

across the street from him in Las Vegas. He had a large entourage and when I'd walk in he'd say, 'OK, there's a lady present, be quiet,' and boy, they listened to him." Barbara spent the '60s married to actor Michael Ansara, who was featured with her in *Voyage to the Bottom of the Sea* and also in *I Dream of Jeannie* (he played an evil genie). She said later it had been love at first sight when she was introduced in '58 to Ansara, who is twelve years her senior. They were married after knowing each other just

six weeks. Just as *I Dream of Jeannie* was starting to shoot, Barbara found out she was pregnant, and in '65, two weeks before the first episode aired, she gave birth to son Matthew. Divorced from Michael Ansara in '72 after fifteen years, she remarried in '77 and moved to Chicago, then she divorced in '83 and wed again in '91, this time in San Francisco. She and her husband now live in one of the stylish canyons up in the L.A. hills.

BONUS SWINGABILITY: Her moniker—she was born Barbara Jean Moorhead, but as a child she took the last name Huffman from her stepfather ... her nickname is "BJ" ... her exotic birthplace—Tuscon, Arizona ... Barbara is said to be an avid traveler and reader ... before the movie was entitled *Flaming Star*, it was going to be called either *Flaming Lance*, *Flaming Heart*, *Black Star*, or *Black Heart* ...before it became an Elvis movie, *Flaming Star* was slated to have two other stars play the movie's brothers: Marlon Brando and Frank Sinatra ... *Get Smart* debuted on the same night as *IDOJ* ... when Barbara first appeared on the show, she was speaking some exotic language with subtitles; not until the astronaut wished her to speak English did we understand her ... the first season of *IDOJ* was in black and white, all the rest were in color ... in later episodes, Farrah Fawcett played bit parts ...Barbara has performed charity work for the Make-a-Wish Foundation, the March of Dimes, the American Heart Association, and other organizations ... in a TV biography Barbara said about "Jeannie," "If you're going to be defined by one role, that's a nice one" ... Barbara has her own official Web site—http://www.barbaraeden.com.

A DATE WITH BARBARA

August 23, 1934	Barbara Eden is born
October 7, 1957	*How to Marry a Millionaire* debuts
December 20, 1960	*Flaming Star* is released
March 18, 1964	*The 7 Faces of Dr. Lao* is released
September 18, 1965	*I Dream of Jeannie* debuts
September 1, 1970	*I Dream of Jeannie* concludes its five-season run in primetime

BARBARA FELDON

SWINGIN' '60s CREDENTIALS: This deep-voiced seductress played level-headed Agent 99 and tried to keep KAOS to a minimum on the clever TV comedy *Get Smart*.

WORKIN' IT: The sound of Barbara Feldon's deep, sultry voice is enough to bring back fond memories. It's a voice that's been heard in over thirty years of commercials, TV shows, and movies. She was modeling and doing commercials in New York when *Get Smart* came along in '65. Initially she turned down a starring role in the series because she didn't want to leave New York for Hollywood, but after making the successful pilot episode she agreed to co-star as Agent 99, patient partner-in-crime-fighting to nutty Agent 86.

Created by Mel Brooks, Buck Henry, and Leonard Stern, *Get Smart* was one of the wittiest comedies of the '60s. Brilliantly spoofing the decade's Bond-mania, the show gave its characters Bond-like numbers, high-tech gadgetry (the two most famous devices were the shoe-phone and the Cone of Silence), and accented opponents who worked for an acronymed crime organization (KAOS). Whereas Bond always had the quickest quip in the West, Maxwell Smart had "Would you believe," his signature response every time one of his

feeble explanations went awry. Barbara, a bright, attractive, elegant actress, was the perfect foil for Don Adams, the unintelligent intelligence agent. The show was strong in the ratings and strong at the Emmy ceremonies, where it won seven trophies during its five-year run (including two years as Outstanding Comedy Series). In '67, Barbara brought her charms to *Fitzwilly*, a caper-comedy in which she

made her movie debut as Dick Van Dyke's love interest. Back at *Get Smart*, with ratings starting to sag in '68, the season began with the engagement of 86 and 99; two months later, they were married (86 + 99 = 185?). The next season, still trying to boost ratings, 99 had twins. Nevertheless, *Get Smart* became *Get Canceled* in '70.

Barbara continued with some commercials and TV appearances—she was in the underrated *Marty Feldman Comedy Machine* in '72, then a decade later she was a smart, smooth rendezvous for Sam Malone on an episode of *Cheers*. She also made a a dozen TV movies, notably *Playmates* in '72 and *Get Smart, Again* in '89. *Smile* in '75 was her best big-screen role. With that voice, she's always had steady work doing voiceovers and narrations, and late in the '90s she performed a one-woman Off-Broadway show. As post-99 screen work came less frequently, she became an astute investor and a stock broker. But *Get Smart* has never been far away, reappearing on TV for a quick five weeks in early '95. By this time 99 had become a member of Congress, one of the kids had grown up to be an agent, and Max was Chief!

HER '60s LOOK: She had the eyes, cheekbones, and wry smile of a sophisticated beauty. She later admitted that the hair was nearly always a wig or a fall of some sort. As a long tall elegant superspy, she was sort of an American Diana Rigg and a precursor to the slinky Bond models of the '80s and '90s.

BEHIND THE SCENES: Before she got famous as spy with a number for a name, Barbara, like young Patty Duke, won $64K on a '50s quiz show. Barbara invested her winnings in a New York art gallery; invested her heart, too, because in '58 she married her partner, Lucien Feldon. After nine years together, they divorced in '67.

BONUS SWINGABILITY: She uses her married moniker—her real name is Barbara Hall … her exotic birthplace—Pittsburgh, Pennsylvania … *Get Smart* and *I Dream of Jeannie* debuted on the same night on the same network … like *Jeannie* the early episodes were in black and white … in one episode Barbara went by the name Susan Hilton instead of 99.

 A DATE WITH BARBARA

March 12, 1941	Barbara Feldon is born
September 18, 1965	*Get Smart* debuts
November 16, 1968	Agents 99 and 86 get married
November 14, 1969	Agent 99 gives birth to twins
September 11, 1970	*Get Smart* concludes its five-season run in primetime

PEGGY LIPTON

SWINGIN' '60s CREDENTIALS: A slim-bodied straight-haired doe-eyed teen, Peggy jumped from small TV roles to big TV stardom on *The Mod Squad*.

WORKIN' IT: A successful New York model, in her late teens Peggy made TV appearances on mid-'60s episodes of *The Virginian* and *Bewitched*, and she was a regular on the short-lived *John Forsythe Show* in '65. Her minor movie output during the decade included *Mosby's Marauders* with Kurt Russell in '66 and John Derek's *A Boy...a Girl* in '69. But when you talk about Peggy Lipton's '60s career, there's really only one thing to talk about.

Debuting in '68 and running for five years, *The Mod Squad* was a hip, happenin' police show that was based on the actual experiences of the show's creator, Bud Ruskin, a former undercover cop. Peggy played pretty Julie, one of three young criminals whose terms of probation included an assignment with an unarmed undercover unit, the Mod Squad. Her partners on the show were Michael Cole, playing curly-haired pretty boy Pete Cochran, and Clarence Williams III, playing the ultra-cool ultra-afro'ed Linc Hayes. Each character had committed a crime that got them time on the Squad. Julie Barnes, the daughter of a San Francisco hooker, had run away from home and been arrested for vagrancy. Aimed at a young audience (it came on at 7:30 on a school night), and mixing groovy counter-culture heroes with slam-bang police action, the show was a sturdy Tuesday-night hit, finishing in the top-25 of the Nielsen ratings three years out of its five-year run. The show also got an Emmy nomination as Best Dramatic Series, and Peggy received four Golden Globe nominations (with one win) from '70-'73. The show's premise remained popular for decades. A two-hour TV movie, *The Return of the Mod Squad*, ran in '79, and in '99 there was a big-budget movie (with all-new stars replacing the three '60s leads).

For Peggy, the post-Mod Squad years brought some failed films (*Purple People Eater* and *I'm Gonna Git You Sucka*, both in '88), *True Identity* in '91, and Kevin Costner's *The Postman* in '97. Her best work was in early-'90s role of kindly café-owner Norma Jennings, the sanest of the odd squad in David Lynch's quirky TV series *Twin Peaks*. She served what Agent Cooper called "damn fine coffee." Peggy reprised this popular role for the movie, *Twin Peaks: Fire Walk with Me* ('92).

HER '60s LOOK: Peggy was probably a little more mod and a little less squad than your average L.A. cop. She had long straight straw-colored hair, the bedroom eyes of a bonged-out beauty, and the face of an innocent angel. A cute hippy chick, she was also a long lean hipster machine, with groovy patterned dresses and big bell bottoms adorning her lissome frame.

BEHIND THE SCENES: It's unclear who or what her relationships were during the decade, though we can imagine what the social life was like for a 21-year-old who was starring on one of the decade's hippest shows. Bill Zehme's *The Way You Wear Your Hat* casually notes a brief fling Peggy had with Frank Sinatra around '72 (his opener, according to Zehme, was "Would you let an old man buy you a cup of coffee?").

Buying her coffee as of '74 was her new husband Quincy Jones, the famous composer who's won dozens of Grammies and been nominated for six Oscars. With Quincy she had two kids and an '89 divorce.

BONUS SWINGABILITY: Her exotic birthplace—New York City ... her brother Robert is also an actor; he appeared in several '60s movies and was a regular on *As the World Turns* in the early '80s ... in the first season the Mod Squadders drove a classic '50s woody, but they drove it off a cliff in season two ... the show was one of the first hits for producer Aaron Spelling; later he produced dozens of shows ranging from *Charlie's Angels* to *Melrose Place* ... among the guest stars on *The Mod Squad* were David Cassidy, Richard Dreyfuss, Margot Kidder, Martin Sheen, and Anne Archer ... in the '99 movie, Claire Danes starred as Julie; updating the characters with '90s sensibilities, the movie made Julie a recovering cocaine addict.

 A DATE WITH PEGGY

August 30, 1947	Peggy Lipton is born
September 13, 1965	*The John Forsythe Show* debuts
September 24, 1968	*The Mod Squad* debuts
August 23, 1973	*The Mod Squad* concludes its five-season run in primetime

SALLY FIELD

Lawrence on *Gidget*, the sitcom version of the '59 Sandra Dee movie. Sally was a popular, natural actress, lively and personable, and in fact, on the show she would talk directly to the camera as if the TV audience were comprised of good pals spending the night for a slumber party ("Toodles" was her signature goodbye). When the show got canceled after just one season, surfer girl went cowgirl in a little-seen western, *The Way West*, but bigger success was in the air. Literally.

In '67 Sally got a new series that once again keyed on her winning personality and warm charm, though the premise was a little more fanciful. Based on a book by Tero Rios called *The Fifteenth Pelican*, *The Flying Nun* posited Sally as Sister Bertrille, a nun. A nun who lived in the Convent San Tanco in Puerto Rico. A nun who could fly (an ability explained by her low weight—only ninety pounds—and the stiff, elaborately winged cornets the nuns wore). Remember how she often crooned a tune on the show? Sally cut an album, singing the show's theme "Who Needs Wings to Fly?" and a dozen more gentle songs in '67 (her idol, she said in the liner notes, was Julie Andrews).

An interesting development came with the '68–'69 season—Sally got pregnant. Obviously her condition had to be concealed, since she was, after all, playing a celibate nun. She took a quick timeout to deliver a son in November '69 and went back to work in December to film the last episodes. While it's easy to mock her two lighter-than-air '60s comedies, she herself saw them as great training. "Those series didn't hurt me, they gave me the greatest education in the world," she said in Jason Bonderoff's bio *Sally Field*. "There isn't anything I can't do in front of a TV camera as a result of the experience I gained from them. I could stand on my head right now if necessary and spit wooden nickels."

SWINGIN' '60s CREDENTIALS: This ever-perky brown-eyed girl-next-door went from high school cheerleading to sitcom stardom in *Gidget* and *The Flying Nun*.

WORKIN' IT: Best known for her impressive body…of Oscar-winning filmwork, Sally Field enjoyed considerable success in the '60s as one of the few actresses ever to star in two successful shows. Back then she wasn't the well-respected dramatic presence that she is now; she came across more like your nutty kid sister, all freshness and cuteness and innocence. The daughter of actress Margaret Field and the step-daughter of actor Jock Mahoney, adorable Sally was a wholesome all-American teen in the early '60s, cheerleading at L.A.'s Birmingham High and starring in school drama productions.

Everything changed at age 19 when she beat out at least seventy-five other actresses for the role of beachy-teen Frances "Gidg"

Her breezy TV roles in the '60s led to a breezy '73 sitcom, *The Girl with Something Extra*, some good parts in small movies, and even a night hosting *Saturday Night Live* in '75. Finally, in the mid-'70s, her movie career kicked in.

The breakthrough was *Sybil*, a disturbing psychological study of a tortured girl who displayed

seventeen different personalities. The role brought her an Emmy and new-found respect as a serious actress. Soon followed some genuine big-screen hits, especially the entertaining Burt Reynolds flix *Smokey and the Bandit* in '77, *Hooper* in '78, and *The End* in '78. She hit her stride with the dramatic *Norma Rae* in '79 (her first Oscar win), then the equally powerful *Absence of Malice* in '81 and *Places in the Heart* in '84. (When she won the Oscar for *Places*, she gave that heartfelt "You like me, you really like me" speech, generously supplying comedians everywhere with a decade's worth of material.) Balancing her dramas with comedies, she also starred in the wonderful *Murphy's Romance* ('85), *Punchline* ('88), *Steel Magnolias* ('89), *Soapdish* ('91), *Mrs. Doubtfire* ('93), and *Forrest Gump* ('94). Another acting Emmy nomination came her way in '95 via *A Woman of Independent Means*, and since '78 she's gotten a total of eight nominations/victories at the Golden Globes. She's also had several behind-the-camera gigs, including producing/directing a TV movie, *The Christmas Tree*, in '96, and directing one of the episodes of Tom Hanks' *From the Earth to the Moon* in '98. From a flying nun to moon rockets—what a ride for the girl next door.

HER '60s LOOK: With those big brown eyes, smiley cheeks, and flippy hair, Sally would've made a great Disney girl. She herself has said, "I look like the people you might have grown up with," and even in her grown-up sexy '70s roles with Burt Reynolds, she still looked like a kid, not at all like the bombshells one might've expected in those macho *Bandit* movies. In '95 she told *In Style* magazine that when it comes to dressing, "I try to look like the last person I saw that looked good." To that end she converted one bedroom in her Southern California house to a home gym, and she jogs 20–25 miles a week. The work's paid off because she still has only a hundred or so pounds on her 5' 2" frame.

BEHIND THE SCENES: Though she once described herself as having "crippling shyness," in the mid-'60s Sally dated several of Hollywood's young stars, such as Monkee Davy Jones, Pete Deuel, Chris George, Paul Peterson, and Jerry's kid, Gary Lewis. In '68, all of 21 years old, she eloped to Vegas with her high school sweetheart, Steven Craig. Within a few years they had two sons, and in '75 they had a divorce. The well-tabloided Burt Reynolds Era lasted for about five years in the mid-to-late '70s. Sally married producer Alan Greisman, the man behind *Soapdish*, in '84. Within a decade they had a son and a divorce of their own.

BONUS SWINGABILITY: She uses a fake moniker—her real name is Sally Mahoney ... her exotic birthplace—Pasadena,

California ... her mother starred in the '51 film *The Man from Planet X,* her step-dad made lots of westerns and *Tarzan* movies ... Sally appeared as a contestant on *The Dating Game* in '65 ... she wasn't the only future Oscar winner on *Gidget*: in the episode "Ego a Go-Go" in '66, the part of Norman "Durf the Drag" Durfner was played by 19-year-old Richard Dreyfuss ... Farrah Fawcett appeared on two episodes of *The Flying Nun* ... in the mid-'60s Sally tested for the role of Elaine in *The Graduate*, but her lack of film experience cost her the part ... Sally made the cover of *Playboy*, March '86 ... in '98 she made a guest appearance as one of the ever-changing secretaries on *Murphy Brown* ... Sally has said that on movie sets, she usually does lots of needlework between takes ... the décor in her Mediterranean-style house includes an elephant tusk that's a souvenir from an '84 ballooning trip over Tanzania for *The American Sportsman* show... in an interview she summed up her philosophy with a quote from Rilke, the German poet—"One must always go toward what is difficult" ... she added to that quote a comment about her own restless desires: "I ask myself where is the next dream that I haven't tapped into yet, I feel I have so many unseen places I need to go, quickly, I've always felt that way, that there's something calling."

 A DATE WITH SALLY

November 6, 1946	Sally Field is born
September 15, 1965	*Gidget* debuts
May 24, 1967	*The Way West* is released
September 7, 1967	*The Flying Nun* debuts
September 18, 1970	*The Flying Nun* concludes its three-season run in primetime
April 14, 1980	Sally wins the Best Actress Oscar (*Norma Rae*)
March 25, 1985	Sally declares "You like me" after winning her second Oscar

CAROLYN JONES

SWINGIN' '60s CREDENTIALS: TV's most sweetly sinister seductress played a dozen '60s roles that took her from drama (*How the West Was Won*) to comedy (*The Addams Family*) to camp (*Batman*).

WORKIN' IT: Carolyn Jones was not a major star, but she was always an interesting one. She was versatile enough to handle romantic, dramatic, and comedic roles and was capable of playing a gangster's moll, a nutty bongo player, a West-taming frontier wife, and a Gomez-seducing French-speaking Japanese-singing 'Tish.

Born in Texas in the year of the stock market crash, Carolyn used her voice before she used her looks and acting talent. While she was still in high school she worked as a disc jockey for a Texas radio station, and later, when she was still struggling to make her way in Hollywood, she continued to work in radio.

In the '50s she landed small roles in over a dozen prominent movies, including Bob and Bing's *Road to Bali* in '52, Vincent Price's *House of Wax* in '53 (she played the Joan of Arc wax figure), Frank Sinatra's *The Tender Trap* and Marilyn Monroe's *The Seven Year Itch*, both in '55, and Alfred Hitchcock's *The Man Who Knew Too Much* in '56. Playing a bongo-bangin' existentialist, Carolyn flashed in and out of *The Bachelor Party* ('57) like a glimmering meteor, but her six minutes were so incandescent that she got nominated for a Best Supporting Actress Oscar and won a Golden Globe as Most Promising Newcomer. Strong movie roles took her to the end of the decade, including two memorable parts with two twentieth-century kings.

In late '57, Elvis was feeling a draft—Uncle Sam had come knocking, and he was expected to report for induction into the army in January '58. Unfortunately, *King Creole* was scheduled to begin shooting at the same time. The great Michael Curtiz (*Casablanca*) was on board to direct this tale of a New Orleans singer, and Carolyn Jones was set to co-star as a good girl gone bad. Only by grace of a special deferment was Elvis' induction postponed to March 24th, which meant he could still make the film in January and February as planned. Which meant Carolyn's character got to die in Elvis' arms as scheduled. Which meant more resplendent notices for Carolyn: *Variety* praised her performance as "strong" and "moving." Then, teamed with Sinatra in Frank Capra's syrupy *A Hole in the Head* in '59, Carolyn once again stole the spotlight with a convincing performance that was the best thing in the movie.

The '60s brought a flurry of minor movies and appearances in TV Westerns, then in '62 she got a coveted role alongside half the stars in Hollywood in the sprawling blockbuster *How the West Was Won*. Still, even with big stars and big movies on her résumé, big stardom eluded her. It took a popular cartoon to make her a legend.

Charles Addams' famous drawings about a macabre family had been appearing in the *New Yorker* since the '30s. In '64 they got reinvented as a TV series, *The Addams Family*. With its sinister sets and skewed perspectives, the show became one of the most stylish and fascinating comedies of the era. Though it only ran for two seasons and sixty-four episodes, the show firmly cemented its bizarre characters (Lurch, Thing, Cousin Itt) and its signature phrases ("You rang!") into the national consciousness. Carolyn's smooth, seductive, stable Morticia was the perfect partner for joyous, rakishly-mustachioed Gomez (John Astin), whose eyes twinkled with impulsive ideas and whose heart beat with eternal passion for his beautiful *cara mia*. Morticia was a multi-talented character who carved sculptures, sang, and wrote stories ("Cinderella, the Teenage Delinquent" was her take on the classic fairy tale). Just as *Bewitched*, *I Dream of Jeannie*, and *The Patty Duke Show* put their lead actresses in dual roles, so too did *The Addams Family* have a second character for Carolyn. Donning a long blonde wig, she occasionally played Ophelia Frump, Morticia's sister. Though the show left primetime in the fall of '66, it has lived on in reruns, in a TV movie (*Halloween with the New Addams Family* in '77), in two animated versions ('73–'75 and '92–'95, both without Carolyn's voice), and two '90s movies (with Angelica Huston as Morticia and Raul Julia as Gomez).

Carolyn would have a steady career after the show (including five episodes as Marsha, Queen of Diamonds, on *Batman* in '66 and '67), but she would never again play a character as popular as Morticia. She made some more TV movies and was one of the stars on the series *Capitol* in '82, bravely carrying on though her health was failing. Sadly, in '83 Carolyn Jones died of cancer at the age of only 55. Her early death may have been tragic, but her life was triumphant.

HER '60s LOOK: The large blue eyes, smooth porcelain skin, and long straight black wig suited her small face beautifully. And her slinky 5' 5" figure was perfect for Morticia's black-widow gown (her

real talent may have been her ability to stand up and walk in that bewitching "tube dress"). Is it a stretch to say that Morticia presaged the gothic look of the '80s? The look and popularity of *The Addams Family* may also have inspired part of Disneyland's Haunted Mansion. Developed in the mid-'60s while the show was still on the air, the eagerly anticipated attraction opened to wild acclaim in August '69. The creepiest E-

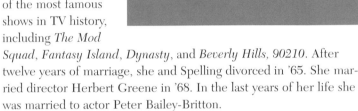

ticket in the park, the Haunted Mansion still features a walk-through gallery of transforming portraits, one of which ("April–December") bears an eerie resemblance to Carolyn's beautiful Morticia.

BEHIND THE SCENES: In '53 Carolyn married Aaron Spelling, who later produced some of the most famous shows in TV history, including *The Mod Squad*, *Fantasy Island*, *Dynasty*, and *Beverly Hills, 90210*. After twelve years of marriage, she and Spelling divorced in '65. She married director Herbert Greene in '68. In the last years of her life she was married to actor Peter Bailey-Britton.

BONUS SWINGABILITY: She used a fake moniker—her real name was Carolyn Baker ... her exotic birthplace—Amarillo, Texas ... she was part Comanche Indian ... Carolyn's famous line in *The Bachelor Party*: "Just say you love me—you don't have to mean it!" ... there must have been something slightly sinister in the air back in '64: *The Addams Family* debut came one week before the debut of another similarly creepy comedy that gave audiences the TV jeebies, *The Munsters*, and then the two shows aired their final episodes within a week of each other in '66.

A DATE WITH CAROLYN

April 22, 1928	Aaron Spelling is born
April 28, 1929	Carolyn Jones is born
April 10, 1953	Carolyn marries Aaron Spelling
May 1, 1958	*King Creole* is released
July 15, 1959	*A Hole in the Head* is released
February 20, 1963	*How the West Was Won* is released
September 18, 1964	*The Addams Family* debuts
April 8, 1966	The "Ophelia's Career" episode airs
September 2, 1966	*The Addams Family* concludes its two-season run in primetime
August 9, 1969	The Haunted Mansion opens at Disneyland

TINA LOUISE

SWINGIN' '60s CREDENTIALS: This red-headed glamour girl spent three years washed ashore as screen-siren Ginger Grant on TV's *Gilligan's Island*.

WORKIN' IT: Though she's known to millions by one role on one show, Tina Louise has had a long, varied career. "Debutante of the Year" in '53, she made lots of TV appearances (including *Studio One*, *The Phil Silvers Show*, and *The Real McCoys*) in the '50s; she also worked on Broadway in *Two's Company* with Bette Davis and in *Li'l Abner* as Appassionata Von Climax (the role later played in the movie by Stella Stevens). Tina also worked as a nightclub singer and even recorded an LP of Cole Porter songs in '57 called *Time for Tina*. Poised for stardom, she won a '59 Golden Globe as the Most Promising Newcomer.

However, she was unhappy in the early '60s with the direction her Hollywood career was heading, so she moved to Italy in search of better roles in foreign films. Eighteen months later she returned to a fruitful '60s career of many TV shows (such as *The Doctors*, *Burke's Law*, *Mannix*, *Ironside*, *Marcus Welby, M.D.*, and *Love, American Style*) and movies (she played a stripper in *For Those Who Think Young* in '64 and worked with Dino in *The Wrecking Crew* in '69). To her lasting chagrin, her greatest fame came as a castaway. When Sherwood Schwartz created *Gilligan's Island*, supposedly Jayne Mansfield was the model for sex goddess Ginger Grant.

When Jayne allegedly rejected the part, 30-year-old Tina got it, and eternal cult popularity was hers. *Gilligan's Island* ran from '64 to '67, totalling ninety-eight primetime episodes and thousands of reruns.

The show raised far more questions than it ever answered: Why would the Howells bring bags of cash with them? Why would everybody pack so many clothes for a three-hour cruise? How come they could build a record player and a car but they couldn't fix a two-foot hole in the *Minnow*? How could such a slight show that was derided by the critics stay so popular for so long? Some thirty-five years after the show left its characters stranded 250 miles (the Professor's estimate) southeast of Hawaii, Tina is still trying to get off *Gilligan's Island*.

In an interview with *Pinup* magazine, she said she doesn't even include the show on her résumé: "Who wants to be known just for that? I don't want to traipse around in an evening gown looking glamorous for the rest of my life." Actually, she did more than that on the show. Though the lightweight plots floated along with buoyant slapstick, Ginger Grant did display a range of talents, from singing (she, Lovey, and Mary Ann performed as the Honeybees in one episode) to seducing (to get off the island Ginger made unfulfilled overtures to virtually every guest star who drifted into view) to sympathizing (one dream sequence showed her as a nurse). Tina got more TV roles in the '70s (*The Love Boat*, *CHiPs*, a recurring role as Julie Grey on *Dallas*) and in the '80s (*Knight Rider*, *Married…with Children*). She was also featured in almost two-dozen post-'60s movies, usually of the unspectacular made-for-TV variety.

In '97 Tina wrote a book about her childhood called *Sunday*, and she now works to promote literacy in grade schools, volunteering twice a week as a reading tutor on the island where she now resides: Manhattan.

HER '60s LOOK: As a castaway Tina did a masterful Marilyn impression. She lured her prey with the same limp-lidded bedroom eyes, and she had the seductive, quivering half-smile that Marilyn perfected. While she didn't quite have the famous figure of Marilyn (few did), Tina always looked delicious no matter which gown or bathing

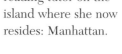

suit or play-acting costume she was wearing. She was curvy enough to be a featured femme in *Playboy* in October '60, November and December '61, January and December '62, December '65, November '66, and January '67.

BEHIND THE SCENES:
"I admit back in Hollywood I used to date some swingers," Ginger Grant once said on *Gilligan's Island*, "but they didn't swing from trees!" According to her interview in *Pinup* magazine, Tina sometimes had a playful attitude about her sexy image when she was a castaway. "In one episode Tina was to take a shower in a makeshift stall...since the bamboo shower door would hide her from the shoulders down and wouldn't show anything but her head, shoulders, legs and feet, Tina announced she would be shooting this scene in the nude. Word got around the set and by the time they were ready to shoot the scene the catwalks above the set were filled with electricians, carpenters, and every grip that suddenly felt they had a job to do above the infamous shower scene. Tina arrived in a sarong-type bathing suit and entered the shower never looking up at the gawking men. While some 45 workers gazed down, Tina removed her bathing suit only to reveal another bathing suit underneath." Back in the real world, Tina was married in '66 to Les Crane, a late-night talk-show host, and they had one daughter. The couple divorced in '70. Tina has gone on to the best starring role of all: "The best movie you'll ever be in is your own life," she said in an interview, "because that's what really matters in the end."

BONUS SWINGABILITY:
She uses a fake moniker—her real name is Tina Blacker ... her exotic birthplace — New York City ... her father owned a candy store, her mom was a former model ... Tina's education included UCLA, the University of Miami in Ohio, the N.Y. Neighborhood Playhouse, and the Actors Studio ... when Tina was in *For Those Who Think Young* in '64, Bob Denver and

Nancy Sinatra were also in the cast ... also in *The Wrecking Crew* with Dean and Tina were Elke Sommer and Sharon Tate ... according to the book *Inside Gilligan's Island*, when Tina was pitched the Ginger role, she was told that the show would be about her, with six others along as supporting players ... in the '78 TV movie *Return from Gilligan's Island* Ginger was played by Judith Baldwin; Tina said at the time that she wanted to break away from the role, but she may have wanted too many simoleons, according to *The Complete Directory to Prime Time Network and Cable TV Shows* ... that book (and *TV Guide* in '93) noted that Gilligan was the *last* name for Bob Denver's character, and that series creator Sherwood Schwartz discussed with Denver a first name for Gilligan—it would've been Willie, but it was never used in the ninety-eight episodes ... Ginger Grant's credits included appearances in *Sing a Song of Sing-Sing*, *The Hula Girl and the Fullback*, and *Housewives from Mars* ... when the *Minnow* ran aground, supposedly Ginger was about to play Cleopatra in Broadway's *Pyramid for Two* ... about the series and its affect on her career: "I don't really feel the series stopped me from doing what I wanted to do. Life is really a period of passages. You're going to arrive where you're going to arrive. The right things are going to find you one way or another."

A DATE WITH TINA

February 11, 1934	Tina Louise is born
September 26, 1964	*Gilligan's Island* debuts
September 4, 1967	*Gilligan's Island* concludes its three-season run in primetime

ELIZABETH MONTGOMERY

SWINGIN' '60s CREDENTIALS: A pretty blonde nose-twitcher, Elizabeth Montgomery worked a spell on audiences for eight years as Samantha Stephens, the lovely stay-at-home suburban witch married to switcheroo husbands on *Bewitched*.

WORKIN' IT: One of the queens of '60s TV, Elizabeth Montgomery reigned longer than any other '60s actress in a major show. Not just the most durable '60s TV star, she was perhaps the most talented. Her magical performance as the spell-binding Samantha Stephens on *Bewitched* brought her Best Actress Emmy nominations every year from '66 to '70.

Elizabeth was born to parents who were both actors. Her father, Robert, made over fifty movies in the '30s and '40s and was nominated for Best Actor Oscars in '38 for *Night Must Fall* and '41 for *Here Comes Mr. Jordan*. Growing up in New York, Elizabeth attended private schools before making her first appearance in the early '50s

on *Top Secret*. Robert Montgomery was also on that show, though it's said that he didn't know his daughter was in the cast until rehearsals had begun. From there they then appeared regularly together on his *Robert Montgomery Show*, which ran for seven years in the '50s. Meanwhile, still in her twenties, she appeared on such classic shows as the *Kraft Television Theatre*, *Studio One*, *Alfred Hitchcock Presents*, and *Wagon Train*. Though she'd later be best-known for her gifted comedic skills, at this point in her career she showed that she had the goods to deliver drama.

She proved herself as a serious stage actress when her first Broadway play, *Late Love*, brought her a Theater World Award. Her performance in the '55 film *The Courtmartial of Billy Mitchell* also received strong critical acclaim. Her TV career in the '60s included appearances on great '60s shows such as *Burke's Law*, *77 Sunset Strip*, *Rawhide*, a classic *Twilight Zone* episode in '61 as the last woman on earth, and a '61 episode of *The Untouchables* that brought her the first of nine Emmy nominations. In '63 she did some big-screen movies, too: *Johnny Cool* and *Who's Been Sleeping in My Bed*. But *Bewitched* in '64 established her once and for all as a TV legend.

Working with her husband, producer William Asher, Elizabeth helped conceive *Bewitched* and its main characters, Darrin and Samantha Stephens. In the show's first episode, "I, Darrin, Take this Witch," Sam and Darrin got married, but not till the honeymoon did he discover her secret. That first year, *Bewitched* became ABC's biggest hit to date, ranking second overall in the '64 Nielsen ratings. Up to that time, most TV shows had positioned their female leads as nutty foils for their wiser husbands (think of Lucy Ricardo on *I Love Lucy*); *Bewitched* gave Samantha all the brains, making her a uniquely appealing heroine. A perplexing change came to the show in '69 that has forever brought bemused smiles to its fans. From '64–'68 Sam's husband Darrin was played by Dick York; from '69–'72 the role was played by Dick Sargent, with no explanation to account for the obvious switch. (York's increasing health problems were the real cause—he had severe back pains, and once he was rushed directly from the set to the hospital.) Other changes on the show included the introduction in the second season of a daughter, Tabitha, who was played by three sets of twins (one set for the '65 season, another set for '66, and a third set for '67–'72). And in '71 Darrin and Sam had a son named Adam (again played by twins).

Just as Barbara Eden did on *I Dream of Jeannie*, Elizabeth sometimes played a mischievous relative to juice the story a little. Introduced in episode 54, "And Then There Were Three" (the same episode that welcomed the newly born Tabitha), Sam's cousin Serena gave Elizabeth a chance to go a little wild with colorful miniskirts and peace signs inked onto her cheek. In fact, her portrayal was so good, many viewers didn't realize that Elizabeth was both Sam and Serena, a conclusion supported by the show's credits, which named Pandora Sparks as the actress playing the cousin. With its bewitching star, goofy supporting cast, and imaginative scripts (one of the show's main writers was Bernard Slade, who would go on to write the hit Broadway play *Same Time, Next Year*), the show enchanted prime-time audiences for almost a decade and conjured up a total of sixteen Emmy nominations (plus four Golden Globe nominations for Elizabeth). The magic didn't end until '72, when *Bewitched* went up against the socially relevent *All in the Family* on Saturday nights. Suddenly the light fantasy/comedy of *Bewitched* seemed outdated, and the show floated over to rerunland.

Elizabeth's post-Samantha work was dominated by two-dozen acclaimed TV movies from the '70s to the '90s, three of which yielded Emmy nominations—*A Case of Rape* ('74), *The Legend of Lizzie Borden* ('75), and *The Awakening Land* ('78). Other TV movies included *Mrs. Sundance* ('74), *Belle Starr* ('80), and *The Black Widow Murders* ('93). She turned up on a few TV shows, including *The Dennis Miller Show* in '92, did commercials for two breakfast cereals, Quake and Quisp, and also narrated the Oscar-winning documentary *The Panama Deception* ('92).

Unfortunately, in '95, at the age of 62, Elizabeth died of cancer. On a TV bio about her remarkable life, she was remembered for her wonderful sense of humor: Author Dominick Dunne said, "She was truly funny. I've had some of the best laughs of my life with her."

HER '60s LOOK: She was the perfect TV wifey for the '60s—a big radiant smile, a pretty and intelligent face, and silken honey hair with a wave worthy of Breck commercials. She could also do that tinkly nose twitch that was both cute and had utterly magical results. Her clothes on *Bewitched* were generally "urban conservative" with a colorful, hip flair, often revealing the great gams that proved what a phenomenal catch she was for the two dufus Darrins. According to ABC press kits, she created many of the outfits on *Bewitched*, and for a time she even designed a *Bewitched* line of coats. Only once did Samantha actually fly around in a classic witch outfit with a black cape—that was in episode 71, "The Catnapper."

BEHIND THE SCENES: Elizabeth's first husband was Frederick Hammond, whom she married when she was 21. He was the Harvard-educated stage manager on her father's show, and they lived on New York's Upper East Side. They divorced within a year because he refused to go west with her when Hollywood beckoned. That's when she hooked up with actor Gig Young, who was twenty years her senior. Early in the '60s she suffered through what became an abusive marriage as alcoholism overtook Young. She finally got a Mexican divorce, and in '63 she took up with producer William Asher. He

produced or directed many important TV shows, notably *Bewitched* and three episodes of *I Love Lucy*. His film credits include five teen-beach movies from '63 to '65 (Elizabeth made a cute cameo in one of them, *How to Stuff a Wild Bikini*). With Asher she had two sons, Willy and Robert, and a daughter, Rebecca Elizabeth, all born between '64 and '69. The marriage split up in '74. Soon after, she met Robert Foxworth, who co-starred with her in *Mrs. Sundance*. Foxworth's credits include *Airport '77*, *Omen II* in '78, a dozen TV movies, and several TV shows, including *Falcon Crest*. He and Elizabeth lived together for nineteen years. They married in '93 and were together until her death in '95.

BONUS SWINGABILITY: Her exotic birthplace—Hollywood, California ... making guest appearances on the show were June Lockhart and Billy Mumy (both from *Lost in Space*); Raquel Welch (playing an airline flight attendant); young Maureen McCormick (who later played Marcia Brady on *The Brady Bunch*); Peggy Lipton from *The Mod Squad* (playing a secretary); and future Oscar-winner Richard Dreyfuss (playing a warlock named Rodney) ... when gay actor Dick Sargent came out of the closet, she supported him by joining with him as Grand Marshall of the L.A. Gay Pride Parade ... as for the longtime popularity of *Bewitched*, Elizabeth explained it this way in *Nick at Nite's Classic TV Companion*: "It's not about cleaning the house with a magic wave...or flying around the living room. It's about a very difficult relationship. And I think people pick up on this. They know there's something else going on besides the magic."

A DATE WITH ELIZABETH

November 4, 1913	Gig Young is born
August 8, 1921	William Asher is born
April 15, 1933	Elizabeth Montgomery is born
November 1, 1941	Robert Foxworth is born
September 17, 1964	*Bewitched* debuts
July 1, 1972	*Bewitched* concludes its eight-season run in primetime
May 18, 1995	Elizabeth dies of cancer

MARY TYLER MOORE

SWINGIN' '60s CREDENTIALS: A leggy reed-thin smiler who played the ideal all-American wife on *The Dick Van Dyke Show*, marvelous Mary then graduated to musicals with *Thoroughly Modern Millie* and a co-starring role in the King's last '60s film, *Change of Habit*.

WORKIN' IT: Though she's best known as the quintessential single career gal on her own '70s sitcom, Mary Tyler Moore was one of the most important TV actresses of the '60s. On *The Dick Van Dyke Show* ('61–'66), she helped to change the roles of women on TV and set the stage for the landmark sitcoms that would follow. On a '99 TV bio, she described what was so important about her character, the funny and talented Laurie Petrie. "Up until *The Dick Van Dyke Show*, the wives were extensions of their husbands…but Laura was a person in her own right."

After *The DVD Show* she proved herself to be the rare quadruple threat who could act, sing, dance, and produce, establishing herself as a television institution and her company, MTM Enterprises, as an entertainment empire. All of this was a far cry from her humble beginnings in Flatbush.

Her dad was a clerk, her mom was a pinball addict, and in '46 they, Mary, and her younger bro and sis moved to L.A. Her first job came at 18 when she played the spritely "Happy Hotpoint," the dancing pixie in the national Hotpoint TV commercials. Joining the Screen Actors Guild, she originally wanted billing simply as Mary Moore, but she added Tyler because there were already a half-dozen Mary Moore's listed in S.A.G. In '59 she got her first real role, as Sam, the sexy secretary to suave David Janssen in *Richard Diamond, Private Detective*. Ironically, the audience never saw her face, only her gams and hands while she spoke in a deep, breathy voice. Earning $90 a week at this point, she asked for a C-note a week and was promptly fired. Fortunately she soon landed roles on *77 Sunset Strip* and also on Broadway. The new decade brought a spirited new presidency and a spirited new show for Mary.

Created by comedian Carl Reiner, *The DVD Show* was based on his experiences as a New York writer on *Your Show of Shows*. The brilliant ensemble cast (which included Reiner himself) and the deft writing made it a classic sitcom and still one of the most watchable of all '60s shows. Not only was Mary one of the cutest housewives in TV history, she was one of the keys to the show's success: Dick Van Dyke called her "the perfect straight man." One of the most talented, too: she got to joke, cry, sing, dance, throw parties, dress up, get her toe stuck in a bathtub faucet, and say "Oh, Rob" a couple of times a week. Mary's obvious gifts were rewarded with an Emmy nomination in '63 and wins in '64 and '66, plus a Golden Globe in '65 as Best TV Star. In '66, while the show was at its peak of popularity and raking in the last of its fifteen Emmy Awards, the cast voluntarily decided to call it quits. Mary quickly jumped to other media.

She'd made her big-screen debut in '61's *X-15* with Charles Bronson. After *The DVD Show* she did four small-to-medium movies: *Thoroughly Modern Millie* alongside Julie Andrews ('67), *Don't Just Stand There* ('68), *Run a Crooked Mile* ('69), and Elvis' *Change of Habit* ('69). The latter was one of the King's strangest flix, casting him as an inner-city doctor and Mary as a nun (with Ed Asner in a supporting role). The results were as unbelievable as you'd imagine, and in '81 she was given a Golden Turkey Award in the category of Worst Performance by an Actor or Actress as a Clergyman or Nun. She also hit Broadway as the star of a 1966 musical version of *Breakfast at Tiffany's*, but it too flopped.

Mary's next big break came in '69 when she sang and danced on a Dick Van Dyke TV special. Suitably impressed, CBS decided to give her a series of her own. She started her MTM Enterprises, run by husband Grant Tinker, to produce the new sitcom. *The Mary Tyler Moore Show* became one of TV's all-time greatest shows, and Mary Richards became one of TV's all-time favorite characters (*TV Guide* named her #21 among the top-50 characters in TV history). Mary was an Emmy perennial throughout the '70s, getting nominations every year from '71 to '77 and awards in '73, '74, and '76. Not every show had the Midas touch, however: Three attempts at another *Mary* series died quick deaths (*Mary* in '78, *The Mary Tyler Moore Hour* in '79, and *Mary* in '85).

Not one to be stymied by temporary setbacks, Mary diversified into other TV arenas. MTM Enterprises produced popular dramas like *Hill Street Blues* and *St. Elsewhere*, and Mary got more Emmy nominations for her performances in TV movies in '79, '85, and '88, and won another Emmy for *Stolen Babies* in '93. Her biggest film success came in '80 when director Robert Redford gave her a departure role as the bitter mother in his directorial debut, *Ordinary People*. Her strong performance brought her an Oscar nomination. In the '80s she made a triumphant return to Broadway with the acclaimed *Whose Life Is It Anyway?*

A true TV legend, Mary Tyler Moore was elected to the Television Hall of Fame in '85, and she remains one of the most popular, durable stars in entertainment history.

HER '60s LOOK: Mary was only 24 when *The Dick Van Dyke Show* debuted in the fall of '61. Her youth, energy, and looks perfectly represented the enthusiastic spirit of the early '60s. With that wide smile and bouncy hair, Mary was pretty without being devastatingly beautiful, making it easier for women to identify with her. Mary looked especially adorable when she was crying, radiating vulnerability and gentleness. In fact, some of *The DVD Show*'s funniest moments came when Mary held in, then surrendered to, total sobbing. Mary's most prominent feature was below the waist—she's got two of the most famous stems in the biz. Of the clothes Laura Petrie wore on *The DVD Show*, she said in a TV bio, "I will take credit for this—I was the one who said 'this is the way she's gonna look,' and I don't wear frocks"; thus she often sported clingy tights and capri pants, showing off her slender shape to sexy effect in ways that more traditional TV housewives never imagined.

BEHIND THE SCENES: Mary was married for nearly the entire '60s, first to Richard Meeker, "the boy next door" whom she had married at age 18 in the mid-'50s. With him she had a son, Richie, who was born in '56. In the mid-'60s Mary's career came between her and her husband, and they separated. She quickly fell for ad exec Grant Tinker—their love-at-first-sight meeting on the set of *The DVD Show* resulted in marriage six months later. That union lasted until the late '70s, when she and Tinker separated, reconciled, and finally divorced. Unfortunately, during the '70s pressures drove Mary to alcohol, and late in the decade she suffered through several terrible traumas: In '78 her sister died of an accidental drug OD,

and in '80 her son Richie accidentally killed himself. Mary rebounded with a marriage to Dr. Robert Levine, fifteen years her junior. More pain awaited her, unfortunately. In '91 her younger brother died of cancer after a botched attempt at assisted suicide. Happily, Mary and her doc are still together.

BONUS SWINGABILITY: Her exotic birthplace—Flatbush, Brooklyn ... Mary brought David Letterman to television, using him in the background on her MTM shows, which is why she regularly turns up on HIS show ... so strong was Mary's impact in the '60s and '70s, even the obscure people around her got famous—witness Hazel Frederick. Hazel was the mesmerized bystander who watched Mary capriciously toss her hat into the air during the opening credits of *The Mary Tyler Moore Show*. She enjoyed years of mild publicity for her lucky appearance. When Hazel died in December '99, her obituary ran in national newspapers ... a diabetic, Mary injects herself with insulin four times daily, and she's a major fundraiser for diabetes research ... her best-selling '95 autobiography, *After All*, was a frank, candid examination of the triumphs and tragedies in her life ... lessons from Mary in a TV interview: "Nobody gets out of this life without paying something...it is the random aspect of life and I use it to give me the strength to be ready for anything else that might happen."

✳	A DATE WITH MARY	✳
December 29, 1936	Mary Tyler Moore is born	
July 1, 1957	*Richard Diamond, Private Detective* debuts	
October 3, 1961	*The Dick Van Dyke Show* debuts	
May 25, 1964	Mary wins the Outstanding Lead Actress Emmy (*The DVD Show*)	
May 22, 1966	Mary wins the Outstanding Lead Actress Emmy (*The DVD Show*)	
September 7, 1966	*The DVD Show* concludes its five-season run in primetime	
March 21, 1967	*Thoroughly Modern Millie* is released	
November 10, 1969	*Change of Habit* is released	
September 19, 1970	*The Mary Tyler Moore Show* debuts	

JULIE NEWMAR

SWINGIN' '60s CREDENTIALS: This graceful goddess got started in '50s musicals, attained TV stardom with her own show in the '60s, and then created the classic Catwoman character on *Batman*.

WORKIN' IT: Julie Newmar has brought style and glamour to every role she's ever played. Her prodigious musical skills have kept her in the theatre spotlight for decades, and her nimble comedic skills have made her a TV fixture. Her lack of starring roles suggests that Hollywood has never fully taken advantage of her considerable appeal.

After studying ballet (still a pursuit to this day) and graduating from high school at only 15, teenaged Julie started getting dance parts in a variety of '50s films, including *Seven Brides for Seven Brothers* ('54) and *Li'l Abner* ('59), the latter presenting her as the show-stoppin' Stupefyin' Jones. She was also starring on Broadway during the '50s, dancing in numerous shows and starring as the bombshell in *The Marriage-Go-Round*, the role that brought her a Tony Award. In the '60s she was a welcome and reliable TV presence who stole any *F Troop*, *Beverly Hillbillies*, *Monkees*, or *Love, American Style* episode she was on. *My Living Doll* ('64–'65) was

a one-season wonder that cast her as a life-like robot that got its education from Robert Cummings. Though the show lasted only a year (it was positioned opposite the all-conquering *Bonanza*, and Cummings left awkwardly mid-way through the season), Julie was nominated for a Golden Globe as the year's Best TV Star, poising her for the part that would make her a lasting TV favorite.

Though it was drubbed by critics, *Batman* debuted with high ratings in the winter of '66 (it finished the season as a top-10 hit). The show was so popular that for the first year ABC showed it in two-part episodes that ran consecutive Wednesday and Thursday nights. When negotiations with Suzanne Pleshette broke down, Julie was offered the part of the show's newest villain, Catwoman. Julie's often told the story that she hadn't ever seen the month-old show and only took the job on the advice of her brother, a devoted Bat-fan. In March of '66 Julie made the first of a dozen co-starring appearances as the purr-fect cat-foil to the Caped Crusader. Sexy, smart, and unrelentingly evil, she often tried to seduce Batman as well as defeat him. She brought some grown-up sexual intrigue to the otherwise cartoony show whose villains were usually absurd, one-dimensional males (the Joker, the Riddler, the Bookworm, etc.). Always humorous (whether she won or lost a battle on the show), always using her flexible voice to great advantage, cat-tastic Julie seemed to revel in her character in every episode. In '97 *TV Guide* listed the best all-time TV episodes on any show in history, and among them were Julie's first two Catwoman appearances. "The first Catwoman remains the best," the magazine wrote, "meow and forever."

She continued playing the part into the second season, but for the third she left to make a movie and was replaced by Eartha Kitt. (A third actress, Lee Meriwether, wore the catsuit in the '66 *Batman* movie.) Julie's movie career in the '60s encompassed five flix, none of 'em blockbusters: *Marriage-Go-Round* with James Mason in '60, *For Love or Money* with Kirk Douglas in '63, the TV movie *McCloud: Who Killed Miss U.S.A.* in '69, Rowan & Martin's *The Maltese Bippy* in '69, and the Gregory Peck western *Mackenna's Gold* in '69.

After the '60s she made many TV appearances (the obligatory *Love Boat* and *Fantasy Island* among them), plus a dozen minor movies, and she also toured in major musicals. Additional credits on her long résumé include TV commercials (in the late '60s she was a sensuous Mother Nature for Dutch Masters cigars), numerous print ads (including Smirnoff Vodka and Coppertone), poses on several romantic album covers (she was Spice on the 101 Strings' *Sugar and Spice* album), the creation in the '70s of her own line of pantyhose (Nudemar), a cameo in George Michael's '92 video "Too Funky," an appearance in the Lands of Lore 2 video game, and more. Her cult immortality was confirmed in '95 when she was deified in the film *To Wong Foo, Thanks for Everything, Julie Newmar*.

the tv

HER '60s LOOK: Cat-tastic: Julie established once and for all the stereotype of the female super-villain. A lithe 5' 11" tall, 135 pounds with 38-23-38 curves, she radiated an intimidating sexuality in her black vinyl catsuit with a zipper up the back (an erotically evil look emulated again in '92 by Michelle Pfeiffer in *Batman Returns*). To emphasize the curves that put fans in a feline frenzy, she wore her Catwoman belt low across her hips, rather than up high across her waist; in his book *Back to the Batcave*, Adam West correctly praised her as "the sexiest woman on TV." After seeing her at an L.A. party, an overwhelmed Grace Slick later described her in her book *Somebody to Love?*: "Julie Newmar, an outstanding example of the kind of beauty that drops your jaw....Standing over six feet, she was taller than most of the men and towered over all of the women. I couldn't imagine what it must be like to be inside such a spectacular body and have a completely stunning effect on everybody within fifty feet of you at all times." Fashion designers have long loved her look, and in fact she modeled in Paris for Theirry Mugler in the '90s. In addition, Julie has been featured, especially early in her career, in many men's magazines, among them *Playboy* (May '68 and September '69). When *Playboy* published its list of the "100 Sexiest Stars of the Century" in January '99, Julie was ranked #88.

BEHIND THE SCENES:

A marriage, a son. But what a rich tale is in those four words. Julie married a lawyer in '77, and five years later, when she was in her late 40's, she gave birth to a son, John, who was diagnosed with Down's syndrome. Within two years Julie was a divorced mom. She intentionally slowed down her career to spend more time with her son, keeping him at home in Brentwood, California, rather than turning him over to an institution. "Yes, I could have put myself first and sent John off to some facility run by doctors," she told the *National Enquirer* in late '99, "but I love this wonderful person who just happens to be my son. I live my life with him, not in spite of him. He can't speak much and can hardly walk, but inside him is a beautiful soul that shines forth in everything he does." They've traveled the world together, and at home she's designed and built for him a serene "secret garden" that's filled with fountains, rocks, lush landscaping, and ceramic animals. "I want John's life to be as complete as possible," she explained to the *Enquirer*. "He fills my life with joy everyday."

BONUS SWINGABILITY:

Her moniker—born Julia Chalane Newmeyer, and she's been credited as Charlene Jesmer (Jesmer was her mother's maiden name), Julie Neumar, and Julie Newmeyer ... her exotic birthplace—L.A., California ... her father (Donald Newmeyer) was a college professor who had once played for the Chicago Bears, her mother (Helen Jesmer) was a Ziegfeld dancer, and her brother, a Harvard Ph.D named John Newmeyer, is a writer and the proprietor of a Napa, California, winery ... also appearing in the *Li'l Abner* movie with Julie were Stella Stevens and Donna Douglas ... Julie's a serious political activist who has triumphed over noisy leafblowers for the good of homeowners everywhere ... successful in real estate and as a producer, the ever-active Julie told us that her latest fancy is writing: "Having the pleasure of being my own boss, I'll probably never retire!" ... she has her own classy Web site—http://www.geocities.com/Hollywood/Academy/8035.

A DATE WITH JULIE

August 16, 1935	Julie Newmar is born
September 27, 1964	*My Living Doll* debuts
September 8, 1965	*My Living Doll* concludes its one-season run in primetime
January 12, 1966	*Batman* debuts
March 17, 1966	Julie debuts as Catwoman on *Batman*
February 23, 1967	Julie's last appearance as Catwoman
March 14, 1968	*Batman* concludes its two-season run in primetime
May 10, 1969	*Mackenna's Gold* is released

stars

NICHELLE NICHOLS

SWINGIN' '60s CREDENTIALS: In '63 this elegant, coolly professional actress appeared on Gene Roddenberry's show *The Lieutenant*; three years later he remembered her when he was looking for an African-American female to be a regular cast member on his newest TV show, *Star Trek*.

WORKIN' IT: How's this for name-dropping: Duke Ellington hired her, Martin Luther King, Jr. advised her, and Whoopi Goldberg and an astronaut took inspiration from her. Even though she was only a supporting character on a TV show, often with simple, single lines (usually something like "Hailing frequencies open"), Nichelle Nichols was the fulcrum for several important changes on the TV landscape.

A successful singer who toured North America and Europe with Duke Ellington and Lionel Hampton, Nichelle had established herself as an accomplished stage actress (putting several big-city productions on her résumé) when she made her TV debut in '63. That show was *The Lieutenant*, a short-lived cop drama. Nichelle was on just one episode, but it was enough to plant a seed in the mind of the show's producer, Gene Roddenberry. In '66 that seed blossomed into Roddenberry's invitation for Nichelle to work on his new *Star Trek* sci-fi series. It was a bold move for 32-year-old Nichelle. The ground-breaking part of Lieutenant Nyota Uhura made her the first African-American woman to have a prominent role on a major network show.

Nichelle worked with Roddenberry to invent a rich background for Uhura. Born in 2239, supposedly the Lieutenant was from the Bantu Nation in the United States of Africa, she was a graduate of

the Starfleet Academy, she could speak Swahili, and her name was a variation on "uhuru," the Swahili word for "freedom." Nichelle impressed others with her hard work and dedication. Wrote Leonard Nimoy in *I Am Spock* ('95): "On the set, Nichelle was always very beautiful and very involved; and though she often was not given many lines in the script, she nevertheless was totally present and made an emotional investment in whatever was happening in the scene."

Despite her professionalism, nothing on the show was ever easy for Nichelle. In '66, on her way to the second day of shooting *Star Trek*, she was in a serious car accident, receiving a badly split lip and leg injuries. Ever the pro, she went to work anyway. Subjected to occasional racial hostility on the set, she soon found out that she alone among the major characters hadn't been given a contract and was being paid on a daily basis. The studio, she discovered, was even withholding her fan mail! As if these humiliations weren't bad enough, her lines and responsibilities were being cut, a final frustration that made her want to quit midway through the show's first season. She changed her mind after Dr. Martin Luther King personally told her he was a fan and praised her as "a wonderful role model."

Much later, Whoopi Goldberg told her that Uhura was the character who made her want to be a star, and the first African-American woman in space, Dr. Mae Jemison, also credited Uhura as an inspiration.

Nichelle released an album during the show's first season called *Out of This World*, which included her interpretation of the show's theme song. Her character was also instrumental to one of the show's most popular episodes—in "The Trouble with Tribbles," it was she who brought the first hermaphroditic furball onto the *Enterprise* from Deep Space Station K-7. Her most controversial moment on the show came in the '68 episode called "Plato's

Stepchildren" when she and series star William Shatner shared what's said to be the first interracial kiss ever shown on TV. *Star Trek* ran for three years and a total of seventy-nine episodes. While it never ranked higher than #52 in the Nielsens, it was the very definition of a cult hit, spawning blockbuster movies, several spin-off TV shows, an animated series, video games, books, and several additions to the pop culture lexicon ("phasers," "trekkies," "Vulcans," and "Beam me down, Scotty" among them).

As creative as the show was, for the most part it never utilized Nichelle's full talents. She sometimes came off kind of wooden, which is probably good for a Starfleet officer but bad if you're an ambitious dramatic actress.

Her post-'60s career has included lots of star trekkin'. Nichelle's been in six of the *Star Trek* movies that came out steadily after '79 (Uhura's gotten promotions to Commander along the way), she's done voices for the *Star Trek* cartoon and video games, and she appears at fan conventions. Outside of the *Star Trek* universe, she has also lived long and prospered. She was in the Isaac Hayes movie *Truck Turner* ('74), she performs voices for cartoon shows (*Gargoyles* and *Spider-Man*), she's continued her stage career, and she's occasionally performed a nightclub act.

Nichelle wrote a frank and fascinating autobiography, *Beyond Uhura: Star Trek and Other Memories*, in '94, and a sci-fi novel, *Saturn's Children*, in '95 (a sequel, *Saturna's Quest*, is in the works). A huge advocate of space travel, she's attended many NASA ceremonies and has helped the agency recruit minorities. Among her many international awards and honors, there's one that's something of a landmark: She was the first African-American to place handprints in front of Hollywood's Chinese Theatre.

HER '60s LOOK: On the show Nichelle's natural attractiveness was made more futuristic by exotic make-up and twenty-third-century wigs. She did fill out her officer's uniform nicely, but the camera seemed to dwell on whatever skimpy outfit the other actresses on the series wore to titillate the predominantly male audience. Which is just fine, thank you—Nichelle and Uhura were more about dignity and professionalism than they were about titillation, and in that they both managed to rise above the show's more juvenile tendencies.

BEHIND THE SCENES: To the surprise of some on the show, Nichelle confessed in her autobiography that she and Gene Roddenberry had fallen in love when she worked on *The Lieutenant* in '63. Roddenberry wasn't boldly going where no man had gone before, however—she'd been a mom since the age of 18. In early '51 Nichelle had married a dancer who was fifteen years her senior. Within four months he left her, and by August '51 Nichelle had delivered a son, whom she raised on her own. Nichelle's autobiography didn't describe any intimacies with Roddenberry during the *Star Trek* years, just a close, professional relationship. Nichelle remarried in '68, this time to a songwriter, but that marriage ended in divorce a few years later. "Nichelle was stunned," wrote *People* magaine in its April 14, 1997 issue, to learn that her brother Thomas had committed suicide in the spring of '97 along with the other Heaven's Gate cult members in Rancho Santa Fe, California.

BONUS SWINGABILITY: Her moniker—she was born Grace Nichols, went by Lynn Mayfair for six months in her early teens, and switched to Nichelle Nichols at about 16 ... her exotic birthplace—Robbins, Illinois, where her father was the mayor ... in her autobiography she described a tense confrontation between her father and Al Capone—and it was Capone who backed down! ... besides writing she also likes to paint and sculpt ... Nichelle gets extra Swingability points for complaining directly to Shatner about his inconsiderate and egotistical behavior ... Roddenberry died of cardiac arrest in '91, and Nichelle sang two songs at the service ... Nichelle has her own informative Web site—http://www.uhura.com.

A DATE WITH NICHELLE

December 28, 1933	Nichelle Nichols is born
September 8, 1966	*Star Trek* debuts
December 29, 1967	"The Trouble with Tribbles" episode airs
November 22, 1968	The "Plato's Stepchildren" episode airs
September 2, 1969	*Star Trek* concludes its three-season run in primetime
Stardate 4523.3	The *Star Trek* date given for the "Trouble with Tribbles" episode
Stardate 5784.2	The *Star Trek* date given for the "Plato's Stepchildren" episode

MELODY PATTERSON

SWINGIN' '60s CREDENTIALS: This cheerful young thang lied about her age to get the plum role as rootin' tootin' cowgirl Wrangler Jane on *F Troop*.

WORKIN' IT: Melody Patterson had plenty o' potential, but she never rose much higher than that first role—a minor role, mind you—on the Western whoopdedo *F Troop*. Much as viewers may have wanted to see more Melody on that show, the *bugler* had more screen time. Besides *F Troop*, her '60s *oeuvre* is pretty insubstantial. She was Ella Mae Chubber, betrothed to Davy Jones, in the "Hillbilly Honeymoon" episode of *The Monkees* in '66, then later she was a blonde receptionist in "The Devil and Mr. Frog" episode of *Hawaii Five-0*. In '69 she appeared in two little-noticed biker flix, *The Angry Breed* with James MacArthur and *The Cycle Savages* with Bruce Dern. In '68 and '69 she did USO tours of Vietnam. Even if there's not much *there* there, feisty Wrangler Jane Anjelica Thrift was

enough fun to warrant inclusion on this list. Not so much for the part but for how Melody got it.

Born in 1949, and an actress in L.A. since she was 5, Melody was only 15 when she auditioned for *F Troop*. The guy she was wooing on the show, Captain Wilton Parmenter, was played by someone over twice her age, 32-year-old Ken Berry. By the time she confessed her true age to the producers (who thought she was 18), seven episodes had already been filmed and it was too late to replace her.

A modest hit throughout its two-year run, *F Troop* blended slapstick with gag-shtick as performed by a roster of experienced show-biz veterans. Besides Berry, the other main actors were sturdy Forrest Tucker, loony Larry Storch, and a gang of guest-starring comedians, including Don Rickles (as, appropriately enough,

Bald Eagle), Milton Berle (as Wise Owl), and Paul Lynde (as Sgt. Ramsden). Rompin' into this motley crew was pretty young Melody, not just the cutest gal, but the *only* gal, in them there parts. In '67 the title question of the last episode, "Is This Fort Really Necessary?," was answered with a resounding no, and the show was canceled.

Melody had a depressingly small amount of post-'60s work: star billing in a feeble horror flick in '71, *Blood and Lace*, an uncredited role in '73's *The Harrad Experiment*, followed by an eighteen-year gap until '91's *The Immortalizer*. Today she's teaching drama and writes "Wrapping with Wrangler," a column for the magazine *Wildest Westerns*.

HER '60s LOOK: She was the best in the West, sort of a frontier Donna Douglas—wrangly blonde hair that was probably a lengthy fall, big rosy lips, friendly smile, and big enthusiastic eyes made her a vision of youthful sex appeal. Though her Western cowgirl outfit didn't really show off her curves, a few still photos at her official Web site suggest she could put the Wild in Wild West. In '98 Larry Storch told People Online that he's still in touch with Melody and she's "as beautiful as ever...she could be acting if she wanted to."

BEHIND THE SCENES: How swingin' is this: As a 16-year-old working on *F Troop*, she fell for a married Warner Bros. producer who was exactly twice her age, causing a scandal within the studio. At 18 she hooked up with and then married actor James MacArthur, the son of theatre legend Helen Hayes. He had played sensible son Fritz in Disney's *Swiss Family Robinson* before *Hawaii Five-0* established him as a TV staple. They split up at the end of the '70s, and Melody married musician Vern Miller in '98.

BONUS SWINGABILITY: Her exotic birthplace—Inglewood, California ... she owned and ran a Honolulu boutique called The Iron Butterfly ... Melody reportedly gave an interview in the early '90s to shock-jock Howard Stern in which she titillated his audience with tales of a motel-room *menage a trois* ... Melody has her own official Web site—http://www.wranglerjane.com.

 A DATE WITH MELODY

December 8, 1937	James MacArthur is born
April 16, 1949	Melody Patterson is born
September 14, 1965	*F Troop* debuts
August 31, 1967	*F Troop* concludes its two-season run in primetime
July 12, 1970	Melody marries James MacArthur

SWINGIN' '60s CREDENTIALS: This sweet blonde went from winning beauty contests to playing Marilyn on *The Munsters* and co-starring with Elvis in *Easy Come, Easy Go.*

WORKIN' IT: Patricia Priest was performing on stage and winning beauty contests from the time she was in her mid-teens. Moving from Washington, D.C. (where her mom served as the U.S. Treasurer) to California to pursue an acting career, Pat performed around the San Francisco Bay Area and was appearing in local commercials when she got the call to go to Hollywood.

The Munsters had debuted in the fall of '64, but after the thirteenth episode Beverly Owen, a brunette who wore a platinum-blonde wig, decided to get married and quit her role as Marilyn. Pat stepped in for episode 14 and continued in the role through the seventieth and final episode in '66. Supposedly the daughter of Lily's sister (who was never named), earnest and sincere Marilyn was the attractive, "normal" college girl among the monstrous Munsters (the show never explained exactly why Marilyn lived at 1313 Mockingbird Lane). Marilyn was usually in the background of the storyline, providing occasional merriment when her dates would come to the door and get a glimpse of Herman. One of the few episodes to showcase her was episode 48, "A Man for Marilyn," in which Grandpa tried to turn a frog into a prince so that the "ugly" Marilyn would be able to land a husband. Thanks to the delightful cast of ol' pros like Fred Gwynne and Al Lewis, plus the great set design (not to mention the rockinest theme song this side of *The Monkees*), *The Munsters* was an instant success. Comparing *The Munsters* with *The Addams Family*, another show with a freakish family confronting the real world, *Variety* declared its favorite after both shows had run a few weeks in '64: "The edge must go to *The Munsters* for, as 'unnatural' shows go, this one is more natural, more credible, it's less frenzied, and doesn't shove its 'way out' quality down the viewer's throat."

Unfortunately, once the *Batman* juggernaut revved up in January '66 in the same timeslot on a different network, *The Munsters* was doomed, and the show was canceled four months later. After *The Munsters* ended, Pat joined another tall, dark leading man with a big house, this time for a major movie. In Elvis' *Easy Come, Easy Go,* she was the bikini-blessed bad girl on hand as the King dove for undersea treasure. The most notable entry on her slim post-'60s résumé is *The Incredible Two-Headed Transplant* in '71. She still makes occasional appearances on TV and at fan conventions.

HER '60s LOOK: Her gentle blonde hair, innocent eyes, and kind smile made her a pretty contrast to the horrific Munsters. She has said that the best part of her '60s look was its simplicity.

Whereas the other characters needed several hours a day to put on and take off their complicated make-up, Pat needed only twenty minutes. *Easy Come, Easy Go* revealed her to be slender and leggy, always a winning combination.

BEHIND THE SCENES: While *The Munsters* was on, Pat was already married and had two sons, both of whom did TV commercials. She and her second husband currently live in Haley, Idaho.

BONUS SWINGABILITY: Her exotic birthplace—Salt Lake City, Utah ... as the U.S. Treasurer during the Eisenhower years, Pat's mom's signature was printed on all paper currency ... all the Marilyns, in order: Beverly Owen (*The Munsters*, '64); Pat (*The Munsters*, '64–'66); Debbie Watson (*Munster, Go Home* movie, '66); Jo McDonnell (*The Munster's Revenge* TV movie, '81); Hilary Van Dyke (*The New Munsters* TV show, '88); Christine Taylor (*Here Come the Munsters* TV movie, '95); Elaine Hendrix (*The Munsters Scary Little Christmas* TV movie, '96) ... Pat once owned Elvis' black '67 Caddy, but two years later she traded it away for a (gulp!) Pontiac ... Pat has her own Web site, run by her son, Pierce—http://www.pscelebrities.com/pp.html.

 A DATE WITH PAT

August 15, 1936	Pat Priest is born
September 24, 1964	*The Munsters* debuts
December 24, 1964	Pat takes over for Beverly Owen as Marilyn on *The Munsters*
November 18, 1965	The "A Man for Marilyn" episode airs
September 8, 1966	*The Munsters* concludes its two-season run in primetime
June 1, 1967	*Easy Come, Easy Go* is released

INGER STEVENS

her late teens, Inger studied with the legendary Lee Strasberg in hopes of being a serious actress.

She got her TV start with the lead role in Broadway show, *Debut*, which quickly closed in early '56. Her TV career, though, was soon underway with some mid-'50s commercials and *The Robert Montgomery Show*, which starred the father of Elizabeth Montgomery (and sometimes Elizabeth herself). More TV appearances led to prominent billing in four late-'50s films: *Man on Fire* ('57), *Cry Terror* ('58), *The Buccaneer* ('58), and *The World, the Flesh, and the Devil* ('59). The '60s started off great for her. She began the decade in January '60 with a *Twilight Zone* episode—"The Hitchhiker"—that is still is considered one of the show's best ever. In '62 she got an Emmy nomination for an appearance on *The Dick Powell Show*. In '63 *The Farmer's Daughter* debuted, and her TV legacy was made.

On *The Farmer's Daughter* Inger played sweet Katrin "Katy" Holstrum, a governess to a congressman, played by William Windom. The gentle show was based on the '47 movie of the same name that had brought Loretta Young an Oscar as Best Actress; in '64 it brought 29-year-old Inger Stevens a Golden Globe as Best TV Star. She also won a *TV Guide* popularity poll that year, and she got her second Emmy nomination. Just as *I Dream of Jeannie* and *Get Smart* would do at the end of the decade, in '65 the show married off its two leads in a failed attempt to juice the ratings.

Returning to the big screen, her movie career started to gather momentum, and she made four films in '68 alone. Late-decade highlights included Clint's *Hang 'Em High* in '67, the delightful *A Guide for the Married Man* in '67, and Dino's *5 Card Stud* in '68. Two TV movies ran in '70: *Run, Simon, Run* and *The Mask of Sheba*.

Sadly, Inger's long battle with depression finally defeated her. In '70 a house-guest found Inger in her Hollywood home unconscious from a barbiturate OD. She was declared DOA at the hospital, a death ruled a suicide by the L.A Coroner's office.

She died never having fulfilled her full star potential, and today she's often overlooked when TV stars of the '60s are recalled. Her career, however, proved she could play comic, dramatic, and romantic roles with skill and subtlety. Just before her death she had signed a contract to do a new Aaron Spelling series, *The Most Deadly Game*, which eventually flickered to brief life in '70–'71 with Yvette Mimieux as the star.

SWINGIN' '60s CREDENTIALS: This blue-eyed blonde with a pretty, yet sad, face came from Sweden to become an American TV star on *The Farmer's Daughter*, but her late-'60s movie career came to a depressing end in '70.

WORKIN' IT: Of all the actresses described in this book, Inger Stevens was probably the unhappiest. The product of a broken home in Sweden, her father brought her to America at age 10. She grew up in two Manhattans—first in New York, then in Kansas, where her father taught at Kansas State. A part-time model and chorus girl in

HER '60s LOOK: Inger Stevens was pretty, at times spectacular, though she herself once described her face as "crooked." For glamorous events she usually wore her blonde hair piled high á la

Tippi Hedren. While Inger often wore long, conservative frontier dresses for her period films, she had a fit figure and long legs, all revealed to controversial effect in the mid-'60s when she wore a mini to the Oscars. Her sexiest role may have been *A Guide for the Married Man*, which opened with closeups of her doing exercises in a leotard and trying to tempt her neglectful husband, Walter Matthau. Later scenes placed her in tight pants and a bikini, showing Matthau what a wonderful wife she'd be if he only paid attention.

BEHIND THE SCENES: Inger was married to her agent from '55 to '57. After their divorce, stories circulated of affairs she was having on the sets of her movies. The stars she was allegedly involved with included Bing Crosby, James Mason, Anthony Quinn, and Harry Belafonte. Wrote Inger, "I often feel depressed. I come from a broken home, my marriage was a disaster, and I am constantly lonely." The press reported that she attempted suicide in '59 with a combo of sleeping pills and ammonia. In '61 she secretly married African-American actor/musician Ike Jones in Tijuana. Jones was later one of the producers of Sammy Davis, Jr.'s *A Man Called Adam* in '66. Their marriage struggled at the end of the decade, and rumors aligned Inger with Dean Martin and then Burt Reynolds. After she died, her body was cremated, the ashes scattered over the Pacific.

boards and charities, and she was chairwoman of the California Council of Retarded Children ... William Windom once described her as "a lady of many secrets" ... at the Internet's Inger Stevens Memorial Site, she's quoted as saying, "I had a terrible insecurity, an extreme shyness, that I covered up with coldness. Everybody thought I was a snob. I was really just plain scared" ... and this too from Inger: "Sometimes when I'm doing a part, I think: 'My heavens, I'm not really capable of doing any of this. Someday they're going to find out I just can't do it'" ... and finally: "If I took a test, I would probably find I'm in the wrong field" ... those and other Inger Stevens quotes and stories can be found at http://www.geocities.com/Hollywood/Boulevard/7484/main.html.

BONUS SWINGABILITY: She used a fake moniker—her real name was Inger Stensland ... her exotic birthplace—Stockholm, Sweden ... while vacationing in '61, she was on a jetliner when one of the jet's wheels collapsed on the runway, forcing her and other passengers to flee as their burning plane exploded behind them ... she served on various medical

A DATE WITH INGER

October 18, 1934	Inger Stevens is born
January 22, 1960	Inger stars in "The Hitchhiker" episode of *The Twilight Zone*
December 2, 1960	Inger stars in "The Lateness of the Hour" episode of *The Twilight Zone*
November 18, 1961	Inger marries Ike Jones
September 20, 1963	*The Farmer's Daughter* debuts
November 5, 1965	Katy marries her congressman on *The Farmer's Daughter*
September 2, 1966	*The Farmer's Daughter* concludes its three-season run in primetime
May 25, 1967	*A Guide for the Married Man* is released
July 31, 1968	*Hang 'Em High* is released
April 30, 1970	Inger commits suicide
May 5, 1970	Inger is cremated, her ashes scattered over the ocean

stars

MARLO THOMAS

SWINGIN' '60s CREDENTIALS: This lively kite-flyin' dock-runnin' go-go-boot-wearin' voice-crackin' cutie was best-known in the '60s for one key role—wannabe actress Ann Marie on TV's *That Girl*.

WORKIN' IT: Marlo Thomas was a natural. And given her parentage, is it any surprise? She was born the daughter of entertainment legend Danny Thomas, who had his own popular '50s show, *Make Room for Daddy* (later *The Danny Thomas Show*).

Though famous for *That Girl*, Marlo made appearances on several other shows in the '50s and '60s, most notably as recurring character Stella Barnes on *The Joey Bishop Show* ('61–'62). Late in the decade she was the unmarried, pregnant title character taking up with Alan Alda in the soapy *Jenny* ('69), which brought her a Golden Globe nomination as the Most Promising Newcomer. But *That Girl* was the show that brought her the most acclaim (a Golden Globe in '67 as Best Actress and four Emmy nominations).

Though not considered a classic comedy, *That Girl* was something of a breakthrough in that it was about a modern single woman, thus paving the way for such other acclaimed shows as *Julia*, *The Mary Tyler Moore Show*, and *Rhoda*. Produced by her powerful papa, and created by Bill Persky and Sam Denoff (former writers of *The Dick Van Dyke Show*), *That Girl* focused on young, wholesome, fashionably dressed forward-thinking model/actress Ann Marie (Marie was her last name), who navigated the Big Apple with Don

Hollinger (Ted Bessell), her patient boyfriend and a writer for a magazine called *Newsview*.

When the show debuted in '66, Marlo was somewhere in her late twenties, depending on which source you believe (her birthyear is usually given between '34 and '38; the latter seems to be generally accepted). The zany gags often revolved around the zany gigs Ann would get to support herself while waiting for her big break, including one commercial where she dressed as a chicken and other temporary jobs as a meter maid, chef, and door-to-door salesperson. But more impressive to viewers was her strong stance on women's rights, making her perhaps primetime's first feminist and a role model for young women.

Before Ann Marie, young women on TV were often portrayed as dependent and silly, as on *I Dream of Jeannie*, which concentrated all the show's powers in Barbara Eden's character and then made that character subservient to a male master. Single career women were usually middle-aged wise-crackers, such as *The Dick Van Dyke Show's* Sally (played by Rose Marie). Ann Marie gave young female viewers someone with whom they could identify. Like many viewers, she had left a small town (Brewster, New York, where she was a meter maid) in hopes of making it in the big city. She was approximately the same age as her loyal fans, she wore their same hip clothes, and, like her audience, she had to juggle jobs, dates, and family obligations. Ann Marie was smart, warm-hearted, ambitious, and liberated. She probably even read *Cosmo*. Viewers followed her romantic relationship from its beginning (passerby Donald rescued her from what he thought was a kidnapping) to matrimony (almost). Borrowing a familiar storyline technique, Ann Marie and Donald (as she called him) got engaged in '70. (Other shows that married

the tv

off the leads included *The Farmer's Daughter*, *Get Smart*, and *I Dream of Jeannie*.) Ann and Donald never did marry, however (in fact, Ann almost lost the engagement ring in some cake batter), and *That Girl* became Canceled Girl in '71.

Ann Marie resurfaced in '73, however, with Marlo doing the vocals for the animated TV special *That Girl in Wonderland*, which put her in the roles of various fairy tale heroines.

Marlo then shifted from her classy TV show to lots of classy TV movies and specials, including *It Happened One Christmas* in '77, *Nobody's Child* in '86 (bringing her an acting Emmy), and *Held Hostage* in '91. Generations of children have been influenced by her two remarkable multi-media children's projects: Marlo co-produced, performed in, and won an Emmy for, the landmark children's special *Free to Be…You and Me* in '74 (also creating the classic children's book), and she won another Emmy for hosting *The Body Human: Facts for Girls* in '80. Other entertainment achievements include several starring roles on Broadway (her '74 Broadway debut was in *Thieves*, a role she reprised for the '77 film), and an episode of *Friends* that brought her another Emmy nomination in '96.

Off-screen, she continues to support numerous social causes and charities, especially one, St. Jude's Children's Research Hospital, that was founded by her father. That Girl of the '60s is now That Woman of the twenty-first century, as energetic and idealistic and accomplished as ever.

HER '60s LOOK:
The brunette flip, the sunny smile, the pretty face—young Marlo was the ultimate in kookie urban charm. Because Ann Marie always wore such gear fashions, including bright dresses and great go-go boots, the eternal question was about her income. How could this often-unemployed character afford so many new clothes? Bog down with that, though, and you'll start lying awake nights wondering about the number of suitcases brought to *Gilligan's Island*, the number of Marilyns on *The Munsters*, and the number of Darrins on *Bewitched*.

BEHIND THE SCENES:
Like Jill St. John, Shirley MacLaine, Candice Bergen, and other beautiful actresses, Marlo was briefly linked with Henry Kissinger in the '70s. She met talk-show host Phil Donahue on his show in '77, and they married in '80.

BONUS SWINGABILITY:
Her moniker at birth was Margaret Julia Thomas … her exotic birthplace—Detroit, Michigan … her brother Tony is also a TV producer, with dozens of post-'60s shows on his résumé … among the recurring guest stars on *That Girl* were Dabney Coleman as a neighbor, Ruth Buzzi as a pal, Billy De Wolfe as her drama teacher, George Carlin as her agent, and Bernie *Get Smart* Kopell as Don's friend … someone else who made several appearances on the show was her own father, Danny Thomas; in the third season he played a priest in the "My Sister's Keeper" episode, and when Ann Marie bumped into him she said, "Excuse me, father," to which he replied, "That's all right, my child" … in season five Danny showed up in the "Those Friars" episode with Milton Berle, both playing themselves, and Danny and Marlo performed a musical number at the end … a character Ann Marie shared much in common with was Laura Petrie of *The Dick Van Dyke Show*. Although Laura was married, she still had many of Ann Marie's best qualities: they both lived in or around New York, they had similar dark features and slender builds, and they both got their toe stuck in something (Laura's in a bathtub faucet, Ann Marie's in a bowling ball) … despite struggling to earn a living, Ann Marie managed to have nice Manhattan apartments, first at 344 West 78th Street, and then at 627 East 54th Street … she's one of the few actresses of the '60s immediately identified by her own theme song, though it's unclear what the four elements of the song's first line—diamonds, daisies, snowflakes, and *That Girl*—have in common.

 A DATE WITH MARLO

December 21, 1935	Phil Donahue is born
November 21, 1938	Marlo Thomas is born
September 8, 1966	*That Girl* debuts
September 25, 1970	Donald proposes to Ann on *That Girl*
September 10, 1971	*That Girl* concludes its five-season run in primetime
March 11, 1974	*The Free to Be…You and Me* special airs

stars

DAWN WELLS

SWINGIN' '60s CREDENTIALS: This sweet, brown-eyed beauty-pageant winner played Mary Ann, the Kansas farm girl who booked a three-hour tour and got shipwrecked for three years on *Gilligan's Island*.

WORKIN' IT: Dawn Wells wasn't always a castaway. Miss Nevada and a Miss America contestant in '59, Dawn's early light was shining in lots of '50s and '60s TV shows. But not until that fateful trip on the *S.S. Minnow* did she become a star.

Legend has it that when *Gilligan's Island* was being cast in '64, Raquel Welch was one of the actresses who auditioned for the Mary Ann part. Dawn, however, was the very personification of a naïve Kansas cutie, something akin to Dorothy in *The Wizard of Oz* but without the dog.

Mary Ann was rarely at the center of the show's plots; in fact, she and the Professor weren't even mentioned in the original version of the theme song. The storylines revealed that she had an Aunt Martha and Uncle George back home in Winfield, Kansas, and she usually did all the cooking on the island (coconut cream pie was a specialty, though who knows where the dairy products came from). Dawn spent her mid-twenties shipwrecked through ninety-eight episodes and three seasons ('64–'67), returning a decade later to do the three TV movies (*Rescue from…* in '78, *The Castaways on…* in '79, and *The Harlem Globetrotters on…* in '81) and the animated *Gilligan's Planet* in '82 (she did the voices of both Mary Ann and Ginger).

Her screen résumé is fleshed out with minor movies (*The Town That Dreaded Sundown* and *Winterhawk* in '76, *Return to Boggy Creek* in '78), and over 100 appearances on TV series and talk shows. She's also produced children's TV broadcasts, and late in the '90s she hosted her own fishing show called *Dawn Wells' Reel Adventures*.

Branching into other arenas, she's created her own line of clothes for the physically challenged, called the Wishing Wells Collection and touted as "special clothes for special people." She tours as a motivational speaker, and she teaches acting at the Dawn Wells Film Actors Boot Camp, located on her Teton Wells Ranch near Jackson Hole, Wyoming (one week of classes, room and board at the ranch=$2500). In '93 Dawn published *Mary Ann's "Gilligan's Island" Cookbook* (sprinkling recipes like Ginger's Snaps and Gilligan Stew with show anecdotes), and later she did a national commercial for Western Union in which she played Mary Ann and revealed that she had married—ta da!—the Professor!

HER '60s LOOK: Though not the dazzler that Tina Louise's Ginger was on the show, Dawn's Mary Ann was definitely cute. She had the timeless country-girl appeal that still works today. On *Gilligan's Island* her clothes weren't always demure gingham, however; some of her best outfits put her in boots and a short skirt (yet another example of the castaways' bizarre packing strategy). But no matter what she wore, Mary Ann always looked appealing, quite a feat when you consider that the meals on the island usually involved variations on the coconut theme.

BEHIND THE SCENES: In lieu of actual lovelife info about Dawn, we present this mental exercise about Mary Ann. Had the castaways actually been rescued on the show, think for a second what Mary Ann said she would do upon her return to civilization: "The first thing I'll do when I get back home is bake an apple pie, milk the cow, and feed the chickens."

BONUS SWINGABILITY: Her exotic birthplace—Reno, Nevada … the first thirty-six episodes of *Gilligan's Island* were in black and white, the next sixty-two were in color … Mary Ann's last name on the show was Summers; other character names on *Gilligan's Island* were Skipper Jonas Grumby, Thurston's wife, Lovey Howell, plus high school science teacher Professor Roy Hinkley … the one-season *Gilligan's Island* cartoon placed the castaways on another planet trying to get back to Earth; the professor couldn't even fix a boat, but he was supposed to fix a rocket ship? … Dawn with the Wind: she's done some remarkable traveling all around the world, which is described (along with her business ventures) at her official Web site—http://www.dawn-wells.com.

 A DATE WITH DAWN

October 18	Dawn Wells is born
September 26, 1964	*Gilligan's Island* debuts
September 4, 1967	*Gilligan's Island* concludes its three-season run in primetime

the tv

THE TV STARS:
CARTOON CUTIES

We couldn't end a presentation of '60s actresses without men-
tioning a coupla fictional TV trixies who gave us reasons to get up
early on Saturday mornings. Just because they only existed as ink
drawings didn't mean they couldn't have lives and romances and
careers. These two girls were as real as any character on the
campy Batman series, and they never once gained weight, got
arrested, or demanded a bigger trailer.

JUDY JETSON

SWINGIN' '60s CREDENTIALS: The pony-tailed Miss Jetson had one role in the '60s as the boy-crazy cast member of *The Jetsons*, a primetime cartoon that in '62 became ABC's first color TV show.

WORKIN' IT: Unfortunately, like other animated actresses, Judy Jetson was pretty two-dimensional, and though *The Jetsons* was a long-running hit, Judy started out in a supporting role and never rose above it to branch out into a solo career. Judy was one of the four members of the family headed by George Jetson, who worked at Spacely Space Age Sprockets; others in the Jetson clan included Jane, his wife, his boy Elroy, and later Rosie the robot maid. The family dog was named Astro (another pet, the slinky-like Orbitty, came later). As a student at Orbit High School, Judy's main interests were boys, shopping, boys, the phone, and boys, although in one later episode she showed a talent for sculpting. On the show, Judy's vocals were performed by veteran actress Janet Waldo, who did voices for many other cartoon characters, including Granny Sweet on *Atom Ant*, Jenny on *The Space Kidettes*, and Josie on *Josie and the Pussycats*. Janet reprised her Judy vocals in the '87 TV movie *The Jetsons Meet the Flintstones*, but in the 1990 *Jetsons* movie, Judy's vocals were done by pop star Tiffany, who sang three songs: "You and Me," "I Always Thought I'd See You Again," and "Home."

HER '60s LOOK: Judy was cute 'n' perky with that ponytail 'do; to her credit, she never seemed to age. Perhaps that's due to her swingin' threads: A futuristic femme, she always wore the height of twenty-first century fashions on her slender model's figure.

BEHIND THE SCENES: That she lived in the Skypad Apartments in Orbit City throughout the decade was pretty swingin', but that she was living there with her parents and little brother wasn't. Judy did get a boyfriend in the "Rosie's Boyfriend" episode, and later she tried to elope with Mr. Spacely's nephew Samuel, who was a student at M.I.T. (the Moon Institute of Technology). She also got three jobs in the "9 to 5 to 9" episode: construction worker, dog-walker, and fast-food server.

BONUS SWINGABILITY: *The Jetsons* show was an early proponent of recycling: The first season (the only one in primetime) had only twenty-four episodes, which were repeated over and over on Saturday mornings for the next twenty years (new episodes weren't created until the mid-'80s); what's more, the show's formula—a wacky suburban family in the future—was Hanna-Barbera's variation on the successful formula of *The Flintstones*—a wacky suburban family in the past—which had debuted two years earlier ... no year is specified as the setting for *The Jetsons*, but Judy tips us off that it's after the millennium when she criticizes George's dancing as being "practically twentieth century!"

A DATE WITH JUDY

September 23, 1962	*The Jetsons* debuts
September 8, 1963	*The Jetsons* concludes its one-season run in primetime
June 2	George and Jane's wedding date, year unspecified

VERONICA LODGE

SWINGIN' '60s CREDENTIALS: This lanky raven-haired vixen was the object of Archie Andrews's affections in the *Archie* comic books and on the Saturday-morning cartoon series *The Archie Show*; her main rival was sweet golden-hearted blonde Betty Cooper, but everybody usually went daffy for Veronica because she was rich and played hard to get.

WORKIN' IT: Veronica Lodge made her debut into the Archie comic book universe in '42, four months after Archie and Betty first appeared. She worked all through the '60s, though rarely on her own—when she wasn't paired with Archie, she was usually with Betty. Veronica did jump to different media during her career, going from a supporting role in the comic books to a supporting role in *The Archie Show*, which ran on Saturday mornings in '68 and continued in various incarnations (*The Archie Comedy Hour*, *Archie's Funhouse*, *Archie's TV Funnies*, *Everything's Archie*, *The U.S. of Archie*, *The New Archie/Sabrina Hour*, *The Bang-Shang Lalapalooza Show*, and *The New Archies*) for the next decade. On the original show in '68, Veronica and Betty's voices were provided by the same actress—Jane Webb, who later played Ginger Grant on *The New Adventures of Gilligan* series from '74 to '77. The live-action *Archie: To Riverdale and Back Again* (AKA *Return to Riverdale*) TV movie reunited the gang in '90 (Karen Kopins played Ronnie, Lauren Holly was Betty). More than just an Archie graphic, though, the character of Veronica was part of the fictional Archie sound. In the cartoon rock band the Archies, Ronnie sang back-up, chiming in on the saccharine "Sugar Sugar" with the line "I'm gonna make your life so sweet." Astonishingly, that song hit #1 for four weeks in '69, the same year that saw hit records by the Who, Led Zeppelin, the Beatles, and Elvis.

But acting and singing weren't Veronica's true talents. For any guy's romantic compass, Ronnie was the true north where their needles perpetually pointed. Often she dated rich wiseguy Reggie Mantle, a louse who was rapid with a dollar, and big hunky types, who did the mummy stumble when Ronnie walked by, all while still flirting with Archie, just to keep him dangling. Vain and arrogant, she was great at flaunting her wealth and social status by buying the best and most of everything. Still, despite her long career in various entertainment arenas, today her name barely registers on the impact-o-meter. Mention the name "Veronica Lodge" and most people will think you're talking about a great vacation destination—and in a way, they'd be right.

HER '60s LOOK: Truly beautiful, Veronica was more like a '40s vamp, which was appropriate since the comic started in '41; actually, she looked suspiciously like Betty Cooper, and they would've been identical twins except for the hair. She and Betty both had knockout figures, all sleek legs and flat stomach. Unlike the other girls, who wore teenage styles like sweats and jeans, Veronica usually wore expensive designer fashions. She was beautiful, rich, well-dressed, and had every dude in Riverdale except Moose and Jughead acting like punch-drunk saps as they competed for her affections. It's a wonder she had any girlfriends.

BEHIND THE SCENES: Supposedly a senior at Riverdale High, Veronica lived at home all decade. But who wouldn't, given that the home was the biggest mansion in Riverdale (her dad's favorite magazine was called *Moolah Monthly*).

BONUS SWINGABILITY: Her moniker—she often went by the nickname "Ronnie" ... in '94 Veronica lost Archie to newcomer Cheryl Blossom, a saucy redhead who was even richer than Ronnie ... Ronnie's gal pals were Midge and Ethel ... among readers, Betty is generally the most popular in head-to-head Internet polls ... when a new live-action *Archie* movie was first announced in the late '90s, the part of Veronica Lodge was supposedly going to be played by Shannon Doherty ... there's an official Archie comics Web site—http://www.archiecomics.com.

A DATE WITH VERONICA

September 14, 1968	*The Archie Show* debuts
August 16, 1969	"Sugar Sugar" enters the *Billboard* charts (it will hit #1)
August 30, 1969	*The Archie Show* concludes its one-season run
September 6, 1969	*The Archie Comedy Hour* debuts
December 20, 1969	"Jingle Jangle" enters the *Billboard* charts (it will hit #10)
September 5, 1970	*The Archie Comedy Hour* concludes its one-season run

THE ATHLETES

Women athletes took giant strides in the '60s. Not only were some of the most memorable women athletes of all time performing at their peaks during the decade, but a movement towards equality for all athletes, male and female, gained momentum and power. And thanks to the sharp surge in TV sports coverage, athletic achievements could be witnessed live all around the planet. After the '60s, women's athletics were never the same again.

PEGGY FLEMING

SWINGIN' '60s CREDENTIALS: If Grace Kelly had been a figure skater, she would've been Peggy Fleming; this exquisite, ethereal elegant beauty won the hearts of the world—and the only U.S. gold medal—at the '68 Winter Olympics.

WORKIN' IT:

Peggy Fleming's figure skating career can be summarized in a word: domination. She won five straight U.S. figure skating championships from '64 to '68 and three straight world titles from '66 to '68, culminating with the gold medal at the '68 Winter Olympics. Her awards during the '60s included the ABC Athlete of the Year Award in '67 and the Babe Didrickson Zaharias Award in '68. What makes her accomplishments all the more astonishing is the disaster that shook America's Olympic skating team in the early '60s.

Peggy had been been skating since she was 9 years old, winning various amateur titles around the country in anticipation of joining the U.S. figure skating team for the '64 Olympics. Tragically, in '61 that entire team, including her own coach, Bill Kipp, was wiped out in an airplane crash in Belgium on the way to the World Championships in Prague. Eleven-year-old Peggy was left behind without experienced peers to practice with and without the trainers and coaches she'd relied upon. "I didn't have anyone to look up to

and guide my training," she later said, "but that was good in a way. To try to copy someone is never a good thing. There were a lot of special feelings when I won, feelings that I was more than just another champion, that I was the first to rise above the tragedy." Rise she did. A 14-year-old Olympic rookie suffering from a fever, she finished sixth at the '64 Games in Innsbruck. But she was now poised for her triumph at the '68 Olympics, for which she trained five to eight hours per day. Peggy, still a teenager, was rivaled only by French skier Jean-Claude Killy as the superstar of the '68 Games held in Grenoble, France.

These were an especially significant Olympics, because they were the first to be televised live and in color to a global TV audience. Skating to Tchaikovsky's *Pathetique*, Peggy delivered a graceful, impeccable performance, leaving her closest competitor almost ninety points behind and winning America's only gold medal of the Games. Skating expert Dick Button described her delicate style: "She is not a fiery skater, and she shouldn't be made to be. With some skaters, there is a lot of fuss and feathers but nothing is happening. With Peggy, there's no fuss and feathers, but a great deal is happening." What was happening was the coronation of a new Ice Queen and a sudden surge in the sport's popularity. "She made it appear so easy and lovable," said former champion Carlo Fassi. "A lot of little girls fell in love with it."

After the '68 Games Peggy turned pro and performed in five TV specials, worked as a commentator for ABC Sports at several subsequent Olympics, hosted an African wildlife special, appeared on shows such as *Diagnosis Murder* and *Newhart*, and did commercials for Trident gum, Canon cameras, fitness and skin care products. Herself the subject of numerous books, she wrote her own, *The*

me over the years…I don't know if I'd change anything in my life—maybe if I had more time, if we could extend the day a little longer, that would really help me out."

BONUS SWINGABILITY: Her exotic birthplace—San Jose, California … besides being the first Olympics shown in color on global TV, the '68 Games were also the first to have more TV personnel than athletes, the first to have portable typewriters for journalists, the first to have East and West Germany competing separately, and the first to have drug and gender testing for the athletes …the U.S. Olympic Committee's Olympic Hall of Fame has enshrined only two women figure skaters (besides Peggy): Tenley Albright (gold medalist at the '56 Olympics) and Dorothy Hamill (gold medalist at the '76 Olympics) … always a competitor, thirty years to the day after she won her gold medal she had successful surgery for breast cancer. "The life Olympics," she called it in a written statement, explaining "this is another kind of competition, but I'm being coached by an excellent team, and I've got a real strong competitive spirit" … "In training, you have to have positive thoughts," she told *People*. "I totally believe that everything I learned as [an athlete] helped me get through this"… to *More* magazine she said, "If you're a competitor, you can't let the negative vibes come in. If you skate on eggshells and think, 'Oh, God, I hope I don't fall on this difficult jump,' then you are going to fall" … always a contributor, she has done much charity work for Easter Seals, the American Cancer Society, the March of Dimes, the Diabetes Foundation, and the Kidney Foundation, among many other organizations … the quotable Peggy: "The first thing is to love your sport. Never do it to please someone else. It has to be yours" … Peggy has her own Web site—http://www.peggyfleming.net.

Long Program: Skating Towards Life's Victories, in '99. She's continued to tour in ice shows, even into her fifties. Recognition of her illustrious career and myriad contributions has continued unabated. She was the first skater asked to perform at the White House, she was elected to the U.S. Olympic Committee Hall of Fame in '83, and at the end of the millennium *Sports Illustrated* put her in the top-20 of the greatest female athletes of all time. To this day she remains one of the most popular (and most admired) athletes America has ever produced, a glowing symbol of the Olympic ideal and the kind of role model that is sorely missed in twenty-first-century sports.

HER '60s LOOK: Peggy's beauty amplified the appeal of her Olympic skating achievements—a smitten *Sports Illustrated* said she had "the face that launched a thousand Zambonis." Her slender frame belied her strength and endurance. The skating costumes came from Peggy's mother, who designed and sewed them herself. When Peggy won the gold, she was wearing a bright chartreuse chiffon mini-dress, a great '60s style and color.

BEHIND THE SCENES: Single during the '60s, in '65 Peggy met her future husband, who was also a skater. He later became a dermatologist. They married in '70 and are still together, living with their two kids in Los Gatos, a toney suburb of San Francisco. Family is what's most important to her, and time with her family is what's most precious, as the always-busy Peggy explained in a TV bio: "I'm extremely grateful for all the wonderful things that have happened to

A DATE WITH PEGGY

July 27, 1949	Peggy Fleming is born
February 15, 1961	The U.S. figure skating team is killed in a plane crash
February 13, 1965	Peggy wins the U.S. figure skating championships
March 4, 1967	Peggy wins the world figure skating championships in Vienna, Austria
February 10, 1968	Peggy wins the gold medal at the '68 Winter Olympics
February 23, 1968	Peggy makes the cover of *Life* magazine
March 2, 1968	Peggy wins the world figure skating Championships in Geneva

CATHY RIGBY

SWINGIN' '60s CREDENTIALS: America's first gymnastic pixie, this sensational sprite soared to Olympic fame as the highest-scoring American gymnast—and one of the TV audience's favorites—at the '68 Mexico City Games.

WORKIN' IT: Though she didn't win a medal at the '68 Olympics, Cathy Rigby's youthful all-American pig-tailed beauty and superlative skill brought unprecedented popularity to her sport and helped

women gain more attention as Olympians. The Olympics haven't always been the wonderful forum for women's sports that they are now. Women couldn't even compete in the first modern games in 1896, and in the '60s women comprised less than one-quarter of all the Olympic athletes. Cathy helped change that.

Born in '52, she was only 15 when she finished fourth at the '68 Olympics. As Peggy Fleming had done some ten months before, Cathy's remarkable routines riveted a global audience to their TV sets. Cathy's athletic career was studded with so many impressive accomplishments—she was the first American woman to medal at the World Championships—that she made the *Wide World of Sports* list of the "25 Most Influential Women Athletes."

After competing in the '72 Games in Munich, Cathy trained for a whole new arena—entertainment. By the late '70s she was ready, and the starring roles tumbled in. She's made three TV movies: *The Great Wallendas* in '78, *Challenge of a Lifetime* in '85, and *Perfect Body* in '97. Even more spectacular have been Cathy's roles on the musical stage, where's she proven herself to be a top draw. She made

her musical debut as Dorothy in *The Wizard of Oz* in '81, then performed in *Annie Get Your Gun, Meet Me in St. Louis,* and *Paint Your Wagon,* among others. When she came to Broadway with *Peter Pan* in '91, she was nominated for a Tony Award and set box-office records. By now she's logged more "frequent flyer" miles than any other actress who's played Peter. Crowed the *Boston Globe,* "[Cathy] is remarkably talented…she sings wonderfully, with precision, with range, with style…Rigby will lift you out of your seat!" When not performing on a Broadway stage Cathy has headlined in Vegas (winning the George M. Cohan award there for Best Specialty Act), narrated videos (such as *Cathy Rigby on Eating Disorders* in '98), and been a national spokesperson for the Fast Track exercise machine. Maybe she didn't win the gold for gymnastics, but she's certainly won it for versatility.

HER '60s LOOK: In the '60s, Cathy's cute Disney-girl face was made even more adorable and innocent by the blonde pigtails that became her trademark. At only 4' 11" tall and a mere ninety pounds, she was probably the tiniest, and certainly the fittest, of all the stars of the '60s. Later, however, pressures got to her and she struggled to overcome eating disorders. To her credit, she wasn't afraid to discuss these problems publicly, in hopes of helping others.

BEHIND THE SCENES: This Olympic hero had no awful scandals in the '60s (she was only in her mid-teens for the '68 Games, for cryin' out loud). Cathy has married two Toms. The first, Tom Mason, from '72 to '81, ended in divorce but brought her two sons. The second, Tom McCoy, from '82 onward, has brought her two daughters. Tom McCoy has teamed with Cathy to create a company called McCoy/Rigby entertainment, based in Southern California.

BONUS SWINGABILITY: Her moniker—she's sometimes billed as Cathy Rigby-McCoy … her exotic birthplace—Long Beach, California … Cathy devotes time to the Special Olympics, the Boy and Girl Scouts of America, and The National Center for the Prevention of Sudden Infant Death Syndrome.

A DATE WITH CATHY

December 12, 1952	Cathy Rigby is born
October 12, 1968	The 19th Summer Olympic Games begin in Mexico City
October 27, 1968	The 19th Summer Olympic Games close
May 5, 1972	Cathy makes the cover of *Life* magazine

THE YOUNG STARS

With the emphasis on youth in the '60s, it's only natural that young actresses would achieve stardom. The girls shown here enjoyed long, full careers before they reached adulthood—we literally watched them grow up before our very eyes. To paraphrase Mick, time was on their side.

ANGELA CARTWRIGHT

HER SWINGIN' '60s CREDENTIALS: A popular big- and small-screen presence, this cute young actress played memorable supporting roles on *The Danny Thomas Show*, in the film *The Sound of Music*, and then on *Lost in Space*, always displaying a charming sincerity and a dignified intelligence.

WORKIN' IT: Angela Cartwright's '60s career spanned most of the decade and covered movies, TV, and music. Though she was never a trend-setter, a lead, or a "love interest" in any of her roles, she was always a warm, wholesome, welcome personality in any project she undertook.

Born in '52, Angela made her professional debut at age 3 as a child model.

Then she was in the '56 boxing flick *Somebody Up There Likes Me* with a coupla mugs named Paul Newman and Steve McQueen. Playing Linda Williams, she joined the cast of *The Danny Thomas Show* in '57, the year when the four-year-old series changed its title from *Make Room for Daddy*. Still a pre-teen, she released a record, *Angela Cartwright Sings*, with billing as "America's Little Sweetheart." In '64 she had to be excused from the last episode of *Danny Thomas* so she could film *The Sound of Music* ('65). The Oscar-winning classic took her to Austria and made a singin' Von Trapp out of her. Next came three years *Lost in Space* ('65–'68), with Angela as the youngest daughter of parents John and Maureen Robinson (Guy Williams and June Lockhart). Unfortunately, Angela had prominent screentime in only about ten percent of the *Lost in Space* episodes; aliens, the Robot, and the pusillanimous Dr. Smith dominated this TV universe. Perhaps the Penniest episode was "The Magic Mirror," sending Angela through a mirror into a fantasy world (à la Lewis Carroll's *Through the Looking Glass*). Though she was underused, Angela was still an important ingredient in the *Lost in Space* recipe. This amiable space fantasy was really a kids' show (it came on at 7:30 p.m.), as pointed out in Mark Cotta Vaz's *Lost in Lost in Space*. Since the show was aimed at a young audience, the Penny character was vital to the show's creators. Whoever played her had to be someone kids could identify with, respect, and really like, making it easier for them to accept the show's far-out fantasy adventures. Already familiar from other successful shows and major movies, Angela was the perfect Penny. The show lasted for eighty-three episodes, and like the original *Gilligan's Island*, which was also running about this time, *Lost in Space* never did bring its castaways home to stay. Angela's post-'60s post-teen appearances included another run as Linda Williams in Danny Thomas's one-season series *Make Room for Granddaddy* ('70–'71), plus a role in *Beyond the Poseidon Adventure* ('79). Commercials, especially for Soft & Dri, United, and milk, con-

tinued to give her national and international exposure through the '70s. More recently, she made a cameo appearance in the '98 *Lost in Space* movie, playing a reporter alongside her *Lost in Space* TV sister, Marta Kristen. Since '76 Angela has run Rubber Boots, a "haven where gifted artists have created unique items." The gift boutique existed first as an actual storefront in Toluca Lake, California, but since '99 it's lived exclusively on the Internet (http://www.rubber-boots.com). Angela's also an acclaimed photographer and author (*My Book: A Child's First Journal*), she's co-written a fantasy novel called *To What Purpose* with Billy Mumy, and she's got her own wonderful Web site with lots of great old photos and stories.

HER '60s LOOK:

Angela was what parents wished teens would be: cute, wholesome, freckly, and intelligent. She would've made a great Mouseketeer. In *Lost in Space*, the other Robinson daughter, Marta Kristen as Judy, had the parabolas to properly fill out the aluminum-foil outfit of the show's first season. Angela didn't become a spaceboy's dream until the Robinsons broke out the groovy velour suits in the last season. She has written at her Web site that when she got taller on the show, the producers stopped putting her in velour pants suits and switched her to minis. No matter what she wore, she was always a friendly find on the TV dial. At 18 she cut her hair short, which was "quite liberating," her Web site says, and she went to Italy for modeling jobs. Today, photos of Angela show that her teen cuteness has blossomed into adult beauty.

BEHIND THE SCENES:

Angela was too young and too smart for the typical '60s drug busts and broken relationship with a rock star, which is all good news for our Penny. Instead, her remarkable childhood was filled with travel, friends, and lots of camera time. She probably even managed to get good grades. Angela married in '76 and has raised two children, Rebecca and Jesse. Compare her life to another young actress of the '60s, Anissa Jones. Anissa was only 8 when she started playing Buffy, the Mrs.-Beasley-owning, pigtail-wearing young 'un on *Family Affair*. By age 11 Anissa was in an Elvis movie, *The Trouble with Girls* ('69), by 13 she'd published *Buffy's Cookbook*, and by 18 she was dead of a drug overdose.

BONUS SWINGABILITY:

Her exotic birthplace—Altrincham, England ... she's the younger sister of Veronica Cartwright, the short-haired crew member who got munched in *Alien* ... *Lost in Space* was originally to be called *Space Family Robinson*, but the studio changed it because of the similarity with the Disney movie *Swiss Family Robinson* ... a decade before he would write the *Star Wars* music, John Williams penned the *Lost in Space* theme ... *Mad* magazine honored *Lost in Space* with one of its patented parodies; this one was called *Loused Up in Space* and the family was called the Boobinsons ... on the show 12-year-old Penny Roberta Robinson was said to have an I.Q of 147 ... in '83 Angela joined fellow *Lost in Space* cast members on *Family Feud*, where they faced off against Yvonne Craig and cast members from the *Batman* TV series; each team won one match ... Angela's official Web site, where her son Jesse is the Webmaster—http://www.angela-cartwright.com.

A DATE WITH ANGELA	
September 9, 1952	Angela Cartwright is born
March 11, 1958	Anissa Jones is born
March 2, 1965	*The Sound of Music* is released
September 15, 1965	*Lost in Space* debuts
February 16, 1966	"The Magic Mirror" episode of *Lost in Space* airs
September 12, 1966	*Family Affair* debuts
September 11, 1968	*Lost in Space* concludes its three-season run in primetime
September 3, 1969	Elvis' *The Trouble with Girls* is released
September 9, 1971	*Family Affair* concludes its five-season run in primetime
August 29, 1976	18-year-old Anissa Jones dies of a drug overdose
September 9, 1985	On *Lost in Space*, Penny Robinson was supposedly born on this date
October 16, 1997	On the *Lost in Space* pilot episode, the first adventure supposedly took place on this date

HAYLEY MILLS ✻

Walt's wife, Lillian, had seen *Tiger Bay* ('59), Hayley's first starring role and one which brought her rave reviews and two international film awards. When Walt was looking for a young actress for his upcoming film, Lillian suggested that he go meet Hayley. He flew to England and was immediately smitten by the bright, charming girl, and he quickly cast her in *Pollyanna* ('60). The sunny hit brought her an honorary Oscar for Juvenile Performance and a Golden Globe as 1961's Most Promising Newcomer. Things only got better for Hayley and Walt. They teamed up in '61 for *The Parent Trap*, at the time his most successful film ever. So popular was Hayley, her recording of the movie's song, "Let's Get Together," raced up the music charts. A natural charmer as an actress, she later said, "I was lucky. I always liked the camera. It was like a friend, I just trusted it." Maureen O'Hara, her co-star in *The Parent Trap*, praised her as being "fun, professional, and a hard worker." *Whistle Down the Wind* (based on her mother's book) in '61, and four more from Disney—*In Search of the Castaways* in '62, *Summer Magic* (alongside Deborah Walley) in '63, *The Moon-Spinners* in '64, and *That Darn Cat!* in '65—established Hayley as the most popular young actress of the decade.

In her late teens she started to stretch into more mature roles. In '64 she gave a stirring performance as a disturbed girl in *The Chalk Garden* (which co-starred her father), and in '66 she played a mentally slow teen in *Gypsy Girl* (which her mother scripted and her father directed). The famous culmination of this gradual break from her Disney days was *The Family Way* ('66), in which she smoked and swore and drank and even did a scene partially nude (Paul McCartney wrote the score of this controversial comedy). Perhaps because she had been so endearing as a girl, audiences didn't want to accept that she (and they) were getting older. Though she continued to work for the next ten years, her momentum definitely slowed. Three *Parent Trap* TV movie sequels in the late '80s, plus shows like *Love Boat* and

SWINGIN' '60s CREDENTIALS: An adorable Disney doll with a British accent, a ready smile, and a spunky attitude, Hayley moved from her classic juvenile filmwork in the first half of the decade, which included Disney delights *Pollyanna* and *The Parent Trap*, to more serious adult films like *Gypsy Girl* and *The Family Way*.

WORKIN' IT: Like Mia Farrow and Vanessa Redgrave, Hayley Mills was born into a show-biz family. She's the daughter of Sir John Mills, one of the world's top movie stars in the early '60s (he played the tanned dad in Disney's *Swiss Family Robinson* in '61), and writer Mary Hayley Bell, who wrote the novel *Whistle Down the Wind*. Hayley's older sister is Juliet Mills, who was nanny Phoebe Figalilly on TV's *Nanny and the Professor* ('70–'71).

The family lived on a 200-acre farm in Sussex, England, where 13-year-old Hayley was visited one day by Walt Disney himself.

Murder She Wrote, typified her post-'60s screen roles. She did, however, continue to perform on stage, co-starring with her sister in the Noel Coward play *Fallen Angels*, and touring Australia and the U.S. in the '90s as the singing, dancing "I" in *The King and I*. She has also written introductions for several books, and in '88 she co-edited *My God: Letters from the Famous on God and the Life Hereafter*.

HER '60s LOOK: Her sweet, open face, featuring big expressive blue eyes and immense, cushiony lips, was topped by a kicky 'do, all thick and blonde and bouncy and bangy. A natural in period costumes, as in *Pollyanna*, she was also well-suited for active tomboy parts like the twins in *The Parent Trap*. Her biggest problem back then was her sudden growth spurt—during the filming of *The Parent Trap*, she shot up two inches, and all her costumes had to be altered. After she left her teens behind she began to battle her weight, and for a ten-year period she was bulimic. She's emerged into the twenty-first century as a beautiful adult who still has the lively twinkle in her blue eyes that made the world adore her some forty years ago.

BEHIND THE SCENES: Hayley's first crush was on Elvis, and she has said that she actually saw him driving his big Caddy in Hollywood in '62. Her first kiss, she claimed, was with Peter McEnery in *The Moon-Spinners*. Eighteen-year-old Haley was so nervous, she said, "I forgot to close my eyes." At 20 she met her future husband, Roy Boulting. He was the director of *The Family Way*, he was thirty-three years her senior, and he already had a wife and six kids (two of them older than Hayley). When they moved in together, her parents were outraged by the age difference, and movie magazines treated their pairing like a major international scandal. Everybody was bothered by the age difference, it seemed, except for the two people involved. Explained Hayley in an interview, "You are either old souls who connect and share the same interest…or you are not." They finally married in '71, had a son (Crispian, who is now the lead singer of the rock group Kula Shakur) in '73, and divorced in '77. She then took up with actor Leigh Lawson and had his son, but she and Lawson split up in the mid-'80s (he went on to marry Twiggy). Later she had a relationship with the brother of Maxwell Caulfield, the actor who married her sister. She now lives in a 200-year-old cottage in Hampton, England.

BONUS SWINGABILITY: Her full moniker—Hayley Catherine Rose Vivien Mills … her exotic birthplace—the swingin'est, London, England … she was considered for the lead in Kubrick's *Lolita* but she didn't pursue it because the sexy role didn't fit her squeaky-clean image … when Hayley went to Hollywood for *Pollyanna*, Walt gave

her a personal two-day tour of Disneyland … here's what she said about him in the book *Remembering Walt*: "Looking back, I appreciate even more now what Walt was trying to do with his movies. He told me that he wanted to show people the best in themselves. Certainly, he achieved that. You always come out of his movies feeling happier than when you went in, and you feel better about humanity and the human condition" … actress Joan Hackett once said about her: "Hayley Mills was my favorite actress for a long time. As a kid and a teen, she had tremendous talent, and personality to spare" … on a TV biography she said, "All the things I've been through—the good, the bad, and the ugly—they were all things I had to learn," adding that "it's all been a great mystery and a wonderful adventure."

 A DATE WITH HAYLEY

November 21, 1913	Roy Boulting is born
April 18, 1946	Hayley Mills is born
May 19, 1960	*Pollyanna* is released
June 13, 1960	Hayley Mills makes the cover of *Life* magazine
April 17, 1961	Hayley is given a special Juvenile Award at the Oscars
September 18, 1961	"Let's Get Together" enters the *Billboard* charts (it will reach #8)
December 21, 1962	*In Search of the Castaways* is released
April 14, 1962	"Johnny Jingo" enters the *Billboard* charts (it will reach #21)
May 21, 1964	*The Chalk Garden* is released
July 8, 1964	*The Moon-Spinners* is released
December 2, 1965	*That Darn Cat!* is released
October 16, 1998	Disney names her an official Disney Legend

SUE LYON

SWINGIN' '6Os CREDENTIALS: She was the luscious title character in *Lolita*, making her the very definition of tantalizingly precocious jail bait.

WORKIN' IT: "How did they ever make a movie of *Lolita*?" That was the ad line used to publicize the controversial '62 movie in which Sue Lyon made her big-screen debut. First published in '55, Vladimir Nabokov's book had already been hailed as a literary masterpiece, with the focus less on the 12-year-old title character and more on the author's brilliant prose ("Wild, fantastic, wonderfully imaginative, it is a style which parodies everything it touches," wrote *The Atlantic Monthly* in '58). But the book's love affair between a pre-teen and a middle-aged man was still scandalous and had caused the book to be temporarily banned in France. ("I'm going to put off reading *Lolita* for six years," joked Groucho Marx. "I'm waiting until she turns 18.") When director Stanley Kubrick was casting for the movie, he knew film audiences wouldn't accept the love affair at the core of the story. Thus he made the character 14 and put 16-year-old Sue Lyon, whom he'd seen on *The Loretta Young Show*, in the role of the bikini-wearing lollipop-sucker. While still thirty-seven years younger than James Mason, who played Humbert Humbert, Sue's Lolita wasn't quite the shock that Nabokov's original

pre-pubescent child had been. Sue, who looked older than she really was, was an inspired choice. She perfectly captured the essence of a teen on the cusp between innocent adolescence and jaded adulthood—not too old to play with a hula hoop but already bored by her older lover's advances.

Her career off and running, she won the Golden Globe in '63 as the Most Promising Newcomer and was soon whisked away to Mexico to shoot *The Night of the Iguana* with Hollywood heavyweights Richard Burton and Ava Gardner. Unfortunately, as she matured, starring roles came less frequently (*The Flim-Flam Man* in '67, *Evel Knievel* in '71), minor movies replaced the high-profile films she'd done as a teenager, and after a decade of unremarkable projects she left the screen for good in the mid-'80s.

HER '6Os LOOK: A big-eyed blonde with a knowing smile, young Sue was a perfectly pouty teenie bopper for *Lolita*, her alluring bikini action making her seem older and wiser than her years (her measurements were given in '63's *Movie Life Yearbook* as 34-22-35). Sue's sweet-but-seductive face landed on the August '62 cover of *Cosmo*. In *The Flim-Flam Man*, she looked better in blue jeans than anyone until a decade later when nothing came between Brooke Shields and her Calvins.

BEHIND THE SCENES: In '64 Sue married her long-time boyfriend Hampton Fancher III (an actor who later wrote the screenplay for *Blade Runner*), but they divorced in '65. She had another one-year marriage from '70 to '71, and another from '73 to '74 when, according to legend, she married and divorced a convicted murderer who was serving a life sentence in prison. A fourth marriage, this one in '85, has lasted to the present.

BONUS SWINGABILITY: Her exotic birthplace—Davenport, Iowa ... in her early teen years, one of Sue's best friends, and the person who introduced her to the book *Lolita*, was young Michelle Phillips ... supposedly Sue beat out Tuesday Weld for the role of Lolita Haze ... according to an article about her in *Movielife Yearbook* in '66, 20-year-old Sue was in a serious car accident that caused her "to realize she's in the wrong business" and to briefly consider becoming a teacher.

A DATE WITH SUE

July 10, 1946	Sue Lyon is born
June 13, 1962	*Lolita* is released
August 6, 1964	*The Night of the Iguana* is released

THE GUIDING LIGHT

Watching, commenting, and guiding was Helen Gurley Brown.

Many important, memorable writers championed sexual liberation

and women's rights in the '60s, but none was as fun as Helen.

HELEN GURLEY BROWN

SWINGIN' '60s CREDENTIALS: Though Helen Gurley Brown didn't invent sex, she sure made it more fun for generations of women. The ultimate *Cosmo* girl, she is arguably one of the most influential women of the decade, perhaps even the century, and she did it all with her pen.

WORKIN' IT: Since the early '60s Helen Gurley Brown has been instructing, helping, advising, liberating, promoting, and cheering for women, giving them new role models to emulate and a new manual for the sexual revolution.

Like many revolutionaries who seek out better lives and new worlds to conquer, she came from humble beginnings. She was born in 1922 in Arkansas to parents who were both schoolteachers. Tragedy came early to the family. Helen's father died in an accident when Helen was young, and her sister, a victim of polio, was an invalid from the time she was 19. As a young working woman, Helen herself was the embodiment of the "mouseburger" she would later help to emancipate. Working as a secretary for the prominent ad agency Foote, Cone & Belding in the '50s, she impressed her boss with her entertaining letters and was moved to the copywriting department. By the early '60s she was one of the country's highest-paid ad copywriters.

Her big breakthrough came in '62 with the publication of *Sex and the Single Girl*, which remained on bestseller lists into '63 and became a Natalie Wood movie in '64. She wrote three more books in the '60s—*Sex and the Office* in '65, *Outrageous Opinions of Helen Gurley Brown* in '67, and *Helen Gurley Brown's Single Girl's Cookbook* in '69. More importantly, in '65 she joined the editorial staff of *Cosmopolitan* magazine.

At the time, *Cosmo* was a struggling, underachieving literary magazine trying to find its voice in an era of rapid change and new freedoms. Helen seized the reins for the July '65 issue and, as editor in chief, immediately established *Cosmo* as a powerful advocate for women's sexual liberation. Suddenly women everywhere had a new best friend. *Cosmo* rooted endlessly and unconditionally for women, educated and advised them with underlined insider information, encouraged self-analysis with monthly quizzes, offered them glamorous *Cosmo* girls to emulate, and (thanks to the newest birth-control technology, the pill) encouraged them to take control of their sexual destinies. Gone was the old double standard that taught women to be virginal while men could be predatory, replaced by frank discussions of how women could get the most pleasure out of sex. Probably the closest parallel is Hugh Hefner, who did for men in the '50s what Helen was doing for women in the '60s, with equal passion and commitment.

For the next thirty-two years she continued at the helm of *Cosmopolitan*, guiding it to spectacular circulation figures and making it the most successful woman's magazine ever (it's now one of the five largest-selling periodicals on U.S. newsstands). Stylish and witty and positively bubbling with spunky personality, she was a natural for the talk-show circuit, of course. She's been a frequent visitor to everything from *60 Minutes* and *20/20* to *The Tonight Show* and *Entertainment Tonight*. For a while she had her own show, *View from Cosmo*, on the Lifetime Network, and for three years she had a weekly spot on *Good Morning America*. She's also continued to write books, following up her four '60s tomes with *Sex and the New Single Girl* in '70, *Having It All* in '82, *The Late Show: A Semi Wild but Practical Guide for Women Over 50* in '93, *The Writer's Rules: The Power of Positive Prose—How to Create It and Get It Published* in '98, and *I'm Wild Again* in early 2000.

In '97, at the age of 73, Helen left *Cosmo's* editor-in-chief position in New York to oversee the more than three-dozen international editions of the magazine. Her life now is spent flying from one exotic city to another, bringing the *Cosmo* philosophy to the locals. And she picks up awards, too. Among them are the 1996 American Society of Magazine Editors' Hall of Fame Award, the 1995 Henry Johnson Fisher Award from the Magazine Publishers of America (the first time this award was ever given to a woman), and writeups in *Who's Who of American Women*, *Who's Who in America*, *Who's Who in the World*, and the *World Book of Facts*. She was even declared a "living landmark" by New York's Landmark Commission. Mouseburger? Maverick. Marvelous!

HER '60s LOOK: In the '60s, Helen was always tastefully and intelligently conservative with her look. Despite the fashion craziness going on around her, she stayed smart, urban, chic, stylish, and glamorous. Always impeccably and expensively dressed, she wasn't one for jeans or sweats, preferring instead tailored short dresses, fashionable suits, colorful prints, and beautiful French gowns. What's more, she's kept her look going long after other women have given up, so that her long successful career has been matched by her long successful life as a woman of fashion. Today she still looks cultured and careful, poised and professional, a woman who instantly commands respect whether she's meeting with a famous writer or a pompous maître d'.

BEHIND THE SCENES: Talk about marrying well. She's been married since the '50s to David Brown, the successful producer of big-time movies like *The Sting*, *Jaws*, *The Verdict*, *Cocoon*, *A Few Good Men*, *Driving Miss Daisy*, and *Angela's Ashes*. What an ally

he's been: at his urging she wrote *Sex and the Single Girl*, and he encouraged her to take the *Cosmo* job. For over thirty years he even wrote all the coverlines that accompanied the sensational *Cosmo* cover photos. They've lived a fast-paced, jet-set life together for over four decades. And if you want to talk friends and connections, Helen's got 'em. One of her closest friends was Jacqueline Susann, she of *Valley of the Dolls* fame. A regular on the celebrity scene, Helen is as good with Hollywood royalty as she is with European royalty; in fact, she and her husband were once presented to the Queen of England.

BONUS SWINGABILITY: Her exotic birthplace—Green Forest, Arkansas ... her replacement at *Cosmo* was Bonnie Fuller, former editor in chief of the U.S. *Marie Claire* and a woman whom Helen tutored for eighteen months before she left ... one of the most famous *Cosmo* issues appeared in April '72, with Burt Reynolds as

the first nude male pin-up (remember who followed Burt as a *Cosmo* pin-up? John Davidson) ... Helen describes herself as a health nut, a feminist, a workaholic, and someone who's passionately interested in the man-woman relationship, which she has called "the most exciting, dramatic thing in the world."

 A DATE WITH HELEN

July 28, 1916	David Brown is born
February 18, 1922	Helen Gurley Brown is born
May 23, 1962	Helen's *Sex and the Single Girl* is published
December 25, 1964	The film *Sex and the Single Girl* is released
January 17, 1996	Helen announces her resignation as editor in chief of *Cosmo*

SELECTED BIBLIOGRAPHY

*The Addams Chronicles: Everything You Ever Wanted to Know
About the Addams Family*
  by Stephen Cox (NY: Harper Perennial, 1991)

After All
  by Mary Tyler Moore (NY: Dell Publishing, 1995)

Ann-Margret: My Story
  by Ann-Margret with Todd Gold (NY: G.P. Putnam's Sons, 1994)

Audrey Hepburn: A Biography
  by Warren G. Harris (NY: Simon & Schuster Books, Inc., 1994)

Audrey Style
  by Pamela Clarke Keogh (NY: HarperCollins Publishers,
  Inc. 1999)

The Avengers Dossier
  by Paul Cornell, Martin Day and Keith Topping (London: Virgin
  Books, 1998)

Baby Doll: An Autobiography
  by Carroll Baker (NY: Arbor House, 1983)

Back to the Batcave
  by Adam West with Jeff Rovin (NY: Berkley Publishing
  Group, 1994)

Bardot: An Intimate Portrait
  by Jeffrey Robinson (NY: Donald I. Fine, Inc., 1995)

The Beatles: The Authorized Biography
  by Hunter Davies (NY: McGraw-Hill Book Company, 1968)

The Beverly Hillbillies
  by Stephen Cox (NY: Harper Perennial, 1993)

Beyond Uhura: Star Trek and Other Memories
  by Nichelle Nichols (NY: G.P. Putnam's Sons, 1994)

Billboard Book of Top 40 Hits
  by Joel Whitburn (NY: Billboard Publications, Inc., 1996)

Billboard Book of Number One Hits
  by Fred Bronson (NY: Billboard Publications, Inc., 1997)

Blown Away: The Rolling Stones and the Death of the Sixties
  by A.E. Hotchner (NY: Simon and Schuster Books,
  Inc., 1990)

The Book of Bond, James Bond
  by Hoyt L. Barber and Harry L. Barber (CA: Cyclone
  Books, 1999)

California Dreamin': The True Story of the Mamas and Papas
  by Michelle Phillips (NY: Warner Books, Inc., 1986)

Call Me Anna: The Autobiography of Patty Duke
  by Patty Duke and Kenneth Turan (NY: Bantam Books, 1987)

Captain's Logs, The Complete Trek Voyages
  by Edward Gross and Mark A. Altman (London: Boxtree
  Limited, 1993)

Cary Grant: The Lonely Heart
  by Charles Higham and Roy Mosele (NY: Harcourt Brace
  Jovanovich, Publishers, 1989)

*Classic Sitcoms: A Celebration of the Best in
Prime-Time Comedy*
  by Vince Waldron (NY: Collier Books, 1987)

*The Complete Directory to Prime Time Network and
Cable TV Shows*
  by Tim Brooks and Earl Marsh (NY: Ballantine Books, 1999)

The Complete James Bond Movie Encyclopedia
  by Steven Jay Rubin (Chicago: Contemporary Books, 1995)

Cult Movies
  by Danny Peary (NY: Gramercy Books, 1981)

Diahann! An Autobiography
  by Diahann Carroll with Ross Firestone (Boston: Little, Brown
  and Company, 1986)

Dick Clark's The First 25 Years of Rock & Roll
by Michael Uslan and Bruce Solomon (NY: Dell Publishing Co., 1981)

Don't Tell Dad: A Memoir
by Peter Fonda (NY: Hyperion, 1998)

Drama Queens
by Autumn Stephens (CA: Conari Press, 1998)

Dreaming of Jeannie
by Steve Cox with Howard Frank (NY: Griffin Trade Paperback, 2000)

A Dream Is a Wish Your Heart Makes: My Story
by Annette Funicello with Patricia Romanowski (NY: Hyperion, 1994)

The Early Stones
by Michael Cooper and Terry Southern (NY: Hyperion, 1992)

Edie: An American Biography
by Jean Stein, edited with George Plimpton (NY: Dell Publishing Company, Inc., 1983)

Elvis and Me
by Priscilla Beaulieu Presley with Sandra Harmon (NY: G.P. Putnam's Sons, 1985)

Elvis Day by Day
by Peter Guralnick and Ernst Jorgensen (NY: Ballantine Publishing Group, 1999)

The Encyclopedia of Animated Cartoons
by Jeff Lenborg (NY: Checkmark Books, 1999)

The Essential Bond
by Lee Pfeiffer and Dave Worrall (NY: Harper Entertainment, 1998)

Faithfull: An Autobiography
by Marianne Faithfull with David Dalton (NY: Cooper Square Press, 1994)

Fantastic Television
by Gary Gerani with Paul H. Schulman (NY: Harmony Books, 1977)

The Films of the Sixties
by Douglas Brode (NY: Citadel Press, 1980)

The First Time
by Cher as told to Jeff Coplon (NY: Pocket Books, 1999)

Golden Girl
by Shirley Eaton (London: B.T. Batsford Ltd., 1999)

Helter Skelter: The True Story of the Manson Murders
by Vincent Bugliosi with Curt Gentry (NY: W.W. Norton & Co., 1994)

Hollywood Babylon II
by Kenneth Anger (NY: Plume Publishing, 1985)

Hollywood Wits
edited by K. Madsen Roth (NY: Avon Books, 1995)

Inside Gilligan's Island
by Sherwood Schwartz (NY: St. Martin's Press, 1994)

I, Tina: My Life Story
by Tina Turner with Kurt Loder (NY: Avon Books, 1993)

The James Bond Girls
by Graham Rye, (NY: Citadel Publishing Group, 1998)

Jane Fonda: An Intimate Biography
by Bill Davidson (NY: Dutton, 1990)

Jayne Mansfield and the American Fifties
by Martha Saxton (Boston: Houghton Mifflin Company, 1975)

Laughing on the Outside, Crying on the Inside
by Judy Carne (NY: Rawson Associates, 1985)

Looking for Gatsby
by Faye Dunaway with Betsy Sharkey (NY: Simon & Schuster Books, Inc., 1995)

Lost in Lost in Space
by Mark Cotta Vaz (NY: HarperCollins Publishers, Inc., 1998)

Matter of Survival
by Chris Noel (MA: Branden Publishing Company, Inc., 1987)

Model: The Ugly Business of Beautiful Women
by Michael Gross (NY: William Morrow & Company, Inc., 1995)

My Life
by Burt Reynolds (NY: Hyperion, 1994)

My Lucky Stars
by Shirley MacLaine (NY: Bantam Books, 1996)

Natalie: A Memoir by Her Sister
by Lana Wood (NY: G.P. Putnam's Sons, 1984)

Nick at Nite's Classic TV Companion
edited by Tom Hill (NY: Fireside, 1996)

The Playboy Book: The First Forty Years
by Gretchen Edgren (L.A.: General Publishing Group, 1998)

Playing the Field: My Story
by Mamie Van Doren with Art Aveilhe (NY: G.P. Putnam's Sons, 1987)

Pure Goldie
by Marc Shapiro (Secaucus, NJ: Carol Publishing Group, 1998)

Reel Elvis: The Ultimate Trivia Guide to the King's Movies
by Pauline Bartel (TX: Taylor Publishing Company, 1994)

Rock Wives: The Hard Lives and Good Times of the Wives, Girlfriends and Groupies of Rock and Roll
by Victoria Balfour (NY: Beech Tree Books, 1986)

Sophia Loren: Living and Loving
by A.E. Hotchner (NY: William Morrow & Company, Inc., 1979)

Somebody to Love?: A Rock-and-Roll Memoir
by Grace Slick with Andrea Cagan (NY: Warner Books Inc., 1998)

That Book About That Girl
by Stephen Cole (L.A.: Renaissance Books, 1999)

This Life
by Sidney Poitier (NY: Alfred A. Knopf, 1980)

Vanessa Redgrave: An Autobiography
by Vanessa Redgrave (NY: Random House, 1994)

They Went That-a-Way
by Malcolm Forbes with Jeff Bloch (NY: Ballantine Books, 1988)

Totally Uninhibited: The Life and Wild Times of Cher
by Lawrence J. Quirk (NY: William Morrow and Company, Inc., 1991)

Total Television
by Alex McNeil (NY: Penguin Books, 1996)

Trouble Girls: The Rolling Stone Book of Women in Rock
edited by Barbara O'Dair (NY: Random House, 1997)

Up and Down with the Rolling Stones: The Inside Story
by Tony Sanchez (NY: New American Library, Inc., 1980)

The Way You Wear Your Hat: Frank Sinatra and the Lost Art of Livin'
by Bill Zehme (NY: HarperCollins Publishers, Inc., 1997)

What Falls Away
by Mia Farrow (NY: Nan A. Talese, Doubleday, 1997)

ACKNOWLEDGEMENTS

My thanks go to these people who provided contacts, information, or encouragement above and beyond the call of duty: Peter Alles, Greg Altenberger, Janey Bain, Mike Bartlett, Joe Doyle, Dragonfly, Sophie-Francoise Faithfull, Ernest Farino, Kiki Hernandez, Hal Horn, Lester Isa, Elle Kensington, Frank Liberman, Hal Lifson, Philip Molyneux, Tara Pollard, Kim Rosenthal, Bob Rush, Tom Simon, Camilla Twigg, Brigitte Urbina, Will the Thrill Viharo, Brian Walker, Glynis Ward, and Jeannine Yeomans.

Several of the wonderful women profiled in this book (or in other Swingin' Chicks of the '6Os projects) deserve an extra mention for the personal assistance they gave me. For all their generous help, I am indebted to Carroll Baker, Lisa Baker, Helen Gurley Brown, Grace Coddington, Angie Dickinson, Shirley Eaton, Linda Harrison, Anne Helm, Linda Lawson, Donna Loren, Barbara Mason, Julie Newmar, Chris Noel, Julie Parrish, Michelle Phillips, Mary Quant, Cathy Rigby, Stella Stevens, Mamie Van Doren, and Deborah Walley.

Every single one of the creative, hard-working professionals in every single department of Cedco Publishing has contributed in one way or another to this book's success. Special thanks go to Charles Ditlefsen, Mary Sullivan, Brooke Peterson, Shiffra Steele, Susan Ristow, Julia Dvorin, designer extraordinaire Teena Gores, the ever-resourceful photo expert Krista Osteraas, Larry Noggle, Rob Northen, Leslie Patrick, Michael Arnaud, Russ Dailey, Janet Hekking, Liz Kalloch, Jay Young, Lisa Bartlett, Kathy Knaap, Marc Fevre, and most of all Lara Starr, who is a fount o' fun facts, and the patient and wise Shari Lejsek.

Endless, eternal praises for my mom, still ageless, still swingin'.

Finally, this book would not have been possible without the research, ideas, and support provided by Sheryl Patton.

PHOTOGRAPHY CREDITS

(alphabetical by source)